SOUNDING THE BOOKSHELF 1501

Sounding the Bookshelf 1501

Music in a Year of Italian Printed Books

Volume 1

*Tim Shephard, Oliver Doyle,
Ciara O'Flaherty, Annabelle Page,
and Laura Ștefănescu*

https://www.openbookpublishers.com

©2025 Tim Shephard, Oliver Doyle, Ciara O'Flaherty, Annabelle Page, and Laura Ştefănescu

This work is licensed under a Creative Commons Attribution-NonCommercial 4.0 International (CC BY-NC 4.0). This license allows you to share, copy, distribute and transmit the text; to adapt the text for non-commercial purposes of the text providing attribution is made to the authors (but not in any way that suggests that they endorse you or your use of the work). Attribution should include the following information:

Tim Shephard, Oliver Doyle, Ciara O'Flaherty, Annabelle Page, and Laura Ştefănescu, *Sounding the Bookshelf 1501: Music in a Year of Italian Printed Books. Volume 1.* Cambridge, UK: Open Book Publishers, 2025, https://doi.org/10.11647/OBP.0473

Further details about CC BY-NC licenses are available at http://creativecommons.org/licenses/by-nc/4.0/

Copyright and permissions for the reuse of many of the images included in this publication differ from the above. This information is provided in the captions. Every effort has been made to identify and contact copyright holders and any omission or error will be corrected if notification is made to the publisher.

All external links were active at the time of publication unless otherwise stated and have been archived via the Internet Archive Wayback Machine at https://archive.org/web

Digital material and resources associated with this volume are available at https://doi.org/10.11647/OBP.0473#resources

Information about any revised edition of this work will be provided at https://doi.org/10.11647/OBP.0473

Paperback: 978-1-80511-632-5
Hardback: 978-1-80511-633-2
PDF: 978-1-80511-634-9
EPUB: 978-1-80511-635-6
HTML: 978-1-80511-636-3
DOI: 10.11647/OBP.0473

Cover image: Dario Tiberti, *Epithome Plutarchi* (Ferrara: Lorenzo Rossi, 1501), fol. [iii] v. Augsburg, Staats- und Stadtbibliothek, 4 Bio 1139, urn:nbn:de:bvb:12-bsb11210570-1
Cover design by Jeevanjot Kaur Nagpal

This research was generously funded by the the Leverhulme Trust.

LEVERHULME
TRUST

Table of Contents

0. Introduction	1
0.1 Methodology	3
0.2 Authors and Readers	8
0.3 The 1501 Corpus and Contemporary Libraries	14
0.4 Everyday Musical Knowledge	19
0.5 Structure and Editorial Policies	24
1. Lifestyle	29
1.1 Education	32
1.2 Conduct	51
1.3 Health and Wellbeing	77
1.4 Astrology	99
1.5 Conclusions	116
2. Poetry	121
2.1 Indications of Performance	132
2.2 Landscape	140
2.3 The Beloved	156
2.4 The Author	167
2.5 Conclusions	181
3. Scholarship	183
3.1 Natural Philosophy	187
3.2 Rhetoric	207
3.3 Literature	228
3.4 History	268
3.5 Law	295
4. Conclusions to Volume 1: A Musical Life in Italy c.1501	303

Appendix: 1501 Excerpts	311
Bibliographies	333
1. 1501 Books	333
2. Other Primary Sources	340
3. Modern Literature	345
Index	365

0. Introduction

This book presents the results of the project "Sounding the Bookshelf 1501: Music in a Year of Italian Printed Books" (2020–23), funded by the Leverhulme Trust and hosted at the University of Sheffield. The project asked a simple, if somewhat contrived, question: standing in an Italian bookshop towards the end of the year 1501, what information about music might you encounter as you browse the new printed titles available for purchase? The USTC (Universal Short Title Catalogue; www.ustc.ac.uk) lists 358 books printed in Italy in 1501. Very few of them are "about" music, but many of them mention music in passing, and sometimes at length, whilst discussing something else. These kinds of casual, fragmentary comments on music were probably encountered by many more people than the specialist music theories associated with plainchant and counterpoint, the audience for which (and especially for the latter) must have been relatively small. To recover these comments, and to characterise the contradictory and incoherent field of everyday musical knowledge they comprise, we have read every book printed in Italy in 1501, excerpting every passage mentioning music, sound, or hearing.

The main purpose of this study is to report what we found in our 1501 corpus. Accordingly, in the pages that follow we will present and excerpt a great deal of material from our sources that we have judged to be relevant in some way to music and sound, giving our new findings priority over the review of secondary literature. This material represents a kind of cross-section of the textual circulation of musical knowledge in print, rather like a slice through the stem of a plant in a school biology class. Taken together, we believe, our varied and numerous 1501 examples comprise a collage that suggests the parameters and affordances of a "musical worldview" that is, with many provisos and qualifications, characteristic of Italian culture at that time. We aim to contextualise our sources, their creators, and the notions we have found in them sufficiently to facilitate a well-informed discussion, and to develop some well-founded suggestions concerning how they may have inflected musical lives in Italy at the turn of the sixteenth century. But inevitably, given that 358 is a large number of sources, on both fronts this work is only begun in our book and not completed. The process of working out, in detail and in specific contexts, the implications of our findings for our understanding of Italian Renaissance musical culture will extend well beyond the last page, and require the contributions of many other researchers.

Overall, we hope that our findings will prompt a dramatic expansion in the range of books considered relevant to the circulation of musical knowledge in the period around 1500. Musicologists working on Italy around 1500 have, understandably and inevitably, developed a distinct canon of roughly contemporary excerpts that are used when contextualising musical sounds and practices: Johannes Tinctoris' *De inventione et usu musice* (especially the passage on the "effects" of music); the first few sections of Franchino Gafori's *Practica musicae*; Vincenzo Colli detto Il Calmeta's brief biography of the famous singer-songwriter Serafino Aquilano; the excerpt from Paolo Cortesi's *De Cardinalatu* published by Nino Pirrotta; and a few pages from Baldassare Castiglione's *Book of the Courtier*—at a stretch, also two or three musical episodes and images from the *Hypnerotomachia Poliphili*, and both the overall mise-en-scène and a few specific passages from Jacopo Sannazaro's *Arcadia* and Pietro Bembo's *Gli Asolani*.[1] We have arrived at this canon not after an exhaustive survey of musical discussions circulating in the period, but by collecting things encountered serendipitously because they seem particularly interesting and relevant to the point we want to make. There is no question that these sources are valuable and important, but equally

---

1   Key interventions in the development of this canon include Nino Pirrotta, "Music and Cultural Tendencies in 15th-Century Italy," *Journal of the American Musicological Society* 19 (1966), 127–61; James Haar, "The Frontispiece of Gafori's *Practica Musicae* (1496)," *Renaissance Quarterly* 27.1 (1974), 7–22; and Haar, "The Courtier as Musician: Castiglione's View of the Science and Art of Music," in *Castiglione: The Ideal and the Real in Renaissance Culture*, ed. Robert Hanning and David Rosand (New Haven, CT: Yale University Press, 1983), 165–90. This canon of excerpts (or at least, a very similar one) is effectively crystallised in Oliver Strunk and Leo Treitler ed., *Source Readings in Music History*, rev. edn (New York: Norton, 1998), in the Renaissance section, edited by Gary Tomlinson.

it is clear that using a handful of passages assembled more-or-less by accident and because they fit our interests as a complete characterisation of a musical context is not wholly satisfactory. Our project, we believe, takes a big step towards a more comprehensive view of the textual circulation of musical thinking beyond the specialist discourse of music theory in Italy around 1500.

0.1 Methodology

In our project, we looked at each of the 358 books listed by the USTC as printed in Italy in 1501, and transcribed all the passages we came across relating to music, sound or hearing. 1500 is a Goldilocks moment for our project; a time at which print is well established in Italy, but not sufficiently well established to generate a surviving annual production that is obviously beyond the capacity of five people to read in three years. The USTC produces a very cluttered dataset for the year 1500, however, because it includes many books with vague date ranges, such as 1500–49 or 1500–99; therefore, we chose 1501 as our sample year. We achieved our book list very simply by running a blank search in the USTC, then entering "1501" in both the "From" and "To" boxes, and limiting the "Region" to "Italians States."[2] We have therefore accepted at face value the definitions of "1501" and "Italian States" that are built into the USTC database (to do otherwise would have been impractical). In this respect, it is important to note that the books listed by the USTC for 1501 use a mixture of *more Veneto* and New Style dating, and we have not attempted to bring everything into calendrical alignment.

By defining our sample in this simple way, we do not mean to imply that books printed in 1501 were the only books available to read in Italy in that year, or even that the 358 editions listed in the USTC were the only titles printed in Italy that year.[3] Books printed in previous years remained

---

2   This search yielded 358 results during the period that we worked on the primary research for this project, in 2020–23. By the time this book was on its way to the press, in 2025, the number had grown to 372, thanks to the continuing work of the USTC team; we made no attempt to account for the extra 14 books. No doubt the number will grow again in future.

3   A recent attempt to understand the relationship between the number of early printed books of which we have knowledge, and the number that were actually produced, is Jonathan Green, Frank McIntyre, and Paul Needham, "The Shape

in the book-chests and on the shelves of readers, and in the catalogues of booksellers; and Italian readers could also acquire books printed abroad—not to mention the continuing ownership and production of manuscripts. It seems obvious, though, that taking account of all books available to read in Italy in 1501 would pull our project well beyond the bounds of practicality, and therefore we have chosen more limited terms in which to define our sample.

As we read through our corpus, we captured basic bibliographic information on each book, noting briefly its physical proportions and typographical design, checking how often its title-page texts were printed in Italy across a period from 1480 to 1520, and observing where music-related illustrations or handwritten annotations appear in our copy. But, although we are fortunate to benefit from the insights of a recent wave of new studies on the early printed book, this is not a bibliographic project, and we are interested in such matters only to the extent that they are necessary to a nuanced discussion of a book's printed contents.[4] Books of manageable size we read from cover to cover in their 1501 editions. With commented editions of classical texts and textbooks, usually printed in folio with the commentary in small text, and running in some cases to well over half a million words, we have necessarily taken a more targeted approach, reading the main text, often in a modern edition or translation, and only consulting the commentary to check the treatment of a particular word or phrase. In these cases, our final findings were always drawn from the 1501 edition, and we made sure to investigate its paratexts and reference apparatus, as well as reading around our excerpts, so that we could understand how a reader might have encountered them in 1501.

The USTC, although a wonderful and indispensable tool, inevitably contains imperfect data, including duplicate and mis-dated entries, and moreover some of the titles listed for 1501 are lost, so our sample was in

---

of Incunable Survival and Statistical Estimation of Lost Editions," *The Papers of the Bibliographical Society of America* 105.2 (2011), 141–75. Their conclusion, very approximately, is that the surviving editions may amount to around half the number originally produced.

4   Key examples relevant to the Italian context include Brian Richardson, *Printing, Writers and Readers in Renaissance Italy* (Cambridge, UK: Cambridge University Press, 1999); Andrew Pettegree, *The Book in the Renaissance* (New Haven, CT: Yale University Press, 2010); and Angela Nuovo, *The Book Trade in the Italian Renaissance*, trans. Lydia G. Cochrane (Leiden: Brill, 2013).

reality a few dozen smaller than is indicated by the 358 search hits. Our corpus is also slightly diminished because we have deliberately avoided looking at the handful of books that are obviously and explicitly musical. 1501 is celebrated by musicologists as the year in which Ottaviano Petrucci published his first songbook, *Harmonice musices odhecaton*, regarded rather approximately but tenaciously as marking the inception of "proper" music printing.[5] The same year also saw Petrucci's sequel, *Canti B numero cinquanta*, as well as the first edition of Bonaventura da Brescia's *Regula musice plane*, a short vernacular singing tutor, written by a Franciscan primarily for other religious, which is the only "music theory" book that can rightly be regarded as a print bestseller in Italy in the first decades of the sixteenth century, reaching twenty editions by 1527.[6] Our corpus also includes several service books (specifically, four missals and an antiphonary) containing notated plainchant.[7] In a project expressly designed to investigate what people write about music when they are not really writing about music, these books are the least relevant. Certainly they are important—in some cases crucially so—to the history of music in Italy in this period; but for that very reason musicology already has them covered.[8] All in all, accounting also for the 1501 books that turned out to contain little or nothing of interest concerning music, sound or hearing, or which offered only unnecessary

---

5   *Harmonice musices odhecaton* ([Venice: Ottaviano Petrucci, 1501]).
6   *Canti B. numero cinquanta* (Venice: Ottaviano Petrucci, 1501); Bonaventura da Brescia, *Regula musice plane* (Milan: per Leonhard Pachel ad impensas Giovanni Da Legnano, 1501).
7   *Antiphonarium Romanum* ([Venice: Johannes Emericus] per Lucantonio Giunta, [c.1501–02]); *Missale Romanum* (Venice: sumptibus & iussu Nikolaus von Frankfurt arte itemque & industria Peter Liechtenstein & Johann Hertzog Hamann, 1501); *Missale Romanum* (Venice: Antonius de Zanchis, 1501); *Missale romanum noviter impressum* (Venice: per Lucantonio Giunta, 1501); and *Missale secundum morem Romane Curie* (Venice: iussu & impensis Antonio Zanchi, 1501).
8   On Petrucci, see for example the two substantial volumes arising from quincentennial conferences held in 2001, Giulio Cattin and Patrizia Dalla Vecchia ed., *Venezia 1501: Petrucci e la stampa musicale* (Venice: Fondazione Levi, 2005); and Peter Reidemeister ed., *Ottaviano Petrucci 1501–2001*, published as *Basler Jahrbuch für historische Musikpraxis* 25 (2001); as well as Stanley Boorman's fundamental monograph, *Ottaviano Petrucci: A Catalogue Raisonné* (New York: Oxford University Press, 2006). Early printing of chant in Italy is extensively surveyed in Mary Kay Duggan, *Italian Music Incunabula: Printers and Type* (Berkeley, CA: University of California Press, 1992). Bonaventura da Brescia has not been afforded the same attention by musicologists, therefore we do include his book in Chapter 1.1 below.

repeat examples, across the two volumes of this study we will mention around 150 titles from our corpus.

We divided the corpus between five members of project staff, using four broad and very approximate thematic categories, which are represented in the three chapters of the present volume, plus Volume 2. Oliver Doyle took on "lifestyle literature," the most ambiguous and diffuse category, which accounts for around 20% of our sample. Here we find books telling you how to lead a good and healthy life, such as books on how to educate your children, texts explaining how to behave in a manner befitting your rank (i.e., conduct literature), works describing the regimen and diet that will result in good health and wellbeing, and books revealing what you could expect in your character and life circumstances thanks to the influence of the stars. A second 20% category, tackled by Ciara O'Flaherty, is poetry, among which she developed a particular focus on contemporary and near-contemporary verse. Scholarly books comprise roughly 30% of the corpus, including ancient, medieval, and new works on natural philosophy, literature, rhetoric, history, and civil law, often commented, printed primarily on behalf of university professors for the use of their students; these were Tim Shephard's responsibility, with the exception of law, which fell to Annabelle Page. Finally, Laura Ștefănescu took charge of religious books, which make up roughly 30% of the whole and will appear in the second volume of our study. These include devotional literature such as saints' lives, sermons, confession manuals, and advice on pious lifestyle; patristic literature and theology; canon law; the handful of liturgical books already mentioned; and one monastic rule.

These categories create numerous overlaps and relationships which should be acknowledged briefly here. Some of the religious literature sitting within Ștefănescu's book pile is written in verse, suggesting that it could also be placed within O'Flaherty's domain. O'Flaherty's "poetry" could also be taken to encompass classical Latin verse, such as that of Virgil and Ovid; but as the majority of such editions in our 1501 corpus are commented by university professors reflecting the teaching of the university classroom, their primary discussion comes under Shephard's "scholarship." Doyle's "lifestyle literature" includes medical books, which could equally be categorised as "scholarship;" we placed them with health and wellbeing under "lifestyle" because the particular medical books printed in 1501 have, for the most part, a practical (e.g., diagnosis and treatment) rather than a theoretical (e.g., natural-philosophical) character. The same can be said for Doyle's astrological literature, and the same reasoning explains our decision. Grammar books, meanwhile, are placed with education under "lifestyle" rather than with university-oriented "scholarship" because their primary role was in school-age education. And several of Ștefănescu's many devotional works could easily be considered "lifestyle literature," or even, more specifically, conduct literature. We see these overlaps and knotty allegiances not as problems, but as opportunities to build synergies and highlight relationships across the chapters and volumes of our study.

Although the central focus of our project is music, in reading through the books we have cast the net of musical relevance quite wide, noting discussions of sound and hearing as well as those directly addressing music. This is partly for pragmatic reasons: at the beginning of the project, it was by no means clear that we would find a large fund of material directly concerned with music, thus we aimed for the largest possible haul of material in which we might find musical relevance. However, there are also sound intellectual reasons for our approach, for, as many studies over the past one or two decades have shown, music was and is practised and perceived as a distinctive component within a broader field of sound production and sound perception, its meaning-making affordances and habits significantly interleaved with a wider sonic culture.[9] Reading for musical relevance in this way is not an activity easily accommodated to a completely systematic process, as it relies quite heavily on the judgement of the reader, and it is partly for this reason that we have read the books ourselves, rather than using an approach relying on Optical Character Recognition (OCR).

In fact, our wide net of relevance threatened to become unmanageably broad, and had to be drawn in a little as the project progressed. We quickly found that our 1501 corpus was full to bursting with voices and

---

9   Key examples of relevance to Italy in our period include Niall Atkinson, *The Noisy Renaissance: Sound, Architecture, and Florentine Urban Life* (University Park, PA: Penn State University Press, 2016), and several studies by Flora Dennis, including all those listed in our Bibliography. The *locus classicus*, of course, is Emma Dillon, *The Sense of Sound: Musical Meaning in France 1260–1330* (Oxford: Oxford University Press, 2012).

speakers, elements which could be both textual and aural/oral, and whose utterances threatened entirely to dominate our dataset. We turned down the volume somewhat on these contributions, so that in the end we could place music and musical culture at the heart of our interpretation of our findings, surrounded but not overwhelmed by a wider sonic field. Nonetheless, voices and speech remain important topics in this study, for several reasons. At the most fundamental level, the voice is the primary currency in the transaction between text and sound, something that is most clearly evident in our 1501 texts that were intended to be recited or sung, or that report speech and song internally to their textual soundscapes—many examples of these kinds are discussed in Chapter 2 (on poetry) and Chapter 3.2 (on rhetoric), and also in the second volume dealing with the religious books. Furthermore, we have observed that the decorum of voice—the explicit and implicit rules determining what voices ought to do and how—operated in similar ways regardless of whether a voice was speaking or singing; these aspects are picked up especially in the chapter on Lifestyle.

0.2 Authors and Readers

The deliberately simple methodology of our project and the nature of our 1501 sample make our project practicable and easy to understand, but they also present numerous difficulties and complications. Many of the texts in the corpus, although newly printed in 1501, were not newly written, sometimes hundreds or even thousands of years old. The *Problemata* of pseudo-Aristotle, Abu Bakr's *Liber nativitatum*, and Apuleius' *Asinus aureus* are all obvious examples.[10] In most such cases, the text has undertaken a tortuous journey from its initial creation to our 1501 reader, experiencing alterations and adaptations, undergoing translations and retranslations, accumulating commentaries, diagrams, illustrations, dedications and indexes, until they are finally "edited" for

---

10 Included in Aristotle et al., *Problemata Aristotelis cum duplici translatione antiqua & nova Theodori Gaze: cum expositione Petri Aponi. Tabula secundum Petrum de Tussignano Problemata Alexandri Aphrodisei. Problemata Plutarchi* (Venice: per Boneto Locatello haer. Ottaviano Scoto, 1501); Albubather et al., *Albubather. Et Centiloquium divi Hermetis* (Venice: per Giovanni Battista Sessa, 1501); and Apuleius, *Commentarii a Philippo Beroaldo conditi in Asinum aureum Lucii Apuleii* (Venice: per Simone Bevilacqua, 1501), respectively.

the printing press. This process introduces interventions from numerous individuals, often across several centuries, who are not the headline author of the text. Some of these contributors are named, some are misnamed, and some are not named, sometimes resulting in a mismatch between a "correct" modern philological understanding of the text, and the understanding accessible to and accepted by readers in 1501.

For example, a volume containing the *Problemata* attributed to Aristotle, Alexander of Aphrodisias, and Plutarch, names no fewer than ten different contributors (translators, commentators, indexers, editors, encomiasts) in addition to its three headline authors; one of those headline authors (Aristotle) is now thought to be spurious, but 1501 readers thought the attribution accurate.[11] Another similarly labyrinthine case is presented by a volume entitled *Albubather. Et Centiloquium divi Hermetis*, which contains three texts: the *Albubather*, now better known to scholarship as the *Liber nativitatum*, written in Arabic in the ninth century by Abu Bakr, and translated into Latin in Toledo in the thirteenth century by a Paduan canon named Salio and a Jewish scholar named David; the *Centiloquium divi Hermetis*, a collection of one hundred aphorisms derived from the Hermetic tradition, translated from the Arabic by Stephen of Messina during his time at the court of King Manfred of Sicily between 1258 and 1266; and another Hermetic compilation, the *Almansoris Judicia seu propositiones*, translated by Plato Tiburtinus some time after his arrival in Barcelona in 1116.[12] None of the translators are named in our 1501 edition, but the contemporary Venetian priest Antonio Lauro is named as the editor of the anthology. Our 1501 corpus contains many, many books presenting complexities of these kinds. As a result, the contents of our 1501 editions as encountered and perceived by their first readers are rarely adequately captured by modern critical editions of the texts named on their title pages.

For the purposes of our project, we deal with these difficulties by considering that the editions in our corpus are often old texts, but they are all new books. Because we want to write about musical knowledge in

---

11 Aristotle et al., *Problemata Aristotelis*. The details concerning these various contributors can be found in Tim Shephard and Charlotte Hancock, "Looking Up Music in Two 'Encyclopedias' Printed in 1501," *Renaissance Studies* 38.4 (2024), 564–95, at 570–76.

12 Albubather et al., *Albubather*. This book is discussed in more detail in Chapter 1.4 below.

1501, we have focussed on their newness as books, and only view their oldness and messiness as texts through the lens of their new acquisition and reading in particular 1501 editions. In other words, with regard to ancient and medieval authors we are working in the realm of reception history. In fact, the compound nature of the books gives us some interesting starting points in this respect. Relatively recent interventions by indexers, commentators, translators, dedicators, and editors can suggest the audiences and reading strategies that seemed in 1501 to be most pertinent to very old headline texts, in ways that sometimes inflect the musical insights available in the books.

A focus on readers in 1501 has been central to our project. The different books in our corpus are clearly designed to meet the expectations and needs of very different kinds of readers. A highly specialised Latin work with just a couple of Venetian editions, such as the *Liber nativitatum*, probably reached few readers, and only those with a professional interest in astrology. In contrast, the several commented editions of Juvenal's *Satires* that feature in our corpus, issued regularly by printers based in several cities of northern and central Italy, were probably thumbed by many university students as they studied Latin poetry in grammar class, as well as older leisure readers and scholars.[13] In some cases in our 1501 corpus, indications concerning the readers specifically envisaged by authors and editors are preserved in the books themselves or in accessory evidence. For example, some of the treatises by the famous Dominican Silvestro Mazzolini were written for and dedicated to women. In a few cases there are indications that a book was not only (or perhaps primarily) a retail product: instead, or as well, copies were sent by authors and editors as gifts to their friends and correspondents.

Although Venice dominated the book trade (around three-fifths of our 1501 books were printed there), many other Italian cities had their own printers, and some books were angled at local and regional audiences rather than Italy- or Europe-wide circulation. Giovanni Pontano's *Opera*

13　Juvenal, *Argumenta Satyrarum Iuvenalis per Antonium Mancinellum. Cum quattuor commentariis* (Venice: per Giovanni Tacuino, 1501); Juvenal, *Argumenta satyrarum Iuvenalis per Antonium Mancinellum. Cum quattuor commentariis Sebastianus Ducius recensuit* (Milan: per Giovanni Angelo Scinzenzeler sub impensis Giovanni da Legnano, 1501); Juvenal, *Commentarii Ioannis Britannici in Iuuenalem, cum gratia a ducali dominio Venetiarum nequis alius eos intra decennium imprimat* (Brescia: ab Angelo & Giacomo Britannico, 1501).

exemplifies a common publication trajectory whereby a local celebrity is first published by a local printer (in this case, Mathias Moravus in Naples, whose substantial operation was responsible for 61 editions listed in the USTC), primarily for local circulation, and then, if successful, the work is picked up by a larger Venetian printing house (in this case, that of Bernardino Viani, member of a Venetian printing dynasty spanning the entire sixteenth century) and reaches a wider audience.[14]

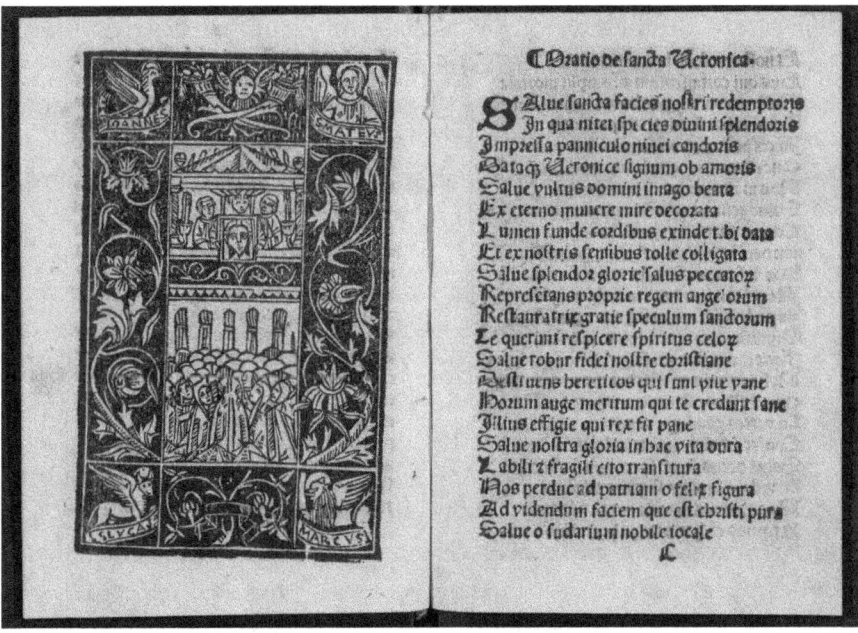

Fig. 0.1 The beginning of the *Oratio de S. Veronica*, with an image showing a crowd venerating Veronica's veil outside St Peter's Basilica on the facing page. *Mirabilia Romae* (Rome: per Johann Besicken, 1501), sigs. [B viii] v–C [i] r. Vienna, Österreichische Nationalbibliothek, 38.193-A. Image © Österreichische Nationalbibliothek, Vienna.

More irrevocably rooted in the local within our 1501 corpus is the so-called *Mirabilia Romae*,[15] an octavo guidebook for pilgrims and tourists

---

14 Giovanni Pontano, *Opera. De fortitudine: libri duo. De principe: liber unus. Dialogus qui Charon inscribitur. Dialogus qui Antonius inscribitur. De liberalitate: liber unus. De beneficentia: liber unus. De magnificentia: liber unus. De splendore: liber unus. De conviventia: liber unus. De obedientia: libri quinque* (Venice: per Bernardino Viani, 1501).

15 *Mirabilia Romae* (Rome: per Johann Besicken, 1501).

visiting Rome—which, coincidentally, contains a prayer on Veronica's veil, the generously indulgenced *Oratio de S. Veronica* or "Salve sancta facies" then attributed to Giles of Rome (see Figure 0.1), versions of which were set to music by Jacob Obrecht and Josquin des Prez. Issued in dozens of editions by German printers based in Rome in the decades either side of 1500, the *Mirabilia Romae* was a local product for local distribution to an international readership.

Although a small, pocket-sized volume, the *Mirabilia Romae* was extensively illustrated, and was available in Latin, Italian or German. It is clear that in this case, as in others, the choice of language and the inclusion of illustrations are directly related to the expected readership. Plain, commented Latin editions of Juvenal's *Satires* surely appealed to a different, though overlapping, group of readers from illustrated, vernacular editions of the lives of saints, such as the *Vita di sancti padri*, which also enjoyed a strong run of editions in the period around 1500.[16] The former was probably purchased for use at university; the latter probably for use at home, or perhaps in a convent library.

Our project is orientated towards readers, but, as we have already observed above, codicology has not been the focus of our research. A sensitive and detailed investigation of the material and textual clues to readership present in all of our 358 editions would have been well beyond the capacity of our team in the time available. Accordingly, in this book we aim to strike a balance: we bring in specific considerations of the readership and use of individual books when they are especially pertinent to the excerpts we want to discuss and the conclusions we want to draw, and when they are exemplary of wider groups or categories of books, or types of readers; but we do not drill down in this way into every book we mention.

The majority of books printed in Italy in 1501—around two thirds— were in Latin. Latin, of course, remained in 1501 the common language of scholarship, and its dominance in the print corpus is inevitable. Nonetheless, writing in Latin rather than the vernacular did limit one's readership, sometimes undesirably, as some of our 1501 authors explicitly acknowledge (for example, the Pavian physician Giovanni Antonio Bassino, as discussed in Chapter 1.3). If some degree of literacy was

---

16   *Vita di sancti padri vulgariter historiada* (Venice: per Otino Luna, 1501).

relatively common in Italy, where elementary schooling was reasonably well established in some regions, Latin literacy sufficient to read classical literature with fluency was largely the preserve of the priesthood, the professional class (lawyers, doctors, accountants, secretaries), and the rich—most of them men. This could easily be viewed as a problem in a project that seeks to chart "everyday musical knowledge" through printed books.

A useful nuance to the Latinity of our 1501 corpus can be discovered by considering the relationship between printed texts and professional practice. It seems likely that the *Liber nativitatum* was mostly read by expert astronomers, for example, but those specialists read it to inform their *viva voce* consultations with clients, and their preparation of advisory horoscopes and prognostications, at least some of which activity was transacted in the vernacular. Similarly, Giovanni de Concoregio's *Practica nova medicine* was clearly written for practicing physicians by a practicing physician, but the information it contained was intended to be used in advising patients on diagnoses and treatments.[17] Thus, ideas written down in Latin need not stay written down, or in Latin, but in some cases and to some extent could make their way quite easily into the wider world of oral, vernacular, and indeed visual discourse.

Another obvious point of interface between the written and the oral can be found in our religious literature, some of which was written by mendicants who were also active as preachers. Mazzolini's three titles printed in 1501 (at which point he was around the middle of his career) furnish a good example.[18] While sermons were often published in Latin, they were usually delivered in Italian, often in public, and sometimes to large crowds.[19] Mazzolini's 1501 titles are all devotional works (in

---

17 Giovanni de Concoregio, *Practica nova medicine Ioannis de Concoregio Mediolanensis. Lucidarium & flos florum medicinae nuncupata. Summula de curis febrium secundum hodiernum modum & usum compilata* (Venice: [Simone Bevilacqua], 1501).
18 Silvestro Mazzolini, *Opere vulgare* (Bologna: per Benedetto Faielli, 1501); Silvestro Mazzolini, *Incominza la vita de la seraphica e ferventissima amatrice de Iesu Cristo Salvatore Sancta Maria Magdalena: ricolta cum molte nove hystorie per il reverendo padre e maestro ne la sacra theologia frate Silvestro da Prierio de l'ordine de frati predicatori* (Bologna: per Caligola Bazalieri, 1501); Silvestro Mazzolini, *Summario per confessarsi brevissimo e doctrinale* (Bologna: Giovanni Antonio Benedetti, 1501).
19 Carlo Delcorno, "Medieval Preaching in Italy," in *The Sermon*, ed. Beverly Mayne Kienzle and René Noël (Turnhout: Brepols, 2000), 449–560; Peter Howard, "A Landscape of Preaching: Bartolomeo Lapacci Rimbertini OP," in *Mendicant Cultures in the Medieval and Early Modern World: Word, Deed, & Image*, ed. Sally

this case in Italian), but it seems reasonable to suppose that the same or similar precepts could also be heard *viva voce* in his sermons. A somewhat similar case is presented by the large portfolio of classical texts in our corpus that were printed with commentaries by one or more contemporary university professors. It has often been observed that these commentaries must be closely related to professors' teaching notes, and moreover we know that university lectures were public events which could in theory be attended also by those who were not studying for a degree.[20] Thus, even the impenetrable thicket of printed words crammed into the margins of an edition of Juvenal or Virgil could also, partially and in some circumstances, be encountered as speech in class.

Considerations such as these indicate that the "readership" for our 1501 books extended well beyond those who had the intellectual and financial capital, and the motivation, to buy and read them—or indeed to write, translate, edit, comment, illustrate, index, or print them. In Italy in 1501, books intersected with lives in a wide variety of ways, both direct and indirect, allowing for a considerable porosity between the written and the oral, the Latin and the vernacular. In this study we often lean on this broader notion of "readership" in discussing the circulation of musical knowledge and in drawing our conclusions.

0.3 The 1501 Corpus and Contemporary Libraries

An obvious step in evaluating our 1501 corpus in relation to readers is to compare it with the contents of actual contemporary libraries documented in inventories, to see if and to what extent it is "representative." This step is not actually necessary to our project, as the foregoing and the following discussion amply explain, because the circulation and currency of the musical ideas found in our corpus did not hinge on whether or not a specific individual physically possessed a particular 1501 title. In fact, recent research has shown that library inventories very imperfectly represent the contemporary culture of books in any case.

Cornelison, Nirit Ben Debby, and Peter Howard (Turnout: Brepols, 2016), 45–64, at 52–53; Pietro Delcorno, *In the Mirror of the Prodigal Son: The Pastoral Uses of a Biblical Narrative (c. 1200–1550)* (Leiden: Brill, 2018), 114.

20 On the relationship between commentaries and teaching, see Paul F. Grendler, *The Universities of the Italian Renaissance* (Baltimore, MD: John Hopkins University Press, 2002), 241–44; and on public lectures, 223.

Perhaps the richest source of data on book ownership is probate inventories.[21] These lists can provide an extraordinary window into everyday life, but they are far from exact. The testator carrying out an inventory was principally concerned with the value of an estate, and objects which were considered of negligible value—which might include printed books—were often imprecisely noted, described as a collection (for instance, "four small books in the vernacular"), or omitted entirely.[22] Texts which were the cheapest and most frequently sold, such as hornbooks, lives of saints, elementary Latin grammars, prognostica, and ephemeral poetry collections, had very little monetary value second-hand, and may well have been present in more homes than records disclose.[23] Meanwhile, thanks to the importance of a "culture of borrowing," not owning a book was not the same thing as not reading it.[24] On the other side of the same coin, the presence of a text in an individual's collection is no guarantee that they ever read it.[25] This becomes particularly apparent when considering that the construction of a library could be but one form of collecting as a means of projecting power, status, or any other facet of one's self image.[26] Thus, there is no proof-of-concept to be found for our project in a booklist; but a brief comparison of our 1501 sample with three roughly contemporary examples will be interesting nonetheless.

When the Portuguese nobleman Gonzalo Gomez purchased over 227 books on behalf of Catherine, Queen of Portugal, from the Milanese

---

21 Malcolm Walsby, "Booklists and their Meaning," in *Documenting the Early Modern Book World: Inventories and Catalogues in Manuscript and Print*, ed. Malcolm Walsby and Natasha Constantinidou (Leiden: Brill, 2013), 1–24, at 6.

22 Sarah Gwyneth Ross, *Everyday Renaissances: The Quest for Cultural Legitimacy in Venice* (Cambridge, MA: Harvard University Press, 2016), 28; and Walsby, "Booklists and their Meaning," 11.

23 On the brisk trade in grammar books, see Cristina Dondi, "From the Corpus Iuris to "psalterioli da puti," in Parchment, Bound, Gilt... The Price of Any Book Sold in Venice 1484–1488," *Studi di Storia* 13 (2020), 577–99.

24 On book lending as a duty of friendship in Quattrocento Florence, see Dale Kent, *Cosimo de' Medici and the Florentine Renaissance: The Patron's Oeuvre* (New Haven, CT: Yale University Press, 2000), 74.

25 Walsby, "Booklists and their Meaning," 5.

26 Angela Nuovo, "Private Libraries in Sixteenth-Century Italy," in *Early Printed Books as Material Objects*, ed. Bettina Wagner and Marcia Reed (Berlin: De Gruyter Saur, 2010), 229–40, at 230–31. For a detailed study of Isabella d'Este's possible use of books as a self-fashioning tool, see Brian Richardson, "Isabella d'Este and the Social Uses of Books," *La Bibliofilía* 114.3 (2012), 293–326.

bookseller Andrea Calvo in 1540, her library—previously assembled piecemeal—more than quadrupled from the size it had been in 1534.[27] The nature of her collection changed, too. As of 1534, it contained a mixture of ancient authors, and moral and religious works, not unlike the reading list recommended for women by Leonardo Bruni more than a hundred years before.[28] The selection purchased in 1540 expanded this into something nearing a fully-fledged humanistic library, replete with texts on rhetoric, medicine, and architecture, a small number of Latin grammar manuals, and two texts dedicated to conduct: Pontano's complete works and Castiglione's *Libro del Cortegiano*.[29] Besides Pontano's *Opera*, this library exhibits numerous concordances with our 1501 corpus. From the ancient world, Cicero's *Epistulae ad familiares*, the works of Cato, Ovid's *Metamorphoses* and *Heroides*, Juvenal's *Satires*, the letters of Pliny the Younger, and the writings of Statius and Terence were all present in Catherine's collection. Among her works in the vernacular, only two concordances are found: the works of Petrarch, and a vernacular commentary on the psalms. Such a library had its uses, in terms of Catherine's own interests and the education of her son, but its categorisation in the 1540 inventory—by language and binding, rather than subject—suggests that Catherine's purpose with her new acquisitions lay not so much in specific titles as in the coalescence of texts which projected a learned ideal.[30]

While Catherine's inventories overlap to a fair degree with the 1501 corpus in terms of the presence of ancient authors, the 1499 and 1529 inventories of Baldassare Castiglione's library reveal a far greater bent towards study. Castiglione's library on both dates was replete with grammars and reference books, many of which were also published

---

27 Kevin M. Stevens, "Books Fit for a Portuguese Queen: The Lost Library of Catherine of Austria and the Milan Connection (1540)," in *Documenting the Early Modern Book World: Inventories and Catalogues in Manuscript and Print*, ed. Malcolm Walsby and Natasha Constantinidou (Leiden: Brill, 2013), 85–116, at 96.

28 Stevens, "Books Fit for a Portuguese Queen," 96; and Leonardo Bruni, "The Study of Literature," in *Humanist Educational Treatises*, ed. and trans. Craig W. Kallendorf, The I Tatti Renaissance Library 5 (Cambridge, MA: Harvard University Press, 2002), 92–125, at 97–99 and 107. Bruni's treatise was printed in Italy in 1477 and 1483.

29 Stevens, "Books Fit for a Portuguese Queen," 96. For a transcription of the inventory of those texts purchased in 1540, see 107–16.

30 Stevens, "Books Fit for a Portuguese Queen," 103–04.

in 1501 (though, of course, he did not necessarily own them in their 1501 editions).[31] Focussing solely on texts of this kind also printed in 1501, in the 1499 inventory we find two copies of Constantine Lascaris' *Erotemata*, Niccolò Perotti's *Cornucopiae* and *Rudimenta grammatices*, Giovanni Tortelli's *Orthographia*, Pliny's *Naturalis historia*, and Johannes de Sacrobosco's *De sphaera mundi*. By the time of his probate inventory in 1529, the list of 1501 concordances had expanded to include Lorenzo Valla's *Elegantiae*, Aldo Manuzio's *Rudimenta Grammatices*, two copies of Pliny's *Naturalis historia*, the complete works of Pontano, and Guarino da Verona's *Erotemata*. Like Catherine of Austria, he owned copies of Juvenal's *Satires*, Ovid's *Metamorphoses*, the writings of Statius, Terence, and Virgil, and the poetry of Petrarch; but in addition he possessed Cicero's *Orator*, Martial's epigrams, Macrobius' *Somnium Scipionis*, Philostratus' *Vita Apollonii*, and of the writings of Apuleius, Aristophanes, and Aristotle, all duplicated in our 1501 list.

Concordances are also found in the inventory carried out sometime after the death of Isabella d'Este, though the number of book purchases described in her letters betrays a library that was once far larger.[32] Like Castiglione, Isabella owned copies of many philosophical, poetic, and historical works by ancient authors found in our 1501 sample—Aristotle's *Problemata*, the writings of Apuleius, Cicero's *Orator*, Philostratus' *Vita Apollonii*, the poetry of Ovid and Martial, two copies of Pliny's *Naturalis historia* (in Italian and Latin), and the writings of Statius and Terence. Like Castiglione, she also owned a copy of Perotti's *Cornucopiae*. Unlike Castiglione, her library also included a *Regimine sanitatis* (perhaps that by Arnaldus de Villa Nova) and Avicenna's *De medicina*, as well as a compilation of prognostica, which, as short, ephemeral prints, might have gone unnoted if not gathered into one sizeable volume. It is interesting to observe that, of the three contemporary libraries considered here, only Isabella's contained a book on music that was listed in an inventory (in

---

31 The following comparison is based on the transcription of several inventories of Castiglione's belongings in Guido Rebecchini, "The Book Collection and Other Possessions of Baldassarre Castiglione," *Journal of the Warburg and Courtauld Institutes*, 61 (1998), 17–52. See especially 26–30 and 35–44.

32 Stephen Campbell, *The Cabinet of Eros: Renaissance Mythological Painting and the Studiolo of Isabella d'Este* (New Haven, CT: Yale University Press, 2006), 270. A full transcription of this inventory can be found on pages 276–79.

this case, a handwritten copy of Franchino Gafori's lost *Fioretti di musica*), even though Castiglione's musical interests are also well documented.[33]

In the end, though, it is not the specific 1501 concordances so much as the disposition of general categories of books in different kinds of libraries that is of interest for our project. Many elite libraries created in Italy in the decades around 1500 contained a selection of classical works across several genres, and copies of the Latin grammars that helped one learn how to read them. Obviously, such works may have been owned more for their look on the shelf than for their contents—although any reader who had undertaken university study, or who cultivated a learned reputation, would certainly have had cause to engage with (some of) them in earnest. Within this broad category, books such as Perotti's *Cornucopiae*, Tortelli's *Orthographia*, and Pliny's *Naturalis historia* were owned widely enough that they must have been valued as reference texts. Works of moral instruction—whether practical or literary, vernacular or Latin in character—were common to many libraries, as was devotional literature; in women's libraries and smaller libraries these categories usually dominated. Books of practical value to the household, such as those touching on health and wellbeing, and prognostications, comprise another important category—although some books of these types were cheap and slim, exactly the kind of volume that a notary might consider irrelevant to an inventory intended to calculate the financial value of an individual's material assets.

This offers an important reminder of the limitations of these inventories as snapshots of a reader's interests. The absence of ephemeral prints of contemporary verse from their collections, for example, certainly cannot be taken to imply that Castiglione and Isabella d'Este took no interest in the genre. We must also acknowledge that books were owned not only by individuals, but also by institutions: a church might well own printed service books, or volumes of patristic theology, for example, and a substantial shelf of devotional literature might be expected in a monastic or convent library. With these and similar considerations in mind, we will be cautious in drawing substantive conclusions about our 1501 corpus from its degree of concordance with contemporary booklists.

---

33 Campbell, *The Cabinet of Eros*, 273. On this treatise see Bonnie J. Blackburn, Edward Lowinsky, and Clement A. Miller ed., *A Correspondence of Renaissance Musicians* (Oxford: Clarendon, 1990), 167 (note 76).

0.4 Everyday Musical Knowledge

Of course, it is incumbent upon us to explain what we mean by "everyday musical knowledge," and why it is reasonable to suppose that a year's printed books can give us access to it. Roughly, we use the phrase "everyday musical knowledge" to capture all the things people could know and think about music in their daily lives, which are different from the "music theory" discussed by musical specialists. Musicologists and cultural historians have already made the Italian music theory of the late fifteenth and early sixteenth centuries the subject of numerous important and substantial studies.[34] Johannes Tinctoris in Naples, Nicolò Burzio and Bartolomé Ramos de Pareja in Bologna, Franchino Gafori in Milan, Giovanni Spataro in Venice, and Pietro Aron in Imola, Venice, then Bergamo, are among the cornerstones of our history of Italian musical culture c.1500. It seems likely that their expert perspective on music overlaps only partially with the musical knowledge and understanding acquired by those engaged more casually in musicking, who, after all, make up the majority of participants in a musical culture. We hypothesise that we might find a closer reflection of *their* musical knowledge if we attend to what is said or implied about music in printed books when music is not the main subject of discussion. We think of this as adding up to a kind of "musical worldview"—which is more a set of affordances than a precise prescription, because it seems unlikely that every Italian in 1501 inhabited it in the same way.

There are, of course, difficulties inherent in using our 1501 corpus to access such a musical worldview. For all its neat chronological coherence and seemingly comprehensive scope, our project has forced us into a highly anachronistic reading practice, because nobody in Renaissance Italy ever purchased every book printed in 1501, *only* 1501, then read them all cover-to-cover. Moreover, a significant number of texts that

---

34 The most fundamental studies include Claude V. Palisca, *Humanism in Italian Renaissance Musical Thought* (New Haven, CT: Yale University Press, 1985); Blackburn et al., *A Correspondence of Renaissance Musicians*; Ann E. Moyer, *Musica Scientia: Musical Scholarship in the Italian Renaissance* (Ithaca, NY: Cornell University Press, 1992); and Bonnie J. Blackburn, "Music Theory and Musical Thinking after 1450," in *Music as Concept and Practice in the Late Middle Ages*, ed. Reinhard Strohm and Bonnie J. Blackburn (Oxford: Oxford University Press, 2001), 301–45.

have plenty to say about music, and went through many printed editions around 1500, happened not to be printed in 1501—Quintilian's *Institutio oratoria*, for example, or Pier Paolo Vergerio's *De ingenuis moribus ac liberalibus studiis*, or the writings of Girolamo Savonarola. Such texts will only appear in our findings piecemeal, helping to flesh out a wider context for the 1501 books that are our main focus, and this may represent a distortion of the everyday musical knowledge we are seeking to chart. Conversely, a handful of texts printed in 1501 that have a particular wealth of musical content were never printed before or since, suggesting that they found few readers. The unique 1501 edition of Giorgio Valla's *De expetendis, et fugiendis rebus opus*, with a long section on ancient Greek music theory, is a good example:[35] in a study of humanist responses to music, Valla's work would be centrally important, but in a study of everyday musical knowledge the book seems of limited interest.[36] In our work we have been careful to resist, or at least to moderate, the lure of texts that are exceptionally musically productive, but probably unrepresentative.

Although our sample is certainly imperfect, there are clear reasons to suppose that it is sufficient to reflect in a general way the everyday musical knowledge we seek, without distorting it beyond an acceptable margin of error. The organisation of the chapters and volumes of this study reflects our observation that, across our 1501 corpus, music inhabits several discrete and approximately coherent discourses, each shared across numerous similar texts. So, for example, there is a musical discourse connected with school-age education (Chapter 1.1); a musical discourse engaged by medical practitioners (1.3); a musical discourse associated with astronomy (1.4); one developed by and for lyric poets (Chapter 2); one arising from commentary on Aristotelian natural philosophy (Chapter 3.1); and one activated by humanities professors when commenting on classical literature (3.3, 3.4)—among numerous others. Within each of these musical discourses, there is a reasonably consistent repertoire of pertinent things one can say,

---

35 Giorgio Valla, *De expetendis et fugiendis rebus opus* (Venice: in aedibus Aldo Manuzio impensa ac studio Giampietro Valla, 1501).

36 As exemplified by Palisca, *Humanism*, 67–87; and Moyer, *Musica Scientia*, 92–100. See also Bonnie Blackburn, "The Fifteenth-Century Afterlives of the *Speculum musicae* by Jacobus of Liege," *Journal of the Alamire Foundation* 16.2 (2024), 244–78, at 262–73.

including illustrative examples. Thus, for our 1501 corpus to produce a representative picture of everyday musical knowledge in print, it need not contain every book then in circulation, and we need not presume that every Italian had read every book in the corpus; it is sufficient that a selection of books representing the range of well-established musical discourses is present, both in our corpus, and in the awareness and experiences of a period reader.

These discrete musical discourses are, of course, not unrelated to each other. There are significant alignments and overlaps between them, for example concerning music's effects on individuals and society (moving the emotions; persuading; bringing to accord), the concepts through which musical sounds are evaluated (variety; sweetness; harmony; joy), and the underlying mechanisms assumed to drive its effective capacities (humouralism and complexion; harmonics), among other elements. However, for all their shared assumptions, these distinct musical discourses are also misaligned, contradictory, or at the very least speaking at cross-purposes, as an inevitable result of the different objectives, the different origins (e.g., Greek, Roman, Arabic, medieval, recent), and the different rhetorical and intellectual traditions characterising the larger discourses of which they form a small part (such as that of poetics, or that of Galenic medicine, or that of Aristotelian commentary). It is interesting to think about the impacts these discontinuities may have had as the different musical discourses rubbed up against each other within the musical worldview of an individual in 1501—the creatively anachronistic accommodations of old ideas to new musical practices, the degree of segmentation or integration attempted between incompatible musical perspectives, the conceptual fudging considered acceptable and necessary to a somewhat coherent total understanding. These discontinuities are not intellectual problems for our project and its objectives, however; rather, they are integral to real human experience in general, and in particular to the real experience of knowing some things about any subject.[37]

We see the musical worldview revealed in our 1501 sources as a contribution to a wider move towards tracing the weave of musical

---

37 These issues are thematised and explored in Shephard and Hancock, "Looking Up Music in Two 'Encyclopedias'."

threads into the fabric of everyday life in Renaissance Italy, which might be said to emphasise a social/anthropological rather than a technical/aesthetic view of our subject. Music studies has shown a marked trend toward the everyday since the turn of the century, led especially by scholars whose methods and research questions are drawn from sociology and social psychology rather than musicology *per se*, and almost always focussed on the present day.[38] Meanwhile, a similar trajectory has emerged within Italian Renaissance studies, spurred on especially by the seminal V&A exhibition *At Home in Renaissance Italy* curated by Marta Ajmar-Wollheim and Flora Dennis and its accompanying catalogue, and underpinned primarily by the methods and perspectives of cultural history.[39] Work investigating the cultures and practices associated with family, sex, health and wellbeing, costume, food, devotion, and many other areas of life, has over the past three decades built an increasingly detailed impression of the texture of daily experience in Italy between the fifteenth and the seventeenth centuries.[40]

Music and sound are already finding their places in this discourse, though often in work conducted outside of the disciplinary frame

---

38 Key studies include Tia DeNora, *Music in Everyday Life* (Cambridge, UK: Cambridge University Press, 2000); and Eric Clarke, Nicola Dibben, and Stephanie Pitts, *Music and Mind in Everyday Life* (Oxford: Oxford University Press, 2010).

39 Marta Ajmar-Wollheim and Flora Dennis ed., *At Home in Renaissance Italy* (London: V&A, 2006).

40 For example, in chronological order by date of publication: Dora Thornton, *The Scholar in his Study: Ownership and Experience in Renaissance Italy* (New Haven, CT: Yale University Press, 1997); Luke Syson and Dora Thornton, *Objects of Virtue: Art in Renaissance Italy* (London: British Museum, 2001); Carole Collier Frick, *Dressing Renaissance Florence: Families, Fortunes and Fine Clothing* (Baltimore, MD: Johns Hopkins University Press, 2002); Patricia Fortini Brown, *Private Lives in Renaissance Venice* (New Haven, CT: Yale University Press, 2004); Evelyn Welch, *Shopping in the Renaissance: Consumer Cultures in Italy 1400–1600* (New Haven, CT: Yale University Press, 2005); Andrea Bayer ed., *Art and Love in Renaissance Italy* (New York: Metropolitan Museum of Art, 2008); Jacqueline Marie Musacchio, *Art, Marriage and Family in the Florentine Renaissance Palace* (New Haven, CT: Yale University Press, 2008); Sara F. Matthews-Grieco ed., *Erotic Cultures of Renaissance Italy* (Aldershot: Ashgate, 2010); Sandra Cavallo and Tessa Storey, *Healthy Living in Late Renaissance Italy* (New York: Oxford University Press, 2013); Jill Burke, *The Italian Renaissance Nude* (New Haven, CT: Yale University Press, 2018); Abigail Brundin, Deborah Howard, and Mary Laven, *The Sacred Home in Renaissance Italy* (Oxford: Oxford University Press, 2018); and Allen J. Grieco, *Food, Social Politics and the Order of Nature in Renaissance Italy* (Florence: I Tatti—The Harvard Centre for Italian Renaissance Studies, 2019).

of musicology. Cultural historian Flora Dennis, for example, has investigated the sounds and musics associated with everyday objects such as fans, cutlery, and cookware, prompting musicologists to engage more fully with the "material turn" in the humanities.[41] Meanwhile, architectural historian Niall Atkinson has documented the "sonic armatures" implemented in the streets and public spaces of Florence, inspiring a new approach to Renaissance urban "soundscapes" that looks beyond the contributions of church and court and the public performance of polyphony.[42] Within musicology, the relevance and importance of everyday musical experience is by now quite well established among those working on the mid and late sixteenth century, as a glance through "Part II—Culture, Place, and Practice" in Iain Fenlon and Richard Wistreich's 2019 *Cambridge History of Sixteenth Century Music* will quickly confirm.[43] Where the fifteenth and early sixteenth centuries are concerned, we are only at the beginning—although inspiring models are already available in the work of scholars such as Anthony M. Cummings and Giovanni Zanovello.[44]

Our findings add to our understanding of the place of music in everyday life in Italy around 1500, to the extent that the books in our 1501 corpus themselves thread in and out of the daily lives of Renaissance

---

41 Dennis, "Resurrecting Forgotten Sound: Fans and Handbells in Early Modern Italy," in *Everyday Objects: Medieval and Early Modern Material Culture and Its Meanings*, ed. Tara Hamling and Catherine Richardson (New York: Routledge, 2010), 191–210; Dennis, "Scattered Knives and Dismembered Song: Cutlery, Music and the Rituals of Dining," *Renaissance Studies* 24.1 (2010), 156–84; Dennis, "Cooking Pots, Tableware, and the Changing Sounds of Sociability in Italy," *Sound Studies* 6.2 (2020), 174–95. See also Tim Shephard, "Musical Classicisms in Italy Before the Madrigal," *Music & Letters* 101.4 (2020), 690–712; and Shephard, "The Domestic Life of the Syrinx," in *The Media of Secular Music in the Medieval and Early Modern Period*, ed. Vincenzo Borghetti and Alexandros Maria Hatzikiriakos (New York: Routledge, 2024), 217–38.

42 Atkinson, *The Noisy Renaissance*. See also Daniel M. Zolli and Christopher Brown, "Bell on Trial: The Struggle for Sound after Savonarola," *Renaissance Quarterly* 72.1 (2019), 54–96; and Tim Shephard and Melany Rice, "Giovanni Pontano Hears the Street Soundscape of Naples," *Renaissance Studies* 38.4 (2024), 519–41.

43 Iain Fenlon and Richard Wistreich ed., *The Cambridge History of Sixteenth Century Music* (Cambridge, UK: Cambridge University Press, 2019).

44 For example, Cummings, "Music and Feasts in the Fifteenth Century," in *The Cambridge History of Fifteenth Century Music*, ed. Anna Maria Busse Berger and Jesse Rodin (Cambridge, UK: Cambridge University Press, 2015), 361–73; Zanovello, "'In the Church and in the Chapel': Music and Devotional Spaces in the Florentine Church of Santissima Annunziata," *Journal of the American Musicological Society* 67.2 (2014), 379–428.

Italians. One could encounter some of our books when attending school or university; others when consulting a physician, astrologer or lawyer; others when diligently pursuing devotional practice or in church; and yet others during leisure time at home. It is through these encounters (which may or may not entail actually owning, borrowing or reading the books in question), and their conventional or likely patterns, that we can most easily draw together the disparate threads of musical knowledge found in our 1501 corpus into something approximating a worldview, and show how that musical worldview might interact with, inform, or play out in everyday life. We return to these ideas in the Conclusions to each volume of this study.

0.5 Structure and Editorial Policies

In a book that presents a snapshot rather than a reel, there is no chronological progression to give a narrative logic to the sequencing of our material. To present our four thematic categories in some sort of coherent order, we have appealed to two interacting notions, both related to the ways in which knowledge was organised in the period. First, we have considered an ordering that reflects a reader's educational and literary life journey in the early sixteenth century; this is what places matters concerning birth, education, and moral formation, discussed by Doyle, and O'Flaherty's analysis of amatory verse, associated especially with youth culture, at the beginning. Second, we have considered period views on the hierarchy of knowledge, which often place theology at the summit, as the science of the divine; this is why Ștefănescu's material comes last, in the second volume, following and superceding the material on natural philosophy, rhetoric, literature, history, and law dealt with by Shephard and Page at the end of the first volume.

These considerations already indicate the division of authorial responsibilities. In the first volume, Shephard is the primary author of the Introduction, with the exception of Chapter 0.3 which was first drafted by Doyle, although in fact the content of the Introduction as a whole is substantially the product of discussion among the entire project team. Doyle is the primary author of Chapter 1 (except for some material on Galen in 1.3, which was first authored by Shephard), and O'Flaherty of Chapter 2, in both cases with guidance and editorial interventions from Shephard. Shephard is the primary author of Chapter 3, with two important exceptions: O'Flaherty contributed significant material on Juvenal to 3.3, and Page co-authored 3.5 on law. The Conclusion is written by Shephard, with editorial interventions from the other co-authors. The second volume as a whole is written by Ştefănescu, with editorial interventions from Shephard.

We have implemented certain policies to ensure consistency, to match our research objectives, and to convenience the reader, which it will be useful to outline here. In all cases, our overriding objective is to put our 1501 books front and centre, and to represent their contents as faithfully as possible without making our study difficult to use. With the exception of the Introductions to each volume, each section of each chapter begins with a bibliography of the 1501 books that are discussed therein. The nature of that "discussion" varies widely, from brief mentions in footnotes to lengthy case studies. These are compiled into the alphabetical Bibliography 1: 1501 Books towards the end of each volume, where the sections at which each book is mentioned are noted; 1501 books that are not discussed in this study are not listed (a complete list can easily be called up on the USTC). The bibliographic entries for our 1501 books are copied almost exactly from the USTC, with only a few small corrections here and there. Our transcriptions from the 1501 books retain the original punctuation, capitalisation, and spelling, but write out abbreviations (including &), and adapt u/v letter substitutions to match modern norms. A small selection of longer passages is given in the Appendix so as not to overburden the main text. When citing passages in our 1501 books, we give folio numbers if they are present in our copy, and in their absence we use signatures.

Translations are ours unless otherwise noted. We are immensely grateful to both Jeffrey Scott Bernstein and David E. Cohen for refining several of our Latin translations, and to Alexandros Maria Hatzikiriakos for help with a few words and phrases in Greek. (Any remaining errors are of course our own responsibility.) Our translations are more direct than literary, because they exist primarily to assist in the navigation of the original. Where published translations are available, we use them, but often with adaptations to reflect the Latin and Italian readings present in our 1501 texts, which sometimes differ from their modern equivalents. For translations of classical literature we default to Loeb, except in cases where a more direct translation is preferable to clarify the discussion. In the case of ancient Greek works, adaptation or retranslation is sometimes necessary to match the medieval Latin translations through which 1501 readers usually encountered them.

Many, many personalities active in Italy in the fifteenth and early sixteenth centuries are mentioned in this study: printers, publishers and authors, of course, but also editors, translators, indexers, dedicatees, and so forth. Conducting exhaustive biographical research into each of these individuals, with appropriate citations, would have been an impossible task, and would have made our study extremely cumbersome without advancing our research objectives. Therefore in almost all cases we have relied on the entries in the immensely useful *Dizionario Biografico degli Italiani*, published online by the Istituto della Enciclopedia Italiana Treccani.[45] We will not cite the individual articles on our protagonists, which readers can easily locate via an online search using the relevant names as keywords; this explanation serves as acknowledgement of our scholarly debt.

We must point out some overlaps between our material presented in this study and that already published in a special issue of *Renaissance Studies* (38.4, 2024) entitled *Reading for Musical Knowledge in Early Sixteenth-Century Italy*. Specifically, some parts of this Introduction are revised and adapted from the Introduction to the special issue; some paragraphs of Chapter 1.4 are reworked from Doyle's article "Musicianship and the Masteries of the Stars: Music and Musicians in the *Liber Nativitatum*;" and some passages of O'Flaherty and Shephard's article "Commenting on Music in Juvenal's Sixth Satire" are further developed here in Chapter 3.3. We are grateful to Wiley, the publisher of *Renaissance Studies*, for permission to reuse our material in these ways.

Finally, it is our great pleasure to acknowledge the impact on this study of all those individuals who discussed our project with us at our various conference panels, invited us to test out our work-in-progress in seminars at their institutions, or kindly read and commented on drafts

---

45 See https://www.treccani.it/enciclopedia/elenco-opere/Dizionario_Biografico/.

for this study. We would like to single out Bonnie Blackburn, Vincenzo Borghetti, Antonio Cascelli, Julie Cumming, Richard Freedman, Elisabeth Giselbrecht, Alexandros Maria Hatzikiriakos, Kevin Killeen, Melinda Latour, Peter Loewen, Evan MacCarthy, Marica Tacconi, Giovanni Zanovello, and the anonymous readers for Open Book Publishers for particular thanks.

1. Lifestyle

Bonvesin de la Riva, *Vita scolastica* (Venice: per Giovanni Battista Sessa, 1501)

Pseudo-Aelius Donatus et al., *Donatus Melior. Catonis Carmen de moribus. De Arte Libellus* (Milan: [Giovanni da Legnano] per Leonhard Pachel, 1501)

Marsilio Ficino, *De triplici vita libri tres* (Bologna: Benedetto Faelli, 1501)

Francesco Maria Grapaldi, *De partibus aedium libellus cum additamentis emendatissimus* (Parma: Angelo Ugoleto, 1501)

Lifestyle literature, if not the largest of the four categories into which we have divided the corpus of texts printed in Italy in 1501, is probably the most diverse, and certainly the most contrived.[1] At its core, we intend the term "lifestyle literature" to encapsulate texts written or read with the intention of informing any facet of the reader's actions, regimen or character—in short, addressing the question of how to live well. The fundamental difference between lifestyle literature and the perhaps more familiar term "conduct literature" lies in this breadth. Past studies of conduct literature in the Middle Ages and Renaissance have often limited themselves to didactic texts, sometimes going so far as to distinguish between texts which deal with morality and those which deal with behaviour. The breadth of our strategically imprecise category of "lifestyle literature" allows us to approach the matter of living well more flexibly, fully recognising that Renaissance readers sought moral instruction and life guidance directly or indirectly from a very wide range of texts.[2] Enea Silvio Piccolomini and Leonardo Bruni, for

---

1 For further critical reflections on the definition and validity of "lifestyle literature" as a category in our project, beyond those presented here, see Oliver Doyle, "Beyond the Courtier: Music and Lifestyle Literature in Italy 1480–1530" (PhD diss., University of Sheffield, 2024), 3–11.

2 Anna Dronzek, "Gendered Theories of Education in Fifteenth-Century Conduct Books," in *Medieval Conduct*, ed. Kathleen Ashley and Robert L. A.

example, both recommended the reading of a variety of ancient poetry, philosophy, and religious texts, in order for boys and girls to develop good morals and an attractive writing style, in their respective treatises on education, *De librorum educatione* (*On the Education of Boys*, 1450) and *De studiis et litteris* (*On the Study of Literature*, c.1422–29).[3]

As Helena Sanson has pointed out, definitions of genre are often applied retrospectively, and as such are porous: in some way, all literature was conduct literature, as any text could influence the reader's perspective or behaviour, whether it intended to or not.[4] This view is borne out in some way by what little we know of how readers might have encountered books on a visit to their local bookshop. By the 1530s, the printer Gabriele Giolito had begun to distinguish manuals of conduct (*comportamento*) from other volumes for sale.[5] In contrast, the bookseller Francesco de Madiis, active in the final decades of the fifteenth century, drew no such distinction: the *Fiore di virtù*, a conduct book proffering exemplars in the form of the lives of saints, finds itself not amongst religious literature (a shelving which did exist in Madiis' shop), and certainly not amongst conduct literature (a category which he did not use), but rather amidst a broad selection of vernacular literature, ranging from translations of the Bible to chivalric romances.[6] Angela Nuovo notes that the *Fiore di virtù* served a dual purpose, in that it was used to teach women to read after they had learned the alphabet, as well as presenting them with examples of virtuous behaviour.[7] The *Disticha Catonis*, which appears in our 1501 corpus within an anthology

---

Clark (Minneapolis, MN: University of Minnesota Press, 2001), 135–59, at 137. Alessandro Arcangeli makes a similar observation about advice specifically on proper leisure: *Recreation in the Renaissance: Attitudes towards Leisure and Pastimes in European Culture, c. 1425–1675* (New York: Palgrave Macmillan, 2003), 1.

3 Enea Silvio Piccolomini, "The Education of Boys," in *Humanist Educational Treatises*, ed. and trans. Craig W. Kallendorf, The I Tatti Renaissance Library 5 (Cambridge, MA: Harvard University Press, 2002), 126–259, at 221–23; Leonardo Bruni, "The Study of Literature," in *Humanist Educational Treatises*, ed. and trans. Kallendorf, 92–125, at 97–9 and 107.

4 Helena Sanson, "Introduction. Women and Conduct in the Italian Tradition, 1470–1900: An Overview," in *Conduct Literature for and about Women in Italy 1470–1900: Prescribing and Describing Life*, ed. Helena Sanson and Francesco Lucioli (Paris: Classiques Garnier, 2016), 9–38, at 13.

5 Sanson, "Women and Conduct in the Italian Tradition," 16.

6 Angela Nuovo, *The Book Trade in the Italian Renaissance*, trans. Lydia G. Cochrane (Leiden: Brill, 2013), 393–94.

7 Nuovo, *The Book Trade*, 394.

for teaching grammar, played a similar dual role for children learning Latin.[8] Thus, acquiring basic literacy and fundamental morality—expressed through one's comportment, language, and regimen—went hand-in-hand.

Overall it is clear that, from the perspective of a reader in 1501, the question of good living was not confined to dedicated manuals of etiquette, but spanned across a wide range of texts associated with different aspects and phases of lived experience. There is a lot to be learned from examining a diverse selection of such texts, and asking what a 1501 reader may have taken from them into the realm of their experiences with music. The materials discussed in this chapter, then, are drawn from books intended for a broad range of readers, from elementary grammars used for teaching Latin to children, to vernacular prognostica, which were amongst the most affordable and ephemeral texts in circulation at the turn of the sixteenth century.[9] Our lifestyle literature is divided into four subcategories. We begin with educational literature, and especially the panoply of Latin grammars published in 1501 (1.1), before moving on to a discussion of texts in which conduct is a central concern and is dealt with critically (1.2). The border between these two subcategories is porous, as there are several moralising texts which were used to teach grammar to schoolchildren, such as the *Disticha Catonis* and Bonvesin de la Riva's *Vita scolastica*; Francesco Maria Grapaldi's *De partibus aedium*, a lexicon which serves equally to present ancient models for good conduct and to provide a storehouse of Latin terminology, may also have been used in this dual manner. Next we deal with books on health and wellbeing (1.3), and then astrology (1.4). This pair of subcategories is also closely tied: Marsilio Ficino's lifestyle guide for scholars, *De vita libri tres*, features prominently in both, for example, and astrology formed a key component of medical training in Italy during this period.

---

8   Roberta L. Krueger, "Introduction. Teach Your Children Well: Medieval Conduct Guides for Youths," in *Medieval Conduct Literature: An Anthology of Vernacular Guides to Behaviour for Youths with English Translations*, ed. Mark D. Johnston (Toronto: University of Toronto Press, 2009), ix–xxxiii, at xiii.

9   On the status of prognostica as "cheap print" see Rosa Salzberg, *Ephemeral City: Cheap Print and Urban Culture in Renaissance Venice* (Manchester: Manchester University Press, 2014), 19.

References to music emerge at every turn throughout this body of literature—but not necessarily the mentions for which musicologists might hope. The absence of evocative descriptions of polyphonic song, technical discussions of harmony, and other similar topics, is noteworthy, if hardly surprising. Instead, when music comes up it is most often discussed in ways that engage pragmatically with human experience, within a conceptual framework dominated by the stars, the humours, the qualities, and a loosely stoic ethical perspective. Our 1501 materials in this vein offer the opportunity, perhaps not to elaborate a more refined music-critical apparatus, but certainly to see how music was worked into the grain of everyday life in Renaissance Italy. Meanwhile, when music turns up in our lifestyle literature as an artful practice, it is usually encountered somewhat indirectly, at the meeting point of musical and literary culture. Here, our 1501 gleanings augment recent work on poetic recitation and "semi-improvised" accompanied solo song, topics that will return in Chapter 2 and then again in Chapter 3.2.

1.1 Education

Alexander of Villedieu, *Doctrinale cum comento* (Venice: per Lazzaro Soardi, 1501)

Alexander of Villedieu, *Doctrinale cum commento* (Venice: per Pietro Quarengi, 1501)

Bonaventura da Brescia, *Regula musice plane venerabilis fratris Bonaventurae de Brixia Ordinis minorum* (Milan: per Leonhard Pachel ad impensas Giovanni da Legnano, 1501)

Pietro Borghi, *Libro de abacho* (Venice: Giacomo Penzio per Giovanni Battista Sessa, 1501)

Giovanni Battista Cantalicio, *Canones brevissimi grammatices & metricas pro rudibus pueris* (Rome: s.n., 1501)

Agostino Dati, *Elegantiolae faeliciter incipiunt* (Venice: per Cristoforo Pensi, 1501)

Roderich Dubravius, *De componendis epistolis* (Venice: Pietro Quarengi, after 24 May 1501)

Stefano Fieschi, *De componendis epistolis* (Venice: per Cristoforo Pensi, 1501)

Johannes de Sacrobosco, *Algorismus domini Ioannis de Sacro Busco noviter impressus* (Venice: per Bernardino Vitali, 1501)

Aldo Manuzio, *Rudimenta grammatices Latinae linguae. De literis Graecis & diphthongis, & quemadmodum ad nos veniant. Abbreviationes, quibus frequenter Graeci utuntur. Oratio dominica, & duplex salutatio ad Virginem gloriosiss. Symbolum Apostolorum. Divi Ioannis Evangelistae evangelium. Aurea carmina Pythagorae. Phocylidis poema ad bene, beateque vivendum. Omnia haec cum interpretatione latina. Introductio per brevis ad Hebraicam linguam* (Venice: Aldo Manuzio, 1501)

Niccolò Perotti, *Rudimenta grammatices* (Turin: per Francesco Silva, 1501)

Niccolò Perotti, *Cornucopie nuper emendatum a domino Benedicto Brugnolo: ac mirifice concinnatum cum tabula prioribus aliis copiosiori: utiliori: faciliorique* (Venice: per Giovanni Tacuino, 1501)

Questo sie uno libro utilissimo a chi se dilecta de intendere todesco dechiarando in lingua latina solennissimo vocabulista utilissimo (Milan: per Alessandro Pellizzoni, 1501)

Domenico Serafini, *Compendium Sinonymorum* (Milan: [Giovanni da Legnano] per Leonhard Pachel, 1501)

Giovanni Sulpizio, *Regulae Sulpitij* ([Venice: s.n., 1501–09])

Giovanni Tortelli, *Orthographia. Ioannis Tortelii Lima quaedam per Georgium Vallam tractatum de orthographia* (Venice: per Bartolomeo Zani, 1501)

The avenues of education available in Italy at the turn of the sixteenth century were numerous. Paul F. Grendler has identified three types of school active in this period: communal schools sponsored by local governments; independent schools run by a master; and ecclesiastical schools, which had dwindled considerably by 1500.[10] Each of these categories is, however, very broad. Independent schools, often operated by a single master, account for everything from "reading" schools teaching the basics of vernacular literacy, such as that operated by Mona Dianora in Florence in 1513, through *abbaco* schools teaching practical calculus to prepare students for work in a trade, as shopkeepers or as merchants, to the prestigious boarding schools teaching a full programme of liberal arts, Latin, and Greek, as exemplified by the schools of Vittorino da Feltre in Mantua—the *Ca' Giocosa*—and Guarino da Verona in Ferrara in the fifteenth century.[11] Specialist music and dance schools, though far less numerous than those teaching literacy or

---

10   Paul F. Grendler, *Schooling in Renaissance Italy: Literacy and Learning, 1300–1600* (Baltimore, MD: John Hopkins University Press, 1989), 5–6.

11   On Mona Dianora see Grendler, *Schooling in Renaissance Italy*, 91.

numeracy and apparently leaving little surviving trace of their activities, also fall within this category.[12] Although Grendler downplays the importance of ecclesiastical schools by the fifteenth century, this category also includes the *Scuole Eugeniae*, a series of twelve cathedral schools founded or reinvigorated by order of Pope Eugenius IV between 1431 and 1446, which supervised the education—musical and otherwise—of hundreds of boys.[13] Indeed, the *Scuola* in Verona, the *Scuola degli Accoliti*, was responsible for the training of Michele Pesenti, Marchetto Cara and Vincenzo Ruffo, and at one time counted among its teachers none other than Franchino Gafori.[14] This category must also include the schooling received by children entering a monastic or convent community. Of course, great numbers of children, particularly girls, were also educated at home, whether by a parent, tutor, or several tutors, depending on the inclination and wealth of their family.

The trace that the curricula of these avenues of education leave in the 1501 printed corpus varies. While *abbaco* schools were among the most popular of the Middle Ages—the chronicler Giovanni Villani estimated that as many as 1200 children were studying *abbaco* and *algorismo* in Florence in 1345, double the number studying Latin grammar—numeracy is represented by only two textbooks, Pietro Borghi's extensive *Libro de abacho*, and Johannes de Sacrobosco's brief *Algorismus*. Similarly, there is no trace in our corpus of the primers, hornbooks, *salteruzzi*, or *psalterioli* that were used to teach children the very basics of reading and phonetics; indeed, there are only two known extant example from the whole period of the fifteenth and early sixteenth centuries, the *Psalterium puerorum* published by Erhard Ratdolt in Venice in the early 1480s, and a *Babuino* printed by Giovanni Battista Sessa in Venice in

---

12   On the presence of such schools in Venice, see Paolo da Col, "Silent Voices: Professional Singers in Venice," in *A Companion to Music in Sixteenth-Century Venice*, ed. Katelijne Schiltz (Leiden: Brill, 2018), 231–71, at 237. Victor Coelho and Keith Polk note a contract drawn up in Florence in 1432 between a lutenist, a harpist, and a singer to establish a music school. See Victor Coelho and Keith Polk, *Instrumentalists and Renaissance Culture, 1420–1600* (Cambridge, UK: Cambridge University Press, 2016), 154.

13   See Grendler, *Schooling in Renaissance Italy*, 6–11.

14   Osvaldo Gambassi, *"Pueri cantores" nelle cattedrali d'Italia tra Medioevo ed età moderna* (Florence: Olschki, 1997), 195; and Giovanni Zanovello, "The Frottola in the Veneto," in *A Companion to Music in Sixteenth-Century Venice*, ed. Schiltz, 395–414.

1505.[15] The owners of prints which aided the teaching of basic literacy and numeracy must have seen little value in keeping them after their contents had been mastered.

The limited number of 1501 introductions to Greek and Hebrew, specialisms reserved for the wealthiest of children or scholars, is more easily understandable. Practical music teaching is similarly represented by a single textbook, a vernacular edition (peppered liberally with material remaining in the original Latin) of Bonaventura da Brescia's *Regula musice plane*, first printed by Angelo Britannico in Brescia in 1497. This was the most popular music treatise of its day, appearing in twenty-one editions before the year 1535, and written specifically with the aim of improving the musical aptitude of "poor and simple people in holy orders, as well as those desiring a true grounding in plainsong" (li poveri e simplici religiosi.necnon de li desideranti de havere vero fondamento de musica plana), meaning its intended readers were primarily those living and working in ecclesiastical institutions.[16] Teaching materials for music, like those for basic literacy and numeracy, must in many cases have been ephemeral, quickly discarded, or reliant on institutionally-owned manuscripts.

In contrast, Latin grammar textbooks are abundant in our 1501 corpus. We know of no fewer than seventeen editions of Latin grammars printed in Italy that year, and many of them had already received numerous editions since the advent of print in Italy—in the case of Niccolò Perotti's *Rudimenta grammatices*, as many as fifty.[17] Accordingly, they were stocked and sold by booksellers in large quantities. A bookshop in Mantua in 1483 held 345 grammatical texts and schoolbooks, which accounted for almost 40% of its stock; the selection included forty-four copies of Alexander of Villedieu's *Doctrinale*, fifty-two *Salteri* and *Salterioli*, fifty-five copies of grammars ascribed to Aelius Donatus, eleven copies of

---

15 Tiziana Plebani, *Alle donne che niente sanno: Mestieri femminili, alfabetizzazione e stampa nella Venezia del Rinascimento* (Venice: Marsilio, 2022), 25–26. Earlier writers on this topic, such as Grendler, *Schooling in Renaissance Italy*, 147, and Nuovo, *The Book Trade*, 338–39, seem to have been unaware of the *Psalterium puerorum*'s survival. The earliest example of an extant primer given by Grendler dates to 1578.

16 Bonaventura da Brescia, *Regula musice plane*, sig. [a i] v. See also Alessandra Ignesti in "Music Teaching in Montagnana: Organization, Methods, and Repertories," in *Music in Schools from the Middle Ages to the Modern Age*, ed. Paola Dessì (Turnhout: Brepols, 2021), 171–94, at 183.

17 Nuovo, *The Book Trade*, 122.

Agostino Dati's *Elegantiolae*, nine copies of Perotti's *Rudimenta*, and 150 copies of Guarino da Verona's *Grammaticales regulae*.[18] During a particularly slow period of six months in 1498, the bookshop owned by Vincenzo Benedetti in Bologna sold only fifty books, almost all of which were grammars or devotional texts.[19] Experiencing a brisker trade which saw the sale of some 25,000 volumes between May 1484 and January 1488, the *Zornale* of Francesco de Madiis records the sale of 258 copies of Donatus' *Ars minor*, 252 copies of Guarino's *Grammaticales regulae*, and 105 copies of Alexander of Villedieu's *Doctrinale*, the first two titles for as little as five and four soldi respectively—less than one would pay for a haircut.[20] The *Doctrinale* sold for as much as nine soldi, presumably because it most commonly appeared, as it did in 1501, in one of two editions which included lengthy commentaries.[21]

While the paucity of surviving music treatises or numeracy textbooks is no indication of their lack of popularity as subjects, the proliferation of Latin grammars is but one attestation of the importance placed on Latin literacy. Reading Latin literature was generally considered to be morally uplifting.[22] Pier Paolo Vergerio, whose treatise on education *De ingenius moribus et liberalibus adulescentiae studiis liber* was printed twenty-six times in Italy before the year 1501, is but one pedagogue to have emphatically promoted a Latin education as a means of productively occupying the mind, offering a crucial distraction from leisurable activities, such as dancing, which he feared would incline young people "to lust and every intemperance," and to weakened states of mind and body stemming from subsequent "premature sexual activity" (inmatura namque Venus).[23] A mastery of Latin was a necessary gateway to the wider *studia humanitatis*, which proffered the reader the moral guidance of the poets and philosophers of antiquity, and numerous historical examples

---

18 Nuovo, *The Book Trade*, 352.
19 Nuovo, *The Book Trade*, 334–35.
20 Cristina Dondi, "From the Corpus Iuris to 'psalterioli da puti' on Parchment, Bound, Gilt... The Price of Any Book Sold in Venice 1484–1488," *Studi di storia* 13 (2020), 577–99, at 589–90.
21 Dondi, "From the Corpus Iuris to 'psalterioli da puti'," 589–90.
22 Robert Black, *Humanism and Education in Medieval and Renaissance Italy* (Cambridge, UK: Cambridge University Press, 2001), 315.
23 "Otium enim ad libidines et ad omnem intemperantiam pronos efficit." *Humanist Educational Treatises*, ed. and trans. Kallendorf, 20–21.

of virtue and vice by which to guide their own conduct.[24] As we will see, this imitation of the great and good was likewise a key constituent in learning eloquence, a crucial signifier of an individual's civic value for its power to change the bent of crown and commoner alike.[25] Indeed, Latin literacy was so valued by the upper echelons of society that being able to read and write in the vernacular was hardly considered literacy at all; the celebrated poet-musician Serafino Aquilano was but one of many public figures branded illiterate for possessing no Latin, or using it poorly.[26]

For these and other reasons, Latin was one of the most commonly taught subjects, after basic numeracy and literacy. The curriculum was divided into two—elementary and secondary grammar—on the model of the late Roman grammarian Aelius Donatus, who composed two treatises, *De partibus orationis ars minor* and the *Ars maior*.[27] Of these, the latter was commonly circulated only as a fragment (a chapter on "barbarisms," common grammatical errors for the astute student to root out), and the former was replaced in Italy by a late-medieval text similar in content but falsely attributed to Donatus, now known as the *Ianua*.[28] Students, having already learned the basics of vernacular literacy, began with simple pronunciation and reading, moving through declensions and syntax, before studying metrics and elements of rhetoric, such as figures of speech, as part of their secondary education.[29] For students studying at a communal or independent school, or at home with a tutor, fees would increase incrementally as the curriculum demanded greater erudition on the part of the teacher, and students might drop out as fees became prohibitive.[30] Boys studying at a *Scuola Eugenia*, or similar cathedral school, would not face this problem: their education was

---

24 *Humanist Educational Treatises*, ed. and trans. Kallendorf, 48–49 and 12–13.
25 *Humanist Educational Treatises*, ed. and trans. Kallendorf, 49.
26 Anne MacNeil, "'A Voice Crying in the Wilderness': Issues of Authorship, Performance, and Transcription in the Italian Frottola," *The Italianist* 40.3 (2020), 463–76, 473.
27 Grendler, *Schooling in Renaissance Italy*, 163.
28 Grendler, *Schooling in Renaissance Italy*, 163. As Black explains (*Humanism and Education*, 45), the naming of the grammar by pseudo-Donatus *Ianua* was introduced by Remigio Sabbadini in the 1890s to distinguish it from the work of Donatus proper.
29 W. Keith Percival, "Grammar, Humanism and Renaissance Italy," *Mediterranean Studies* 16 (2007), 94–119, at 103.
30 Grendler, *Schooling in Renaissance Italy*, 18.

free—including clothing and books—provided they were born in the city, from a poor background but of legitimate marriage, were without physical disability, and had a voice "apt and sufficient for singing."[31] Free or subsidised education was also available in communes where local authorities recognised the potential benefits of an accessible, moralising education.[32] Lucca had a particularly strong tradition: from the late 1460s to 1486 it fell to the cathedral's *Magister cantorum* John Hothby to teach arithmetic and grammar to the poor of the city, as well as to the boys in the cathedral choir.[33] Although a mastery of Latin was very much a mark of distinction applicable to the wealthier echelons of society, in urban areas, and particularly in enlightened communes and for children gifted with a good singing voice, a Latin education was not entirely beyond the reach of the less fortunate.

The relevance of music to the study of grammar and rhetoric was a point made often by musicians in fifteenth-century Italy.[34] As a subject dogged by associations with idleness and lascivious conduct, an affiliation with the moral edification of Latin grammar and the utility of rhetoric gave grounds for the elevation of music in like manner.[35] Those lauding music's educational benefits had venerable, but only recently-available fuel: Quintilian's *Institutio oratoria* and Cicero's *De*

---

31 "Vocem Puerilem aptam et sufficientem ad cantandum." Gambassi, *"Pueri cantores"*, 60. The reporting of this particular relates to the Scuola dei Pueri Cantus di S. Luigi dei Francesi, Rome, in 1591, but is representative of the practice of the Scuole from their inception.
32 Grendler, *Schooling in Renaissance Italy*, 13–14.
33 Benjamin Brand, "A Medieval Scholasticus and Renaissance Choirmaster: A Portrait of John Hothby at Lucca," *Renaissance Quarterly* 63.3 (2010), 754–806, at 771.
34 Of course, suggestions of a link between music and grammar or music and rhetoric were not new in the fifteenth century. Earlier examples are discussed in several studies by Margaret Bent: "Sense and Rhetoric in Late Medieval Polyphony," in *Music in the Mirror: Reflections on the History of Music Theory and Literature for the 21st Century*, ed. Andreas Giger and Thomas J. Mathiesen (Lincoln, NE: University of Nebraska Press, 2002), 45–59; "Grammar and Rhetoric in Late Medieval Polyphony: Modern Metaphor or Old Simile?" in *Rhetoric Beyond Words: Delight and Persuasion in the Arts of the Middle Ages*, ed. Mary Carruthers (Cambridge, UK: Cambridge University Press, 2010), 52–71; and "Performative Rhetoric and Rhetoric as Validation," in *Inventing a Path: Studies in Medieval Rhetoric in Honour of Mary Carruthers*, ed. Laura Iseppi De Filippis (Turnhout: Brepols, 2012), 43–62.
35 Tim Shephard, Sanna Raninen, Serenella Sessini, and Laura Ștefănescu, *Music in the Art of Renaissance Italy 1420–1540* (London: Harvey Miller, 2020), 140.

oratore were rediscovered within four years of each other, in 1417 and 1421 respectively (the latter, but not the former, appears in our 1501 corpus).[36] Cicero makes extensive analogies between music, poetry, and oratory (discussed in Chapter 3.2), while Quintilian's lengthy *laus musicae* (*Institutio Oratoria* 1.10.10–35) proposes that grammar and music were once taught hand-in-hand (grammatice quondam ac musice iunctae fuerunt).[37] Though traditionally thought of as a mathematical discipline—it is as such that music is described by Isidore of Seville in his *Etymologiae*—through its constituent parts of rhythm and metrics it shared common ground with grammar, and placed a foot in both Trivium and Quadrivium.[38] Indeed, Augustine's *De musica* is first and foremost a treatise on poetics, focusing on rhythm and metrics but dispensing with music's first constituent part, harmony.[39]

A detailed study of metrics fell to the latter part of a student's studies, but for many, some understanding of rhythm and meter was unavoidable from an early age. Versification of learning material was a favourite tool of the medieval pedagogue, with whole treatises versified in an attempt to help students commit them to memory; as many as half of all music treatises written between the ninth and sixteenth centuries assume this format.[40] In the field of mnemonic verse, Alexander of Villedieu's Latin grammar in leonine hexameter, the *Doctrinale*, towers over its counterparts in terms of dissemination.[41] It enjoyed a wide circulation in Europe from the thirteenth century onwards, and the USTC lists some sixty-four editions known to have been printed in Italy by the end of the year 1501; our corpus includes two editions. It is commonly described

---

36 On the rediscovery of *De Oratore* see Tim Shephard, "Musical Classicisms in Italy Before the Madrigal," *Music and Letters* 101.4 (2020), 690–712, at 692; on Poggio Bracciolini's discovery of Quintilian, see James Hankins, *Virtue Politics: Soulcraft and Statecraft in Renaissance Italy* (Cambridge, MA: Harvard University Press, 2019), 48.
37 Quintilian, *The Orator's Education, Volume I: Books 1–2*, ed. and trans. Donald A. Russell, Loeb Classical Library 124 (Cambridge, MA: Harvard University Press, 2002), 220–23.
38 Shephard et al., *Music in the Art of Renaissance Italy*, 138–39. On music as a mathematical discipline see Isidore of Seville, *Etymologiae* (Venice: Petrus Löslein, 1483), fol. 12v (*Etymologiae* 2.4).
39 Shephard et al., *Music in the Art of Renaissance Italy*, 139.
40 Anna Maria Busse Berger, *Medieval Music and the Art of Memory* (Berkeley, CA: University of California Press, 2005), 98.
41 Black, *Humanism and Education*, 52–53.

today as an advanced grammar taught to those who had already received a grounding in Latin, but the testimony of the grammarian and printer Aldo Manuzio suggests otherwise: in the preface to his *Rudimenta grammatices*, also printed in 1501, he bewails having been forced to memorise Alexander's "inept" *Doctrinale* (Alexandri carmen ineptum) as a young boy, wishing he had been able to study Cicero and Virgil instead.[42] Manuzio was not alone in his criticism. In his preface to the 1501 edition of Perotti's *Rudimenta grammatices*, the publisher and bookseller Antonio Moreto refers in strikingly similar terms to "barbarous Alexander's inept poem" (Alexandri Barbari carmen ineptum)—playing on the contemporary usage of the term "barbaro" to denote both grammatical errors, and anyone from north of the Alps— deriding it as "nonsense" (ineptias) now rendered obsolete by Perotti.[43] Manuzio and Moreto's criticism of the *Doctrinale* falls within the scheme of a well-known humanist invective against medieval scholasticism, which was seen as having corrupted the true eloquence of the Latin of antiquity. However, such attacks did not preclude the popularity of the *Doctrinale*; Guarino da Verona was known to have asked his students to memorise portions dealing with irregular morphology, and it continued to be printed frequently and copies sold in considerable numbers into the sixteenth century.[44]

Unlike the *Doctrinale*, the grammars of both Perotti and Manuzio return to the classical question and answer format found in Donatus' *Ars minor*, and were designed as comprehensive textbooks, introducing the fundaments of grammar step by step.[45] Indeed, in Manuzio's *Rudimenta grammatices*, the only substantial material thrown at the uninitiated comes in the form of prayers, such as the *Pater Noster*, *Ave Maria*, and *Benedictus*, and other biblical and liturgical texts, such as the Apostle's Creed, the opening of John's Gospel, and Psalm 42, which includes the commendation "I will give praise upon the cithara to thee, o God my

---

42 Grendler, *Schooling in Renaissance Italy*, 139. Manuzio's recollection of his studies can be found in Manuzio, *Rudimenta grammatices*, fol. 2v.
43 "Nec video qua excusatione digni posthac accipiantur: qui Alexandri Barbari carmen ineptum: quod a vera et prisca grammatica prorsus alienum: caeterasque huiuscemodi ineptias legere pergent." Perotti, *Rudimenta grammatices*, fol. 1v.
44 Percival, "Grammar, Humanism and Renaissance Italy," 103.
45 W. Keith Percival, *Studies in Renaissance Grammar* (Abingdon: Routledge, 2016), 70.

God" (Confitebor tibi in cithara, Deus Deus Meus).⁴⁶ These texts had long been established as among the first things which a child would learn to read, and carried immense practical utility in the daily life of the laity. Manuzio includes four prayers of benediction (ad benedicendam mensam) for use before and after meals (*prandium* and *coenam*), and the anonymous Carthusian author of the *Decor puellarum*, a vernacular conduct guide for women published by Nicolas Jensen in Venice in 1471, suggests that women perform similar prayers throughout the day.⁴⁷ In the *Babuino* printed by Giovanni Battista Sessa in 1505, a rare survivor in the field of early printed vernacular primers, the reader is similarly given Latin prayers—the *Ave Maria, Pater Noster, Salve Regina,* and the Apostle's Creed—after an introduction to the letters of the alphabet, a lengthy syllable table, and lists of first names, kingdoms, cities, towns, and their peoples.⁴⁸ Accordingly, an inability to recite the *Ave Maria* in particular was seen as a sure indicator of illiteracy and moral frailty.⁴⁹ These were also among the texts most frequently set to music. If members of the laity sang these texts in public (rather than speak them, as the *Decor puellarum* and documents such as the statutes of various Italian confraternities of this period suggest was commonly bidden), they would almost certainly have done so in plainsong or to a *lauda* setting. It may be precisely because such prayers were among those most commonly used by the laity that they were set so often in polyphony by composers.⁵⁰

---

46 Manuzio, *Rudimenta grammatices*, fols. 2v–5v.
47 One such commendation is for women to say the Benedictus upon waking: "Quando ve levate subito fateve tre volte lo segno de la croce dicendo. Benedicamus patrem et filium cum sancto spiritu in saecula saeculorum amen." *Decor Puellarum* ([Venice]: Nicolaus Jensen, [1471]), fol. 41r.
48 *Questo sie uno libreto utilissimo a chi non sapesse littere de imparare presto elqual se chiama Babuino* (Venice: Giovanni Battista Sessa, 1505).
49 A verse which became popular in the first decades of the sixteenth century, *De vilan non te fidare* (Don't trust the bumpkins), includes an inability to recite an *Ave Maria*, or any other prayer, as a point of ridicule of countryfolk: "el vilan non fa lave maria/ne alcun oration/per sua devotion." *Le malitie dei vilani con alquanti stramotti alla Bergamascha* (s.l.: s.n, undated), fol. 1v.
50 As a very rough measure, a search in the Digital Image Archive of Music Manuscripts (DIAMM; www.diamm.ac.uk), which inventories more than 3,500 sources of European polyphonic music created mostly from the fourteenth to the sixteenth centuries, retrieves 389 Ave Marias, 113 Pater Nosters, and 2,047 Benedictuses (three of the prayers given by Manuzio).

Whether a versified treatise or one modelled after Donatus, musical references pepper the texts of most of the grammars in the 1501 corpus. Often, a musical word is used simply to demonstrate declensions or conjugations. Words such as "cornu" (horn) and "cantare" (to sing) occur with relative frequency, though their occurrence never develops into longer, musically pertinent phrases. One of the few cases in which musical terminology extends beyond a single word comes in the form of a quote from Virgil's *Eclogues* (8.71): "cantando rumpitur anguis" (by singing, the snake bursts asunder). This phrase occurs in four of the grammars printed in 1501 to demonstrate the gerund. Agostino Dati, for example, uses it in his discussion of the gerund in the *Elegantiolae*, one of the most popular grammars of the period due to its promise of a quick road to eloquence:[51]

> Illud ignorandum non est quod gerundius modus ab omni verbo similiter procreatur si quando nobis eo opus foret ut cantando rumpitur anguis. Est enim ut ait Servius dum cantatur et alio loco active dictum est ut cantando tu illum rumpis idest dum cantas id efficere oratores atque usurpare queunt.[52]

> This must not be ignored, that the gerundive form, if ever we should have a need for one, is created from every verb similarly. *Cantando rumpitur anguis* (the snake is rent in pieces by singing) is in fact *dum cantatur* (while there is singing), as Servius says. And in another place it is said actively, as in *cantando tu illum rumpis* (you rend him by singing). Orators are able to produce this form.[53]

The popularity of this particular snippet of Virgil to demonstrate the gerund is twofold. Firstly, it dovetailed the textbook studies of a student of secondary school age or older (here suggested by the admonition to the reader that anyone aiming for the proficiency of an orator should be able to use the gerund correctly) with their wider reading, heavily inflected with Virgil for its perceived morally improving qualities.[54] Secondly, but more difficult to prove, it might have presented a model

---

51   Black, *Humanism and Education*, 360.
52   *Elegantiolae*, fol. 18v.
53   Translation in Christopher J. Warner, "Quick Eloquence in the Late Renaissance: Agostino Dati's 'Elegantiolae'," *Humanistica Lovaniensia* 61 (2012), 65–240, at 225, adapted to reflect the content of the 1501 edition.
54   Grendler, *Schooling in Renaissance Italy*, 237–38.

for the gerund which, through its vividness and the curiosity it must have provoked, was more memorable than a commonplace example, such as *ambulando, vivando,* or *vigilando,* might have been.[55] How could singing force a snake to burst? None of the grammars care to explain, though it is conceivable that the question could have formed a point of departure for discussing the similitude of song and magic through the Latin *carmen,* the supernal quality of music in the hands of the likes of Orpheus, Amphion and Arion, and the sway music held over the mind as described in the philosophical writings of Plato and Aristotle.

A similar mnemonic purpose could be attributed to other occurrences of musical activity or objects in grammatical texts. Returning to the *Doctrinale,* when demonstrating the creation of an agent noun from an object (such as ironmonger or woodworker) Villedieu chooses "tibicen" (piper) and "tubicen" (trumpeter), players often grouped under the hyponymic term *pifferi* during this period, when any number of other objects may have sufficed. The same terms are used to the same end by Giovanni Tortelli in his *Orthographia,* a vast grammar and Latin dictionary first printed in 1471 and included in our 1501 corpus.[56] Perotti likewise turns to *tubicen* and *tibicen* when discussing grammatical gender.[57] There is ample evidence to suggest that these players were amongst the most commonly encountered musicians both in Renaissance Italy and in earlier times in western Europe; they formed civic, courtly and university bands, playing for ceremonial and social occasions both in public and behind closed doors. Indeed, in a list of "sound makers" (sonadori) in the 1501 edition of the first printed Italian-German dictionary, which consciously limited itself to "the words said most commonly" (vocabuli e parole che se posseno dire i piu modi), "Lo pifero/der pfiffer" comes first, followed by "el trombeta/der trometer."[58] Musical instruments and their players may not carry the shock factor of a bursting snake when used as grammatical examples, but they did bring the benefit of being

---

55 These are examples given, alongside *cantando,* by W. H. Kirk in "The Syntax of the Gerund and the Gerundive, II," *Transactions and Proceedings of the American Philological Association* 76 (1945), 166–76.
56 *Doctrinale cum comento,* fol. 46v; and *Orthographia,* fols. 3v and 36v.
57 Perotti, *Rudimenta grammatices,* fol. 5v.
58 *Questo sie uno libro utilissimo,* fols. 1r and 13r. This appears to be a reprint of an earlier edition, *Introito e porta de quele che voleno imparare e comprender todescho a latino cioe taliano,* compiled (compiuto) by Adam von Rottweil (Venice, 1477).

encountered in everyday life, while still being one step away from the mundane.

For the student in 1501, Latin was still very much a living language, and its use included basic legal and notarial functions as much as it did lofty orations and neo-Latin verse. For the aspiring notary, knowing how to refer to musicians and their functions was crucial when drawing up legal documents such as statutes, contracts and wills; for example, it is as *trombatoribus* that trumpeters employed for ceremonial purposes are described in the 1405 statues of the University of Bologna, and as a *cytharista* that the great lutenist Pietrobono Burzelli is recorded in his will of 1466.[59] Texts like Domenico Serafini's *Floridum compendium sinonymorum*, a short, versified compendium of synonyms and antonyms first printed in 1501, might have found their market among such readers (or rather writers). Largely staying clear of erudite discourse on ancient musical practices, Serafini is content to write that "Fistula sambuca psalterium cum simphonia/ Tibia cum cithara lyra soni" are musical instruments (sunt instrumenta), later clarifying for the reader that "Psaltria," "fidicina" and "citharista" are encountered as synonyms (dicitur idem), and that "fistula" might equally refer to a musical instrument or a water pipe.[60] Such texts help us understand not only how a child may have encountered music in grammar class, but also the linguistic tools they acquired to describe the musical world around them.

Ideally, the end of a Latin education was eloquence, and in this respect the objectives of the grammar student overlapped considerably with those of the singer-poet performing *al improvviso*, whether a Latin *cantor ad lyram* or vernacular *cantimpanco*. Indeed, it is more often that praise for the eloquence of such musicians survives, than for their vocal quality or virtuosity. In the 1480s, for example, Michele Verino wrote of the *cantimpanco* Antonio di Guido—by the time Michele was hearing him a man of some age, having first performed in the Piazza San Martino in Florence in 1436 aged eighteen—"I once heard Antonio in Piazza San

---

59 See Nan Cooke Carpenter, *Music in the Medieval and Renaissance Universities* (Norman: University of Oklahoma Press, 1958), 35–37; and Evan A. MacCarthy, "The English Voyage of Pietrobono Burzelli," *Journal of Musicology* 35.4 (2018), 431–59, at 457.

60 *Compendium Sinonymorum*, fols. 7r, 22r, and 25v. The *Compendium* was published three times in Italy between 1485 and 1501.

Martino, singing about the wars of Orlando with such eloquence that you seemed to be hearing Petrarch himself."[61]

It is well-known that a large part of the improvisor's art rested on the power of their memory. Using the example of the fourteenth-century poet Antonio Pucci, Blake Wilson has shown how the *cantimpanco*'s process might have involved the collection of a vast amount of source material—choice excerpts from favoured authors, biblical and chivalric tales—which was stored in commonplace books.[62] This material could then be memorised and performed, either as first encountered by the *cantimpanco*, or woven into new extempore compositions, or its style imitated in the building of the poet's own distinctive manner. Three memory treatises have been found in anthologies linked to Florentine *cantimpanchi*, which appear to draw on complex mnemonic tools, such as the "house of memory" outlined in the *Rhetorica ad Herennium* in the first century BCE, with the aim of memorising the material word for word.[63] Petrarch once wrote to Bocaccio of his annoyance at being asked for verse by street performers, "men of no great talent, but great memory," desperate for new works to perform.[64] Antonio di Guido may have been a greater talent than the performers despised by Petrarch, but there is every chance that when listening to him, Michele Verino was hearing more Petrarch than he realised. Decades after his death, it was Antonio's own poetry which was being performed and printed, alongside works attributed to Serafino Aquilano and Dante, as well as original work, by the itinerant *cantimpanco* Zanobi della Barba.[65]

Although the reproduction of another poet's works may have been the subject of scorn, the corpus of grammars from this period shows that a similar imitation of great authors went hand-in-hand with memorisation as the key tenets of learning from an early age. Two of the first questions posed by Perotti in his *Rudimenta grammatices*—before even the letters of the Latin alphabet have been listed, and long before

---

61 Chriscinda Henry, "Alter Orpheus: Masks of Virtuosity in Renaissance Portraits of Musical Improvisers," *Italian Studies* 71.2 (2016), 238–58, at 247.
62 See Blake Wilson, *Singing to the Lyre in Renaissance Italy: Memory, Performance, and Oral Poetry* (Cambridge, UK: Cambridge University Press, 2020), 65–67.
63 Wilson, *Singing to the Lyre*, 112–23, especially 117 and 121–22.
64 Wilson, *Singing to the Lyre*, 48.
65 *Froctola dilectevole da mandar via lotoi et la malinconia* ([Florence]: Zanobi, undated), contains sonnets attributed to Dante, Serafino, and a poem on the Liberal Arts by Antonio di Guido, alongside a frottola which appears to be by Zanobi himself.

any work on the grammar necessary to arrange them into words and sentences—are clearly intended as a moralising couplet to inform a child's lifetime approach to learning, itself to be memorised as a maxim:

> Quod est primum ingenii signum in pueris? Memoria.
> Quod est secundum? Imitatio.[66]
>
> What is the first sign of intelligence in boys? Memory.
> What is the second? Imitation.

Modern studies of mnemonics have highlighted the use of such tools as "houses of memory," commonplace books, verse, and diagrams as aids in the memorisation process, but the simple act of repetition was the main tool by which beginners were usually taught the rudiments of grammar.[67] In his treatise on the teaching of grammar, *De ordine docendi et studendi* (completed in 1459 and first printed in Ferrara around 1475), Battista Guarini counsels the repetition "over and over" (iterumque iterumque) of grammatical paradigms and poetry to learn the fundaments of Latin grammar and to build awareness of metrical quantity, an activity happily related to the memorisation of Virgil's poetry, which Guarini also advocates.[68] Once a student has obtained fluency, Guarini suggests that they write glosses in their texts, and compile their own commonplace books, excerpting passages from their reading of ancient authors which can be returned to routinely to aid in memorisation.[69]

To the end of obtaining "quick elegance"—perhaps even more quickly than one would by reading Dati's *Elegantiolae*—two texts from the 1501 corpus act as printed commonplace books, providing material to imitate when corresponding in Latin: Roderich Dubravius' *De componendis epistolis*, and the earlier and more widely printed manual of the same name by Stefano Fieschi, also known as *De prosynonymis* or *Synonyma sententiarum*.[70] Unlike Giorgio Valagussa's *Elegantiae Ciceronis* (not

---

66 Perotti, *Rudimenta grammatices*, fol. 3r.
67 Grendler, *Schooling in Renaissance Italy*, 196.
68 *Humanist Educational Treatises*, ed. and trans. Kallendorf, 260–309, at 268–69 and 276–77.
69 *Humanist Educational Treatises*, ed. and trans. Kallendorf, 296–97.
70 Grendler, *Schooling in Renaissance Italy*, 211. While not as popular as some of the grammatical texts mentioned so far, the 1501 edition of Fieschi's manual was its fifteenth edition in print, and some twenty-one manuscript copies are known.

printed in 1501, but by then available in six editions), which excerpts phrases from Cicero's letters for use, neither of these texts follow the humanist principle of reproducing ancient exemplars.[71] Fieschi's manual gives any number of sentences one might require when writing a letter, and supplies several Latin translations in varying degrees of floridity for each, but these appear to have been composed by Fieschi himself.[72] Likewise, Dubravius' exemplars are taken from his own correspondence. As Grendler has noted, it would be entirely possible to construct a letter using Fieschi's examples with only the slightest modification.[73] This suggests that, rather than providing models for imitation, the contents of these texts were designed to be memorised, and phrases replicated wholesale or used as a basis for modified constructions in a reader's own writing.

If this method for collating and memorising material—and the general importance of honing the memory—were instilled in children from a young age, it follows that the ability to extemporise verse to the accompaniment of a stringed instrument was built on foundations laid at the very beginning of a player's education, and that the latinising *cantor ad lyram* relied as much on a *cibaldone* of material as the vernacular *cantimpanco*. Thanks to the assiduous collection and memorisation of material to ensure, in Guarini's words, that a student "may be confident, not only of being able to hold forth elegantly on any subject that arises in day-to-day-speech, but also of having some maxim suitable for every subject," by the time a student was nearing the completion of their schooling, they would have a veritable storehouse of literature at their disposal with which to weave extemporisations on given topics.[74] The moralising nature of the material to which they were directed in grammar class likewise informed the sentiment of their song. In his defence of music, *De musica et poetica*, the celebrated improvisor Raffaello Brandolini credits his practice of Latin lyric with "[restraining] the emotions of the soul that run wild at banquets," in comparison with the "meretricious songs and attractions that are employed so frequently at

---

71 Grendler, *Schooling in Renaissance Italy*, 211.
72 Grendler, *Schooling in Renaissance Italy*, 210–11.
73 Grendler, *Schooling in Renaissance Italy*, 211.
74 "confidat is omnia quae in quotidiano sermone contigerint, non modo ornate proloqui posse, verum etiam ad omnem materiam sententiam aliquam se habiturum." *Humanist Educational Treatises*, ed. and trans. Kallendorf, 288-9.

today's banquets [...] incentives to prodigality, depravity, drunkenness, and lust."[75]

Of course, in order to extemporise Latin poetry, one required a thorough understanding of Latin meter. There is some evidence that singing Latin verse was employed by teachers to cultivate an appreciation of the importance of syllabic quantity to correct *pronuntiatio* in both poetry and prose.[76] Amongst various descriptions of precocity emanating from the school of Vittorino da Feltre in the first half of the fifteenth century are accounts of students singing verse to one another at dinner in order to distract them from bad behaviour, and of boys as young as ten reciting original compositions for guests.[77] Guarini suggests that an understanding of syllabic quantity and meter (syllabarum versuumque) be built after a student has mastered the fundamentals of grammar and syntax, and that this can be done through singing Virgil: "They should also practice reciting [Virgil's poems] so that by constant repetition they may become aware of the quantity of the feet by merely singing the verse."[78]

That a comprehensive understanding of meter might not normally have been taught quite so early in the average grammar school as it was in the hallowed halls of Vittorino's *Ca' Giocosa* is evident in the structure and content of the grammars in our 1501 corpus. The respective *Rudimenta* authored by Perotti and Manuzio omit metrical analysis altogether, although in an effort to secure correct *pronuntiatio* particular attention is often paid to diphthongs. "Are diphthongs long or short?" Perotti's student asks. "Always long" the reply, and of course the example Perotti gives is from Virgil's *Aeneid*.[79] Following this, students are told

---

75 Raffaele Brandolini, *On Music and Poetry*, trans. Ann E. Moyer and Marc Laureys (Tempe, AZ: Arizona Centre for Medieval and Renaissance Studies, 2001), 33.
76 Philippe Canguilhem, "Singing Horace in Sixteenth-Century France: A Reappraisal of the Sources and Their Interpretation," in *Horace across the Media: Textual, Visual and musical Receptions of Horace from the 15th to the 18th Century*, ed. K.A.E Enkel and Marc Laureys (Leiden: Brill, 2022), 422–41, at 430. In this instance, Canguilhem is referring to the methods employed by Conrad Celtis north of the Alps.
77 Wilson, *Singing to the Lyre*, 251–52.
78 "Declamare autem etiam in his oportebit, ut assiduitate pedum numerum etiam solo verborum cantu annotent." *Humanist Educational Treatises*, ed. and trans. Kallendorf, 276–77.
79 Perotti, *Rudimenta grammatices*, fol. 3v. The example Perotti gives is *Aeneid* 7.524: "Virgilium: Stipitibus duris agitur, sudibusve praeustis."

that syllables are short, long, and of middling length (Breve: longum: et medium).⁸⁰ Often, detailed discussion of metrics was the preserve of dedicated textbooks. Of the printed grammars in contemporary circulation, Francesco Negri's complete Latin syllabus, the *Grammatica* (Venice: Theodorus Herbipolensis per Johannes Lucilius Santritter, 1480), is a notable exception for including a complete discussion of metrics, as well as—uniquely amongst grammatical texts of the fifteenth century—five mensural melodies, one for each of the five species of *vocalis harmonia*, which he identifies as "Heroic Grave" (Heroica Gravis), "Heroic Bellicose" (Heroica Bellica), "Elegiac" (Elegiaca), "Sapphic" (Sapphica), and "Lyric" (Lyrica).⁸¹

From among the 1501 corpus, Giovanni Battista Cantalicio's *Canones brevissimi grammatices & metricas* is similarly notable, although it also underscores the separation of metrics from the rudimentary grammar syllabus, in that the *brevissimi grammatices* and the *metricas* are presented as two separate texts, each with its own dedication. Cantalicio proceeds through the metrical feet and their origins (we are told, for instance, that the *Molossus* is based on an Epirot dance), the quality of the syllables, word endings and meter, concluding with the remark that the boy who learns the rules outlined by Cantalicio will soon "speak with Apollo and the muses" (cum Apolline: musisque loquuntur).⁸²

The rhetorician Giovanni Sulpizio includes metrics in his *De versuum scansione*, another component of our corpus, but he specifically calls it music *sine harmonia*, while also confirming that its study was reserved for more advanced students, and was crucial for proper pronunciation:

> Adolescens nichil tibi iam ad latinam musicam: hoc est ad rectam proninciationem deest. Habes de syllabarum quantitate opus exactissimum. Habes de pedibus: et de generibus carminium: Habes ex Servii excerpta centimetro: ipsumque epitomen. Habes de accentibus Priscianum. Superest ut iis invigiles et diligenter incumbas: Quod si egeris os tuum stribiligine non foedabis: et carmen compones ac legantissimum.⁸³

---

80   Perotti, *Rudimenta grammatices*, fol. 3v.
81   Canguilhem, "Singing Horace," 423.
82   *Canones brevissimi*, fols. 61v and 68v.
83   *Regulae Sulpitij*, fol. 33r. Some typographical errors have been corrected using a later edition (Venice: Guilielmum de Fontaneto, 1520).

> When you are young, you have no concern with Latin music; but this is what is lacking for correct pronunciation. Here you have a most exact work on the quantity of syllables; on feet and the genres of song. You have from Servius excerpts of the *centimetro* and the epitome itself. You have accents from Priscian. It is necessary that you watch over them and pay careful attention to them; if you do this, you will not pollute your mouth with shrillness and will compose the most famous of songs.

While Sulpizio does not include any music in the way that Negri does, his final comment on avoiding unpleasant recitation through careful attention to scansion speaks to the importance that the rules of scansion had for the erudite performer and listener. Several studies have examined how closely the few surviving settings of classical Latin lyric we have from the late fifteenth and early sixteenth centuries match the syllabic quantity of their texts, with mixed conclusions.[84] Philippe Canguilhem has suggested, based on the various musical settings included in the editions of Negri's *Grammatica* published in Venice in 1480 and Basel in 1499, and the Latin texts and *modi* for singing Latin verse printed by Petrucci, that the musical performance of Latin poetry may have varied from the strictly syllabic to the accentual depending on the context of performance: syllabic when teaching meters to students, and accentual when performing poetry convivially.[85] Given the strictness with which grammarians counselled students to pay attention to syllabic quantity, it may seem more reasonable that the division between syllabic and metrical performances was not so much based on occasion as on the performer themselves. An amateur learning Michele Pesenti's setting of *Integer vitae* may have lacked the understanding or interest to critique his adherence to syllabic quantity. On the other hand, for the most distinguished *cantor ad lyram* it was a crucial mark of their erudition: what would be the point in carefully choosing a meter suited to a particular subject, only to garble it with superimposed rhythms? Confirming its importance to the musically-minded humanist—if one more actively involved in polyphony than Latin lyric—in his *Practica musicae* Franchino

---

84 See, for instance, Francesco Luisi, *La musica vocale nel Rinascimento: del cantar a libro… o sulla viola: studi sulla musica vocale profana in Italia nei secoli XV e XVI* (Torino: ERI, 1977), 325–438; Camilla Cavicchi, "The cantastorie and His Music in 15th and 16th-Century Italy," *Troja—Jahrbuch für Renaissancemusik* 13 (2017), 105-133; and Canguilhem, "Singing Horace," 422–30.

85 Canguilhem, "Singing Horace," 430.

Gafori described the "careful judgement" (sano prosequentes judicio) followed by "poets and musicians" (poetae atque musici) in determining the note values assigned to syllables based on their duration, long or short, also giving a lengthy, though not exhaustive, list of metrical feet.[86]

Whilst the grammar texts printed in 1501 offer little to help us gauge what role practical music might have played in teaching outside of cathedral schools, it is evident that basic musical knowledge—in the form of the ability to name and conjugate instruments, instrumentalists and the acts of playing and singing—played a role in the Latin education of boys from an early age. Those who continued to study Latin into their later teenage years may have acquired the knowledge of metrics and a storehouse of themes and poetic and rhetorical figures to embroider into their own sung Latin lyric. All of them, and indeed those learning the vernacular too, would have had the need for a strong memory and the importance of imitating excellence instilled in them from their earliest schooling, and in an age in which so much music seems to have been performed *all'improvviso* or *alla memoria*, these skills were also of crucial importance to performers of music.[87]

1.2 Conduct

Aristotle et al., *Aristotelis philosophorum maximi secretum secretorum ad Alexandrum. De regum regimine: De sanitatis conservatione: De physionomia.* [...] *Alexandri aphrodisei Clarissimi peripatetici. de intellectu. Averrois magni commentatoris de anime beatitudine. Alexandri Achillini bononiensis de Universalibus. Alexandri macedonis in septentrione monarche de mirabilibus Indiae Ad Aristotelem* (Bologna: impensis Benefetto Faelli, 1501)

Bonvesin de la Riva, *Vita scolastica* (Venice: per Giovanni Battista Sessa, 1501)

Pseudo-Aelius Donatus et al., *Donatus Melior. Catonis Carmen de moribus. De Arte Libellus* (Milan: [Giovanni da Legnano] per Leonhard Pachel, 1501)

---

86   Franchino Gafori, *Practica musicae* (Milan: Guillaume le Signerre, 1496), fol. 27r. Quoted in Canguilhem, "Singing Horace," 428–29.

87   On the importance placed on memory in vernacular learning, Lisa Kaborycha draws attention to a page in a fifteenth-century manuscript (Biblioteca Nazionale Centrale, Firenze N.A.352, fol. 78v) containing texts on John on Baptist; underneath an alphabet, "in a female hand" are written the words "Most merciful father, give me memory such that I might remember the whole alphabet" (pietossi[si]mo padre dami memoria tale che io mi possa ricordare Di tutto quello Alfabeto). See Lisa Kaborycha, *A Corresponding Renaissance: Letters Written by Italian Women, 1375–1650* (New York: Oxford University Press, 2016), Plate IV.

Francesco Maria Grapaldi, *De partibus aedium libellus cum additamentis emendatissimus* (Parma: Angelo Ugoleto, 1501)

Aldo Manuzio, *Rudimenta grammatices Latinae linguae. De literis Graecis & diphthongis, & quemadmodum ad nos veniant. Abbreviationes, quibus frequenter Graeci utuntur. Oratio dominica, & duplex salutatio ad Virginem gloriosiss. Symbolum Apostolorum. Divi Ioannis Evangelistae evangelium. Aurea carmina Pythagorae. Phocylidis poema ad bene, beateque vivendum. Omnia haec cum interpretatione latina. Introductio per brevis ad Hebraicam linguam* (Venice: Aldo Manuzio, 1501)

Giovanni Pontano, *Opera. De fortitudine: libri duo. De principe: liber unus. Dialogus qui Charon inscribitur. Dialogus qui Antonius inscribitur. De liberalitate: liber unus. De benificentia: liber unus. De magnificentia: liber unus. De splendore: liber unus. De coviventia: liber unus. De obedientia: libri quinque* (Venice: per Bernardino Viani, 1501)

The fact that the educators of the fifteenth century directed readers to a wealth of ancient and religious texts for moral guidance necessarily clouds the distinction between what can be considered conduct literature and what cannot. The conduct manual of the Middle Ages drew on a range of such sources, depending on its target audience, to expound upon the importance of the classical cardinal virtues of courage, justice, prudence, and temperance, the abundance or paucity of which were thought to be evident in all manner of daily actions and interactions.[88] Ideally, such texts carried the benefit of synthesising a vast body of literature and applying it to the everyday concerns of the reader, especially important in cases where the target audience was not equipped with a level of Latin literacy sufficient to comprehend the writings of Aristotle (in Latin translation), Cicero, Ovid, Virgil, Augustine or Jerome. The *Speculum principis*, which sought to provide advice on comportment and government and was often gifted to a ruler upon their ascension, ranks among the most popular and oldest genres of conduct literature.[89] Among our 1501 corpus, an important

---

88   For an overview of the foundation of the conduct manual in religious and classical literature, see Krueger, "Teach Your Children Well," particularly xi–xiii. For a broader overview of conduct books and "how to" manuals in the Italian Renaissance, see Rudolph M. Bell, *How To Do It: Guides to Good Living for Renaissance Italians* (Chicago, IL: University of Chicago Press, 1999).

89   On the breadth and scholarly disagreement on the nature of the genre, see Nasrin Askari, *The Medieval Reception of the Shāhnāma as a Mirror for Princes* (Leiden: Brill, 2016), 6–7; and the introduction to István Pieter Bejczy and Cary J. Nederman ed., *Princely Virtues in the Middle Ages, 1200–1500* (Turnhout: Brepols, 2007), at 1–8.

contribution to the genre is Giovanni Pontano's treatise *De principe* addressed to the author's pupil Alfonso II of Naples, included in a volume of his *Opera*. Drawing partly upon this tradition, Castiglione's *Libro del Cortegiano*—so often cited as the conduct manual *par excellence* of the entire Renaissance—quickly became one of the most widely-distributed books of the sixteenth century following its first publication in 1528.[90]

Those secular texts published in 1501 with the express purpose of informing the decorum of their readers, either through instruction in the imperative or commentary on the conduct of others, are relatively few— no more than six—and can be placed into two categories: those printed for schoolboys learning Latin and Greek grammar, and those written for the ruling classes and aspiring elite.[91] All of those texts intended for didactic use are written in verse, each line or distich representing a maxim whose concise verse form aided memorization. The *Disticha Catonis*, before the mid-sixteenth century attributed variously to Cato the Elder or Younger, was perhaps one of the most widely-read of these in the Latin Middle Ages. Grendler cites its usage in tandem with the *Ianua* to instil a moral code in schoolchildren from an early age; this is exactly what happens in our 1501 edition, which begins with the *Ianua* (entitled *Donatus melior*), continues with the *Disticha Catonis* (entitled "Cato Carmen de Moribus"—Cato's moral song), and concludes with Antonio Mancinelli's *De arte libellus*.[92] The moralising *carmina* attributed to Phocylides and Pythagoras had already enjoyed a high degree of popularity prior to their first appearance in print, appended by Aldo Manuzio to Constantine Lascaris' *Erotemata*, and from the mid-1490s to his own grammar, in parallel Greek and Latin.[93] Bonvesin de la Riva's *Vita scolastica*, a guide to productive study and comportment for students and their teachers, had similarly enjoyed wide circulation since its composition in the late thirteenth century, its value to teachers

---

90 Peter Burke, *The Fortunes of the Courtier: The European Reception of Castiglione's Cortegiano* (University Park, PA: Penn State University Press, 1995), 1–2.

91 Texts primarily concerned with regimen to support health and wellbeing, rather than conduct approached from an ethical perspective, will be discussed in the following section. Texts offering religious guidance are discussed in Volume 2 of the present study.

92 Grendler, *Schooling in Renaissance Italy*, 182.

93 Attilio Russo, "Costantino Lascaris tra fama e oblio nel Cinquecento messinese," *Archivio Storico Messinese* 84–85 (2003–04), 5–87, at 52–54.

suggested by the eleven surviving editions printed in Italy prior to 1501.[94] Not content with the moralising qualities already inherent in the *Vita scolastica*, the printer of our 1501 edition, Giovanni Battista Sessa, has appended a second moralising text for students to reflect on: Thomas Regazola's *De morte carmen horrendum*, a literary *memento mori*.

Of those texts aimed towards the literati and the ruling elite, the pseudo-Aristotelian *Regum regimine*—presented, in the true manner of a *Speculum principis*, as a letter on the ideal conduct of the prince addressed to Alexander the Great—achieved an ever greater circulation following its complete translation from Arabic in the thirteenth century: more manuscript copies survive than of any other Aristotelian text, real or spurious, testifying to a wider readership than princes alone.[95] Giovanni Pontano's works, in contrast, were comparatively new in 1501: the earliest work included in our edition, *De principe*, dates from around the time Pontano became tutor to Alfonso II in 1468, or a little before.[96] Nevertheless, the steady publication of Pontano's works in Naples by Mathias Moravus (*De aspiratione*, 1481; *De fortitudine*, *De principe* and *De oboedientia*, 1490; *Dialogi qui Charon et Antonius inscribuntur*, 1491), and later *De liberalitate*, *De beneficentia*, *De magnificentia*, *De splendore* and *De conviventia* by Johannes Tresser and Martinus de Amsterdam (1498), inspired the publication of a collection of his works by Bernardino Viani in Venice in 1501.

The last conduct text to be considered here, and perhaps the most novel, Francesco Maria Grapaldi's *De partibus aedium*, is nominally a lexicon, using a patrician home and its contents as a premise around which to build a dictionary of Latin terms. Grapaldi draws on the writings of an impressive array of authors, from Aulus Gellius to Nicholas of Lyra; he states in his introduction that he was compelled to take a scythe (falce) to his sources in order to keep his book to a manageable length.[97] In spite of this, and crucially for our purposes,

---

[94] Robert Black has noted that the *Vita scolastica* was amongst the texts assembled by Pietro Crinito for use in his teaching at the turn of the sixteenth century. Black, *Humanism and Education*, 235–36.

[95] Steven J Williams, *The Secret of Secrets* (Ann Arbor: University of Michigan Press, 2003), 1.

[96] Hélène Casanova-Robin, "La rhétorique de la légitimité: Droits et devoirs du prince dans le de Principe de Pontano," *Rhetorica: A Journal of the History of Rhetoric* 32.4 (2014), 348-361, at 348.

[97] *De partibus aedium*, fol. 1v.

Grapaldi also extracts detailed descriptions of the functions of the spaces he describes, providing imitable models, largely from antiquity, for the noble designing or reconfiguring their own residence and for the banquet host, as much as for the Latinist looking to expand their vocabulary.

It should be noted that none of these texts were published with the express intention that women would form part of their readership, and in Pontano's *Opera* and the *Vita scolastica*, women are portrayed either as irrational and foolish adjuncts to male life or as sources of moral corruption to be avoided at all costs. These issues will be addressed in due course, but in order to remedy the paucity of moral direction for women presented by the 1501 corpus, we will also draw on two texts printed in Italy prior to 1501: the *Fiore di virtù*, which is known in no less than fifty-nine editions printed before 1501, and the *Decor puellarum*, printed by Nicolas Jensen in Venice in the 1470s.[98]

Music is a much more prevalent topic in those texts written with an aristocratic (or at least highly educated) readership in mind. Musical activities receive only fleeting mention in the moralising texts aimed at schoolboys and women, but those few passages pertinent to music—as well as their small number—suggest a subtle yet important division in attitudes towards music in the scheme of humanist ethics on the one hand, and clerical moralism on the other. This will become apparent as we consider our texts in turn.

The contents of the 1501 edition of Pontano's *Opera* are diverse in format and subject matter.[99] The book begins with two texts dedicated to Alfonso II, *De fortitudine* and *De principe*. These are followed by two dialogues. *Charon* presents a series of satirical exchanges regarding the dead as they enter the underworld, chiefly between Mercury and the eponymous Charon, and modelled on Lucian's *Dialogues of the Dead*. *Antonius* takes place around an informal meeting of members of the *Accademia Antoniana*, and is dedicated to its recently deceased founder Antonio Beccadelli (Il Panormita, d.1471), whose leading role among

---

98 The date given in Jensen's edition is 1461, an impossibility as there was no printing press in Italy before 1464. Jensen's press was active from 1470 until his death in 1480, making 1471 a more likely date of publication.

99 On this work and its sonic contents, see also Tim Shephard and Melany Rice, "Giovanni Pontano Hears the Street Soundscape of Naples," *Renaissance Studies* 38.4 (2024), 519–41.

Neapolitan intellectuals had been inherited by Pontano.[100] Concluding the opus are six treatises on the virtues of *liberalitate* (liberality), *beneficentia* (beneficence), *magnificentia* (magnificence), *splendore* (splendour), *conviventia* (conviviality), and *obedientia* (obedience).

References to music occur in each of these texts, and it is striking that they bear a considerable similarity to Castiglione's remarks on music made throughout the *Cortegiano*. Perhaps this should be no surprise: as James Haar has observed, Castiglione tells us nothing about music that cannot be found in another source.[101] Castiglione's reliance on the work of other authors in his treatments of other topics is well-known; his discourse on love, for example, which comprises the final night of conversation at Urbino, is rendered a plain tribute to Pietro Bembo through the use of Bembo as an interlocutor to effectively deliver a paraphrase of his own work on love, *Gli Asolani* (Venice: Aldo Manuzio, 1505). That Castiglione knew Pontano's work is evident from several sources, and most obviously from the inventory of his possessions carried out some months after his death in 1529, where copies of Pontano's *De bello Neapolitano*, *De aspiratione*, and a collection of "Opere de Pontano" (perhaps our 1501 edition) appear.[102] The more subtle influence of Pontano on Castiglione's approach to the art of witty conversation has been the subject of several studies.[103] Yet to date the overlaps in their treatments of music have gone unremarked.

The centrality of being able to exert good judgement in all things—music among them—is a well-known facet of Castiglione's fashioning of the ideal courtier.[104] Instances in which the importance of judgement is

---

100 Matthias Roick, *Pontano's Virtues: Aristotelian Moral and Political Thought in the Renaissance* (London: Bloomsbury, 2017), 78-79.

101 James Haar, "The Courtier as Musician: Castiglione's View of the Science and Art of Music," in *Castiglione: The Ideal and the Real in Renaissance Culture*, ed. Robert Hanning and David Rosand (New Haven, CT: Yale University Press, 1983), 165–90, at 20.

102 Guido Rebecchini, "The Book Collection and Other Possessions of Baldassare Castiglione," *Journal of the Warburg and Courtauld Institutes* 61 (1998), 17–52, at 35 and 43–44. Rebecchini supposes the "Opere di Pontano" to be the 1505 "or later" edition of his works printed under the title *Opera*, however there is no immediate reason why his edition could not have been that printed in 1501.

103 See, for instance, Henri Weber, "Deux théoriciens de la facétie: Pontano et Castiglione," *Réforme, Humanisme, Renaissance* 7 (1978), 74–78; and Florence Bistagne, "Pontano, Castiglione, Guazzo: facétie et normes de comportement dans la trattatistica de la Renaissance," *Cahiers d'études italiennes* 6 (2007), 183–92.

104 See, for example, Haar, "The Courtier as Musician."

brought to the fore in his dialogue are numerous, but the reason for its importance in general terms is summed up neatly by Ludovico Canossa when discussing the courtier's prowess in arms:

> Ma sopra tutto accompagni ogni suo movimento con un certo bon giudicio e grazia, se vole meritar quell'universal favore che tanto s'apprezza.[105]
>
> But above all [the courtier] should accompany all of his actions with a certain judgement and grace, if he wishes to merit that universal favour which is so prized.

Returning specifically to the field of music, a caution against poor judgement is delivered in the form of a joke by Cesare Borgia—in the manner of Poggio Bracciolini's popular *Facetiae*—where he recalls having spoken to a Brescian who, when asked about his favourite aspect of the musical entertainments heard in Venice during the feast of the Ascension, recounts his amazement at seeing a trombone player slide the instrument in and out of his throat at a length of two palms (around six inches) in order to play.[106]

This leads us to the first similarity between Pontano and Castiglione's treatment of music: a low valuation of wind instruments, contrasted with a high valuation of string-accompanied song. The Brescian's error is twofold. First, he displays a comical lack of understanding of how a slide trombone functions. Second, of all of the musical marvels he could have highlighted to show his good taste, he chose the efforts of a mere *piffaro*. In an earlier passage, Federico Fregoso had outlined the forms of music with which a man of taste should engage:

> Ma sopra tutto parmi gratissimo il cantare alla viola per recitare; il che tanto di venustà ed efficacia aggiunge alle parole, che è gran maraviglia [...] Dà ornamento e grazia assai la voce umana a tutti questi instrumenti, de' quali voglio che al nostro cortegian basti aver notizia; e quanto piú però

---

105 Baldassare Castiglione, *Il Libro del Cortegiano*, ed. Giulio Preti (Torino: Einaudi, 1965), 39. On the importance of exercising good judgement to avoid the negative judgement of others, see Jennifer D. Webb, "All Is Not Fun and Games: Conversation, Play, and Surveillance at the Montefeltro Court in Urbino," *Renaissance studies* 26.3 (2012), 417–40.

106 "io vidi uno sonar con certa tromba strana, che ad ogni tratto se ne ficcava in gola piú di dui palmi e poi súbito la cavava e di novo la reficcava; che non vedeste mai la piú gran maraviglia." Castiglione, *Il Libro del Cortegiano*, 160.

in essi sarà eccellente, tanto sarà meglio, senza impacciarsi molto di quelli che Minerva refiutò ed Alcibiade, perché pare che abbiano del schifo.[107]

> But above all I consider most estimable the song accompanied by the *viola* for recitation, something which adds such charm and grace to the words, that it is a great marvel [...] The human voice gives such ornament and grace to all these instruments [i.e., stringed instruments and keyboards], of which I would wish for our courtier to have some knowledge, and the more that he excels in them, the better, without busying himself too much with those which Minerva and Alcibiades rejected [i.e., wind instruments], because these seem to have something odious about them.

Here, Castiglione adds a vein of humanist eloquence to Fregoso's reasoning, referring to an episode in Greek myth in which Athena casts aside the reed instrument she invented after seeing her reflection while playing, judging her puffed-out cheeks to be unseemly. In Plutarch's life of the Athenian statesman Alcibiades, he recounts how, inspired by Athena's example, his protagonist refused to learn the pipe as a boy, and indeed turned all of Athenian society against the instrument (*The Life of Alcibiades*, 2.4).

In his treatise on liberality, Pontano expresses his disdain for wind instruments and their players through an anecdote concerning an encounter with a trumpeter upon arriving at an inn in the Umbrian town of Narni, using the episode to illustrate the importance of judging when to be liberal with men of lower social status, and to what extent:

> Quibus tamen minores facultates sunt, hi respicere imprimis debent, ut ipsorum liberalitas quo rarior minusque plane est, eo exactior ab ipsis delectus habeatur eorum in quos pecunias conferunt: nam qui plurimum habent quod dent, iis fortasse concedendum fuerit, si quid dum non multum tamen in delectu peccent, minus autem opulentis in hoc peccare non facile permittitur. Veneram ipse aliquando Narniam: diverteramque ad meritoriam tabernam cum familiaribus qui mecum iter faciebant. Tubicen non malus discumbentibus nobis atrium ingressus est. Invaluit enim mos ut, cum peregrinus quispiam, qui dignitatem prae se ferat aliquam, oppidum ingreditur tubicines postquam tuba eum salutaverint, donari se expectent. Ingredientem igitur tubicinem carleno donavi, atque ut taceret iussi. Causam requirenti cauponi, respondi me cum erga tubicinem

---

107 Castiglione, *Il Libro del Cortegiano*, 108–09.

liberalis esse nequaquam, si caneret, eo carleno redemisse, ne illiberalis dicerer et qui cantum non possem, silentium eo argento mercatus essem.[108]

> Those, however, who are of lesser means, must be attentive in ensuring that their liberality is more select, and less extravagant, by choosing carefully to whom they give, because those who live in abundance may do so, as long as they do not err in their choices, but those who are less wealthy cannot permit themselves any error. I once went to Narni, and diverted to a reputable tavern with my friends, who had made the journey with me. As we sat down a trumpeter—not a bad player—entered our room, for the custom prevailed that, when a stranger came into town whose rank merited some dignity, he would be greeted by trumpeters, who would then expect a gift in return. When we entered, I had given the trumpeter a silver coin, and ordered him to be silent.[109] When the innkeeper asked why, I replied that, not being able to be liberal with a trumpeter by any means, if he had played, I would have recompensed him, lest any question my liberality, and because I could not pay one who played, I paid rather for his silence.

Pontano uses this example to illustrate the need for those with status and means to be generous whenever possible. It nevertheless casts the trumpeter as a man of low status, undeserving of praise for his rude occupation, an unfitting pursuit for the man of taste to engage in voluntarily as a listener or player.

This episode can be contrasted with one in the dialogue *Antonius* describing an encounter with a player of stringed instruments (lyricen), who stops to play for the members of the Academia Antoniana meeting in a portico, on his way to perform at a wedding.[110] Like the poor *tubicen*, the *lyricen* appearing in *Antonius* is diminished by the academicians, who refer to him as a "little man" (homuntio), and (although the player himself tries to dissemble it) he is marked as someone whose musical skill is employed chiefly for pecuniary gain, not, like the courtier, as an ennobling accomplishment. This distinction is made by Aristotle in *Politics* Book 8 (1341a–b), who applies the term βαναυσικός (*banausikós*,

---

108 Pontano, *Opera*, sigs. [o vi] v–p [i] r.
109 A "carleno" was a silver currency in the kingdom of Sicily, first minted in the reign of Charles I of Anjou. Giovanni Pontano, *I libri delle virtù sociali*, ed. Francesco Tateo (Rome: Bulzone Editore, 1999), 98.
110 On this episode see also Shephard and Rice, "Giovanni Pontano," 534–38.

"banausic") to those, musicians included, who ply a trade for a living.[111] However, the *lyricen* otherwise receives nothing but praise from the assembled *literati* who, like Castiglione's ideal courtier, are more than happy to enjoy no less than four songs performed *alla viola*.

James Hankins has previously suggested that the *lyricen* might be a representation of a real *cantor ad lyram*, specifically one versed in the improvisation of Latin lyric to the accompaniment of a *lira da braccio*.[112] The fact that the player is financially rewarded for his efforts by the academicians, however, places him far from the likes of the Brandolini brothers and other proponents of sung Latin lyric, for whom music was, as for the courtier, an accomplishment, and who would not stoop to playing for tips. Furthermore, a petition from one of the academicians, Enrico, for the *lyricen* to perform something new (novuum), suggests that Pontano did not intend for all of the repertoire presented to be representative of improvisatory practice. Rather, the episode as a whole represents the form of musical entertainment most suitable for men of standing: song performed to a stringed instrument, whether plucked or bowed.

All of the musician's songs appear to be by Pontano himself.[113] In subject matter they have been previously described as "amatory."[114] The first is a plea to a woman, Telesina—a protagonist found in Martial's poetry (Book 2, epigram 49)—to recognise her natural beauty, and not apply makeup. The third relates Galatea's escape from the amorous hands of Polyphemus into the waters of the river she created from her

---

111 Stefano Costa, a jurist and professor of Canon Law at Pavia, used this term in describing professional musicians in his *Tractatus de Ludo*, first published by Franciscus de Sancto Petro in Pavia in 1478, and again in 1489 and 1505: "Such persons [professional musicians] make mercenaries of themselves, and are servile, and according to the Philosopher [Aristotle] are banausic, transmitting elegant and noble music for profit, playing or teaching to play for the sake of material gain" (Tales persone corpus suum mercenarium faciunt et seruile et appelantur per philosophum bannci et transmittunt ellegantiam et nobilitatem musice in lucrum in causam questus quia pullant vel pulsare docent causa lucri). Stefano Costa, *Tractatus de Ludo* (Pavia: Franciscus de Sancto Petro, 1478), fol. 5v.
112 James Hankins, "Humanism and Music in Italy," in *The Cambridge History of Fifteenth-Century Music*, ed. Anna Maria Busse Berger and Jesse Rodin (Cambridge, UK: Cambridge University Press, 2015), 231–62, especially 252–54.
113 Pontano, *Opera*, sigs. [l iv] v–[l vi] r.
114 This episode in *Antonius* is briefly described by James Hankins as an example of the humanist preference for song *ad lyram*, and in which he describes the songs performed as amatory. See Hankins, "Humanism and Music," 253–54.

murdered lover Acis. It drew the revulsion of Julius Caesar Scaliger later in the sixteenth century for its description of Galatea's bobbing breasts (Fluitantque nudae/ Aequore mammae), one of a number of examples of what he saw as "fatal licentiousness" (fatalis lasciva) in Pontano's poetry.[115] The final song is an eclogue, perhaps composed with the first of Virgil's *Eclogues* in mind, addressed to Amaryllis, the lover calling on a host of Arcadian delights to tempt her to his grove.

The ubiquity of amatory themes in song led Castiglione, in the guise of Federico Fregoso, to declare that "most of the time" (il più delle volte) sung texts were amorous in nature.[116] The traditional attitude attributed to the humanist cadre is one of revulsion toward anything which might be considered wanton.[117] In his *De amore*, Marsilio Ficino bisected music into that which is "serious and constant" (grave quodam constans) and that which is "soft and wanton" (molle atque lascivum), one beneficial (utile), the other actively harmful (noxium), following a division made by Plato in the *Republic* and *Laws*.[118] More famously, in *De musica et poetica* Raffaello Brandolini uses such a division in the defence of his musical practice, distancing Latin lyric sung *ad lyram* from the "meretricious" songs he describes as common entertainments at banquets, and which he saw as "incentives to prodigality, depravity, drunkenness, and lust."[119] Such strict views were not shared by all among the elite, however. In *De partibus aedium*, for example, Grapaldi draws on two passages from Aulus Gellius' *Noctes Atticae* (13.11 and 19.9) to describe the model banquet, whose entertainments include readings of a philosophical nature by an *anagnostes*, and song, which might indeed be erotic, although not too

---

115 Karl A.E. Enekel, "The Neo-Latin Epigram: Humanist Self-Definition in a Learned and Witty Discourse," in *The Neo-Latin Epigram: A Learned and Witty Genre*, ed. Susanna De Beer, Karl A.E. Enenkel, and David Rijsser (Leuven: Leuven University Press, 2009), 1–24, at 18.
116 Castiglione, *Il Libro del Cortegiano*, 109.
117 On the moral judgement of music in Italy in this period see, among others, Tim Shephard and Patrick McMahon, "Foolish Midas: Representing Musical Judgement and Moral Judgement in Italy c.1520," in *Music, Myth and Story in Medieval and Early Modern Culture*, ed. Katherine Butler and Samantha Bassler (Woodbridge: Boydell, 2019), 87–104, esp. 88–92.
118 Marsilio Ficino, "De Amore," in Plato, [*Opera*], ed. and trans. Ficino (Florence: Lorenzo d'Alopa, [1484–85]), fol. 6v.
119 Raffaele Brandolini, *On Music and Poetry*, 33.

licentious, and should be sung to a stringed instrument.[120] In enjoying such music, Pontano's academicians are simply emulating what they considered to be the rarified standards of their ancient models.[121]

Pontano's songs in *Antonius* are not only amatory. The second song performed by our *lyricen* is a *memento mori*, reminding the listeners of the futility of life's pleasures through the figure of the Sirens, in whom desire is tied directly to death:

Sirenes madidis canunt in antris	The Sirens sing in their sea-drenched caves,
Dum captas male subruunt carinas.	enthralling ships, and running them aground.
Sic mortalibus ipsa vita blande	So too for mortals life sings so sweet,
Illudens canit ut dolosa Siren:	deceiving like the crafty Siren
Donec vel gravis ingruit senecta	until harsh old age bears down
Aut mors occupat, estque nil quod ultra	or death takes hold, and nothing more is left except a tale and emptiness.[123]
Iam restet nisi fabula atque inane.[122]	

Awakened to the moralising potential of the *lyricen*'s song, it is possible to detect similar themes also in the other texts. In the first, Pontano's adoption of the name "Telesina," which has been suggested to translate roughly as "little fulfilment" in Martial's usage, is perhaps a similar warning against the futility of desire.[124] In the third song, Polyphemus' lust is powerless in the face of Galatea's chastity; whilst in the fourth, gifts are prepared for Amaryllis, cruel and disdainful lover from Virgil's first three eclogues, whose arrival is longed for but does not materialise. Thus, while all four songs in some sense adopt erotic themes, in each the

---

120 "Adhibent nonnulli Anagnostem qui legat faciles utilesque ex Philosophia quæstiones. vel Erotica quædam non nimis lasciva Plurimi vero fidium modulamina." *De partibus aedium*, 71v.
121 On Book 19 of the *Noctes Atticae* as a representation of the entertainments preferred by literary men in antiquity, see Charles H. Cosgrove, *Music at Social Meals in Greek and Roman Antiquity: From the Archaic Period to the Age of Augustine* (Cambridge, UK: Cambridge University Press, 2022), 194.
122 Pontano, *Opera*, sig. [l iv] v.
123 Giovanni Pontano, *Dialogues, vol. 1: Charon and Antonius*, ed. and trans. Julia Haig Gaisser (Cambridge, MA: Harvard University Press, 2012), 263.
124 *Martial's Epigrams: Book Two*, ed. and trans. Craig A. Williams (Oxford: Oxford University Press, 2003), 177.

erotic intent is somehow inverted, opening the door to moral readings that might render them licit *otium*. As per Grapaldi, they are erotic, but not too licentious.

A crucial difference between Pontano's *lyricen* and *tubicen* lies in the manner in which they present their performances. In *De liberalitate*, the *tubicen* greets the unsuspecting visitor with a performance unless the visitor is terse enough to stop them. In *Antonio*, the *lyricen* performs only when asked; and under the weight of the academicians' praise, he prefaces his third song with an assurance of his modesty:

> Geretur a me tibi mos. Utinam tamen is essem cuius ingenio musicae ipsi aliquid collatum esset! Ac ne ex eorum sim numero qui, ut ab Horatio iure irridentur, nunquam rogati cantare inducunt animum, etiam hoc accipe, in tuam atque Herrici ipsius, si tibi non displicet, gratiam:[125]

> I am at your service. If only I had the talent to make a contribution to music! And yet in order not to be one of those who (as Horace mocks justly) "never brings themselves to sing when they are asked," hear this as well, in your honour and Enrico's too, if it does not displease you:[126]

As the *lyricen* is a jobbing performer and inherently banausic, he is under no obligation to adhere to the social guidelines of the liberal classes. In spite of this, in his dialogue he displays a crucial mark of learning—the application of witty maxims to add eloquence to his speech—and his modesty bears striking similarity to the ideal conduct of the courtier when performing as described by Castiglione:

> non voglio che 'l nostro cortegiano faccia come molti, che súbito che son giunti ove che sia, e alla presenzia ancor di signori de' quali non abbiano notizia alcuna, senza lasciarsi molto pregare si metteno a far ciò che sanno e spesso ancor quel che non sanno; di modo che par che solamente per quello effetto siano andati a farsi vedere e che quella sia la loro principal professione. Venga adunque il cortegiano a far musica come a cosa per passar tempo e quasi sforzato, e non in presenzia di gente ignobile, né di gran moltitudine; e benché sappia ed intenda ciò che fa, in questo ancor voglio che dissimuli il studio e la fatica che è necessaria in tutte le cose che si hanno a far bene, e mostri estimar poco in se stesso questa condizione, ma, col farla eccellentemente, la faccia estimar assai dagli altri.[127]

---

125 Pontano, *Opera*, sig. [l v] r.
126 Pontano, *Dialogues*, 267.
127 Castiglione, *Il Libro del Cortegiano*, 107–08.

> I would not wish for our courtier to do so many others do, who as soon as they arrive wherever they are, and even in the presence of gentlemen who they have never met, without waiting to be asked begin showing off what they know, and often also what they don't know, so that it seems they are come solely to make known that it is their main pursuit in life. Rather, the courtier should perform music as though it is merely a means of passing the time, and as if compelled [by the present company], and not in the presence of commoners, or of a large crowd; and though it may be that he is accomplished in what he is doing, in this also I want him to dissimulate the study and effort that are necessary for all things that are done well, and show little estimation of his skill, but which, because of its excellence, makes others think very highly of him.

In much the same way that Castiglione recommends, the *lyricen* also makes it clear that music is not his only or even his primary accomplishment: he states that he spent "the best part of his life" (optimam vitae partem) soldiering.[128] His decorum serves to elevate him beyond his means, earning him "nobility" (nobilitatem) in the eyes of the academicians. Indeed, his parting "to sing at a friend's wedding" (ad amici nuptias propero hymeneum decantaturus) leaves open the possibility of comparison with Apollo himself, who in classical myth sang for the nuptials of Thetis and Peleus, and Cupid and Psyche; what more fitting accolade than to compare one who the academicians proclaim to have "saved us from savage music" (ex agresti illa musica sic emerseris) to the very inventor of the stringed instrument.[129]

Pontano's representation of commendable and reprehensible public performance extends, as also in *Il libro del Cortegiano*, to consideration of the age of performers. The debate on this subject in *Il Cortegiano* is well-known; while agreeing that the enjoyment of music is beneficial for the elderly, the public performance of music by elderly men is dismissed by Federico Fregoso, on the basis that even accomplished musicians of advancing years appear ridiculous when singing, as most song is amatory:

---

128 Pontano, *Opera*, sig. [l vi] r.
129 Pontano, *Opera*, sig. [l vi] r. The mythology of the invention of the *cithara* is labyrinthine, but is attributed to Apollo by Isidore of Seville, "according to the opinion of the Greeks." *The Etymologies of Isidore of Seville*, ed. and trans. Stephen A. Barney, W. J. Lewis, J. A. Beach, and Oliver Berghof (Cambridge, UK: Cambridge University Press, 2006), 97–98.

conoscerà l'età sua; ché in vero non si conviene e dispare assai vedere un omo di qualche grado, vecchio canuto e senza denti, pien di rughe, con una viola in braccio sonando, cantare in mezzo d'una compagnia di donne, avvenga ancor che mediocremente lo facesse, e questo, perché il piú delle volte cantando si dicono parole amorose e ne' vecchi l'amor è cosa ridicula.[130]

[The courtier] will acknowledge his age; for it is indeed unseemly and unlovely in the extreme to see a man of any quality—old, grey and toothless, full of wrinkles—with a *viola* in arm and singing midst a company of ladies, even if he did so passably, and this is because most of the time in singing the words are amorous, and in old men love is a ridiculous thing.

Another musical episode in *Antonius* presents a scenario that seems exactly the sort of behaviour Fregoso has in mind. An old man (senex), an octogenarian (octogenarius) no less, is spotted madly serenading (cantans amore insaniens) a young woman from beneath her window.[131] In spite of the agreeable quality of his comportment, referred to by academician Enrico as charming (blande) and generous (larga), the scene is a source of amusement; Enrico ridicules the man as "delirious" (quid hoc sene delirius?), and takes astonished delight in his tears (Etiam lachrymatur).[132] When challenged by Enrico on his actions, the old man launches into a defence of love and the new lease of life it has brought him:

gravissimeque obiurgandos censeo, qui regnum amoris accusant: Bellissimi pueri: laenissimi heri, indulgentissimi Dei. hic munditias: nitorem: ornatum leporem: computum: ludos: iocum: carmen: elegantiam: delitias: omnem denique vitae suavitatem invenit. Me qui senex sum, aetatis huius molestiarum oblitum, non tantum non invitum sed volentem quoque ad suavissima quaeque secum trahit. Sequor convivia, cantus, hymeneos, choreas, pompas, festos dies, theatra.[133]

I consider deserving of the harshest censure those who find fault with the rule of Amor—the most beautiful boy, the gentlest master, the most indulgent god. He has devised elegance, style, fine dress, charm, adornment, sport, jest, song, refinement, delight, in short, every pleasant

---

130 Castiglione, *Il Libro del Cortegiano*, 109.
131 Pontano, *Opera*, sig. i ii r–v.
132 Pontano, *Opera*, sig. i ii r.
133 Pontano, *Opera*, sig. i ii v.

thing in life; he takes me, an old man, forgetting all the troubles of my time of life, not only not against my will, but even with my eager consent, to all the sweetest pleasures with him. I frequent dinner parties, music, weddings, dances, processions, holidays, theatre.[134]

Enrico is unmoved, simply replying "O inane and unstable man" (O inane et lubricum caput), before expressing gratitude for the fact that they live in a city—only recently recovered from conflict between the ruling Trastámara family and the old order of Angevin barons by the point at which *Antonius* is set—which permits its citizens to do as they please.[135]

Another error committed by the old man is the public nature of his performance; by performing in the street, he sets himself on a footing with the bawdy practice of the *mattinata*.[136] As we have seen, Castiglione is explicit in his recommendation that the courtier refrain from playing for large crowds or commoners.[137] The *lyricen*, in happy contrast, performs in the portico where the academicians are gathering, if not physically removed from the street by means of a door, at least symbolically divided from the thoroughfare.[138]

At no point in his writings does Pontano offer any explicit guidance on the ideal comportment of the gentleman performer. Nonetheless, through engaging in music in a space separated from the general public, it is possible that the academicians are abiding by another convention, that of the enjoyment of music only in small circles. In this regard, it is

---

134 Pontano, *Dialogues*, 145.
135 Pontano, *Opera*, sig. i ii v.
136 On the practice of the mattinata in Italy, see, among others, Flora Dennis, "Sound and Domestic Space in Fifteenth- and Sixteenth-Century Italy," *Studies in the Decorative Arts* 16.1 (2008–09), 7–19, at 13–15; and Flora Dennis, "Unlocking the Gates of Chastity: Music and the Erotic in the Domestic Sphere in Fifteenth- and Sixteenth-Century Italy," in *Erotic Cultures of Renaissance Italy*, ed. S. F. Matthews-Grieco (Ashgate: Aldershot, 2010), 223–45, at 235–37.
137 Castiglione, *Il Libro del Cortegiano*, 107–08.
138 The duality of the portico as a space at once separated from public space and yet easily visible from without is exemplified by the Council of Ten's attempts to regulate the operation of music schools in Venice. A decree promulgated on 21 January 1477 bid all tuition at music schools in the city take place in a "room or portico" visible to the public (sallam seu porticum ubi omnes publice doceantur), evidently to deter any impropriety on the part of the teacher. See da Col, "Silent Voices: Professional Singers in Venice," 237–38. For a transcription of the decree, see Francesco Luisi ed., *Laudario Giustinianeo*, vol. 1 (Venice: Edizioni Fondazione Levi, 1983), 508, doc. 16.

notable that in the final episode of *Antonius*, when a trumpet (tubicen) announces the beginning of a sung theatrical performance in the street and benches (subsellia) are pulled up for the assembling crowd, the academicians gladly watch the performance, which is deemed by Enrico a recent import from Northern Italy (recens cisalpina e Gallia allatum est—literally, from Cisalpine Gaul) and the "only thing lacking to the elegant customs of our state" (Deerat unum hoc civitatis nostrae moribus tam concinnis), yet they do not venture outside the confines of the portico, remaining physically removed from the crowd.[139]

The importance of enjoying music only in select company is rendered explicit by the pseudo-Aristotelian *Regum regimine*, which in a chapter on "The musical solace of the king" (De Regis solatio musicali) states:

> Decet imperatoriam maiestatem privatos habere fideles cum quibus delectabitur cum variis instrumentis et generibus organorum, cum fuerit tediosus. Anima enim humana naturaliter in talibus delectatur: sensus requiescit: sollicitudo et curiositas evanescit: et totum corpus vigoratur. Si tu igitur in talibus volveris delctari: ad plus persevera in tali vita tribus diebus vel quatuor secundum quod videris expedire. Et semper melius et honestius et quod hec fiant privatim.[140]

> It is proper for his imperial majesty to have private confidantes, with whom he will amuse himself with various means and kinds of musical instrument, when he is weary. For the human soul will naturally delight in such things: the senses rest, concern and curiosity disappear, and the whole body is invigorated. If, therefore, you wish to indulge in such things, continue in such a life for three or four days, according to what you see fit. And it is always better and more honest to do this in private.

The wide dissemination of the *Regum regimine* in Europe throughout the Middle Ages makes it entirely possible that it was known to both Pontano and Castiglione. At no point in his oeuvre is Pontano compelled to write a *laus musicae* similar to the "sea of praise" (pelago di laude) upon which Count Ludovico embarks in *Il Cortegiano*, invoking music's effects—now bellicose, now soothing—on Alexander the Great, its study by Achilles and Socrates, and its use by the Lacedemonians in war.[141] However, two closely-related passages in his treatises on obedience and the prince

---

139 Pontano, *Opera*, sig. [1 vi] r.
140 *Aristotelis philosophorum maximi secretum secretorum*, fol. 4v.
141 Castiglione, *Il Libro del Cortegiano*, 78–80.

bear some relation to Aristotle's supposed advice to Alexander. In *De principe*, Pontano writes:

> Et quoniam non semper agendis negociis occupati esse possumus: et a libris secedendum est aliquando: faciendaeque sunt intermissiones: ac quaerenda tum animi tum corporis laxamenta [...] In hac cessatione dandus erit locus aliquis iocis: facetiisque quibus animus recreetur. Quodque ait Laberius, facundum comitem in via pro vehiculo esse, ad istam quam dico cessationem transferendum. Adhibendi sunt etiam musici, qui tum cantu tum chordis oblectent animum et curas permulceant.dandum quoque aliquid istrionibus.[142]

> As we cannot always busy ourselves in work, and from books we must sometimes retire, we must create intermissions, and seek relaxation of both mind and body [...] In such cessation place must be given to pastimes and humour, through which the mind will be refreshed. Thus, Laberius said that "a companion on a journey serves for a carriage," which we might transfer to the cessation I speak of. Musicians are also to be employed who with both song and instruments divert the mind and soothe our cares. Time might also be given to actors.

In *De obedientia*, he similarly upholds the validity of musical recreation, particularly listening to stringed instruments:

> Verum cum voluptatis commune quidem nomen sit: et voluptas ipsa semper nec ubique sit turpis, non omnes corporis sensuumque voluptates intemperantes nos efficient:ut dum lyra delinimur: laboremque solamur cantu: aut naribus admovemus flosculos: seu in Iocti alíquas, Gentilisue picturas egregias conversi, in spectandis illis oculis palcimus: et tanquam ipsi reficimur.[143]

> But indeed pleasure is a common name; not all pleasures are shameful, and not all of the pleasures of the body and senses affect us intemperately, such as when we are soothed by the lyre, console ourselves with song, or our noses are drawn to flowers, or we to some amusing or noble paintings turn; in looking at them we nourish our eyes, and are ourselves restored.

This is the closest Pontano comes to a defence of music. Considering Castiglione's use of Gaspar Pallavicino to represent those voices who thought of music as emasculating—Pallavicino calls music a "vanity fit for women" (vanità sia alle donne conveniente)—it is noteworthy that

---

142 Pontano, *Opera*, sig. [e vi] r.
143 Pontano, *Opera*, sig. u ii r.

in *De obedientia* Pontano specifically reminds the reader that employing music to soothe the mind is nothing shameful. Such reasoning explains, perhaps, why the *Regum regimine* cautions the prince only to engage with music in the presence of confidantes, where none can level accusations of impropriety or weakness on account of musical *otium*.

Of similar import in the *Regum regimine*, in the preceding chapter, "De taciturnitate regis" (On the silence of the king), the monarch is counselled that it is "beautiful and honourable in a king to refrain from being garrulous" (speciorum et honorificum est in rege abstinere a multilogo), and that silence is a tool by which he might distance himself from the common man and appear more regal, familiarity breeding contempt of honour (nimia familiaritas hominum parit contemptum honoris).[144] Frequent laughter (risu multum) is similarly censured for "stealing reverence" (tollit reverentia) from the monarch, reflected in Pontano's *De principe* in his description of clapping as "entirely absurd" (omnino inepta) and of profuse laughter as "shameful" (turpes).[145] Rather, the prince must be able to control his actions and speech, in both tone and content. The *Regum regimine* proffers advice on how manners of speech betray a speaker's intellect, counselling that those with loud, sonorous voices (grossam vocem et sonogram) are bellicose, those with "thin" (gracilem) voices stupid and wicked (mendax), and those with sweet voices (dulcem) insidious; the prince must aim to moderate his voice, being not too loud or grandiloquent, in order to show his wisdom, perspicuity, truthfulness and justice.[146] Pontano reserves similar advice for the very end of his treatise on the prince, asking for similarly well-judged (apte) simplicity (simplicitatem) in choice of words, and neither a languid nor a melodious (languens nec canora) tone.[147] All of these qualities are also applied by Castiglione, through the mouthpiece of Ludovico Canossa, to the ideal courtier.[148]

---

144 *Aristotelis philosophorum maximi secretum secretorum*, fol. 4v.
145 Pontano, *Opera*, sig. f ii v.
146 "vero vox est mediocris in subtiliate et grossitie est sapiens pervidus verax est iustus." *Aristotelis philosophorum maximi secretum secretorum*, fol. 5r.
147 Pontano, *Opera*, sig. f iii v.
148 "E questo cosí dico dello scrivere, come del parlare; al qual però si richiedono alcune cose che non son necessarie nello scrivere: come la voce bona, non troppo sottile o molle come di femina, né ancor tanto austera ed orrida che abbia del rustico, ma sonora, chiara, soave e ben composta, con la pronunzia espedita e coi modi e gesti convenienti; li quali, al parer mio, consistono in certi movimenti di

In spite of the thorny ethical and social considerations attending the musical *otium* of the elite, music was of course used ubiquitously to add magnificence to occasions of all kinds—a key concern for the prince, who must be able to display his wisdom and power through personal modesty and material majesty in equal degree.[149] In *Il Cortegiano*, it falls upon Cesare Gonzaga to elucidate this dichotomy:

> Direi ancor che compagnar dovesse con la grandezza una domestica mansuetudine, con quella umanità dolce ed amabile [...] servando però sempre la maestà conveniente al grado suo, che non gli lassasse in parte alcuna diminuire l'autorità per troppo bassezza, né meno gli concitasse odio per troppo austera severità; dovesse essere liberalissimo e splendido e donar ad ognuno senza riservo, perché Dio, come si dice, è tesauriero dei príncipi liberali; far conviti magnifici, feste, giochi, spettacoli publici [...] e tutte l'altre cose che s'appartengono ai piaceri de' gran signori e dei populi.[150]

> I would say also that [the prince] should accompany greatness with a familiar meekness, with humanity sweet and amiable [...] preserving, however, at all times, the majesty appropriate to his rank, not allowing his authority to diminish at all through baseness, nor exciting hate through too austere a severity; he should be very liberal and splendid, and give to all without reserve, because God, as they say, is the treasurer of liberal princes. He should give magnificent banquets, festivals, games, public spectacles [...] and all other things which pertain to the pleasures of great lords and the populace.

From our 1501 corpus, we have already encountered one instance of music's employment in magnificence (or rather, attempted magnificence) in the guise of the *tubicen* attempting to uphold the civic

---

tutto 'l corpo, non affettati né violenti, ma temperati con un volto accommodato e con un mover d'occhi che dia grazia e s'accordi con le parole, e piú che si po significhi ancor coi gesti la intenzione ed affetto di colui che parla. Ma tutte queste cose sarian vane e di poco momento se sentenzie espresse dalle parole non fossero belle, ingeniose, acute, eleganti e gravi, secondo 'l bisogno." Castiglione, *Il Libro del Cortegiano*, 56–57.

149 On musical aspects of the discourse of magnificence in Italy in this period see, among others, Franco Piperno, "Suoni della sovranità: Le cappelle musicali fra storiografia generale e storia della musica," in *Cappelle musicali fra corte, stato e chiesa nell'Italia del Rinascimento*, ed. Piperno, Gabriella Biagi Ravenni, and Andrea Chegai (Florence: Olschki, 2007), 11–36; and Vincenzo Borghetti and Tim Shephard, "Politics," in *A Cultural History of Music in the Renaissance*, ed. Jeanice Brooks and Richard Freedman (London: Bloomsbury, 2023), 91–120.

150 Castigione, *Il Libro del Cortegiano*, 345–46.

dignity of Narni. The practice of using wind instruments to aggrandise a particular party or individual had ancient roots; in *De partibus aedium*, Grapaldi (drawing on Livy, *Decades* 17.3) recounts the case of Gaius Duilius, victor of Mylae, Segesta, and Macella, who was accorded the perpetual honour of being preceded by a torchbearer (funale) and piper (tibicen) on his way home from dinner.[151] In a chapter on obtaining splendour in banquets (De conviviis splendoris gratia susceptis) in his treatise on conviviality, Pontano ascribes a similar role to players of wind instruments in announcing courses during a banquet:

> Recte etiam ac splendide institutum uidetur: ut precedentibus ferculis tubae tibiaeque praegrediantur, quae conviuas astantesque oblectent cantibus et signum dent incendium ferculorum, ut voluptati etiam ipsi ordo videatur adiunctus: qui si defuerit inter turbari atque confundi necesse est omnia. Ordini quoque illud accedet, ut astantium ac ministrorum ea disciplina sit, quae conviviorum est propria: absint non modo dicta, verum etiam gestus, qui tristitiam aut turbationem affere habeant aliquam. Qua e re mihi videtur introductum, ut his in conviviis adhiberentur musici, qui non solum oblectarent cantu, verum ut, dum astantes ad se audiendos trahunt, silentium parerent, atque e silentio tranquillitatem.[152]

> Likewise proper and splendid is the custom that, as the courses are brought in, they are preceded by trumpets and pipes, whose playing entertains the guests and those present, and gives a signal of the approaching courses, so that pleasure may seem to be adjoined to order—which, if it is lacking, everything must be confused and jumbled. Also connected to order, those present and the servants must observe the discipline that is proper to banquets, that not only words, but also actions will be absent which produce some degree of distaste and disturbance. This seems to be the reason the custom of calling musicians to banquets was introduced; their playing not only delights, but, by drawing those present to them to listen, they might obtain silence, and out of silence, calm.

In this instance, trumpets (tubae) and pipes (tibiae) serve three functions: they add magnificence to the proceedings by announcing each course; they clarify the structure of the the evening for participants; and the music, whether in itself, or as part of a spectacle, or both,

---

151 *De partibus aedium*, fol. 63v.
152 Pontano, *Opera*, sig. [t i] v.

entertains the guests.[153] Whether the *tubicens* and *tibicines* are the same players who later calm the diners is unclear, and perhaps unlikely, given Pontano's distaste for the *tubicen* in *De liberalitate*, and a less-than-flattering description of the appearance and sound of a trumpet-playing herald in *Antonius*:

> Sed praeconem hunc audiamus qui tantam sibi facit in populo audientiam.regium videlicet edictum.nunquam vidi turgidiores buccas. Puto ego hominem fermento vesci. quos clamores dii boni?[154]

> But let us listen to this herald who is getting such a hearing in the crowd. It must be a royal edict. I have never seen more puffed-out cheeks. I think the fellow feeds on yeast. Good gods, what a noise!"[155]

It is, rather, "sweet song" (suavissimos cantus) which Pontano recommends be played at banquets after dining, giving the example of a banquet arranged by King Alfonso of Naples in the 1450s in honour of an emissary from the court of Charles the Bold.[156] Given the praise heaped upon the *lyricen* in *Antonius* by the academicians, it is much more likely that he envisioned a performer or performers playing stringed instruments employed for this purpose, and more generally for the purpose of calming guests at banquets.

Moderation and temperance are principles and objectives that are held in common between the texts aimed at the elite and those read by children in grammar class. Concision is advocated by the *Disticha Catonis*, itself a brief and pithy text, in its final distich: "Do you marvel at the few words with which I write these verses?/ This brevity designs: to share one thought in two lines."[157] The *Poema admonitiorum* attributed to Phocylides counsels moderation in even more abrupt terms, simply stating "Exercise temperance; abstain from indecent acts" (Temperantiam vero exerce. turpibus vero operibus abstine).[158] Much like the precepts

---

153 For a wider view on the role of music in fifteenth-century banquets and feasts, see Anthony M. Cummings, "Music and Feasts in the Fifteenth Century," in *The Cambridge History of Fifteenth-Century Music*, ed. Anna Maria Busse Berger and Jesse Rodin (Cambridge, UK: Cambridge University Press, 2015), 361–73.
154 Pontano, *Opera*, sig. [i] i r.
155 Pontano, *Dialogues*, 135.
156 Pontano, *Opera*, sig. t ii v.
157 "Miraris verbis nudis me scribere versus./ Hos brevitas sensus fecit coniungere binos." *Donatus Melior*, fol. 32r.
158 Manuzio, *Rudimenta grammatices*, fol. 31v.

advanced in the conduct literature for the courtier and prince, moderation is the product of good judgement, and good judgement is symptomatic of keen intelligence. In the body of moralising verse for schoolboys this is rendered nowhere more plainly than in regard to speech. The tenth distich of the *Disticha Catonis* admonishes, "Do not trade words with the verbose:/ Speech is given to all, wisdom to few."[159] In the *Vita scolastica* Bonvesin de la Riva devotes seventeen distichs to the moderation of speech. The *Vita scolastica* appears originally to have been through-composed, without division into books or chapters, however the 1501 edition follows an established practice of dividing the verse with subheadings. In a chapter "On the restriction of speech and tongue" (De locutione et lingue restrictione), Bonvesin details the power of the voice, writing that one should "direct their tongue with discretion" (Eloquio sapiens discreto dirige linguam), for "the tongue, though soft, can a hard thing break" (Lingua licet mollis frangere dura potest), and that the "sweet tongue" (lingue dulcedo) can banish poison (dira venena fugat).[160] The next couplet is a warning to put that power to noble ends, and for the reader not to become a slanderer (detratrix), flatterer (adulatrix) or boaster (falsa superba loquax).[161] Rather, speech should be "humble, discreet and modest" (humilis discreta modesta); in a colourful reworking of the *Disticha Catonis*—which Bonvesin had surely learned himself as a child—and driving home the importance of discretion, he counsels that speech should not be wasted, "for before swine nothing has value" (Nam coram porcis nil preciosa valent).[162]

If the ideal masculine parlance is considered, upright, and sparing, the portrayal of feminine speech and thought in the conduct literature printed in 1501 is the opposite. Women only occur in the *Disticha Catonis* in the guise of the mother or hypothetical future wife of the reader, and

---

159 "Contra verbosus noli contendere verbis:/Sermo datur cunctis animi sapientia paucis." *Donatus Melior*, fol. 26v.
160 *Vita scolastica*, fol. 2v–3r. Perhaps using a difference Ms source to the Sessa, a Brescian edition (Brescia: Baptista Farfengus, 1495) instead choses the rather less severe "De Venusto et Honesto sermones" (on attractive and honest speech) for a title.
161 *Vita scolastica*, fol. 2v–3r.
162 *Vita scolastica*, fol. 2v–3r. The *Disticha Catonis* was among the most popular schoolroom texts of the Middle Ages. For evidence of the use of material from the distichs in medieval song, see Mary Channon Caldwell, "Singing Cato: Grammar and Moral Citation in Medieval Latin Song," *Music and Letters* 102.2 (2021), 191–233.

references to the speech of the latter are always pejorative; distichs 21 and 23 of the third book ask the reader "not to fear the words of an irate wife/ for a woman lays a snare with tears, when she weeps," and to "Remember to bear your wife's tongue, if it is useful to do so/ For it is evil not to be willing to suffer and not to be able to keep silent."[163] The *Vita scolastica* portrays women only as a source of distraction from study and from God through the arousal of carnal desire (Doctrine zelo carneus obstat amor).[164] It is noteworthy that the women described by Pontano in *Antonius* are similarly depicted as belligerent or inspiring lust. Pontano's son Lucio is a vector for a "spewing poem" (carmen evonium) which he describes Pontano as reciting to his angry wife, upon hearing which she vomits bile—the humoural source of anger—and is pacified.[165] Of a similar nature is an episode featuring another woman, Euphorbia, about whom the academicians gossip after she passes them in the street. Her anger is manifested in a range of bellicose sounds, audible throughout the neighbourhood: "She screams, yells, snarls, gnashes her teeth, whinnies, quarrels, rages."[166] Embellishing both the warlike and the bestial nature of her vocalisations, Enrico likens her to the monster which Livy (*Decades* 21.22) describes Hannibal Barca as having seen desolating Italy in a dream, foreshadowing his own devastation of the peninsula:

> Memor es hospes belvae illius quam dux poenorum Annibal vidit in somnis, silvas, agros, villas, oppida, quaque incederet cuncta vastantem? Hæc illa est belva: nequaquam tamen ut illa somnium, sed historia, et vera quidem belva.[167]

> Do you recall, visitor, the beast that Hannibal, the Carthaginian general, saw in his sleep laying everything waste—forests, fields, farms, towns— wherever it went? She is that beast, but definitely not a dream like the other, but a reality and an actual beast.[168]

---

163 "Coniugis iratae noli tu verba timere./ Instruit insidias lachrymis dum foemina plorat." "Uxoris linguam si fugi est ferre memento:/ Nam quae malum est non velle pati nec posse tacere." *Donatus Melior*, fol. 29v.
164 *Vita scolastica*, fol. 2v–3r, fol. 4r.
165 Pontano, *Opera*, sig. [l iv] v.
166 "Clamat. Inclamat, frendit, dentironat: hinnifremit, rixatur, furit." Pontano, *Opera*, sig. i ii v.
167 Pontano, *Opera*, sig. i ii v.
168 Pontano, *Dialogues*, 145.

Unlike the carefully moderated speech of the intelligent man, women are painted as of lesser intelligence, and thus unable to control how their emotions—in this case anger—affect their speech, leading to an unchecked effluence of noise. It is perhaps no accident that Pontano chose to name his most obstreperous female character "Euphorbia," the name given to a poisonous plant native to Mauritania during the reign of King Juba II, which in small doses was a well-known emetic and cathartic.[169]

Texts written for the prince and the courtier indicate that judgement is of crucial importance when engaging in musical practice: an individual should know what type of music to engage in or employ, when to do so, with whom, and to what extent, in order to avoid appearing foolish or libertine. Conduct texts for the lower orders contain no such qualifications. Instead, music is routinely dismissed as a licentious activity to avoid almost completely. The *Vita scolastica* never mentions music as such, but does warn against dance in a section entitled "On the avoidance of frequent dancing:"

De crebris choreis evitandis	On the avoidance of frequent dancing
Te rursus moneo crebras vitare choreas,	I advise you again to avoid frequent dancing,
Cordis ut a studio non vagetur amor	So that love does not draw the heart from study.
Usu cor vanum reddunt spectacula vana	The heart is rendered vain by vain spectacle,
Fundamen stabile fert studiosus amor	A stable heart is stolen by fervent love.
Hec sub luxurie vitio predicta tenentur	These are held under the aforesaid vice of luxury,
Que nisi vitentur littus arare petis.[170]	Unless avoided, you seek to till the shore.

---

169 Dioscorides 4.177 describes Euphorbia and its uses. Efraim Lev and Zohar Amar, *Practical Materia Medica of the Medieval Eastern Mediterranean According to the Cairo Genizah* (Leiden: Brill, 2008), 487. Grendler notes that Ermolao Barbaro, who met Pontano during his time in Naples between 1471 and 1473, completed a new Latin translation of Dioscorides around 1481. Paul F. Grendler, *The Universities of the Italian Renaissance* (Baltimore, MD: John Hopkins University Press, 2002), 344.

170 *Vita scolastica*, fol. 5r. The act of ploughing the shoreline is an established metaphor for any futile activity; Odysseus famously does so in the *Cypria* F 19 in order to

Bonvesin classifies dance under the bracket of *luxuria*, that is, indulgent activities which induce lascivious behaviour. In a separate section of the text devoted to the subject of *luxurie*, he begins: "All luxury flee, he who longs to learn" (Omnem luxuriam fugiat qui discere gliscit), but stops short of providing a list of those activities which might be classed as luxurious.[171] A list is, however, provided by another well-known moralising text: the *Fiore di virtù*. One of the most commonly printed texts of the fifteenth century in Italy and in many ways a mirror of the *Vita scolastica* for women, the *Fiore di virtù* describes *luxuria* in similar terms, but extends it specifically, and without any leeway, to singing and playing music, as well as dancing:

> chi vuole perfectamente lavirtu della castita siconviene guardare da sei cose [...] La quinta sie guardarsi di non stare ne conversare dove si facci overo si parli di luxuria: et pero sancto Silvestro dice. El vitio de la luxuria e dinatura discimia perche ella vuol fare cio che lavede fare adaltri. La sexta si e guardarsi de udire cantare: sonare et ballare. Pithagora dice: lherbe verde nasce apresso lacqua: el vitio della luxuria nasce del ballare cantare et sonare.[172]

> she who would perfect the virtue of chastity must take note of six things [...] The fifth is to neither see nor converse with those who practice or speak of *luxuria*. For as St Sylvester says, the life of *luxuria* is by nature that of a monkey, because it seeks to do that which it sees others do. The sixth is to avoid hearing, singing, playing [musical instruments] and dancing. Pythagoras says that "the greenest grass grows by the water," and so the life of *luxuria* too is born of dancing, singing and playing.

The similarly conservative *Decor puellarum* mirrors this tersely in a text otherwise devoted to meticulous descriptions of how a woman—by implication, one of sufficient means to hire a servant, but not one so wealthy as to be able to delegate the running of a home entirely—should conduct and comport herself from first light to sleep. It bewails the praise (laude) given to women who spend their time in playing chess (zocho de scachi), "those who sing and play like whores" (cantar et sonar come meretrice), and the miserable parents (misero quello padre et miserissimo

---

convince Palamedes of his unfitness to join the Greek expedition bound for Troy.
171 *Vita scolastica*, fol. 4r.
172 *Fiore di virtù* (Florence: [Bartolommeo di Libri], 1489), fols. 35v–36r.

quella madre) who allow their daughters to divert themselves in such activities—particularly those who arrange dance lessons.[173]

Thus, for the authors of the *Fiore di virtù* and *Decor puellarum*, music is a threat to a woman's chastity just as it is a threat to a man's studies in the *Vita scolastica*. The elite man must engage with music but must use his judgement to do so in a fitting manner. The middle-class man or woman, in contrast, has no need to display magnificence, and is assumed to lack the judgement required to practice music safely for personal recreation—or perhaps to lack the wealth and power required to protect them from ill repute; therefore they had better avoid music altogether. One might observe, however, that this precept would not have needed articulating if it were already being consistently followed.

1.3 Health and Wellbeing

Pseudo-Albertus Magnus, *De secretis mulierum cum commento* (Venice: per Giovanni Luigi Varisio, 1501)

Aristotle et al., *Problemata Aristotelis cum duplici translatione antiqua & nova Theodori Gaze: cum expositione Petri Aponi. Tabula secundum Petrum de Tussignano Problemata Alexandri Aphrodisei. Problemata Plutarchi* (Venice: per Boneto Locatello haer. Ottaviano Scoto, 1501)

Giovanni Antonio Bassino, *Modo e ordine securo da preservarse e curarse dal pestifero morbo* (Pavia: s.n., 1501)

Giovanni de Concoregio, *Practica nova medicine Ioannis de Concoregio Mediolanensis. Lucidarium & flos florum medicinae nuncupata. Summula de curis febrium secundum hodiernum modum & usum compilata* (Venice: [Simone Bevilacqua], 1501)

Mario Equicola, *De mulieribus ad d. Margaritam Cantelmam* (Mantua: s.n., 1501)

Giovanni Matteo Ferrari et al., *Tabula consiliorum d. Ioannis Mathei Gradi Mediolanensis, secundum ordinem ac viam d. Auicene ordinata, et Papie anno MCCCCCI impressa. Additis etiam De regimine sanitatis Rabi Moysi ad sultanum, necnon doctissimi Rainaldi ex Villa Nova ad Aragonum regem inclitum* (Pavia: per Giovanni Andrea Bosco impensis Bernardino Scoto, 1501)

Marsilio Ficino, *De triplici vita libri tres* (Bologna: Benedetto Faelli, 1501)

---

173 "Misero quello padre. che a sue figliole over a parente tale cosse content: de imprendere a ballare bem e licito non domentre che sonno donzelle per honesta de la virginita." *Decor puellarum*, fol. 57r–v.

Galen et al., *Commentum in veterem librorum Techni Galeni translationem. Expositio Ja. Forliviensis in nouam librorum Techni Galeni translationem. Quaestiones Ja. Forlivensis super tribus Techni Galeni libris* (Pavia: impensis ac iussu Luigi Castello, Baldassarre Gabiano & Bartolomeo Trotti: arte et industria Michele & Bernardino Garaldi, 1501).

Juvenal and Persius, *Iuvenalis. Persius* (Venice: Aldo Manuzio, 1501)

Macrobius, *De Somno Scipionis: nec non de Saturnalibus libri: summa diligentia suo nitori restituti sunt: in quo plusquam ter mille errores corriguntur: Graecumque quod in olim impressis deerat fere omnibus locis reponitur. Macrobius lectoribus. Qui mutilus dudum & crebris erroribus auctus. Macrobius nulli pene legendus eram Taberii ac Pyladae cura magnoque labore. Nunc iterum mihimet redditus ecce legor* (Brescia: per Angelo Britannico, 1501)

Bartolomeo Platina, *Platina de honesta voluptate et valitudine vulgare* (Venice: Giorgio Rusconi, 1501)

Pliny the Elder, *Libro de l'historia naturale* (Venice: per Albertino da Lessona, 1501)

Al Rhazes (Almansore), *Libro tertio delo Almansore chiamato Cibaldone* (Venice: per Giovanni Battista Sessa, 1501)

The medical practitioners of our period relied largely on a theoretical framework set out in Greek antiquity by Hippocrates, Aristotle, and most importantly Galen, whose writings represent Greek practice at its most consummate.[174] No less important, however, were the authors of the Arab world—particularly Abu Bakr al-Razi (known as Rhazes in the West), Ali ibn-'al-Abbas al-Majusi (known as Haly Abbas), Ibn Sina (known as Avicenna), Ibn Rushd (known as Averroes), and Abu al-Qasim Khalaf ibn al-Abbas al-Zahrawi (known as Albucasis)—who had far greater access to Greek texts through the Arabic translations rendered in the eighth and ninth centuries, and whose writings were in turn translated into Latin from the twelfth century on.[175] Towards the end of the fifteenth century in Italy, efforts were made to strip medical practice of its reliance on Arabic sources, the Latin renditions of which unavoidably included substantial departures from the original Greek following two and sometimes three rounds of translation.[176] This

---

174 Nancy G. Siraisi, *Medieval and Early Renaissance Medicine: An Introduction to Knowledge and Practice* (Chicago, IL: University of Chicago Press, 1990), 4.
175 Siraisi, *Medieval and Early Renaissance Medicine*, 11–12; and Grendler, *The Universities*, 315.
176 Grendler, *The Universities*, 327–28. For instance, in a surviving manuscript source for the pseudo-Aristotelian *Secretum Secretorum* discussed in Chapter 1.2 of the

movement was symbolised by the medical humanist Niccolò Leoniceno, who was vituperous in his criticism of Avicenna in particular, but it only came to fruition a year after his death, with the publication of an *editio princeps* of the Greek Galen in 1525 by the Manuzio press (promised as early as 1495).[177] Thus, in 1501 the medical tradition in Italy remained firmly rooted in the Arabic synthesis of Greek thought; indeed, the majority of the space in the only edition of Galen's works printed in 1501 is taken up with a commentary by the eleventh-century Egyptian physician Ali ibn Ridwan.[178]

Medicine, as taught at universities in Italy at the turn of the sixteenth century, was conceived of as three disciplines: theoretical medicine (dominated by Avicenna and Galen), practical medicine, and surgery.[179] The divide between theoretical and practical medicine is clearly evident in our 1501 oeuvre. Those publications which deal principally with practical medicine—identifying, treating and preventing ailments ranging from depression (melancholia) to the plague (pestifero)—are few, but represent a diverse authorship and readership. The most "learned" of these are two texts likely intended for medical students (and certainly for doctors) by the Milanese physicians Giovanni Matteo Ferrari and Giovanni de Concoreggio, who taught medicine at the universities of Padua and Pavia respectively around the middle of the fifteenth century. These both feature comprehensive *Tabula consiliorum*, providing diagnostics and treatments in an easily searchable format; Ferrari's arranged by *consilium* (numerated advice per ailment), and Concoreggio's by prognostication (prognosticatio) and prescription (recipe). Ferrari's *Tabula consiliorum* appears in our 1501 edition as the first of three texts, its companion works being two earlier treatises on regimen, one by the Jewish physician to Saladin, Maimonides (known as

---

present study, the translator writes that they translated from Yunani (Greek) into *Rumi* and thence into Arabic. Williams supposes *Rumi* to be Syriac. Williams, *The Secret of Secrets*, 19.

177 Grendler, *The Universities*, 325–26.
178 Our 1501 book was the fourth printed edition of Galen issued in Italy: his Latin *Opera* was printed in 1490; an edition of the medieval medical textbook known as the *Articella* (which included Galen's *Techne* or *Ars medica*, the text printed in 1501) appeared in 1493; and an edition in Greek of the *Therapeutica* was issued in 1500.
179 Grendler, *The Universities*, 319–20. As Grendler notes, surgeons were usually trained through apprenticeships, and the number of degrees conferred in this field was consequently small during this period.

Rabi Moysi), and the other by Arnaldus de Villa Nova, who served Pope Clement V at the turn of the fourteenth century. Like his predecessors, Ferrari too counted potentates among his clients, giving consultations—detailed as exemplars in the *Tabula*—to Sforza and Gonzaga rulers, and the king of France.

Straddling the fields of practical medicine and philosophy, as the author himself explains it, is the *De secretis mulierum*, a treatise on conception then supposed to have been composed by Albertus Magnus, but most likely compiled from a selection of his writings by a disciple some time in the late thirteenth or early fourteenth century.[180] Pseudo-Albertus has very little to say about music, but he does proffer useful information on how the body was presumed to function, and particularly regarding the supposed differences between men and women.

The remaining texts of *practica medicina* printed in 1501 are intended to inform the practice of the patient, rather than that of the doctor. The first is a "secure method and routine for the preservation and curing of oneself from the plague" (Modo e ordine securo da preservarse e curarse dal pestifero morbo), written by a physician, Giovanni Antonio Bassino, working in Pavia, which was that year in the grip of an epidemic. Bassino states that he chose to present his advice in the vernacular as those who were not Latin literate would be unlikely to "lend their ears" if it were given in Latin.[181] Similarly charming is a vernacular versification of the third book of the *Almansore*, the common European title for Rhazes' medical treatise *Kitāb al-Manṣūrī* first translated into Latin by Gerard of Cremona in the late twelfth century, presented as a *cibaldone*, or commonplace book. The brief preface to the 1501 edition, which bears significant divergences from the numerous earlier editions in structure and content, states that the work was rendered into tercets by a "learned

---

180 Pseudo-Albertus describes the text as written in "stilo phylosophico et in parte medicinali." *De secretis mulierum*, fols. 1v–2r. On the composition of the *De secretis mulierum*, see Pseudo-Albertus Magnus, *Woman's Secrets: A Translation of Pseudo-Albertus Magnus' De Secretis Mulierum with Commentaries*, trans. Helen Rodnite Lemay (New York: State University of New York Press, 1992), 1–16. While Lemay's translation is based largely on editions printed in Lyons in 1580 and Venice in 1508, the commentary of the 1501 edition corresponds with Lemay's 'Commentary B'.

181 "Ma pur per essere alcuni di loro in lingua latina tersa e bene rimata e il piu di loro per modo che la gente plebea non essendo capace del loro dittato non li prestano orechie." *Modo e ordine securo*, fol. 1r.

philosopher in medicine" (un philosopho dotto in medicina) "for your memory [...] and for good doctrine" (per sua memoria [...] et per bona dotrina).[182] The fact that the author of the preface supposes Almansore not only to have been the author of the treatise (rather than its dedicatee) but also Greek, perhaps exemplifies the necessity for vernacular guides to self-care through healthy diet, the ownership and comprehension of Latin originals being beyond the capacity of the majority of the populace, and consultation of a doctor for such quotidian necessities being impractical for those without extensive means.

Wellbeing through diet is also the chief concern of Bartolomeo Platina's *De honesta voluptate et valetudine*, noted for being "the first printed cookbook," but which also discusses the value of various pastimes and their effect on health, particularly regarding digestion.[183] Composed around 1465 and running to nine editions before 1501, the publication of a vernacular translation in 1487 (Venice: [Hieronymus de Sanctis and Cornelio]) is a similar representation of the market for comprehensive advice on regimen and diet amongst those not possessing refined Latin literacy. Adding to this is the vernacular translation of Pliny the Elder's *Naturalis historia*, entitled *Libro de l'historia naturale*, effected by Cristoforo Landino in 1475 and published the following year in Venice by the Jensen press; the 1501 edition, printed by Albertino da Lessona, represents the third publication of Landino's translation. As an encyclopedia, informing the regimen of its readers is not perhaps the *Libro de l'historia naturale*'s first concern, but it nonetheless contains methods and ingredients for strengthening the singing voice, warnings about the activities and foodstuffs which damage it, and one example—that of Xenophilus—of how engagement with music can prolong life, an example cited by the physician Gabriele Zerbi in advocating musical practice as a means of delaying the onset of old age in his *Gerontocomia* (Rome: Eucharius Silber, 1489).[184]

---

182 *Libro tertio delo Almansore*, fol. 1r.
183 Anne Willan and Mark Cherniavsky, *The Cookbook Library: Four Centuries of the Cooks, Writers, and Recipes That Made the Modern Cookbook* (Berkeley, CA: University of California Press, 2012), 39.
184 "Adunque per miracolo et solo exemplo siraconta che Xenophilo musico vixe ccv anni senza alchuno incomodo di corpo." *Libro de l'historia naturale*, fol. 54v. Our 1501 edition bestows Xenophilus with an additional 100 years of life beyond the 105 years reported by Pliny elsewhere. Zerbi, *Gerontocomia* (Rome: Eucharius Silber, 1489), fol. 117r. For more on music and aging in Italy in this period, see,

The last of the texts on practical medicine discussed here, and perhaps the most familiar to modern readers, is Marsilio Ficino's *De vita libri tres*, a guide to health and regimen for scholars, of which the 1501 edition was the fourth to appear in print.[185] Its contents are wide-ranging, from advice on diet and the avoidance of sexual intercourse, which is commonly encountered in ancient and contemporary literature on medicine and conduct, to instruction on how one might "obtain life from the heavens" (De vita coelitus comparanda) through the "accommodation of song to the stars" (cantum sideribus accomodaturas), a practice which, in the field of musicology, has become more-or-less synonymous with Ficino alone.[186] Scholarship on Ficino's musical practice has tended to focus on the esoteric elements of his output, but in fact a sizeable portion of his writings on the utility of music represents no particular divergence from other medical practitioners of the Middle Ages and early Renaissance.

Two kinds of reference relevant to music occur in these texts: first, those where music forms part of the regimen of a healthy individual; and second, those where aspects of regimen and diet are explicitly linked with the care of the voice, whether in relation to singing specifically or to vocality more generally. In both cases, the mechanisms driving the efficacy of the suggested interventions are rooted in humoural and complexion theory, which reached its apex, like so many other aspects of ancient Greek medicine, in the work of Galen. The precepts of humoural theory are well-known, but it seems sensible to summarise them briefly here in order to trace precisely their relevance to two individuals for whom the medical advice in our 1501 oeuvre might be musically pertinent: the singer looking to care for their voice, and the individual

---

among others, Sanna Raninen, "No Country for Old Men? Aging and Men's Musicianship in Italian Renaissance Art," in *Music and Visual Culture in Renaissance Italy*, ed. Chriscinda Henry and Tim Shephard (New York: Routledge, 2023), 268–80.

185 Marsilio Ficino, *Three Books on Life: A Critical Edition and Translation with Introduction and Notes*, ed. and trans. Carol V. Kaske and John R. Clark (Tempe, AZ: Medieval & Renaissance Texts and Studies, 1998), 3.

186 *De triplici vita libri tres*, fol. 83r. "De vita coelitus comparanda" is the subject of the third book of *De vita*. The musicological literature on Ficino is large; see, among others, Gary Tomlinson, *Music in Renaissance Magic: Towards a Historiography of Others* (Chicago, IL: The University of Chicago Press, 1993); Jacomien Prins, *Echoes of an Invisible World: Marsilio Ficino and Francesco Patrizi on Cosmic Order and Music Theory* (Boston: Brill, 2015); and Angela Voss, "The Music of the Spheres: Marsilio Ficino and Renaissance Harmonia," *Culture and Cosmos* 2.2 (1998), 16–38.

pursuing music as part of a comprehensive regimen promoting good health in general.[187] There are four humours, each a bodily fluid intrinsic to the function of a given organism: blood, phlegm, bile (variously called red or yellow), and black bile (also called melancholy). Each of these has an associated blend of the four qualities—that is, hot, cold, moist, and dry; and the balance of the qualities within an individual can in turn affect their complexion, or temperament, rendering them prone to certain behaviors, and to particular mental and physical illnesses.[188]

This balance is affected by six "non-naturals," that is, things not considered constituent within the human body but which affect it: air, food and drink, exercise and rest, sleep and waking, excretion and sex, and "accidents of the soul"—often referred to, as they are by Concoreggio, as passions.[189] Much like the humours, all foodstuffs were thought to have their own balance of qualities, which would then affect the balance of one who ate them; and any activities—from playing chess to listening to music—could similarly affect the balance of qualities within the body through the passions they arouse or dispel. Galen writes on the importance of avoiding emotional extremes in order to maintain balance within the body: "Obviously it is necessary for people to keep away from the imbalance of all the psychic affections—anger, grief, joy, passion, fear and envy—for these bring changes and also change the normal composition of the body."[190] Listening to and making music is regularly said to prompt several of these specific affections in contemporary texts—most commonly joy, but also passion, anger, and tranquility. Although Galen does not mention music, at least in this case, we might reasonably extrapolate that, as Vergerio puts it, "the use

---

187 This following summary is indebted to Siraisi, *Medieval and Early Renaissance Medicine*, 100–06.
188 As will become apparent, a division between mental and physical health is arguably anachronistic, as for the physician of the Middle Ages both were caused by very physical imbalances within the body.
189 Saul Jarcho, "Galen's Six Non-Naturals: A Bibliographic Note and Translation," *Bulletin of the History of Medicine* 44.4 (1970), 372–77, at 372.
190 "Abstinere vero manifestum est quoniam ab intemperantia oportet omnium anime passionum sicut ire tristitie et guadii et furoris et timoris et invidie et sollicitudis. Exterminant enim hec in mutant corpora ab ea que est secundum naturam consistentia." *Commentum in veterem librorum Techni Galeni*, fol. 49v. Translation in Galen, *On the Constitution of the Art of Medicine. The Art of Medicine. A Method of Medicine to Glaucon*, ed. and trans. Ian Johnston, Loeb Classical Library 523 (Cambridge, MA: Harvard University Press, 2016), 245.

of musical modes is highly effective in [...] calming the passions," and understand this to be a comment with a precise medical foundation and purpose.[191]

The effect of a balance or imbalance, *krasis* and *dyskrasia* to use Galen's terminology, was considered both on a bodily level—that is, regarding the overall complexion of an individual—and with regard to the normative functions of each of the organs. To the singer active in 1501, the most important of these might have been the means of vocal production, that is, the lungs and throat, and the ear and the sense of hearing. In his *Techne* (now usually called *Ars medica*), printed in 1501, Galen deduces that sensory perception takes place in the brain, and specifically in the cerebrum. This is because he perceives that a majority of the motor nerves attach at the back of the brainstem and are associated with the cerebellum, whereas a majority of the sensory nerves attach at the front of the brainstem proximate to the cerebrum.[192] Because sensation is a primary role of Galen's brain, the proper function of the senses and of the sensory apparatus located on the head (eyes, ears, nose) is indicative of general brain health.[193] The brain is particularly associated with phlegm, and excess humour gathered in the head is expelled via the eyes, ears, nose and palate.[194] The influence of the four qualities upon the brain is central to the proper function of the senses and the voice. A dry brain will be predisposed toward sharp sensations, a moist brain toward dim.[195] A cold brain will produce a susceptibility to catarrh and a runny nose (coryza).[196] The qualities also act in combination. Thus, a brain that is both hot and dry will result in

---

[191] "ad remissionem animi sedandasque passiones plurimum valeat modulationis usus." *Humanist Educational Treatises*, ed. and trans. Kallendorf, 52–53.

[192] "Ex ipsa autem non ordinatur nisi pauci nervi numero ad sensum: multo vero ad motum: sicut ex altera parte que est in anteriori nascuntur nervi multi avlde numero ex nervis motus." *Commentum in veterem librorum Techni Galeni*, fol. 13v.

[193] "Et tertium est rectification actionum eius sensibilium et earum corruptio." *Commentum in veterem librorum Techni Galeni*, fol. 12v.

[194] "quando cerebrum est temperatum in qualitatibus quattuor: tunc omnes res quas diximus sunt in eo secundum equalitatem: et superfluitates quas expelit ad fauces: et ad aures: et ad nares: et oculus sunt secundum equalitatem." *Commentum in veterem librorum Techni Galeni*, fol. 14v.

[195] "Siccioris vero cerebri cognitiones. Non superfluum est in efiluxionibus. Et sensuum perfectio [...] humidioris vero cerebri capilli fiunt plani [...] et sensus hebetes sunt." *Commentum in veterem librorum Techni Galeni*, fol. 16v.

[196] "Et cito adveniunt corriza et catarrus." *Commentum in veterem librorum Techni Galeni*, fol. 18v.

sharp sensations and an absence of catarrh and coryza, whereas a brain that is both cold and moist will produce the opposites. A brain that is both cold and dry will result in sharp sensory perception during youth but dimming quickly with age.[197] Galen further explains that the nature of the brain substance impacts its affordances in function. A substance that is soft readily takes impressions and thus produces a quick learner, its opposite a slow learner; a substance that is stable results in a sound memory, its opposite in forgetfulness.[198]

Galen gives a fairly detailed discussion of the voice when he comes to deal with the lungs, trachea, and throat. The balance of the qualities in each component controls a different aspect of the voice. Hot lungs produce a loud voice, cold lungs a soft one, not because of the heat alone, but because the hot individual inhales and exhales more air than someone of a cooler complexion.[199] With dry lungs the voice will be clear, whereas with moist lungs it will be hoarse, "contaminated by superfluities"—something which also happens when somebody raises their voice often.[200] From a rough trachea, resulting from dryness, a rough voice will issue; whereas from a smooth trachea, which is necessarily moist, smooth tones will emerge.[201] A smaller, "sharp" (i.e., high and

---

197 "Complexio autem frigida et sicca quando vincit super cerebrum tunc ipsa ponit caput frigidum mali caloris secundum que facit ei necessarium hec complexio [...] et sensus eius in adolescentia sunt clari cum quibus non est infirmitas omnino. Cum ergo protenditur cu meo etas extinguuntur et debilitantur velociter." *Commentum in veterem librorum Techni Galeni*, fol. 18r.

198 "Et velocitas discendi significat que substantia eius est substantia in qua velociter suscipit sigillatio rerum. Et bonitas servationis.in.memorie significat que substantia eius est substantia enim est firmitudo [...] Facilitas vero discendi est mollis. Et memoria permanentis [...] Et similiter etiam tarditas discendi significat quod substantia eius est substantia in qua difficile suscipitur formatio rerum." *Commentum in veterem librorum Techni Galeni*, fol. 14v.

199 "Sed propter horum caliditatem sitientes inspirant amplius: et exuffiant longius." *Commentum in veterem librorum Techni Galeni*, fol. 36v.

200 "Eius autem cuius est pulmo siccus non est superfluitas quam expuit: et vox eius est clara. Illus autem cuius pulmo est humidus vox est non clara rauca. Et quando utitur ex voce que est miaor et acutior currunt in canam eius pulmonis superfluitates [...] Siccitates vero pulmonis sine superfluitate sunt: et pure a flegmate: et vocem habent claram: quemadmodum et humiliditates obscuram quidem et raucam operantur vocem. Incurrunt autem eis superfluirates magis et acutius loqui volentibus." *Commentum in veterem librorum Techni Galeni*, fol. 36v.

201 "Inde est que vox lenis sequitur lenitatem canne pulmonis. Et vox aspera sequitur asperitatem eius. Et lenitas canne pulmonis sequitur equalitatem complexionis sue. Et asperitas eius sequitur siccitatem ipsius." *Commentum in veterem librorum Techni Galeni*, fol. 36v.

piercing) voice is the result of a narrow throat, whose narrowness arises from its cold; a deep voice is the product of a wide throat, whose width is attributable to its heat.[202]

Galen takes it as self-evident that the ideal body would exhibit a perfect balance of qualities in all of its parts. However, he also acknowledges that a moderate imbalance of the qualities in some parts of the body might be desirable or even necessary in some occupations. Taking this as an invitation, we might hypothesise that a singer would benefit from a brain that is somewhat hot and dry, resulting in acute hearing and a nose and palate not marred by secretions. Hot and dry lungs would also be favourable, producing a voice that is clear and projects well, although the softer voice generated by cold lungs might be preferable in some circumstances. In either case, the trachea had better be moist to ensure smoothness. A singer with a wide throat might be more capable of singing lower parts, whilst the higher and more penetrating voice of a narrow-throated singer might be preferable for the upper parts.

Because Galen sees the proper function of the memory, hearing, and voice as outward signs of the qualities and substance of the brain, we can also infer that a singer exhibiting facility in learning songs, sound memory, sharp hearing and a clear, resonant, and smooth voice would be understood by any competent fifteenth-century physician to possess a brain that was somewhat hot and dry, and of soft but stable substance, lungs that are somewhat hot and dry, and a moist but uncongested trachea. Equally, a singer failing to exhibit these qualities need not despair, because Galen owns that most imbalances can be corrected, slowly and over a long period of time, through a diet and regimen that are opposite to the excess.[203] Thus, if a singer suffers continually from coryza marring their voice, a physician could advise them that this may result from an excessively cold brain, which can be corrected

---

202 "Et similiter iterum vox acuta natura non est possibile ut fiat nisi cum constrictione canne pulmonis et epigloti. Vox gravis non sit nisi cum amplitudine eius. Et strictura eius generatur ex frigore eius innato. Et amplitudo eius generatur ex caliditate ipsius innata." *Commentum in veterem librorum Techni Galeni*, fol. 36v.

203 "Si vero permutare vult et transire ad melius aliud et genus salubrium causarum contrarium quidem supradictis: e quale vero distans ab altera crasi eucratarum et mediarum quas optimis naturis convenire dicebamus [...] tunc medicus intendit in ea ad illud genus occasionum; et permutat corpus paulatim a complexione sua ad complexionem que est melior: quoniam natura non tollerat alterationem subito." *Commentum in veterem librorum Techni Galeni*, fol. 50v.

through dietary and other lifestyle interventions that promote heat in the appropriate region of the body. Or again, if a singer suffers a rough voice, a physician could advise them to take steps that promote a moist trachea. A singer who finds that the lowest notes in a part-song are out of reach at the performance pitch preferred by the other chorus members could take advice from a physician on measures that will open out their throat. In a similar manner, a singer already possessing the imbalances that favour musical performance can reinforce them. One could not, however, change their voice drastically: to a certain extent, the complexion of the vocal organs was innate.[204]

The overwhelming majority of advice on the care of the voice present in the 1501 corpus is dietary. A notable exception is found in Pliny's *Libro de l'historia naturale*, where the emperor Nero, infamous for the decadence of his musical and theatrical leanings, is described as practicing singing whilst wearing a leaden plate (teneva una piastra di piombo in sul pecto) "to maintain the voice" (con quella mantenava la voce)—presumably exercising the diaphragm in order to maintain vocal strength.[205] An element of Nero's diet is also mentioned by Pliny to a similar end in Book 19:

> Diremo ancora de porro maxime: perche Nerone imperadore novamente ha dato auctorita alporrho sectivo: perche con lolio ogni di distate nemangiava senza pane o altra cosa per havere optima voce.[206]

> We will speak also of the leek, especially as emperor Nero has newly given importance to the chive; for on certain days he would eat them with oil, and without bread or anything else, to have the best possible voice.

Pliny is one of many authors to advocate the use of alliums, namely leeks, chives, and garlic, for vocal health. His authority lies behind Bartolomeo Platina's discussion of the subject in *De honesta voluptate*:

---

204 "Non ergo opum semper ut sequatur magnitudo vocis et eius pervitas caliditatem et frigiditatem: neque etiam quando cum magnitudine vocis eius sunt caliditas et frigiditas est illud ex eis ipsius signum. Verum tamen non est ex eis nisi per accidens: et sequitur illud complexio naturalis: con complexio accidentalis." *Commentum in veterem librorum Techni Galeni*, fol. 37r.

205 *Libro de l'historia naturale*, fol. 235r. A similar passage can be found in Suetonius' *Life of Nero* (20). For more on Nero's musicianship see Chapter 3.4.

206 *Libro de l'historia naturale*, fols. 141r–42v.

Porri sonovi di duo sorte: cioe sectivo et capitato: il sectivo Nerone cesare. Li diede auctorita mangiandovi ogni giorno cum olio per cagione di conservarsi la voce cantava lui non solamente privatamente. Ma et in publico. et in elle scene cioe inele feste solemne si ralegrava cum il cantare diceva essere molto obligato al porro cunciosia che el canto e bene et conserva la voce[207]

Leeks are of two kinds: cut and headed.[208] The cut kind emperor Nero gave importance, eating them every day with oil in order to preserve the singing voice [for use] not only in private, but also in public. And in theatrical representations and the solemn feasts in which he loved to sing it was said that he was indebted to the cooked leek, which is good for singing and conserves the voice

Aristotle attributes leeks' ability to clean the pharynx to their "stickiness" when cooked, in *Problemata* 11.39.[209] The *Cibaldone* of the properties and uses of ingredients compiled from the third book of the *Almansore* gives what was perhaps a more widely-known rationale. Almost always confining the information imparted on a given ingredient to a single tercet, the author of the *Cibaldone* nevertheless ensures that the quality—hot, cold, most or dry—of each ingredient is communicated, along with a handful of notable effects it might produce when ingested. On leeks, the *Cibaldone* says:

Il porro e caldo e secco da apetito	The leek is hot and dry, stimulates appetite
il capo fa doler e fa soniare	gives a headache and makes you dream
e chi dal caldo e offeso non de usare[210]	and whoever is hurt by heat should avoid it

The *Cibaldone* makes no division between chives and leeks, but it does differentiate other alliums, giving separate entries for garlic (allio) and onion (cipolla). All three share hot and dry qualities which, in Galenic terms, would be conducive to singing when ingested, as Aristotle suggests, in order to free the pharynx of phlegm, caused by

---

207 *Platina de honesta voluptate*, fol. 26r.
208 "Cut leek" (sectivo) was the term used for chives, and "headed" (capitato) for the leek proper.
209 *Problemata Aristotelis*, fol. 136v.
210 *Libro tertio delo Almansore*, fol. 2v.

the dominance of cold and moist qualities; for the same reason Platina suggests that garlic is useful when dealing with coughs (tosse) and respiratory ailments (suspiratione).[211] As a result of their ability to heat the body (riscalda il corpo), the *Cibaldone* also gives *luxuria* as an unfortunate side effect of garlic and onions.[212]

Other ingredients described in the *Cibaldone* as having a positive effect on the instruments of the voice share similar qualities.[213] Pomegranate and sweet almond (mandorla dolce), both dry in nature, open the throat (fa largare la gola). Bitter almond (mandorla amara) consumes humours (consuma li humori) and opens the lungs. Rosemary similarly purges the lungs of humours (li humori discaza dal pulmone petto). Borage (boragio), described as warm and humid, if only by one degree (un grado caldo e humido), aids both throat and lungs. Platina, while rarely naming the humoural qualities of the ingredients he discusses, gives several recipes for the clearing of catarrh and phlegm, curing hoarseness, or strengthening the voice, using as active ingredients honey and thyme, eggs, and cockerel respectively.[214] The only ingredients explicitly described as negatively impacting the voice are nuts: in the *Cibaldone*, walnuts (nose) are described as generating catarrh (el cataro ingenera la nose); and hazelnuts (nizola), having a similar effect (la simel fa), also "rob the voice" (tol la vose), rendering them unhelpful for those who like to sing (per questi che si dilecta di cantare).[215] Little reason for this is given, though in the *Gerontocomia* Zerbi describes walnuts as inducing hoarseness due to their oily nature.[216]

The *Cibaldone* is undeniably disadvantaged by the need to function as a piece of poetry when it comes to identifying which ingredients are of use to singers and why; some ingredients described as beneficial for the voice in other texts in circulation at the turn of the sixteenth century, including other editions of the *Cibaldone*, are omitted, and the "degree" to which food is hot, cold, moist or dry—a key tenet of medical theory

---

211 Platina *de honesta voluptate*, fol. 25v.
212 *Libro tertio delo Almansore*, fol. 2v.
213 *Libro tertio delo Almansore*, fol. 2r–v.
214 Platina *de honesta voluptate*, fols. 30r–v, 20r, and 42v respectively.
215 *Libro tertio delo Almansore*, fol. 1v. We are grateful to Antonella Fabriani Rojas for her help in clarifying which nuts are mentioned in this passage.
216 Gabriele Zerbi, *Gerontocomia*, ed. and trans. L. R. Lind (Philadelphia: American Philosophical Society, 1988), 239.

rigorously reported for foodstuffs in Zerbi's *Gerontocomia*—is almost never given.²¹⁷ What it does contain, however, is enough to suggest that the prevention of congestion was chief among the singer's concerns, as far as diet permitted, and that this could be achieved through the ingestion of gently drying foods and herbs, and the avoidance of humid ones.

One other aspect of regimen and the voice is explicitly cautioned in the 1501 literature: the danger of sexual intercourse. That the sexual act damages the voice is mentioned briefly in two of our sources. In his *Libro de l'historia naturale*, Pliny writes that "with sex one loses their voice" (con venere si rivoca la voce). Juvenal's sixth Satire, meanwhile, refers to a singer named Chrysogonus, translating from the Greek as "golden gonad," whose singing career was impeded by female admirers, who paid to have a clasp which prevented him from ejaculating—in order to preserve his voice—removed.²¹⁸ This very passage is used by Nicolò Burzio, the only contemporary music theorist to write of the care of the voice, as evidence of the dangers of sex, adding that it should be avoided totally during summer, and that the religious—which comprised many of the men in Italy's cathedral and court chapel choirs at the time—need not concern themselves with the matter at all thanks to their vow of chastity.²¹⁹

The danger of sexual intercourse is not limited to the voice. In *De vita libri tres* 1.7, Ficino describes it as the first of five "monsters" (monstra) which are inimical to scholars for their power to adversely affect cognitive power:

---

217 *The Book of Degrees*, translated from the Arabic by the eleventh-century physician Constantinus Africanus, proposed four degrees by which to measure food, the first being mild in its effects and the fourth dangerously unbalanced. See Lynn Thorndike, *A History of Magic and Experimental Science, Vol. 1* (New York: Columbia University Press, 1923), 750–51.

218 *Libro de l'historia naturale*, fol. 195r; *Iuvenalis. Persius*, sig. C iii v. On the significance of the name "Chrysogonus" see Chiara Sulprizio, *Gender and Sexuality in Juvenal's Rome: Satire 2 and Satire 6* (Norman, OK: University of Oklahoma Press, 2020), 107. This passage of Juvenal is further discussed in Chapter 3.3.

219 Nicolò Burzio, *Musices opusculum*, trans. Clement A. Miller (Neuhausen-Stuttgart: Hänssler-Verlag, 1983), 75–76. Burzio's comments on the care of the voice appear in Book 2, chapter 30 of his *Musices opusculum* (Bologna: Ugo Rugerius per Benedictus Hectoris, 1487), and are discussed in Howard M. Brown and Rebecca Stewart, "Workshop IV. Voice Types in Josquin's Music," in *Proceedings of the Josquin Symposium. Cologne, 11–15 July 1984*, published as *Tijdschrift van de Vereniging voor Nederlandse Muziekgeschiedenis* 35.1–2 (1985), 97–193, at 190–91.

> Primum quidem monstrum est venereus coitus: praesertim si vel paulum vires excesserit. Sub ita namque exhaurit spiritus praesertim subtiliores: cerebrumque debilitat labefactat stomachum atque praecordia. Quo malo nihil ingenio adversius esse potest.[220]

> The first monster is sexual intercourse, especially if even slightly strenuous. Immediately it drains the spirits, especially the finer ones, and debilitates the brain; it ruins the stomach and heart. No evil can be more adverse for the intelligence.

Giovanni Matteo Ferrari draws on long-established reasoning when issuing similar warnings against sexual intercourse in his *Tabula consiliorum*, describing the chief cause of harm as "the great effusion of sperm" (magnam spermatis effusionem), which required no small amount of nourishment to make, and without which the body is left susceptible to melancholy, a cold, dry humour approximately equivalent to modern-day diagnoses of anxiety disorder and depression.[221] Among the symptoms of melancholy, Ferrari later lists "weakness of voice and breathing" (debilitas vocis et hanelitus), confirming that, though the singer might prefer to be free of superfluous phlegm or catarrh, the healthy balance of heat and moisture were considered crucial for the production of a strong voice, and that sex was long supposed to hinder that equilibrium.[222]

At this stage it becomes evident that both Ferrari and Ficino's advice is directed at men, rather than the human species in general. How might regimen advice differ for the female singer? Pseudo-Albertus notes that women, by nature, are "cold and humid" (frigida et humida), while men are "hot and dry" (calidus et siccus).[223] A man's heat is imparted through intercourse to the woman, leaving the man unhealthily cold and the woman more temperate, providing her with the balance of heat

---

220 *De triplici vita libri tres*, sig. c ii v.
221 "Pro parato ad melancolicam passionem [...] In passionibus animalibus gaudendum quantum possible est et per idem cavendum est a cogitationibus tristibus et humorosis. Standum est cum dilectis amicis. A coytu maxime cavere debet quam in eo propter magnam spermatis effusionem forte aquisita est in cerebro et membris sibi coniunctis ficitas que non parva est nocumenti causam. Et hiis sum contentus quantum ad regimen in dieta non comemorans plura propter ipsius hominis intelligentiam." *Tabula consiliorum*, fol. 6v.
222 *Tabula consiliorum*, fol. 76v.
223 *De secretis mulierum*, fol. 9v.

and moisture necessary for life.²²⁴ For this reason, Pseudo-Albertus' commentator admonishes that the heat of intercourse, both that caused by the motion of the body and the heat of sperm, makes women stronger, and for them intercourse is therefore beneficial rather than harmful.²²⁵ The supposedly phlegmatic nature of women is questioned by Mario Equicola in his *De mulieribus*—familiar to musicologists for its praise of Isabella d'Este's musical prowess—where he critiques the idea as a bankrupt rationale for the dismissal of women's abilities and intellect.²²⁶ Nonetheless, the female singer taking her phlegmatic nature for rote might seek to counter her comparatively colder and wetter complexion with foods and activities of a heating nature, potentially including sex.

Whilst the care of the voice through diet and regimen in the Renaissance has received little attention from musicologists or historians of medicine, much has been written about music's own therapeutic role.²²⁷ Several theories existed for why music was an effective part of regimen, either generally, or to help overcome or avoid a particular ailment. The first is tied intrinsically to the notion of the harmonic universe. Pythagoras is credited with having first conceived of the distances between the planets as musical intervals, a notion developed by Plato in the *Timaeus* into a theory of harmony encompassing music, the universe as a whole, and the human body—although Pliny describes it in the *Libro de l'historia naturale* as "more playful than factual" (piu gioconda

---

224 Pseudo-Albertus describes all animal life as dependent on heat and moisture ("vita animalium consitit in calido et humido"). *De secretis mulierum*, fol. 53v.

225 "Nota quod quanto mulieres magis coeunt tanto magis fortificatur quia ratione suppositionis calefiunt propter motum qui sit tempore coitus per virum et etiam sperma viri." *De secretis mulierum*, fol. 44r.

226 "pec plane conspiciamus plurium mulierum actiones argumenta maioris caliditatis et siccitatis." *De mulieribus*, fol. 4v. On Equicola's discussion of Isabella d'Este's musicianship, see William Prizer, "Una 'Virtù Molto Conveniente a Madonne': Isabella d'Este as a Musician," *Journal of Musicology* 17 (1999), 10–49, at 45–46.

227 See, among others, Penelope Gouk, "Raising Spirits and Restoring Souls: Early Modern Medical Explanations for Music's Effects," in *Hearing Cultures: Essays on Sound, Listening and Modernity*, ed. Veit Erlmann (New York: Routledge, 2004), 87–105; Gouk, "Harmony, Health and Healing: Music's Role in Early Modern Paracelsian Thought," in *The Practice of Reform in Health, Medicine, and Science, 1500–2000*, ed. Margaret Pelling and Scott Mandelbrote (New York: Routledge, 2005), 23–42; the relevant chapters in Peregrine Horden ed., *Music as Medicine: The History of Music Therapy since Antiquity* (New York: Routledge, 2016); and Remi Chiu, *Plague and Music in the Renaissance* (Cambridge, UK: Cambridge University Press, 2017).

che necessaria).²²⁸ For Macrobius, this explained why humans enjoyed music, which mirrored the perfect harmony of heaven, from whence the soul derives: "in this life every soul is captivated by musical sounds [...] because it bears in the body the memory of the music which it knew in heaven."²²⁹ Ficino expounds a like doctrine in *De vita libri tres*, adding that it is through "tempered things" (res temperatas) that the soul can be conformed to the perfection of heaven:

> Nihil in mundo temperatius est quam coelum: nihil sub coelo ferme temperatius est quam corpus humanum. Nihil in hoc corpore temperatius est quam spiritus. Per res igitur temperatas vita permanens in spiritu recreatur. Spiritus per temperata coelestibus confurmatur.²³⁰

> Nothing in the world is more tempered than heaven; nothing under heaven more tempered than the human body; nothing in this body more tempered than the soul. Therefore by tempered things the life which endures in the soul is revived. The soul, through tempered things, is conformed to the heavenly.

Ficino later confirms his belief in the benefit of music to wellbeing, as a *res temperata*, by comparing it to contemporary advice on diet (such as that discussed above). He emphasises the value of engaging in music-making for the elderly in particular, addressing them here in the voice of Mercury:

> si vapores exhalantes ex vita duntaxat vegetali magnopere vitae vestrae prosunt: quantum profuturos existimatis cantus: aerios quidem: spiritui prorsus aerio harmonicos harmonico: calentes adhuc vivosque vivo: sensu praeditos sensuali: ratione conceptos rationali. Hanc ergo vobis a me fabricatam trado lyram: cantumque cum ipsa Phoebeum: solamen laborum diuturnae vitae pignus. Sicut enim res qualitate temperatissimae simulque aromaticae: tum humores interse: tum spiritum naturalem secum ipso contemperant. sic odores eiusmodi vitalem spiritum: sic rursum similes quoque concentus spiritum animalem. Dum igitur

---

228 Prins, *Echoes of an Invisible World*, 5. *Libro de l'historia naturale*, fol. 16v.
229 "in hac vita omnis anima musicis sonis capitur [...] quia in corpus defert memoriam musicae: cuius in caelo fuit conscia." Macrobius, *De Somno Scipionis*, fol. 35r. Quoted in translation in Nancy Siraisi, "The Music of Pulse in the Writings of Italian Academic Physicians (Fourteenth and Fifteenth Centuries)," *Speculum* 50.4 (1975), 689–710, at 701. The notion of reminiscence turns up again in Chapter 3.1.
230 *De triplici vita libri tres*, sig. k ii r.

fides in lyra sonusque: dum tonos temperatis in voce: similiter spiritum vestrum intus contemperari putate.[231]

> if the vapours exhaling from a merely vegetable life are greatly beneficial to your life, how much more beneficial do you think will be the songs which are made of air to a spirit wholly aerial, songs which are harmonic to a spirit which is harmonic, warm and still living to the living, endowed with sense to the sensitive, songs conceived by reason to a spirit that is rational? Therefore I pass on to you this lyre which I made, and with it a Phoeban song, a consolation of travail, a pledge of long life. For just as things which are most tempered in quality, and at the same time aromatic, temper both the humours among themselves and the natural spirit with itself, so odours of this kind do for the vital spirit; so again harmonies of this kind do for the animal spirit. While therefore you temper the strings and the sounds of the lyre and the tones in your voice, consider your spirit to be similarly tempered within.[232]

The idea that conforming the soul with the heavens through resemblance can be beneficial to life occurs repeatedly in *De vita* and throughout Ficino's wider oeuvre; a favourite analogy proving this is the fact that one lute will echo another if similarly tuned, shaped, and placed opposite the other.[233] Crucially, in this passage Ficino also exposes a second thread of scientific understanding of music's therapeutic efficacy: like tangible objects such as leeks or borage, music has a complexion, and it is warm. It thus has the power to temper a listener or player's complexion, warming the frigid and drying up the excess moisture of the phlegmatic, or conversely perhaps helping to ameliorate the excess heat of the hot-tempered by presenting a stimulus that is only moderately warm. Its benefit to the elderly arises precisely from its warmth, old age being caused by a gradual cooling of the body, leading to symptoms of

---

231 *De triplici vita libri tres*, sig, l [i] r.
232 Ficino, *Three Books on Life*, 213.
233 For instance, "Nonne sonante cithara quadam altera reboat? Ob id tantum: si et ipsa similem figuram Habeat: atque e conspectu sit posita: et fides in ea positate et intentae similiter. Quidnam hic efficit: ut cithara subito pariatur a cithara: nisi situs aliquis et quedam figura conformis?" (Is not one sounding lute echoed by another? For reason only if that it has a similar figure, is placed nearby, and if its strings are placed and tuned similarly. Why is it that lute answers immediately to lute, if not that their placement and figure conform?) *De triplici vita libri tres*, sig. x ii v. On the importance of resemblance or similitude in the philosophy of Ficino and others, see Tomlinson, *Music in Renaissance Magic*, esp. 84–89.

aging such as greying, hair loss, and the dimming of faculties, until the body is so cold and dry that it cannot sustain life.[234]

Prescriptions built upon the moderate warmth of music are readily found in the 1501 corpus. Music is most commonly encountered alongside a litany of other forms of *otium*, such as walking or conversing with friends, which counter the ill effects of sadness (tristitia) and fear (timor).[235] In the *Tabula consiliorum*, Ferrari describes these negative emotions as having a cooling (infrigidationem) effect on the body, which is harmful (nocens), and can be corrected by cheering (lectificantes) activities:

> et ita letari et gaudere cum dilectis et induere vestes scarlatinas et desirico et deferre annulos gemmatos et loqui de rebus placibilibus et audire sonos and cantus delectabiles et gratos et speculari in pulchris formis hec omnia multum in casu iuvant.[236]

> thus to make glad and rejoice with dear ones, and to put on scarlet garments and silk, and to wear jewelled rings, and to speak of pleasant things, and to listen to pleasant and agreeable sounds and songs, and to look at beautiful figures, all help a lot in this case.

Ferrari's patient in this case was a Venetian patrician (veneto viro patricio), Domenico Moro; Domenico was suffering from a form of dropsy (ydrope asclite), but Ferrari's prescription of good cheer was more about preventing the fear and sadness caused by the disease from further unbalancing his complexion, which might worsen Domenico's complaint or render him susceptible to further ailments.[237] This advice is given several times throughout the *Tabula*, and again in the tract which follows it in our 1501 anthology, Maimonides' *Regimine sanitatis*, which counsels similar activities in order to maintain good health when a doctor cannot be consulted:

> Similiter quoque confortet virtutem vitalem et naturalem cum instrumentis musice et cantis et recitando sermones qui ipsum letificant et eius animam dilatant. Societate gaudeat. Omnia hec oportet esse in

---

[234] For a detailed description of this process, see Zerbi, *Gerontocomia*, 29–37.
[235] Sources taking a similar approach to health are discussed by Chiu in *Plague and Music in the Renaissance*, 15–19.
[236] *Tabula consiliorum*, fol. 36v.
[237] *Tabula consiliorum*, fol. 36r.

quodlibet egro quando medicus non est ad disponendum necessaria que quidem iusserunt antiqui cuilibet medico.[238]

> In like manner he reinforces his vital strength and his nature with musical instruments and singing, and reciting speeches which delight him and magnify his soul. He enjoys company. All these must be observed when there is no doctor nearby, as the ancients commended to every physician.

Elsewhere in our 1501 corpus, these activities are prescribed using "gaudium" (joy, with the quality of sensual delight) as an umbrella term. In Concoreggio's *Practica nova medicine*, *gaudium* is prescribed alongside quality sleep and moist foods to combat the overly cold and dry complexion that characterises melancholy.[239] When Concoreggio prescribes music explicitly, it is similarly as a distraction. Delight helps to balance the complexion of the insomniac in a chapter on *vigilia*; "fables sung sweetly" (fabule modulate suaves et dulces), alongside the extinguishing of light (accesio candelarum et illarum extinctio subita), help to lull a patient to sleep.[240] Meanwhile, to break a fever (ephimera), Concoreggio advocates the removal of "cogitation" (cogitatione) through "happy song" (letium cantibus) as the first step in the recovery process.[241] The importance of distraction from anxious thoughts is highlighted elsewhere in the need for "delightful new songs" (cantilenis delectabilibus novis), suggesting that music which is well-known to the fevered patient might have a lesser efficacy.[242]

In texts offering advice on surviving outbreaks of plague (pestifero) throughout the Renaissance, worrying about becoming ill was often

---

238 *Tabula consiliorum*, fol. 85v.

239 "Item cum impinguantibus et humectantibus ut cum balneis et embrocationibus humidis capiti approximatis ante cibum et. cum humectatione aeris habitaculi sui et unctionibus tenerum et humidum facientibus corpus. et cum cibis et potibus humectativis et generantibus laudabiles humores et cum quiete somno et gaudio et super omnia confert delectari et iocundari corrigi et moneri a prudentibus viris ne a fixis accidentibus anime et cogitationibus variis molestentur etiam capiti in principio et augmento licitum est apponere repercussiva." *Practica nova medicine*, sig. e 2 v.

240 *Practica nova medicine*, sig. [E 3] v. "Fabule" could perhaps be translated more straightforwardly as "poems" here.

241 "Consiit ergo cura huius primo in abscisione cause et ipsius remotione cum suis letium cantibus introducentibus gaudium divertendo a tali cogitatione." *Practica nova medicine*, sigs. A 2 v–[A 3] r.

242 *Practica nova medicine*, sig. A 2 v. The same formulation appears again at sig. [A 3] r.

thought to induce illness, and happy diversions were consequently often advised.[243] However, attempting to counter an outbreak in Pavia in 1501, the physician Giovanni Antonio Bassino warned against those—by Bassino's reckoning the greater part of the population (la mazor parte)—who show the first symptoms of illness but "enjoy themselves a little, and pretend themselves well and hide it in order to avoid restraint."[244] Indeed, in his *Consiglio contro la pestilenza*, Ficino judges that those of a cold, dry nature are less prone to plague, because the inflammation and putrefaction which characterise the buboes synonymous with infection require a hot and humid environment.[245] In spite of his musical leanings, Ficino's final words of advice to the denizen of a plague-ridden locale are simple: leave quickly, go far away, and come back as late as possible.[246]

Similar caution is suggested by Concoreggio, who writes that while *gaudium* can cure a fever, the excessive heat of too much *gaudium* can also induce one, the imbalance of the qualities causing the very sadness that heat was meant to banish.[247] Just as Ficino suggests that "tempered" things can help temper the soul, so Concoreggio writes that care must be taken to ensure that *gaudium* is "tempered" (temperata) in order to avoid the cure becoming a cause of illness.[248] Other treatises advise certain times of day for engagement with music in order to best benefit the body. Maimonides suggests that music following dinner can help induce good sleep, while Ferrari suggests that music and conversation should not take place until three or four hours after eating.[249] In *De honesta voluptate*, Platina nuances this, writing that one should sit without

---

243 Chiu, *Plague and Music*, 16–17.
244 "febre continua: dolore di tesa: vomito: o vero graveza de stomaco [...] avisando che la persona non se debe inganare semedesmo.perho vhe la magor parte voleno fare del gaiardo et existimare de non havere il male et asconderlo per non essere refutati." *Modo e ordine securo*, fol. 2v.
245 Marsilio Ficino, *Consiglio contro la pestilenza* (Florence: Jacobum de Ripolis, 1481), fols. 4v–5r.
246 "Fuggi presto & dilungo & torna tardi." Ficino, *Consiglio contro la pestilenza*, fol. 49v.
247 "illo gaudio simul aliqualis tristitia insurguret in eo." *Practica nova medicine*, sig. [A 3] v.
248 *Practica nova medicine*, sig. [J 4] v.
249 *Tabula consiliorum*, fol. 89v: "sedendo audiat non amara nequam subtilia sed placida. Qua fuerint facilius intellectus ut sunt regum et sanctorum patrum istorie: vel musice melodie." And *Tabula consiliorum*, fol. 52r: "De animalibus quoque passionibus dicatur breviter que omnes conpassiones nocent preter gaudium et leticiam quibus iterdum uti convenit. Unde conversatio cum amicis et audire instrumenta sonora et cantus suoaves vel melodias si hora convenient afferantur

serious movement or thought for two hours in order to allow digestion, a process which was thought to require the better part of the body's heat, rendering anything that might require serious effort or provoke affects which would draw that heat from the stomach to other members unadvisable.[250] Platina says nothing of music's place in his regimen, but does forbid the employment of mummers (mumarie), on account of their propensity to provoke indignation or laughter, both activities which draw heat away from the stomach, amongst the dining party.[251] Rather, he prefers quiet card games or chess, so long as players don't take winning or losing too seriously, thereby disturbing their digestion.[252] Thus, although music might be beneficial for health, nothing should impede digestion, which Ficino cites Avicenna as calling "the root of life."[253]

One other passage from amongst the 1501 medical literature describes an episode in which music is actively harmful. In a chapter on curing pustules, Concoreggio berates "ignorant doctors" (ignorantes medici) who force their patients to stay awake, processing them through the city with "bells, other instruments and voices" (Et campanis et aliis instrumentis et vocibus), instead counselling good rest.[254] Amongst the

---

conveniunt. Non afferantur imediate post cibum sed transactis tribus vel quattuir horis a cibo."

250 *Platina de honesta voluptate*, fol. 4r: "Elle da soprassedere per duo hore doppo ricevuto il cibo da ogni movimento corporeo che sia grande. & da agitatione di mente. Almeno fina che la prima concotione si faci." On the importance of heat to the digestion, see below.

251 "Non voglio Mumarie: non pertervia non dicteria: non convitii da liquali la ira & la indignatione. et molte volte grande risse suoleno nascere." *Platina de honesta voluptate*, fol. 4r. We take these "mummers" to be performers whose practice combined elements of theatre, song, dance, storytelling and humour, similar to the *histrio*, the *mimus*, and the *ioculator* discussed in Chapter 1.4.

252 "Ma che el sia questo cioe. Scachi: carte de varie imagine depincte. Cessi sopratutto in zuocho ogni ingano & avaritia. Per laquale il zuocho si riputato sensa alcuna liberalita: et e da sir detestato. et non produce alcune dilecto dil zugare. Concio sia che la paura dil perdere et imensa cupiditate del guadagnare per varii modi crucia li zugatori. Se le da zuzare. non sia doppo il cibo ma doppo che haverai padito. Impero che il calore naturale per commotione et per agitatione de mente si retrato dal stomacho o vero si riducto piu debile a fare la concoctione." *Platina de honesta voluptate*, fol. 4r.

253 "Quamobrem Avicenna corrumpi sanguinem inquit: ubi digestio ipsa corrumpitur. secutusque Galienum: appellat digestionem: vitae radicem." *De triplici vita libri tres*, fol. 26v.

254 "Non tamen in totum abstineant a somno sicut ignorantes medici ipsos cogunt et prohibent ne aliquo modo dormiant cum cunabulis tintinabulis. Et campanis

medical literature, he is rare in detailing the use of certain types of songs, whether sweetly-sung fables, new tunes, or happy ones, as part of the healing process. In general, however, music is prescribed as part of the ideal regimen of a healthy individual, engaged in with moderation in order to temper the complexion and keep unhealthy emotions at bay—whether sadness or anxiety, caused by a lack of heat which might be corrected by *gaudium*, or other passions caused by too much heat.[255]

1.4 Astrology

Albubather et al., *Albubather. Et Centiloquium divi Hermetis* (Venice: per Giovanni Battista Sessa, 1501)

Francesco degli Allegri, *Tratato di astrologia: prima di uno iudicio vero approbato: elqual dura in perpetuo dele calamita: abondantie: carestie. Item trata de li di infelici li quali sono pericolosi da far tutte le cose* (Venice: per Bernardino Vitali, 1501)

Marsilio Ficino, *De triplici vita libri tres* (Bologna: Benedetto Faelli, 1501)

Luca Gaurico, *Ex regno Neapolitano Prognosticon anni 1502* (Venice: per Bernardino Vitali, 1501 [= January 1502])

Livy, *Titi Livii Decadis* (Venice: per Giorgio Rusconi, 1501)

The overlap between musical and astrological thought and practice in the Italian Renaissance, and indeed more widely, has been the subject of several studies since the publication of D. P. Walker's seminal book *Spiritual and Demonic Magic: From Ficino to Campanella* in 1958.[256] Marsilio Ficino is a central figure in this overlap: the interplay between music and the stars in his *De vita libri tres*, flowing from his belief that a musician could "accommodate" music to celestial bodies in order to draw their beneficial influence, has become a well-known focal point for musicologists.[257]

---

et aliis instrumentis et vocibus infirmos ducendo per civitates et castra: unde debilitantur et agitantur." *De triplici vita libri tres*, fol. 147v.

255 On dance as part of this preventative regime, see Alessandro Arcangeli, "Dance and Health: The Renaissance Physicians' View," *Journal of the Society for Dance Research* 18.1 (2000), 3-30, esp. 3–4.

256 D. P. Walker, *Spiritual and Demonic Magic: From Ficino to Campanella* (London: Warburg Institute, 1958).

257 "Sed iam ad regulus cantum sideribus accomodaturas perveniamus." *De triplici vita libri tres*, sig. [z iv] v.

A byproduct of this focus has been to direct attention away from how the wider panoply of astrological texts in circulation in Italy during the Middle Ages and Renaissance might both reflect and have influenced attitudes towards music.[258] Strongly tied to this, and perhaps influenced by modern viewpoints, has been a historical tendency to view astrology as an occult discipline, on a par with witchcraft, and highly esoteric.[259] No doubt its complexity rendered a deep understanding of the methods of the astrologer beyond the grasp of most people, but only in the same way that the art of any specialist appears opaque to a layperson. In our period, astrology was very much considered a science, and whether or not it was widely and uniformly understood, the vast majority of people gave credence to the influence of the stars upon life on earth.[260]

Astrology was widely taught at Italian universities in the late fifteenth century, with institutions commonly employing one or two professors who could lecture on astrology as a component of mathematics or medicine.[261] For the qualified physician, the positioning of the celestial bodies could determine the timing of any number of procedures, from drawing blood to taking a laxative.[262] In the political sphere, the reliance on astrology of such rulers as Ludovico Maria Sforza, who chose his generals according to astrological predictions, and Giovanni Bentivoglio, who tortured the astrologer Luca Gaurico for predicting—accurately, as it happened—his downfall at the hands of Pope Julius II, is well known.[263] Less well-recorded are the interactions

---

258 A notable exception to this is Lynn Thorndike's study of Julius Firmicus Maternus' *Mathesis*, which posits that the *Mathesis* reflects attitudes to various occupations in the Roman world, musicians included. See Lynn Thorndike, "A Roman Astrologer as a Historical Source: Julius Firmicus Maternus," *Classical Philology* 8.4 (1913), 415–35. For a more detailed study of the *Mathesis'* musical contents in the context of the Italian Renaissance, see Doyle, "Beyond the Courtier," 47–57.
259 See, for example, Wayne Shumaker, *The Occult Sciences in the Renaissance: A Study in Intellectual Patterns* (Berkeley, CA: University of California Press, 1979).
260 Monica Azzolini, *The Duke and the Stars: Astrology and Politics in Renaissance Milan* (Cambridge, MA: Harvard University Press, 2013), 2.
261 Azzolini, *The Duke and the Stars*, 27; and Grendler, *The Universities*, 415.
262 Azzolini, *The Duke and the Stars*, 12–13; and Brendan Dooley, "Introduction," in *A Companion to Astrology in the Renaissance*, ed. Dooley (Leiden: Brill, 2014), 1–16, at 1.
263 Azzolini, *The Duke and the Stars*, 2; and Anthony Grafton, *Cardano's Cosmos: The Worlds and Works of a Renaissance Astrologer* (Cambridge, MA: Harvard University Press, 1999), 124.

of the lower orders with practitioners.²⁶⁴ The survival of the records of the astrologer Simon Forman, which indicate that 10,000 clients sought his advice at his practice on Philpott Lane in London between 1597 and 1601, represents a stroke of fortune for which an Italian counterpart has yet to be found.²⁶⁵ Nonetheless, other sources hint at the importance astrology held at all levels of society. In casting doubt on the efficacy of judicial astrology in his commentary on Plotinus, Ficino wrote that farmers, as well as physicians and astrologers, often attempted—and failed—to use the stars to judge the future success of various crops.²⁶⁶ Indeed, in 1501, Bernardino Vitali published a brief and accessible, if eclectic, selection of short treatises by Francesco degli Allegri, who had been a student of philosophy (arte philosophice studente) in Bologna around 1495, promising "scientifically approved" methods (per scientie approbate) for judging the fate of a man or woman through a wheel of fortune or chironomy; the success of crops and bees; determining when Easter would fall in future years; and a description of the pitfalls and boons proffered by star signs.²⁶⁷

The most widely disseminated literature of this kind came in the form of prognostica, that is, predictions for the coming year based on the movements of the heavens. The statutes of the University of Bologna enshrined a need for the production of an annual prognostication by the lecturer on spherics and theorics in 1404, and from the mid-1480s these were printed and dispersed in Latin and vernacular editions, rendering the complex workings and assimilation of numerous scholarly texts of the astrologer in plain Italian over no more than a few folios; other universities in northern and central Italy soon followed suit.²⁶⁸ While the most notable preoccupation of the majority of prognostica is with the likelihood of various disasters—war, famine and pestilence—afflicting Italy and the wider Mediterranean, they often include predictions for the commoner, too. Stations and occupations are routinely associated with

---

264 Azzolini, *The Duke and the Stars*, 4.
265 William Eamon, "Astrology and Society," in *A Companion to Astrology in the Renaissance*, ed. Brendan Dooley (Leiden: Brill, 2014), 141–92, at 157.
266 Don Cameron Allen, *The Star-Crossed Renaissance: The Quarrel about Astrology and Its Influence in England* (London: Frank Cass, 1966), 16.
267 *Tratato di astrologia*, fols. 1r and 6r.
268 Robert S. Westman, *The Copernican Question: Prognostication, Skepticism and Celestial Order* (Berkeley, CA: University of California Press, 2011), 90.

certain celestial bodies, and the fate of their occupants is consequently tied to the fortunate or unfortunate disposition of their celestial patron. In the visual sphere this is portrayed in popular so-called "Children of the Planets" prints, where various trades and activities are depicted as taking place under the influence of a particular planet.[269] The wide dissemination of prognostica and the theme of the Children of the Planets suggests that, whether people believed a particular prognostication or not, many would have understood that their profession was associated with a specific planet, and that this association, as we shall see particularly regarding music, bore social and moral connotations.

In much the same manner as the dietary *Cibaldone* discussed above, these vernacular and visual astrological ephemera ensured that some astrological knowledge passed through the wider population, and that many people might have had some basic knowledge of planetary influences and star signs, even if they had never consulted an astrologer. One task for which a trained astrologer would have been a necessity, however, was in the drawing up of a birth chart. Casting birth charts, or nativities, required the astrologer to map the heavens on the night of birth or conception onto a square, before analysing the interrelationship of celestial bodies and star signs in an attempt to form a judgement, predicting the fortune and the mental and physical attributes of the newborn child (termed the "native").[270] Plotting the chart accurately required a complete understanding of celestial movements, of the influence which each celestial body would exert on the native, and of the significance of their positioning in relation to other bodies. Printed examples of such charts exist in several sources, most notably Johannes Engel's *Astrolabium planum* (Augsburg: Erhard Ratdolt, 1488; reprinted in Venice for Lucantonio Giunta in 1494 and 1502), but they also survive in far more opulent forms, such as that painted for Agostino Chigi in the Villa Farnesina.[271] In his *Gerontocomia*, Gabriele Zerbi advocates seeing an astrologer to obtain a birth chart, enabling the native to look out for

---

269 On this image type see Dieter Blume, "Children of the Planets: The Popularisation of Astrology in the 15th Century," *Micrologus* 12 (2004), 549–63.

270 Several detailed examples of this process are given in Helena Avelar de Carvalho, *An Astrologer at Work in Late Medieval France: The Notebooks of S. Belle* (Leiden: Brill, 2021).

271 Giangiacomo Gandolfi, "Two Illustrated Horoscopes of the Italian Renaissance," *Paragone: Past and Present* 4 (2023), 45–69, at 48.

pitfalls which might lead to an untimely demise, and to construct a regimen which complements their nature as imparted by the stars.[272]

In order to understand the effects that the heavens would later have on the native, the astrologer could rely on a *Book of Births*, texts which detail the "masteries" of each planet—meaning the characteristics they represent and which they might impart to the native, as well as the effect they might have when aspected or in trine with another planet, situated within a certain star sign, or when in ascent, descent or retrograde. The judgements such texts render are of particular interest, as they tie any number of personal characteristics and future professions—musical inclination and skill included—to certain dispositions of the heavens, and whether a characteristic or profession was viewed as desirable or undesirable can be inferred from its cause, located in a fortunate or unfortunate disposition of the stars.

One such book of births was published in Venice in 1501, the second printed edition of the ninth-century Persian astrologer Abu Bakr al-Hassan ibn al-Khasib's *Kitāb al-mawālīd*, known in Latin Europe as the *Liber nativitatum* or *Albubather* (a corruption of its author's name).[273] The *Liber nativitatum* circulated in Europe from the early thirteenth century, translated by Canon Salio of Padua in 1218, one of a number of scholars who travelled to Toledo in the early thirteenth century to benefit from the aid of Arabic readers there. It forms part of an oeuvre of astrological tracts translated from Arabic during the twelfth and thirteenth centuries; the translation school in Toledo founded by Alfonso X was symptomatic of a concerted effort to render astrological texts available to the Latin world, though the school was responsible for only a portion of the translations completed at that time.[274] The 1492 and 1501 editions of the *Liber nativitatum*, edited by Venetian prelate Antonio Lauro, were printed as anthologies, also containing two shorter treatises translated

---

272 Zerbi, *Gerontocomia*, ed. and trans. Lind, 35
273 Martin Gansten, "Samarasiṃha and the Early Transmission of Tājika Astrology," *Journal of South Asian Intellectual History* 1 (2018), 79–132, at 101. A more detailed musicological treatment of this text can be found in Oliver Doyle, "Musicianship and the Masteries of the Stars: Music and Musicians in the *Liber Nativitatum*," *Renaissance Studies* 38.4 (2024), 494–518, which forms part of the basis for the following paragraphs.
274 Mariano Gomez-Aranda, "The Contribution of the Jews of Spain to the Transmission of Science in the Middle Ages," *European Review* 16.2 (2008), 169–81, at 170.

from the Arabic during the same period: the *Centiloquium divi Hermetis*, a collection of one hundred aphorisms derived from the Hermetic tradition, translated from the Arabic by Stephen of Messina during his time at the court of King Manfred of Sicily between 1258 and 1266; and a similar summary, the *Almansoris Judicia seu propositiones*, translated by Plato Tiburtinus some time after his arrival in Barcelona in 1116.[275]

A significant parallel between these astrological treatises and the medical knowledge introduced to Europe through the translation of Arabic texts lies in the fact that much of their theory derives from Hellenistic sources, most notably the *Tetrabiblos* of Ptolemy of Alexandria. This debt is acknowledged throughout the *Liber nativitatum*, as well as in its frontispiece which depicts Ptolemy seated on a throne flanked by Astrologia and the Muse Urania (usually associated with astrology), canopied by the zodiac. At the simplest level, there are seven planets—the Sun, Moon, Venus, Mercury, Mars, Jupiter, and Saturn—and each of them is assigned two of the four qualities—hot, cold, moist, and dry—which govern whether each is considered beneficent, granting positive qualities, or maleficent, actively harming the individual under their influence. Due to their moderately hot or moist nature, Jupiter, Venus, and the Moon are beneficent, while the excessively hot and cold natures of Mars and Saturn and their shared dryness, qualities considered destructive, make them maleficent.[276] Mercury and the Sun are considered mutable, and especially susceptible to conferring positive or negative characteristics depending on their position.[277] Each of these is also gendered, and assigned a diurnal or nocturnal nature along gender lines: Venus and the Moon are feminine and nocturnal, Jupiter and the Sun masculine and diurnal, whilst Mercury again receives aspects of both.[278] Mars and Saturn, although both masculine, are assigned nocturnal and diurnal natures respectively in order to moderate their

---

275 Paolo Lucentini and Vittoria Perrone Compagni, *I testi e i codici di Ermete nel Medioevo* (Florence: Edizioni Polistampa, 2001), 27; and Josep Puig, "The Transmission and Reception of Arabic Philosophy in Christian Spain (Until 1200)," in *The Introduction of Arabic Philosophy into Europe*, ed. Charles E. Butterworth and Blake Andrée Kessel (New York: Brill, 1994), 7–30, at 11.
276 Claudius Ptolemy, *Tetrabiblos*, trans. F. E. Robbins, Loeb Classical Library 435 (Cambridge, MA: Harvard University Press, 1940), 39 (1.5).
277 Ptolemy, *Tetrabiblos*, 39 (1.5).
278 Ptolemy, *Tetrabiblos*, 43 (1.7).

inhospitable natures: the moist night balances Mars' excessive dryness, and the heat of the day Saturn's frigidity.[279]

Each planet governs a month of the gestation period, and the planet's positioning during this time is crucial in determining whether it imparts its best characteristics, or actively harms the native. The potential impact of each planet is modified considerably by its position in the sky, with the characteristics of the native enhanced or diminished depending on whether a planet is in ascent or descent, is aspected by another planet, or is positioned in a favourable "House" (the signs of the zodiac, of which each planet rules two).[280] With this mutability in mind, the astrologer Abu Ma'shar al-Balkhi (Latinized as Albumasar) warned against categorising planets rigidly as good or evil.[281] Nonetheless, in the *Liber nativitatum* the natures of Saturn and Mars make them inimical to musical ability, and indeed to communication in general. Saturn's influence is commonly conceived as detrimental to the native with few exceptions, and this is never more evident than in passages discussing the voice, hearing and musicianship, where it is the favourable positioning of the beneficent and mutable planets that grant the most desirable traits.

In forecasting the musicality of an individual, the influence of Venus, fortunately disposed, is a necessity. Venus is the only planet discussed in the *Liber nativitatum* as signifying any sort of music without the additional influence of other celestial bodies, her mastery resulting in the birth of a "light singer" (cantor letus).[282] This is tied strongly to her role in determining the physical beauty of the native; though Abu Bakr describes music as one of Venus' masteries, her powers in her assigned month of gestation are limited to the disposition of the native's beauty and happiness. In favourable combination with other planets, her powers render the masteries of other planets more desirable. In his base form, Abu Bakr describes Mercury as follows—gifted with the intelligence

---

279 Ptolemy, *Tetrabiblos*, 43 (1.7).
280 The "aspect" is the angle planets make between one another in a horoscope. Those angles used by Ptolemy were the conjunction (0°), sextile (60°), square (90°), trine (120°), and opposition (180°). Ptolemy, *Tetrabiblos*, 73 (1.13).
281 Richard Lemay, *Abu Ma'shar and Latin Aristotelianism in the Twelfth Century: The Recovery of Aristotle's Natural Philosophy through Arabic Astrology* (Beirut: American University of Beirut, 1962), 97–98.
282 *Albubather*, fol. 11v.

requisite for eloquence, but inherently of servile nature, reflecting his traditional role as messenger of the gods in the Greco-Roman pantheon:

> [Mercurius] est planeta doctrine eloquentie: ac scientie. Cum ergo in mense .6. mercurius in ascensione sua fuerit: natus erit bone eloquentie: ac hominibus verba eius placebunt: eritque magnorum virorum ac potentum secretarius.[283]

> [Mercury] is the planet of teaching, eloquence, and knowledge. When therefore in the sixth month Mercury were in his ascension, the native will be of good eloquence, and his words will please men, and he will be secretary to great and powerful men.

Venus' positive influence serves to improve Mercury's main boon—eloquence—still further, rendering the native "a wondrous speaker, of gentle words."[284] Jupiter's effect on the eloquence of Mercury is even more pronounced. Reflecting his omnipotence in Greco-Roman religion, in his ascension Jupiter's beneficence grants the native sincere and considered speech, and knowledge culminating in prophetic powers:

> Iuppiter habet dispositionem mensis secundi a casu seminis in matricem et ipse significat fidem: sensum: intellectum: et scientiam. ⁋ Cum ergo in mense secundo fuerit fortis ac in sua ascensione id est ascendens in circulo suo: et addens in numero: disponet sensum nati et eius simplicitatem intellectum et sapientiam: et secundum eius ascensionem et elevationem disponet in eo sapientiam et fidem in dictis suis: et dabit ei scientiam quam non audivit: nec aliquis docuit sibi. ⁋ Et si cum hoc in auge sua fuerit: significat quod erit recitator rerum: quas aliis nesciunt: et ponet in eis radices a se ipso: loquetur cum providentia: et quasi propheta reputabitur.[285]

> [Jupiter] will dispose the native's sense and their simplicity, intellect and understanding, and according to his ascension and elevation, he will dispose in them understanding and faith in their speech, and will give them knowledge of that which they did not hear, nor that they have been taught. And if also he is in his apogee, it signifies that he will be a reciter of things which others know not; and he will put the root of this in himself: he will speak with providence, and will be reputed to be like a prophet.

---

283 *Albubather*, fol. 3v.
284 "Si mercurius in domo vel termino veneris fuerit erit i sermone et lingua mirabilis mansuetus verbo." *Albubather*, fol. 3v.
285 *Albubather*, fol. 3r. For an explanation of the role of the symbol "⁋" see Chapter 3.1 below.

Jupiter's effect on Mercury's eloquence is to similarly elevate it:

> Et si mercurio sic disposito Iuppiter ipsum aspexerit: erit eloquentissimus: in libris sapiens et mirabilis sermocinator: ac multa super uno verbo proferens. Et si mercurius in domo vel termino Iovis fuerit: erit eloquentie bone: sapiens ac subtilis ingenii.[286]

> If Mercury, so disposed, were aspected by Jupiter, he will be wonderfully eloquent: well-read and a marvelous speaker, and many words over few will he proffer. And if Mercury were in the house or bound of Jupiter, he will be well-spoken, knowledgeable and of a keen mind.

Conversely, Jupiter in descent "signifies the detriment of the native and the paucity of his intellect; neither will he do or say that which he has heard or seen in others."[287] Mercury's descent, similarly, signals one who "will be almost mute, especially so if he is in a sign without a voice."[288] Such traits are linked to the malefic planets, Saturn and Mars, throughout the *Liber nativitatum*; Saturn in particular is linked with a lack of communicative abilities and miserliness, which separate the Saturnine native from their peers, and nowhere in the text is Saturn linked with musical practice. Throughout the *Liber nativitatum*, eloquence is portrayed as the most valued product of intelligence, and a lack of the former is often followed by a paucity of the latter, a continuation of ideas from antiquity linking civic virtue and utility with rhetorical prowess.[289] Indeed, the *Liber nativitatum* effectively stratifies society based on eloquence in a single sentence:

> Preterea sciendum est quod aliqui sunt qui habent magisteria in loquela uoce et lingua: et alii qui operantur manu sicut scriptor: et alii qui

---

286 *Albubather*, fol. 3r.
287 "Et si Iuppiter in eius descensione fuerit: significat detrimentum nati et paucoitatem sui intellectus nec facit aut dicit quicquid ab aliis audivit ac vidit." *Albubather*, fol. 3r.
288 "Quando si mercurius sic dispositus in descensione sua fuerit: natus erit quasi mutus maxime si in signis voce carentibus collocent." *Albubather*, fol. 3v. Those signs without a voice are described at fol. 10r as Pisces, Cancer, and Scorpio.
289 Most notably in Cicero and Quintilian, but following a chain of political thought extending back to Plato. For an extensive discussion of civic utility and rhetoric in Renaissance Italy, see James Hankins ed., *Renaissance Civic Humanism: Reappraisals and Reflections* (Cambridge, UK: Cambridge University Press, 2000). See also Chapter 3.2.

operantur in computationibus venditionibus et emptionibus: et alii sunt qui sunt pigri sine magisterio.[290]

Therefore know that there are those who have majesty in voice and speech; and others who work with the hand, such as a writer; and others who work in the calculation of sales and purchases; and those who are lazy and without instruction.

Mercury and Jupiter's power to impart eloquence and intelligence upon the native has a similar bearing when it comes to musical skill. As previously noted, Venus, while signifying music, only has the power to create the *cantor letus*. In the most sustained discussion of music, chapter 100, "On the birth of jongleurs [Ioculatores]," Mercury, Venus, Mars, and the Moon all exert influence on the formation of the performer:

Quando Luna et Mercurius cum Marte et Venere fuerint et unus alteri vim suam prebuerit: natus erit citharizator aut rotator. Et si dicti planete ab angulis recedentes fuerint: natus ioculando saltabit. ℂ Et si Mercurius et Venus in terminis suis fuerint: natus erit saltator maxime si unus eorum in Capricorno fuerit. ℂ Quando Mars et Mercurius in angulo terre fuerint: natus erit de illis qui vadunt super cordas. ℂ Quando Venus cum Mercurio in doma sua fuerit, ac in angulis: natus erit mimus aut ioculator talis quod instrumentum manibus et lingua tanget. ℂ Quando Mercurius et Venus ad invicem se firmaverint et Venus in angulis fuerit aut in 4 domo a Mercurio et Venus in termino alterius aut orientalis existens in domo exaltatione vel triplicitate sua fuerint: natus ioculator vocis et saltator ac palmarum percussor erit.[291]

When the Moon and Mercury are with Mars and Venus, and one to the others has shown its power: the native will be a cithara player or rotta player.[292] And if the said planets were receding from the angles: they will be born one who jokes while dancing. And if Mercury and Venus were in their bounds: the native will be a dancer, especially if one of them is in Capricorn. When Mars and Mercury are in the angle of the earth: the native will be one of those who goes upon the strings.[293] When Venus is

---

290 *Albubather*, fol. 11v.
291 *Albubather*, fol. 12v.
292 By 1501, *rotta* was an ambiguous term that referred loosely to stringed instruments.
293 "Vadunt super cordas." This seems to refer to a *funambulus*, or tightrope walker. In a letter to Isabella d'Este, reporting on the performance of an eclogue at the Ferrarese court in 1508, Bernardino de' Prosperi mentions that Cardinal Ippolito d'Este had such a performer in his retinue. For the full text of the letter in

with Mercury in her house, and in the angles: the native will be a mime or jongleur such as play instruments with the hand and tongue.[294] When Mercury and Venus have firmed themselves in turn in the angles or in the fourth house, or Mercury and Venus appear in another's bound or orient, exaltation or triplicity: the native will be a comic, a dancer, and a clapper of the hands.

The benefit of finding such performers discussed in relative detail through the lens of an astrologer lies in their stratification: it is relatively safe to presume that those influenced by the celestial bodies in their most favourable dispositions are considered the most artful. Thus, with the beneficial disposition of the similarly nocturnal and feminine Moon on Venus, balanced by the heat and dryness of Mars and enhanced by Mercury's intellect and eloquence, the entertainer is an instrumentalist. When Venus and Mercury are receding from the angles (losing their influence on the native, in astrological terms), their signifiers of basic musicality, beauty, intelligence and eloquence recede too, the native instead becoming merely one who "makes jokes while dancing."

The influence of Mars in this chapter is seemingly linked to the visual aspects of performance. Ptolemy describes Mars as a lover of dance when allied to Venus, and the planet plays a crucial role in the birth of the performers who "go upon the strings."[295] Mars plays an equally important role in a chapter describing another entertainer: the *histrio*. This term is ambiguous, often translated simply as "actor," and Mars' ability to signify one skilled in imitation when positively disposed with Venus, as also described by Ptolemy, would seem to confirm this.[296] However, both Livy's account of a performance in Book 7 of the *Decades* (whence the term *histrio* derives) and subsequent uses in the Middle Ages suggest that these could be any manner of performers, and

---

translation, see Giuseppe Gerbino, *Music and the Myth of Arcadia in Renaissance Italy* (Cambridge, UK: Cambridge University Press, 2009), 63–64.
294 This seems to imply wind instruments, played with both hand and tongue, rather than two distinct families of instruments.
295 Ptolemy, *Tetrabiblos*, 355 (3.13).
296 Ptolemy, *Tetrabiblos*, 355 (3.13).

most likely hybrid actors, singers and instrumentalists, perhaps better expressed by the ambiguous term "player."[297]

Mercury's commonality to all of these performers is perhaps threefold. Mercury is the planet of knowledge and science, and thus requisite for a theoretical understanding of music, building upon the base musicality provided by Venus. It is also the planet of pleasing and entertaining others. Mercury's notable role in the Greco-Roman pantheon as god of commerce plays no overt part in the *Liber nativitatum* until chapter 107, when the birth of various merchants is discussed, but in the chapters on the *ioculator* and *histrio* Mercury's influence affirms that these performers, however skilled or unskilled, are very much professionals, performing to make a living. Although "good" music and performance is inherently linked to the eloquence and intelligence embodied by Mercury, so too is its servile nature as a profession.

The absence of Jupiter from the discussion of professional musicians is perhaps further confirmation of their servitude. His influence on the base musicality of Venus, however, is mentioned twice, both times instilling the native with the ability to move the listener to tears:

> Et si in domo vel termino Veneris fuerit: natus erit sermocinator et praedicator: pulchriter loquens erit et cantor: ita quod per cantum et verba sua homines ad lachrymas provocabit.[298]

> And if [Jupiter] were in the house or bound of Venus: he will be born a giver of sermons and a preacher; he will speak beautifully and be a singer; so that by his song and words men will be moved to tears.

> Et si loco Martis lupiter eos aspexerit libros legis ac eorum lecturam necnon dulces cantus in rebus fidet atque voces quasi flentium et orantium dominum indicat. Et si Mercurius eos aspexerit compositionem instrumentorum musicalium portendit.[299]

> And if Jupiter rather than Mars aspected [Venus and the Moon], it indicates legal books and their teaching, as well as sweet songs in matters

---

297 *Titi Livii Decadis*, fol. 54v. The relevant passage is presented and discussed in Chapter 3.4. For a detailed discussion of cases in which "hystrio" and its variant spellings have been used to explicitly denote a musician, see Abigail Anne Young, "Plays and Players: The Latin terms for performance," *Records of Early English Drama* 9.2 (1984), 56–72.
298 *Albubather*, fol. 3r.
299 *Albubather*, fol. 12v.

of faith, with voices almost weeping, beseeching God. And should Mercury aspect them [instead of Jupiter] it portends the birth of a maker of musical instruments.

Interestingly, these passages are the only instances in the *Liber nativitatum* in which music is described as provoking an emotional response from the listener. Working on the premise that this is the result of a combination of Jupiter and Venus' signifiers, music capable of moving so deeply would be beautiful by virtue of Venus' association, but also, and more importantly, is the product of a musician of keen intelligence, sincerity, and piety, arising from Jupiter. It is telling that the substitution of Jupiter for an intelligent, yet servile Mercury, results not in the birth of a performer, but of an instrument maker: an alliance between the god of scientific pursuits (scientie) and goddess of beauty results in the construction of beautiful objects manufactured with a high degree of mathematical precision, but not necessarily the ability to play them in a way which moves the soul. This is something only a deeper sense and a higher power, that of Jupiter, can imbue.

With all this in mind, it is possible to see a tripartite division of music in the *Liber nativitatum*: light music and base musicality, influenced by Venus; competent musicianship and musical understanding, such as is required for the skillful playing and construction of instruments, influenced by Mercury; and a "higher," more affective and serious musicianship, influenced by Jupiter. It is important to acknowledge that this scheme represents a view on musicianship considerably more complex than that encountered in most other astrological literature in circulation in 1501.[300] The *Flores astrologie*, a translation of the *Kitāb taḥāwīl sinī al-'ālam*, or *Kitāb al-nukat* (*Book of Revolutions of the World Years*) of Albumasar, prepared by John of Seville in the twelfth century, accords all musical skill to Venus.[301] In a chapter on the significance of the planets in forming a child in the *De secretis mulierum*, Pseudo-Albertus equates

---

300 For an overview of the representation of musicians in astrological literature printed in the decades around the turn of the sixteenth century, see Doyle, "Beyond the Courtier," 57–61.

301 "Venus cum fuerit domina anni et descenderit in arietem aut eius triplicitatem apparebit in civitatibus quibus pre est petitio ludorum et cantilenarum et opera instrumentorum et doctrina hominum in ipso tempore et cupiditas divitum et rusticorum in hoc." Albumasar, *Flores astrologie* (Venice: Giovanni Battista Sessa, c.1500–06), fol. 7r.

music almost solely with Venus, and disparagingly ties the beauty of her natives, their dance, and their music with lascivious pleasure.[302]

A similarly reductive version of the musical influence of the planets can also be found in prognostica of this period. In his predictions for the fortunes of various social groups and professions for the year 1502, Luca Gaurico places "histrios, musicians and singers" under Venus and alongside "suitors, youths, girls [...] and the wanton cohort."[303] When writing their predictions for the years 1494 and 1506 respectively, Augustus Moravus and Ludovico Vitalis both dispensed with Gaurico's eloquence, listing musicians alongside whores (lenones).[304] Those texts which do treat music with a greater degree of nuance suggest that the Venus-inspired *cantor letus* of the *Liber nativitatum* could be understood specifically as a wanton, rather than a simple and untrained, musician. Engel's *Astrolabium planum* depicts musicians in several guises, positive and negative, but among them the *cantor letus* is obviously a source of condemnation, being linked closely with vice. Depicting an unfortunate Jupiter as the third decan of Venus' house of Libra, the accompanying caption reads: "The third face is Jupiter, and [symbolises] gluttony, sodomy, light song, and following bad tastes."[305] Depictions of musical practice under Venus in Children of the Planets prints commonly show it taking place amidst amorous pursuits, although none link music explicitly with prostitution.[306] The *Liber nativitatum* may well lift the art of music from its lascivious associates when performed by people blessed by the influence of Mercury or Jupiter, but the association of music with wanton behaviour was seemingly as prevalent in astrological literature,

---

302 "Venus est stella benivola. et facit natum pulchrum magnis oculis et superciliis carnosum et mediae staturae. Secundum animam vero blandum facit efficacem loquacem et studentem in operatione ornato corporis musicalia diligentem voluptatem gaudium et choream disderantem." *De secretis mulierum*, fol. 25v.

303 "Venerii ut sunt Proci Juuvenes Puelle Histriones Musici Cantores: et petulantium cohors." *Ex regno Neapolitano Prognosticon*, fol. 2v.

304 "Secta Venera. Citharedi Cantores Phonasci Utricularii Lenones Mechi Mirobrecharil Phrigiones." Augustus Moravus, *Iudicium Anno Domini 1494* (Padua: s.n., 1494), fol. 2r; "Qui Veneris Radio iaculantur: sicut Cantores: Cytharedi: Lenones: iuvencule: Pictores." Ludovico Vitalis, *Prognosticon in annum Domini 1506* (Bologna: s.n., 1505/6), fol. 2r.

305 Johann Engel, *Astrolabium planum in tabulis ascendens* (Venice: per Lucantonio Giunta, 1502), fol. 69r.

306 See, among others, Tim Shephard, "24. Venus," in *The Museum of Renaissance Music*, ed. Vincenzo Borghetti and Tim Shephard (Turnhout: Brepols, 2023), 119–24.

especially that written for a wider readership than the learned owners of a *book of births*, as it was in conduct literature of this period.

Although reductive astrological views of musicianship were clearly common, there are indications that the more refined scheme found in the *Liber nativitatum* was known to some Renaissance authors. For Ficino, musical practice can be divided into three parts, with Venus representing "light" music, Jupiter and the Sun representing serious music, and Mercury the music which falls in between.[307] In later discussing how the musician might fashion their music in accordance with the planets, he clarifies the style of each:

> Memento vero totam procedere musicam ab Apolline. Atque eatenus Iouem esse musicum: quatenus est cum Apolline concors. Venerem insuper et Mercurium Musicam vicinitate Apollinis reportare. Item ad hos quatuor duntaxat attinere concentus. Tres vero reliquos uoces quidem habere non cantus. Iam vero voces: tardas: graves.raucas: querulas Saturno tribuimus. Marti vero contrarias: veloces, acutasque: et asperas: et minaces. Medias vero Lunae. Concentus autem loui quidem graves: et intentos dulcesque et cum constantia laetos. Contra Veneri cum lascivia et mollitie voluptuosos cantus adscribimus. Inter hos vero medios Soli tribuimus et Mercurio. si una cum gratia suavitatemque sunt venerabiles: et simplices et intenti. Apollinei iudicantur. Si una cum iocunditate remissiores quodammodo sunt: strenui tamen atque multiplices: Mercuriales existunt.[308]

> Remember that all music proceeds from Apollo; that Jupiter is musical to the extent that he is consonant with Apollo; and that Venus and Mercury claim music by their proximity to Apollo. Remember that song pertains to only these four; the other three planets have voices but not songs. Now we attribute to Saturn voices that are slow, deep, harsh, and plaintive; to Mars, voices that are the opposite—quick, sharp, fierce, and menacing; the moon has the voices in between. The music, however, of Jupiter is deep, earnest, sweet, and joyful with stability. To Venus, on the contrary, we ascribe songs voluptuous with wantonness and softness. The songs between these two extremes we ascribe to the Sun and Mercury: if with that grace and smoothness they are reverential, simple, and earnest, the songs are judged to be Apollo's; If they are somewhat more relaxed along with their gayety, but vigorous and complex, they are Mercury's.[309]

---

307 "vero musicam gravem quidem Iovis Solisque esse, levem Veneris, mediam vero Mercurii." *De triplici vita libri tres*, fol. 46r.
308 *De triplici vita libri tres*, sig. & ii r–v.
309 Ficino, *Three Books on Life*, 361.

Ficino's description of his three types of music bears striking resemblance to descriptions of music in the *Liber nativitatum*, whereby Venus inspires the lightest music, Mercury a more intelligent song, and Jupiter song which is the most serious and emotionally compelling. He confirms something implicit in the *Liber nativitatum*: that the most edifying music comes from a musician of greater intelligence than one inspired by Venus alone, something which chimes with Bartolomé Ramos de Pareja's comment that licentious music (cantus potius lascivia) rarely follows the rules to which ecclesiastical music should be harnessed—that is, those governing harmony and counterpoint.[310] Likewise, though Ficino accords Saturn and Mars voices, he does not link them to music, in accord with Saturn's absence from musical discussion in the *Liber nativitatum*, and Mars' role only in the birth of *ioculatores*.

In this context, the astrological basis for Ficino's recommendation of music to preserve the health of those approaching older age (given by Ficino as fifty years old, but by Zerbi in the *Gerontocomia* as thirty, thirty-five or forty) is reinforced.[311] Assuming the role of Mercury addressing the elderly (senes) in Book 1.13, Ficino gives a lengthy speech warning those of advancing years to flee Venus and venereal activities, on the basis that sex is an incredibly damaging activity for the body (a medical view discussed above in Chapter 1.3). However, in Book 2.8, Ficino gives music as one of the activities linked with youth, governed by Venus, which help to prevent the overt influence of Saturn, who governs old age, and whose cold and dry nature was widely considered inimical to life.[312] The warmth of music—part of the mechanism driving its use in recovery from illness—plays a key role in tempering the savage effects of Saturn; Ficino similarly prescribed himself musical solace in an attempt

---

310 "Sed ista ponimus, ne doctrina fiat confusa et cantus ecclesiasticus intelligatur, qui regulariter est ordinatus. Alii vero cantus potius lascivia quam venustate compositi numquam vel raro regulam servant, de qua paulo post loquemur." Bartolomé Ramos de Pareja, *Musica Practica* (Bologna: [Balthasar de Ruberia and Henricus de Colonia], 1482), fol. 19v.

311 *De triplici vita libri tres*, sig. [h iii] v; and Zerbi, *Gerontocomia*, fol. 6v. 'cuius pars una senectus prima appellatur: quem in homine a trigesimo vel trigesimoquinto aut quadragesimo incipiens anno fere'.

312 "Qui septimum iam septenarium impleverunt quinquagesimum attingentes annum. Cogitent. Venerum quidem significare iuvenes. Saturnum vero senes [...] Musicam repetant: si forte interniserin.nunquam intermittendam." *De triplici vita libri tres*, sig. [h iii] v.

to counter his own melancholy, caused by black bile, and through its cold quality also linked with Saturn.[313]

Beyond simple engagement with music as a means of negating Saturnine influence, Ficino also counsels performing music which is "accommodated" to the stars, in order to attract their positive influence by means of the similitude between the musician's song and the song of the celestial body in question. Ficino gives three rules for this practice:

> Prima est exquirere quas in se vires quosve ex se effectus stella quaelibet et sidus et aspectus habeant, quae auferant, quae ferant; atque verborum nostrorum significationibus haec inserere, detestari quae auferunt, probare quae ferunt. Secunda considerare quae stella cui loco maxime vel homini dominetur; deinde observare qualibus communiter hae regiones et personae tonis utuantur et cantibus, ut ipse similes quosdam una cum significationibus modo dictis adhibeas verbis, quae sideribus eisdem studes exponere. Tertia situs aspectusque stellarum quotidianos animadvertens, saltus, mores, actus incitari homines plerique soleant, ut talia quaedam tu pro viribus imiteris in cantibus coelo cuidam simili placituris similemque suscepturis influxum.[314]

> The first is to inquire diligently what powers in itself or what effects from itself a given star, constellation, or aspect has—what do they remove, what do they bring—and to insert these into the meaning of our words, so as to detest what they remove and to approve of what they bring. The second rule is to take note of what special star rules what place or person and then to observe what sorts of tones and songs these regions and persons generally use, so that you may supply similar ones, together with the meanings I have just mentioned, to the words which you are trying to expose to the same stars. Thirdly, observe the daily positions and aspects of these stars and discover to what principal speeches, songs, motions, dances, moral behaviour, and actions most people are usually incited by these, so that you may imitate such things as far as possible in your song, which aims to please the particular part of heaven that resembles them and to catch an influence that resembles them.[315]

---

313 Angela Voss, "Diligentia et divina sorte: Oracular Intelligence in Marsilio Ficino's Astral Magic," in *Innovation in Esotericism from the Renaissance to the Present*, ed. Georgiana D. Hedesan and Tim Rudbøg (London: Macmillan, 2021), 33–62, at 43. See also Melissa Meriem Bullard, "The Inward Zodiac: A Development in Ficino's Thought on Astrology," *Renaissance Quarterly* 43.4 (1990), 687–708.

314 *De triplici vita libri tres,* sig. [h iii] v.

315 Ficino, *Three Books on Life,* 357–59.

In an effort to decipher what "tones and songs" might have been used for the purpose of attracting astral influence, scholars have previously worked to align Ficino's tripartition of music (that of Venus, that of Jupiter and the Sun, and that of Mercury) with the *musica mundana, humana,* and *instrumentalis* described by Boethius, taking note also of the pairing of church modes with celestial bodies in the books on *Musica practica* by Ramos and Gafori.[316] However, in light of what we have here learned, it would seem reasonable to contend that Ficino's thinking operates not in the realm of specialist music theory, but in that of a kind of astral ethnography. Ficino is clear that the music which the reader should emulate must be sought from the people and regions which are governed by the star in question. To find out to which regions and musicians to train their hearing, the reader need look no further than a book of births, such as the *Liber nativitatum*, or one of the suites of Children of the Planets images, or even a simple prognosticon, in which they could find handy information identifying particular individuals, qualities, skills, and trades—including those related to music—with particular governing planets.

1.5 Conclusions

The fragments of musical knowledge we find scattered amidst this loose coalition of texts are as diverse in nature as the texts themselves. One also finds, perhaps unsurprisingly given the diversity of authors and intended readers, no shortage of difference and disagreement among views on music's value. In the medical literature surveyed for this study, engagement with music is often described as part of a healthy lifestyle. In our conduct literature, it is sometimes given as a useful diversion, and elsewhere as wholly deleterious, one author's healthful *gaudium* being another's insalubrious *luxuria*. Indeed, it would have been difficult for a child receiving a Latin education to avoid the association of music with *luxuria*, while a girl reading the *Decor puellarum* might be disconcerted

---

316 See, for example Voss, "The Music of the Spheres"; Prins, *Echoes of an Invisible World*, 201–05; Tomlinson, *Music in Renaissance Magic*, 67–100; James Harr, "The Frontispiece of Gafori's *Practica Musicae* (1496)," *Renaissance Quarterly* 27.1 (1974), 7–22; and Claude V. Palisca, "Mode Ethos in the Renaissance," in *Essays in Musicology: A Tribute to Alvin Johnson*, ed. Lewis Lockwood and Edward Roesner (Philadelphia: American Musicological Society, 1990), 126–39.

to find herself labelled a "whore" and her parents shamed for paying for her music lessons. Where Latin study was associated with moral rectitude and industriousness, music was symptomatic, in some eyes, of idleness and wantonness. It is perhaps telling that the rhetorician Giovanni Sulpizio describes a grounding in scansion—the route to true eloquence—as "the Latin music," devoid as it is in his treatise of the *harmonia* required to make it music proper. Nevertheless, we routinely see musical words, such as the names of instruments and musical verbs, used as subjects in the grammatical texts printed in 1501. The act of singing (*cantare*), the players of wind instruments (*tibicines* and *tubicines*) and their instruments (for example, *fistula* and *cornu*) were evident enough in daily life to warrant providing children with the means to name them in Latin.

Of course, we know that music's negative connotations did not prevent people from seeking a musical education for themselves or their children. In the case of the *Decor puellarum*, the author's invective against music and dance lessons serves to confirm their popularity. Conduct texts like the pseudo-Aristotelian *Regum regimine* and Pontano's *Opera* evidence, with rather more nuance, the double nature of music in a decorous life. No text surveyed in this chapter contains anything akin to a *laus musicae*—such as that which Count Ludovico de Canossa delivers in Castiglione's *Cortegiano*—but in both the *Regum regimine* and Pontano's *Opera* music is granted a utility which is absent in moralising texts written for schoolboys and women. Both honour the ancient adage that music be used to refresh the weary mind, turned to in moments set aside for repose and, in the case of the *Regum regimine,* not enjoyed in public. The *Regum regimine's* chief concern is for the security of the princely reader's power, and a public display of the need to rest (and by that token, of weakness), runs contrary to a projection of that power. Although the academicians in Pontano's *Antonius* are not potentates, they seemingly abide by a similar precept: they are entertained by a *lyricen* in select company, and in the semi-private space of a portico. The *Regum regimine* gives little detail as to what sort of music the prince should be playing or listening to, but in *Antonius*, Pontano casts the musical diversion in a humanist mould: Latin song, sung to the accompaniment of a stringed instrument. If the *lyricen's* song has erotic content—straying, as we might think, into the bounds of *luxuria*—, Aulus Gellius provides an excuse, found repeated in our 1501 corpus within Grapaldi's *De partibus aedium*, in his condonement of music which is "erotic, but not too lascivious."[317]

Another case of music's utility in Pontano's *Opera* is the role given to it in the ideal banquet, with trumpets and wind instruments ("tubae tibiaque") preceding each course, simultaneously entertaining guests and signalling to the kitchens to begin heating food.[318] In the case of the *tubicen* and *tibicen*, utility goes hand-in-hand with the utilitarian way in which they are viewed by Pontano and many other writers of this period and before; the trumpet player who greets Pontano at Narni is paid not to play, and the trumpet-playing herald in *Antonius* is a figure of ridicule. For Castiglione, wind instruments "abbiano del schifo," and the courtier had better not be seen playing them.[319] Where engagement with music in general is presented by some of the texts surveyed here as a threat to basic morality, the issue with wind instruments and their players is entirely social: they are of and for the lower social orders, ubiquitous and utilitarian.

Medical literature and conduct literature are rarely mentioned in the same breath, but on musical matters they present interesting parallels. Medical tracts such as Concoreggio's *Practica nova* and Ferrari's *Tabula consiliorum* grant music a humoural quality, heat, in line with its position as one of the many sensory activities which comprise *gaudium*. In moderation, these activities can relax the body and mind and dispel illness. In excess, they can lead to illness and an inclination toward sexual activity through the overheating of the body. These tracts are as free from moralising judgements as the conduct literature is free from detailed medical judgements, but here they concur neatly in linking music with both useful relaxation and *luxuria*.

From a purely peptic perspective—and most interestingly, from the perspective of a medical layman—Bartolomeo Platina's *De honesta voluptate* provides grounds to ask whether there were medical, as well

---

317 "Erotica quædam non nimis lasciva." Grapaldi, *De partibus aedium*, 71v.
318 Pontano, *Opera*, sig. [t i] v.
319 It is interesting to note that in spite of the warning Castiglione gives in *Il Cortegiano*, the only musical contents of Castiglione's household upon his death, at least according to the surviving inventory, were a harpsichord (*clavicembalo*) and a chest for storing recorders (*cassa da flauti*). Guido Rebecchini, "The Book Collection and Other Possessions of Baldassare Castiglione," *Journal of the Warburg and Courtauld Institutes* 61 (1998), 17–52, at 35.

as moral, grounds for the choice of musical entertainments at banquets, and indeed whether all music could be considered to possess the same humoural qualities. Platina counsels against entertainments which could provoke anger on the grounds that anger draws heat away from the stomach, rendering it unable to digest. By the same token, all manner of other activities could cause similar peptic issues, whether their content be overly erotic, sad, or cerebral. Between these extremes, arguably, lies the music described by the likes of Pontano and Grapaldi.

The virtue of this well-tempered music, and the pitfalls of lesser forms, is expressed most clearly in our astrological literature. In the *Liber nativitatum*, it is the most well-tempered individual, subject to the influence of the beneficent planets Venus and Jupiter, who produces the most powerful music, wheras the musician guided by Mercury might be technically proficient but lacking in gravitas and sincerity, and the musician guided by Venus alone capable only of wantonness. That this codification is not limited to the *Liber nativitatum* is suggested by its similarity to Ficino's description of three types of music—one healthful, one middling, and one noxious—to which it is much more alike than the Boethian tripartition of music, which has previously been used by scholars to explain Ficino's discussion.

We return several times throughout this volume to the fact that our findings often differ from the material a musicologist might hope for in our 1501 corpus—such as a reference to singing as taught in classrooms buried within a Latin grammar, or perhaps a detailed description of Galeazzo Maria Sforza's star-studded chapel choir in a treatise on princely splendour, which might enrich our understanding of musical education and performance practice at the turn of the sixteenth century. What the texts surveyed in this chapter do instead is elucidate the skills and personal traits that were securely attached to the practice of music in this period, key constituents of the finest performer: an excellent memory, a command of poetic meters, grace, gravitas, and sincerity. They further suggest that a person living at the turn of the sixteenth century might consider sound musical judgement as important for their health as their *buona fama*, and that cultivating that judgement might, therefore, be as important a part of their musical education as learning how to play an instrument or sing.

2. Poetry

Publio Fausto Andrelini, *Amorum libri quattuor* (Venice: per Bernardino Vitali, 1501)

Serafino Aquilano, *Soneti del Seraphin* (Brescia: per Bernardino Misinta, [1501])

Matteo Maria Boiardo, *Sonetti e Canzone del Poeta Clarissimo Matheo Maria Boiardo Conte di Scandiano* (Venice: per Giovanni Battista Sessa, 1501)

Henrique Caiado, *Aeglogae et sylvae et epigrammata Hermici* (Bologna: Benedetto Faelli, 1501)

Benedetto Gareth, *Opera nova del Chariteo* (Venice: per Giorgio Rusconi, [1501–09])

Benedetto Gareth, *Opere di Chariteo stampate novamente* ([Venice]: per Manfredo Bonelli, [1501–09])

Lamento di Roma fato novamente ([Milan: Alessandro Minuziano, 1501])

Le Battaglie date in Faienza dal duca Valentino ([Rome: Eucario Silber, 1501–09])

Questa e la discordia de tutti quanti li fati che sono stati in Italia e simel di quelli signori che sono distruti ([Venice: Manfredo Bonelli, 1501])

Questa sie la venuta del imperatore ([Venice]: s.n., [1501])

Panfilo Sasso, *Strambotti del clarissimo professore dele bone arte miser Sasso Modoneso* (Rome: per Johannem Besicken & Martinum de Amsterdam, 1501)

Panfilo Sasso, *Opera del praeclarissimo poeta miser Pamphilo Sasso modenese. Sonetti. CCCCVII. Capituli XXXVIII. Egloge V.* (Venice: Bernardino Viani, 1501)

Giacomo de' Sorci and anon., *La historia e la guerra del populo genovese e gentilhomini e del re di Franza. E una barzelletta dela discordia de Italia* (Naples: s.n., [1501])

Agostino Staccoli, *Sonecti et canzone de miser Agostino da Urbino* ([Rome: Johann Besicken & Martin van Amsterdam, 1501])

Storia overo cronica come il signor Ludovicho que duca de Milano si parti di Millano e ando in terra todesca e como torno con exercito el paese che conquistò e como al fine e stato preso (Bologna: [Giustiniano da Rubiera, c.1501])

Antonio Tebaldeo, *Soneti, capituli et egloghe* (Milan: per Giovanni Angelo Scinzenzeler, 1501)

The focus of this chapter is contemporary poetry—that is, verse publications whose authors and contents were contemporary to the late fifteenth and early sixteenth centuries. We will also refer to older poetry printed in 1501, when it is clear that it has informed the approaches to sound and music taken by our contemporary poets; but older and, in particular, ancient poetry is discussed in a more systematic fashion in Chapter 3.3 below. That said, one of the most significant poetic publications from 1501 is difficult to align with this scheme, and its importance and popularity make it impossible to overlook. 1501 was the year of the Aldine edition of Francesco Petrarca's vernacular works, titled *Le cose vulgari di messer Francesco Petrarcha*, edited by Pietro Bembo, which marked the beginning of a new phase of engagement with Petrarch's vernacular works, and also the first time they were printed without commentary, exposition, or notes. We will refer to the model furnished by Petrarch's *canzoniere* and its influence several times over the course of this chapter.

Our corpus of contemporary poetry contains an array of vernacular lyric poets writing in the exaggerated Petrarchan style of the late fifteenth century, including some of the most recognisable names from this canon, such as Serafino Aquilano, Antonio Tebaldeo, and Benedetto Gareth (better known as "Il Cariteo"). In addition to these three blockbusters, we also have works from lesser-known lyric poets, such as Agostino Staccoli and Panfilo Sasso, as well as the lesser-known lyric production of the celebrated epic poet Matteo Maria Boiardo. Alongside this vernacular lyric corpus, there are two anthologies of neo-Latin verse, by Henrique Caiado and Publio Fausto Andrelini, as well as half a dozen short vernacular verse histories concerning the Italian wars.

All of our contemporary poetic forms find their basis in the realm of oral delivery and performance, ranging from court performers and the growing popularity of the *cantare ad lyram* idiom, to the traditions of street singing and the rising pamphlet trade.[1] For our lyric poets, most of whom had courtly careers of some kind, there is a notable difference between general *opera* editions functioning as comprehensive anthologies of their known work, and more carefully curated *canzonieri* which, in imitation of Petrarch, worked to create an overarching narrative throughout the publication.[2]

Our analysis of sound and music in this poetic oeuvre will weave together three distinct but richly interrelated themes, all of which are inspired by studies of earlier medieval lyric verse. On the one hand, we will amplify the sonic component of a poetic task that Olivia Holmes has described as the "assembling of the lyric self," investigating how poets used sound within their written verse to construct a distinct persona as both poet and performer.[3] On the other hand, we will analyse what Brigitte Cazelles has termed the "soundscape" internal to the verse, which in the case of our 1501 verse means a close focus on what we might call the psychoacoustics of pastoral landscape, including its population with sounding and listening characters from classical myth.[4] In discussing both of these themes, our overriding objective will be to keep in the foreground the relationship between the written form of printed verse and its sounding form as song or speech, taking

---

[1] The substantial and growing recent literature on this topic includes Brian Richardson, "*Recitato e Cantato*: The Oral Diffusion of Lyric Poetry in Sixteenth-Century Italy," in *Theatre, Opera, and Performance in Italy from the Fifteenth Century to the Present: Essays in Honour of Richard Andrews*, ed. Brian Richardson, Simon Gilson, and Catherine Keen (Leeds: Society for Italian Studies, 2004), 67–82; Luca Degl'Innocenti and Massimo Rospocher, "Street Singers: An Interdisciplinary Perspective," *Italian Studies* 71.2 (2016), 149–53; Degl'Innocenti and Rospocher, "Urban Voices: The Hybrid Figure of the Street Singer in Renaissance Italy," *Renaissance Studies* 33.1 (2019), 17–41; Blake Wilson, *Singing to the Lyre in Renaissance Italy: Memory, Performance, and Oral Poetry* (Cambridge, UK: Cambridge University Press, 2020); and James K. Coleman, *A Sudden Frenzy: Improvisation, Orality, and Power in Renaissance Italy* (Toronto: University of Toronto Press, 2022).

[2] This is a distinction commented upon in the *Atlante dei canzonieri del Quattrocento*, ed. Andrea Comboni and Tiziano Zanato (Florence: Edizioni del Galluzzo, 2017). This very useful book features all of our 1501 lyric poets, with the notable exception of Serafino Aquilano, who is not known to have created any manuscript compilation of his work during his lifetime. Although other poets were published posthumously, Serafino is alone in this regard.

[3] Olivia Holmes, *Assembling the Lyric Self: Authorship from Troubadour Song to Italian Poetry Book* (Minneapolis, MN: University of Minnesota Press, 2000).

[4] Brigitte Cazelles, *Soundscape in Early French Literature* (Tempe, AZ: Arizona Center for Medieval and Renaissance Studies, 2005).

our cue from Sylvia Huot's classic analysis of textual performance and "audiovisual poetics" in medieval French poetry anthologies.[5] In the remainder of this introduction to the chapter, we will review the principal authors, genres and titles represented among our 1501 editions of contemporary verse, forming a kind of *dramatis personae*, as well as clarifying the performance practices (so to speak) associated with these protagonists and their verse, so that these essential points can inform but not burden the verse analysis that follows.

The famed strambottist and performer Serafino Aquilano died suddenly in 1500, prompting an avalanche of publications capturing his verse and capitalising on his fame through the first decade of the sixteenth century.[6] In 1501 we see the publication of a collection of *strambotti*, entitled *Soneti del Seraphin* and printed in Brescia by Bernardino Misinta. This early edition has been overlooked by scholars of Serafino, with most citing the 1502 compilation of his work edited by Francesco Flavio as the first printed after his death.[7] The authorship of some poems in our 1501 edition is dubious—for example, the opening *strambotto* is later attributed to Tebaldeo, and the concluding *capitolo* to Panfilo Sasso— but for the purposes of reflecting on contemporary impact, it is more significant that these works were received by some readers in 1501 as Serafino's.[8] The difficulties of attribution and the dispersed distribution of Serafino's work at the time of his death were highlighted by Flavio

---

5   Sylvia Huot, *From Song to Book: The Poetics of Writing in Old French Lyric and Lyrical Narrative Poetry* (Ithaca, NY: Cornell University Press, 1987), particularly Part Two.
6   For more on Serafino see in particular Antonio Rossi, *Serafino Aquilano e la poesia cortigiana* (Brescia: Morcelliana, 1980); Francesco Saggio, "Improvvisazione e scrittura nel tardo-quattrocento cortese: Lo strambotto al tempo di Leonardo Giustinian e Serafino Aquilano," in *Cantar ottave: Per una storia culturale dell'intonazione cantata in ottava rima*, ed. Maurizio Agamennone (Lucca: LIM, 2017), 25–46; and Blake Wilson, *Apollo Volgare: Serafino Aquilano and the Performance of Vernacular Poetry in Renaissance Italy* (Lucca: Libreria musicale italiana, 2024).
7   Serafino Aquilano, *Opere del facundissimo Seraphino Aquilano collette per Francescio Flavio. Sonetti LXXXIX. Egloghe III. Epistole VI. Capitoli IX Strammotti CCVI Barzellette X* (Venice: Manfredo Bonelli, 1502). This is recorded as the first publication of Serafino's work in both Wilson, *Singing to the Lyre*, 382; and Francesca Bortoletti, "Serafino Aquilano and the Mask of *Poeta*: A Denunciation in the Eclogue of *Tyrinto e Menandro* (1490)," in *Voices and Texts in Early Modern Italian Society*, ed. Stefano Dall'Aglio, Brian Richardson, and Massimo Rospocher (New York: Routledge, 2017), 139–52, at 140.
8   Giuseppina la Face Bianconi and Antonio Rossi, *Le Rime di Serafino Aquilano in Musica* (Florence: Olschki, 1999), 30.

in the 1502 Roman edition.⁹ Although inconvenient for the editor, these factors clearly demonstrate Serafino's great influence and appeal across the Italian peninsula, recognised as one of the greatest poet-performers of his age. He spent both his early and some of his later years at the Aragonese court in Naples, where he was influenced by the style of Cariteo's vernacular verse and performances, as well as the court's tradition of theatrical productions.¹⁰

Two editions of verse by Cariteo himself are listed by the USTC as having been published in 1501 and therefore feature in our 1501 corpus, even though closer examination suggests they date from 1506.¹¹ These volumes contain a variety of verse forms, including sonnets, *strambotti*, *frottole*, *capitoli*, *canzoni*, and *sestine*.¹² Spanish by birth, Cariteo moved to Aragonese Naples in the late 1460s, where he held a number of courtly positions, and received his moniker from the Accademia Pontiniana in recognition of his skills in the composition and performance of vernacular poetry.¹³ Cariteo's level of contemporary fame is harder to judge than that of Serafino, though his skills were obviously great enough to win admiration from the younger poet. Cariteo turned to publishing his work after a long performance career, first with an "open songbook" style of publication that collected his work together, but later editing and forming his work into a true *canzoniere* in the Petrarchan tradition.

Antonio Tebaldeo is frequently cited alongside Cariteo and Serafino for the Petrarchan tendencies of his vernacular verse, all three belonging to the era of Petrarchan poets that flourished before the advent of Bembo's new Petrarchan model. Tebaldeo's vernacular verse was first

---

9   Francesco Flavio's editor's note to Serafino, *Opere*, given in translation in Wilson, *Singing to the Lyre*, 383.
10 Wilson, *Singing to the Lyre*, 306; Wilson, *Apollo Volgare*, 85.
11 For more on this see William J. Kennedy, "Citing Petrarch in Naples: The Politics of Commentary in Cariteo's Endimione," *Renaissance Quarterly* 55.4 (2002), 1196–221, at 1197; and Kennedy, *The Site of Petrarchism: Early Modern National Sentiment in Italy, France, and England* (Baltimore, MD: Johns Hopkins University Press, 2003), 67.
12 The *strambotti* were removed for the subsequent 1509 edition. See Enrico Fenzi, "Benet Garret, detto Cariteo," in *Atlante dei canzonieri del Quattrocento*, ed. Comboni and Zanato, 348–57, at 355.
13 Benedetto Gareth, *Le Rime di Benedetto Gareth, detto il Chariteo*, ed. Erasmo Percopo, 2 vols. (Naples: [Tipografia dell'Accademia delle scienze], 1892). The introduction to this edition remains the principal source for much of the detail on Cariteo's life.

printed in an unauthorised edition in 1498, with a further eight editions produced before our 1501 issue, suggesting the immense popularity of his verse at the turn of the century. Tebaldeo's work would go on to receive over a dozen further reprints before his death in 1537. Tebaldeo did not favour the *strambotto*, and his oeuvre consists primarily of sonnets, *capitoli*, and *epistole*, as well as a number of vernacular eclogues. Also in contrast with his fellow vernacular lyric poets, Tebaldeo was not renowned for his performance abilities, though it seems likely that he would have performed his verse; instead, the documented musical settings of his words are connected with the initiative of Isabella d'Este and her musicians Bartolomeo Tromboncino and Marchetto Cara. Ferrarese by birth, Tebaldeo kept close relations with the Este family, serving as tutor to Isabella and later secretary to Lucrezia Borgia, before moving to the court of Pope Leo X in Rome.

Four 1501 editions of poetry, three of which are essentially identical, bear the name of the Modenese poet Panfilo Sasso as author. His 1501 publications were the first editions of his vernacular works: one is an *Opera* volume featuring sonnets, *capitoli*, and eclogues; the other a separate edition of his *Strambotti*. The *Strambotti* were printed three times in 1501: in Brescia alongside his *Opera* by Bernardino Misinta, and also in Rome by Johann Besicken and Martin van Amsterdam, and in Milan by Leonardo Pachel (though only the Roman edition is recorded by the USTC).[14] Sasso is frequently noted as a "follower" of Serafino, despite being his senior, and the large quantity of celebratory material dedicated to Serafino by Sasso after his passing has no doubt prompted this reception. The decision to collect his *strambotti* in a separate edition, printed in the same year and location as those of Serafino, makes us wonder whether Sasso's own edition was in emulation of Serafino's, or if Sasso had some part in the first edition of Serafino's work, given his close ties to the printer.[15] Unlike the other lyric poets, Sasso is notable for his avoidance of the courts, and has been labelled a "courtier without

---

14 For a detailed history of the editions of the sonnets see Panfilo Sasso, *Strambotti*, ed. Folke Gernert (Trier: Romanica Treverensis, 2017).

15 Sasso's close ties to the area have been noted, and between 1499 and 1501 he published five separate works with the printer. Stephen D. Bowd, *Venice's Most Loyal City: Civic Identity in Renaissance Brescia* (Cambridge, MA: Harvard University Press, 2010), 35–43.

a court" by modern scholars.[16] Instead, he spent the majority of his early life in the area surrounding Brescia and Verona, where he may have been a street singer, as he himself implies in a letter to Cassandra Fedele in the early 1490s where he states that whilst living in Raffa, near Verona, he has caused "men to stop and marvel, beguiled by [his] extemporaneous poems which are sung in meters and accompanied on the lyre or cithara."[17] Sasso later moved to Longiano, a small village near Cesena, where he was Governor and *Podestà* from the early 1510s until his death in 1527.

Matteo Maria Boiardo is better recognised for his contribution to the genre of the chivalric epic, the *Orlando innamorato*, yet it is his lyric work that features in the 1501 corpus. His *Sonetti e canzone* were published first posthumously in 1499, and for the second and final time in 1501. The work is split into three books, mirroring Ovid's *Ars amatoria*, though this inspiration is seen only in the structure of the publication and not in the content. Boiardo's lyric poetry is believed to have been written during the 1470s, appearing collected together for the first time in manuscript form in 1477; the imagined romance that it portrays is indicated to have taken place between 1469 and 1472.[18] In this work, Boiardo exhibits a wide range of verse types and an experimental poetic style, playing with form, internal rhyme structures, and visual formats such as acrostics. Boiardo spent the entirety of his life between his family home in Scandiano and the Este court at Ferrara, entering the service of Ercole I d'Este in 1476.

---

16   See in particular Massimo Malinverni, "Un caso di incrocia fra tradizione autorizzata e letteratura populare: I 'sonetti e capitula' di Panfilo Sasso e un opuscolo sulle guerre di fine '400'," *Diacritica* 5.6 (2019), 45–53; and Sasso, *Strambotti*, ed. Gernert.

17   "Iccirco cum in praesentia huius Veronensis agri vicum nominee Rapha incolat Pamphilus Saxus Mutinensis octavum et trigesimum circiter agens annum, qui, ut tu, bonis leteris Philosophia et Theologia, et utroque extemporanco poemate lyra citharave, et canta modulis interpolatos stupere mortals facit, ad quem elogium de te meum transmisi aliquid laudem tuarum superaddens." Panfilo Sasso, as found in Cassandra Fedele, *Clarissimae Feminae Cassandrae Fidelis venetae Epistolae et orationes*, ed. Jacopo Filippo Tomasini (Padua: Franciscus Bolzetta, 1636), 184; translation from Cassandra Fedele, *Letters and Orations*, ed. and trans. Diana Robin (Chicago, IL: University of Chicago Press, 2000), 81.

18   Andrea di Tommaso, "Introduction," in Boiardo, *Amorum Libri: The Lyric Poems of Matteo Maria Boiardo*, ed. di Tommaso (Binghampton, NY: Medieval & Renaissance Texts and Studies, 1993), 1–26, at 9.

The *Sonecti et canzone* of the much more obscure Agostino Staccoli were similarly published only after their author's death. The title of this edition is not the poet's own, with the original title missing from the manuscript source.[19] Staccoli's publication features mainly sonnets, over 90 in total, in addition to two *sestine* and two *canzoni*, and was arranged by the poet himself in manuscript form before his death, in the 1480s. Staccoli was a lawyer and poet born in Urbino, and spent most of his life between Urbino and Rome, where he was a secretary in service to the Apostolic Chancery. We learn from his poems and letters of his friendship with contemporaries such as Serafino and Tebaldeo.

Publio Fausto Andrelini's *Amorum libri quattor* was first published in Paris in 1490; our 1501 edition was its first and only Italian issue. The work contains a number of love elegies in Latin, split into four books each containing between ten and twelve poems. This work is believed to have been written in Italy around a decade before its first publication, while the author was a member of the Roman academy of Pomponio Leto in the 1480s. Andrelini writes in elegiac couplets, one of the most prevalent verse types for neo-Latin poetry, and one commonly used in Latin improvisation. After his time at the Roman academy, Andrelini moved to Paris in the 1490s, where he taught rhetoric, poetry, and history at the university, remaining in the city for the rest of his life.

Six of the eclogues by Henrique Caiado featured in our 1501 publication were first printed separately in 1496; the 1501 edition adds to these a further three eclogues, three *sylvae*, and two books of epigrams. Both Caiado's published editions were dedicated to the King of Portugal, Emanuel I. Portuguese by birth, Caiado was sent to Bologna to study law in 1485, but found himself more interested in poetry and literature, studying at the University of Florence under Angelo Poliziano, and coming to be considered one of the best neo-Latin poets of his time. Poliziano's influence can be seen in some of Caiado's poetic choices; Poliziano was one of the first to encourage the use of Statius' *Silvae* as a model for poetic imitation, of which we see three examples in this printed compilation. The *sylvae* represented a precedent for

---

19   For more on this, see especially Italo Pantani, "Agostino Staccoli," in *Atlante dei canzonieri del Quattrocento*, ed. Comboni and Zanato, 565–74.

improvisational freedom, a draft composed quickly in a moment of great inspiration that the poet could later refine.[20]

Alongside these star lyric poets, a distinct category within our 1501 poetic corpus comprises a small collection of contemporary histories, short works written mostly in *ottava rima* that give accounts of recent battles in a manner emulative of the popular chivalric style.[21] The authors of these works are largely unknown, and given their short nature, most of them are now found bound into compilations combining histories printed throughout the sixteenth century. We have five of these histories surviving from 1501; the USTC lists an additional history which is now lost.[22] It is likely many more were lost due to their small and fragile nature, and that those surviving did so because they were "saved" by their inclusion in larger compilations.

The content of these short works is quite formulaic and, in comparison to the imagined soundscapes found in the other 1501 poetic works, sonic elements are sparse. These sonic references are meant to represent real sounds, transmitting, albeit in a grand style, the soundscape of war, and as such they do not connect to a constructed soundscape representative of the author such as we see in the lyric verse. One of the most common references is to cries of alarm produced by townspeople and onlookers at the sight of an oncoming battle or army—this is seen extensively in *Le Battaglie date in Faienza dal duca Valentino*, for example, where cries of alarm from various sources are listed.[23] A similar idea is explored in the history by Jacopo Cortenese, who speaks of how "at the cry of alarm, every valley resounds."[24] In this context, the resounding of the landscape suggests the volume and diffusion of the cries, and establishes the very real landscape of the battle. This idea of a resounding landscape no doubt takes inspiration from the imagined landscapes of the lyric and neo-Latin poets, as we will later see. However, the purpose of these texts is not to create an imagined world but to give a dramatic and compelling

---

20 Wilson, *Singing to the Lyre*, 221.
21 Only one history is not written in *ottava rima*, being instead written as a ballata: *Questa sie la venuta del imperatore*.
22 This is the *Storia overo cronica come il signor Ludovicho*.
23 See in particular verse 67, which consists solely of these cries. See Julia Benavent, Maria Josep Bertomeu, and Alessio Bonafe, "Le battaglie date a Faienza dal duca Valentino," *Revista Borja* 1 (2007), 63–102.
24 "Al crido alarme ogni valle rinbomba." Sorci, *La historia e la guerra*, sig. A [i] v.

recollection of events, and so the device does not serve the same purpose in the soundscapes of the histories as it does elsewhere.

Musical sounds are also present in these texts, though they are rare. For example, in *Questa e la discordia di tutti*, we meet a "trombettino," referring not to a small trumpet but to a trumpeter acting as a herald.[25] In *La historia e la guerra del populo genovese e gentilhomini e del re di Franza*, we are given an interesting scene in which the clergy move in procession, accompanied by song, to receive the French king:

Larcivcecovo de genova e abati	The archbishop of Genoa and the abbots
Per ricever el re mesonse in via	
E canonici e preti e molti frati	Set out in order to receive the king
Procession canti de dolce armonia[26]	And canons, and priests, and many friars,
	Process with songs of sweet harmony.

Here, music features as part of the procession, but the focus of the text is more on detailing the scope of the procession than providing data about the music being performed. 1501 readers experienced in the public musical culture of an Italian city could no doubt fill in the missing information in their mind's ear without difficulty—at least with regard to the sonic event, if perhaps not with reference to specific repertoire.

Our corpus of 1501 poets is dominated by known poet-performers, ranging from posthumous publications, as after the death of Serafino, to editions published by the poets themselves appearing after decades of acclaim, as in the cases of Cariteo and Sasso. The majority of these works can be situated within the tradition of *cantare ad lyram*, the practice of solo singing to the "lyre," which had attained great popularity by the late fifteenth century within the courtly settings and humanist circles in which many of these poets moved. With this tradition already comes the implicit understanding that poems published as words on a page also existed in performance, despite the range of verse forms and languages used. Indeed, poetry in general was understood as musical; it was the combination of words harmoniously according to metre, rhyme, and

---

25 *Questa e la discordia de tutti*, fol. 2r.
26 Sorci, *La historia e la guerra*, sig. [A iii] r.

stress.²⁷ The *cantare ad lyram* practice drew elements from the older *canterino* or *cantimbanco* tradition, and they both shared the features of singing to the accompaniment of a string instrument, typically played by the performer, and the improvisation and oral delivery of poetry. It is also from the older *canterino* tradition that many of the poetic forms and structures were drawn, such as the *strambotto* and *capitolo*, which provided short and accessible scaffolds for composition and experimentation.²⁸ However, humanist culture's cultivation of neo-Latin, seen in our editions of Caiado and Andrelini, sets it apart from the *canterini*, despite their shared practices of both improvisation and performance.²⁹

Although musical skill was essential in the performance of these works, contemporary accounts of such performances vary in their detail. Occasionally, we see references to the verse as "sung," using the verb *cantare*, but we also find accounts that suggest a style closer to recitation. As both Blake Wilson and Timothy McGee have concluded, the resultant vocal style may often have been a mixture of the two, intoning verse with some level of rhythmic and melodic variation, helped by the metre and rhyme of the verse, and producing something halfway between strict song and normal speech.³⁰ The poet-performers would most commonly accompany themselves on a stringed instrument, often the *lira da braccio*, which gained popularity in the later half of the fifteenth century.³¹ Notably, there may still have been instances in which the older and more traditional instrument of the *canterini*, the *viella*, was used; and the rising popularity of the lute meant that it too was an attractive option for the poet-performer.

Performance is also entailed in the verse histories in our 1501 corpus, which were created to be performed and sold in the streets and piazzas of towns across Italy. This verse was aimed at a wider public than the neo-Latin poetry and the courtly *strambotti*, combining the popular structures of the oral tradition of chivalric epic with "real" information about

---

27 Nino Pirrotta and Elena Povoledo, *Music and Theatre from Poliziano to Monteverdi*, trans. Karen Eales (Cambridge, UK: Cambridge University Press, 1982), 22.
28 Coleman, *A Sudden Frenzy*, 9.
29 Wilson, *Singing to the Lyre*, 177.
30 Blake Wilson, "The Cantastorie/Canterino/Cantimbanco as Musician," *Italian Studies* 71 (2016), 154–70, at 157–58; Timothy J. McGee, "Cantare all'improvviso: Improvising to Poetry in Late Medieval Italy," in *Improvisation in the Arts of the Middle Ages and Renaissance*, ed. Timothy J. McGee (Kalamazoo, MI: Medieval Institute Publications, Western Michigan University, 2003), 31–70.
31 Wilson, *Singing to the Lyre*, 104 (note 4).

current battles and political situations.[32] These short and popular prints were often recited or sung in order to attract customers, and were pre-composed pieces requiring little to no improvisational skill on the part of the singer as seller.[33] We can see evidence of this in our own corpus, in a book from Naples, where a few lines refer to the nature of the verse as a public musical performance for the purpose of generating sales:

> E qui so fine al mio parlar e al canto
> Ma se volete la lystoria ornate
> Per un soldo ele bona derata.[34]
>
> And here, I can end my words and my song
> But, if you would like this tuneful history
> For just a soldo, it is a good deal.

In the performance of this text, the seller finishes by suggesting that his audience buy the little work, giving a price, and even suggesting it is a bargain. The reference to both speech (parlar) and song (canto) could be to allow multiple sellers of varying performative abilities to present the work without adaptation, executing the same verse in a variety of manners from spoken recitation to fully sung.

2.1 Indications of Performance

Publio Fausto Andrelini, *Amorum libri quattuor* (Venice: per Bernardino Vitali, 1501)

Serafino Aquilano, *Soneti del Seraphin* (Brescia: per Bernardino Misinta, [1501])

Claudian, *Commentarius primus in Raptum Proserpinae Cl. Claudiani* (Milan: in aedibus Lucio Cotta dexteritate Guillame Le Signerre, 1501)

---

32 Massimo Rospocher, "Songs of War: Historical and Literary Narratives of the 'Horrendous Italian Wars' (1494–1559)," in *Narrating War: Early Modern and Contemporary Perspectives*, ed. Marco Mondini and Massimo Rospocher (Bologna: Mulino, 2013), 79–98, at 90.

33 Rospocher, "Songs of War," 90; Massimo Rospocher and Rosa Salzberg, "An Evanescent Public Sphere: Voices, Spaces, and Publics in Venice during the Italian Wars," in *Beyond the Public Sphere: Opinions, Publics, Spaces in Modern Europe*, ed. Massimo Rospocher (Bologna: Mulino, 2012), 93–114, at 102; Rosa Salzberg, "In the Mouths of Charlatans: Street Performers and the Dissemination of Pamphlets in Renaissance Italy," *Renaissance Studies* 24.5 (2010), 638–53, at 640; Salzberg, *Ephemeral City*, 100.

34 Sorci, *La historia e la Guerra*, sig. [A iii] v.

Benedetto Gareth, *Opera nova del Chariteo* (Venice: per Giorgio Rusconi, [1501–09])

Francesco Petrarca, *Le cose vulgari di messer Francesco Petrarcha* (Venice: Aldo Manuzio, 1501)

Panfilo Sasso, *Strambotti del clarissimo professore dele bone arte miser Sasso Modoneso* (Rome: per Johannem Besicken & Martinum de Amsterdam, 1501)

Panfilo Sasso, *Opera del praeclarissimo poeta miser Pamphilo Sasso modenese. Sonetti. CCCCVII. Capituli XXXVIII. Egloge V.* (Venice: Bernardino Viani, 1501)

Antonio Tebaldeo, *Soneti, capituli et egloghe* (Milan: per Giovanni Angelo Scinzenzeler, 1501)

Fazio degli Uberti, *Opera di Faccio Degliuberti Fiorentino Chiamato Ditta Mundi. Vuolgare.* (Venice: Lucantonio Giunta per Cristoforo Pensi, 1501)

Valerius Flaccus, *Argonautica diligenter accurateque emendate & suo nitori reddita in hoc volumine continentur* (Venice: per Cristoforo Pensi, 1501)

Virgil, *Vergilius cum commentariis quinque, videlicet Servii, Landini, Ant. Mancinelli, Donati, Domitii* (Venice: s.n., 1501)

In the introduction to this chapter we have already briefly examined the performative nature of much of the poetry found in our 1501 corpus. As we have seen, the work of these poets is rooted in a known and documented performative reality, with many of the poets recognised not only for their poetic output but also for their abilities as performers. This quality means that when discussing the references to sound and music found within their pages, we must account for their potential relationship to the real-life sounds of the musical performance of the work. In the case of many of the sonic and musical references in these books, that relationship is quite direct: the written texts refer to their own sounding performance. This is done through a wide range of suggestions and concepts that have a dual purpose, serving to create the imagined soundscape of the work whilst also commenting on its real performative soundscape. In this respect, to some extent we can differentiate between elements that are connected to the "real" aural nature of the work and its performance, and those serving to construct the fiction of performance that is conventionally present in the rhetoric of a *canzoniere*, although this demarcation is frequently and deliberately ambiguous.[35]

One of the most prevalent sonic features is the indication at the opening of the work that the poetry being presented is audible in nature; that is, that the work is being heard rather than read. Different versions of these "audible openings" can be found across poetic genres and styles, neatly demonstrating the performative nature of nearly all of our 1501 poetic corpus. Many of these come from the longer narrative and epic works, in which we see the continuation of ancient poetic traditions configuring the act of poetic composition as singing. Here, of course, the presence of "singing" as a conventional opening to epic verse stems from a much older tradition of poetic orality and live performance, which served in the fifteenth century as an enabling trope in the humanist practice of *cantando ad lyram*. This convention can be seen in the epics of classical literature, some of which we find reprinted in our 1501 corpus, such as Virgil's *Aeneid*, which opens "Arma virumque cano" ("I sing of weapons and a man"), and Claudius Claudianus' *De raptu Proserpinae*, which begins "audaci promere cantu / Mens congesta iubet" ("My crowded mind bids me boldly sing").[36] In both these examples, the poet as author introduces the work as sung, and indicates that their voice is the one we will hear narrating the work. This convention has its roots in a genuinely aural tradition of poetry, in which epic verse was transmitted through performance rather than writing.[37] However, by the time of Virgil and other Roman authors, poets were not always referring to the literal singing of the work, but rather using the verb "to sing" as a configuration of their poetic talents, and as a way of connecting themselves to the epic tradition, bringing that tradition to mind for the reader.[38]

We can see the continuation of this tradition into the work of the fourteenth-century writer Fazio degli Uberti, whose *Dittamondo*, a loose imitation of Dante's *Divina commedia*, was printed for the second time

---

35 Holmes, *Assembling the Lyric Self*, 174.
36 *Vergilius cum commentariis quinque*, fol. 113r; *Commentarius primus in Raptum Proserpinae*, sig. A ii r. Of course, this is not an exhaustive list.
37 For more on this see especially the classic study of Eric A. Havelock, *The Muse Learns to Write: Reflections on Orality and Literacy from Antiquity to the Present* (London: Yale University Press, 1986), 79–117.
38 Minna Skafte Jensen, "Performance," in *A Companion to Ancient Epic*, ed. John Miles Foley (Oxford: Blackwell, 2005), 45–54, at 54.

in 1501. Written in *terza rima*, the work follows the author through his travels around the world, accompanied by the third-century Roman geographer Gaius Julius Solinus. The opening to the *Dittamondo* does not imitate the "I sing" conceit directly, but still sees Uberti configure his verse as audible, as sung:

Non per tractar gli afanni chio sofersi	Not to treat of the afflictions, which I suffered
nel mio luongo chamin ne le paure	in my long journey, nor the fears,
de rima en rima tesso questi versi.	from rhyme to rhyme I weave these verses.
Ma per voler cantar le cosse obscure.	But from a wish to sing of the things obscure
chio vidi et chio udi che son si nove	that I saw and that I heard, that are so new
che a creder parerano forte e dure.[39]	that credence will seem difficult and hard.

Uberti's opening does not turn to song as quickly as its classical models, in which the act of singing appears almost immediately, sometimes from the opening line. Instead, it is introduced at the beginning of the second tercet, linking the second tercet to the first by connecting the act of composition, his rhymes and verses, with their audible transmission through his voice. Notably, though Uberti's work is written in imitation of Dante's *Commedia*, the addition of this audible opening is his own. There is no suggestion of audibility to Dante's opening until the third tercet, and even then his verb of choice is *dire*, not *cantare*, making Uberti's choice all the more self-conscious, connecting him to the greater epic tradition and to the idea of audible song. Still, for the 1501 reader of Uberti's *Dittamondo*, whose bookshelf probably featured many "audible openings," it seems likely that such differences would have passed without notice, and that they would have categorised this work in the same way as its source material, considering it a form of epic.[40] As Elena Abramov-van Rijk has observed, it could then have been considered appropriate for monodic

---

39 *Opera di Faccio Degliuberti*, sig. a ii r.
40 For more on the genre and performance of Dante's *Commedia* see Elena Abramov-Van Rijk, *Singing Dante: The Literary Origins of Cinquecento Monody* (Farnham: Ashgate, 2014), esp. 35–45.

performance—although the relatively limited transmission of the *Dittamondo* suggests that it was hardly a popular text.[41]

In the contemporary neo-Latin texts we can see the continuation of the Latin epic tradition more clearly, as, for example, in the work of Andrelini:

> Horrida Grandisonis alter canat arma cothurnis:
> Anxia quae gallo Roma sub hoste tulit.
> Vel canat orthysio madefactos sanguine campos:
> Sparsa vel aemathio membra cruenta solo.[42]
>
> One may sing with grand-sounding buskins of the horrid arms,
> That anxious Rome endured under the Gallic enemy.
> Or he may sing of the fields made wet with the blood of Orthrys,
> Or of bloodied limbs scattered on Emathian soil.

These few lines are presented at the start of Andrelini's work, in his first stanza. In this case, Andrelini's opening is very directly imitative of the ancient style, using the traditional "I sing," and creating a sense of audibility whilst introducing the voice of the narrator in the act of poetic composition. However, Andrelini is not writing a Latin epic; instead, he uses this opening to contrast his own lyric to classical epics, suggesting that it deserves the same standing and accolade, but that it will not contain the historical material of battles and heroes that the epic form requires. Indeed, Andrelini uses the conventional opening of an epic to distinguish what he will *not* do; the focus of his lyric is emotion and love, not the far-fetched stories of epic, and so these are precisely not what he will "sing" of.[43]

As this example confirms, audible openings can also be found in contemporary lyric works, however they present themselves differently in line with the different aims and focus of the lyric form. These openings may in part take their inspiration from the Petrarchan canon, calling to mind Petrarch's famous audible opening to his *Canzoniere*, "Voi; ch'ascoltate in rime sparse il suono" ("You, who hear in scattered rhymes

---

41 Abramov-Van Rijk, *Singing Dante*, 35–45.
42 Andrelini, *Amorum libri quattor*, sig. A ii r.
43 Holt N. Parker, "Renaissance Latin Elegy," in *A Companion to Roman Love Elegy*, ed. Barbara K. Gold (Newark: Wiley, 2012), 476–90, at 476.

the sound").[44] This opening presents a different kind of audibility to that we have seen in the longer verse forms. Instead of suggesting that the author is singing, it addresses a collective "you," creating the sense of an audience, and refers to the verse as being heard. Unlike the longer narrative works in which the audibility of the opening presents the voice of the poet as narrator in the first person before moving to the third person for the main body of text, in the vernacular lyric works there is no such requirement to swap perspectives, as the poet continues to feature as the central character in his own verse. Additionally, these lyric audible openings preface much shorter poetic forms, and so their purpose is quickly to define the audibility of the verse, whilst adding to the narrative of the work by imparting an impression of the verse's delivery. As a result, the audible openings we hear in lyric verse are often far more dramatic, adding an emotional dimension to the delivery of the work that goes beyond singing, whilst still making it clear that the verse is being heard and not read.

Even in our short 1501 anthology of Serafino Aquilano's work, there are multiple examples of such audible openings. He opens one *strambotto*, for instance, with the line "You who hear my sweet complaints."[45] This opening, appearing a few pages into the published collection, evokes Petrarch in calling to a collective "you," but swaps Petrarch's scattered rhymes for the poet's own "sweet complaints." This opening makes reference to the verse as sound, with a listener and not a reader, whilst characterising that sound as sweet, and specifying that it arises from his sufferings in love.

Another common indicator that the poet composes his verse with its audibility in mind is the frequent references to both writing and singing, suggesting a duality in the poet's understanding of his work; he configures his poetic ability as a combination of both these media, because in his self-concept as poet his literary and musical talents are entirely intertwined. This means that although singing in the verse can

---

44 Petrarca, *Le cose vulgari*, sig. aii r. This opening presents us with some ambiguities in its imitation, however, given that, whilst certainly it refers to the audibility of the work, Petrarch's own conception of this opening also refers to its fictional performance to an imagined audience. Olivia Holmes explores how audibility in Petrarch's *Canzoniere* refers to both the real and fictional performance of the work; for more on this see Holmes, *Assembling the Lyric Self*, 174.

45 "Voi che ascoltate mie dolce querele." *Soneti del Seraphin*, sig. b ii r.

often be understood as a metaphor for writing poetry, by separating their actions into both writing and song, the poets are alluding to the performative aspect of their work and suggesting that their poetry was written with the intention of performing (or performed with the intention of being written).

Cariteo does this when he opens one sonnet, "Lady, the more I speak, or write, or sing."[46] Here, the separation of his actions into distinct parts, speaking, writing, and singing, is used by Cariteo to show the depth of his love; he is forced to vent about it in multiple media, as no single medium is enough. Cariteo highlights the importance of hearing his verse twice over, both in speech and in song, with the suggestion that this is not the first time he has resorted to these measures—his poetic production is trapped in a cycle of creation and performance as he tries to win the heart of his beloved. In doing this, he uses the writing/singing duality, and suggests the verse's audibility and performance; his verse must exist in all three media, it is spoken, written, and sung, and his own understanding of his poetic production necessarily entails all of these multiple elements.

We can see another example of this from Tebaldeo, who says, "I give you fame, and of you I write and sing."[47] Tebaldeo addresses the subject of his verse, his beloved, and suggests that as the subject of his work, his beloved gains fame—inferring, of course, as well, the skills of the poet in constructing verse capable of conferring such recognition. Again, this duality suggests performance with the conscious separation of the actions of singing and writing; Tebaldeo both writes poetry about his beloved, and also performs it. This holds the additional suggestion that it is through his verse production, both in its written distribution and in performance, that Tebaldeo too hopes to find fame. Just as he raises his beloved up through his work, he hopes it will raise him up alongside her.

An additional quality of verse is its ability to sound musical in and of itself, a quality that can only be understood when the verse is heard aloud, and is perhaps best conveyed when its musicality is emphasised through musical performance. In these cases, the audibility of the verse is important in revealing the sonic aspects of word choice, and how

---

46 "Donna quantio piu parlo: o scrivo: o canto." *Opera nova del Chariteo*, sig. [H iv] v.
47 "Sio vi do fama: e de vui scrivo e canto." Tebaldeo, *Soneti, capituli et egloghe*, sig. [a iv] v.

choices that may seem unusual on the page are actually reflections of poetic choices made for performance purposes. Such is most certainly the case for Panfilo Sasso, who, as mentioned above, was likely a street singer of some kind for much of his early life. Working as an itinerant singer outside the courts, Sasso's work must have held wide-ranging appeal to sustain his career, with a combination of memorable lyrics and a tune that could get stuck in the head of a listener like a modern-day earworm. In a *strambotto* that also circulated in an anonymous musical setting,[48] for example, he writes:

Cridati tutti amanti al focho al focho	Cry all you lovers to the fire, to the fire
al focho che me strugge per amore	to the fire that burns me for love
corriti tutti insieme al locho al locho	run all together to the place, to the place
al locho dove bruscia lo mio core[49]	to the place where my heart burns.

Sasso combines the group invocation ("tutti amanti") with repetitive rhymes that lead from the end of one line to the beginning of the next. The repetition at the ends of the lines provides emphasis from a purely poetic standpoint, but it is perhaps not the most elegant poetic gesture on the page. Instead, it is memorable, easy to repeat, and can be imagined sung by a larger group than just the author, as he sings to a crowd, imploring them for sympathy, and asking them to join in both empathically and also perhaps literally. This repetition could also suggest improvisation on the part of Sasso, with repeated words and

---

48 The incipit "Cridati tutti amanti" appears in the original table of contents of Modena, Biblioteca Estense, MA α.f.9.9 (known to musicologists as ModE), an anthology of musical settings of *strambotti*, probably originating in Padua in the 1490s. Unfortunately the portion of the manuscript that once contained the setting of "Cridati tutti amanti" does not survive. The concordance with Sasso's 1501 anthology is noted in Walter H. Rubsamen, *Literary Sources of Secular Music in Italy (ca.1500)* (New York: Da Capo Press, 1972), at 18–19. On ModE see most recently Giovanni Zanovello, "'You will take this sacred book': The Musical Strambotto as a Learned Gift," *Journal of the Royal Musicological Association* 141.1 (2016), 1–26. Documented notated musical settings of Sasso's verse are listed in Giulio Cattin, "Nomi di rimatori per la polifonia profana Italiana del secondo quattrocento," *Rivista Italiana di Musicologia* 25.2 (1990), 209–311, at 306.

49 Sasso, *Strambotti*, sig. [a iv] r.

phrases allowing for ease of memorisation and repetition, alongside the formulaic structure seen in the two-line rhyming pairs, allowing for three repetitions and a brief expansion upon the idea before moving on.

2.2 Landscape

Publio Fausto Andrelini, *Amorum libri quattuor* (Venice: per Bernardino Vitali, 1501)

Matteo Maria Boiardo, *Sonetti e Canzone del Poeta Clarissimo Matheo Maria Boiardo Conte di Scandiano* (Venice: per Giovanni Battista Sessa, 1501)

Henrique Caiado, *Aeglogae et sylvae et epigrammata Hermici* (Bologna: Benedetto Faelli, 1501)

Benedetto Gareth, *Opera nova del Chariteo* (Venice: per Giorgio Rusconi, [1501–09])

Ovid. *Ovidio Metamorphoseos vulgare* (Venice: per Cristoforo Pensi ad instantia de Lucantonio Giunta, 1501)

Francesco Petrarca, *Le cose vulgari di messer Francesco Petrarcha* (Venice: Aldo Manuzio, 1501)

Panfilo Sasso, *Strambotti del clarissimo professore dele bone arte miser Sasso Modoneso* (Rome: per Johannem Besicken & Martinum de Amsterdam, 1501)

Panfilo Sasso, *Opera del praeclarissimo poeta miser Pamphilo Sasso modenese. Sonetti. CCCCVII. Capituli XXXVIII. Egloge V.* (Venice: Bernardino Viani, 1501)

Antonio Tebaldeo, *Soneti, capituli et egloghe* (Milan: per Giovanni Angelo Scinzenzeler, 1501)

We are often given great visual and sonic detail of the landscapes imagined by the poet in setting the scene of his verse. Presenting us with another world in which the poet can set his verse, these landscapes are often either directly connected to or emulative of contemporary pastoral fashions—many of our 1501 poets, both vernacular and neo-Latin, wrote pastoral eclogues as part of their oeuvres.[50] Beyond simply

---

50 On contemporary pastoral fashions and their links with music, see especially Giuseppe Gerbino, *Music and the Myth of Arcadia in Renaissance Italy* (Cambridge, UK: Cambridge University Press, 2009); and Tim Shephard, Sanna Raninen, Serenella Sessini, and Laura Ștefănescu, *Music in the Art of Renaissance Italy 1420–1540* (London: Harvey Miller, 2020), 260–87.

setting the scene, the noises of nature are frequently employed to reflect the mental state of the author; the establishment of the poet's landscape creates a world that is an extension of the poet himself, and as a result, landscape offers both a reflection of and an insight into the poet's state of mind. Meanwhile, by directly comparing the sound of their poetic performance to the sounds of their imagined landscape, authors weaken the distinction between the two, creating an integrated performative landscape with which the poet actively interacts.

In the neo-Latin poetry of Caiado and Andrelini, the landscape is a sounding board for the voice of the author, as is typical in work that makes use of the pastoral mode. In constructing this "resounding" environment, our 1501 poets take their inspiration from Virgil, who in his eclogues uses the resounding natural environment to represent having the time and space for poetic expression.[51] In the work of Andrelini and Caiado, we see a particular emphasis on the invocation of setting, and this setting frequently mirrors the emotions of the authors, as is typical of pastoral.

These pastoral tropes are especially evident in the Latin eclogues of Caiado, where we hear on multiple occasions how it is "the forests, the hills, and the cliffs" that "were sounding with poems."[52] Caiado's account of this imagined world, although given to us via visual cues, is really meant to tell us more about its sonic properties than its landscape appearance. He suggests the scope of his imagined world—its acoustic boundaries—by invoking landscape elements that are capable of echoing his words back to him. That his voice escapes mention in these poems highlights his connection to this landscape; his vocal performance is entirely dissolved into the resonance of the environment. Indeed, the feedback loop between poetic performance and landscape resonance is explicitly acknowledged when he writes, "And the valleys and steep cliffs will sound out 'Janus,' as long as the pipes are in my hands and there is breath in my mouth."[53] This reference is very directly pastoral, painting the poet as a shepherd playing his instrument in his landscape,

---

51 Ljubica Ilic, "In Pursuit of Echo: Sound, Space and the History of Self," in *Music, Myth and Story in Medieval and Early Modern Culture*, ed. Katherine Butler and Samantha Bassler (Woodbridge: Boydell, 2019), 156–68, at 163.
52 "Carminibus sylvae colles et saxa sonabant." Caiado, *Aeglogae et sylvae*, sig. C vi r.
53 "Et Ianum valles praeruptaque saxa sonabunt/ Fistula dum manibus fuerit, dum spiritus ori." Caiado, *Aeglogae et sylvae*, sig. D ii r.

with the sound of the instrument standing in for both the poet's voice and his written authorship. Caiado also establishes that it is only in death that his sound can be stopped, creating the landscape as both a distinct protagonist that can listen sympathetically, and a stage for his performance. But concurrently, we might read the poet and the valleys that resound with his sighs as ontologically integrated beings, made up of human voice and natural world, so that, with the poet's death, his imagined landscape must die with him.

It is not only in the overtly pastoral poetry printed in 1501 that we can find this conceit. Boiardo too makes a listener of his landscape, in a way that is highly evocative of contemporary pastoral:

Voi monti alpestri (poiche del mio dire	You high mountains (since my tongue gets twisted
La lingua avanti a lei tanto se intrica	When I try to speak while in her presence
E il gran voler mi sforza pur chio dica)	When my great passion forces me to speak)
Voi monti alpestri oditi il mio martire	You high mountains hear my martyr's tale
Se amor vol pur che sisirando expire	If love insists that I expire sighing
Amor che in pianto aeterno me nutrica	Love that nurtures me with endless plaints
Fatti voi moto a quella mia menica	May you make known to her, my enemy
Nanti al mio fin, che io vuo per lei morire.[54]	Before my end, that I would die for her.[55]

Boiardo makes much greater use of his imagined landscape than any of the other 1501 lyric poets, preferring the sounds and images of nature over the invocation of classical characters and scenes that is more commonly found in the vernacular corpus (on which see below). As a result, it is his landscape that must become the sympathetic listener to his plight, and he addresses the high mountains, suggesting the way in which his voice in its despair must carry to the edges of his fictional world. At these edges, the landscape is marked by towering peaks, providing both a visual boundary,

---

54 Boiardo, *Sonetti e Canzone*, fol. 30r.
55 Boiardo, *Amorum Libri*, trans. di Tommaso, 175.

and also a sonic one, as they echo the poet's words back across his poetic world while also preventing them from travelling beyond its borders. Boiardo emphasises additionally that it is only because he cannot talk to his beloved that he is forced to turn to the mountains to hear his plight, conflating his sound in performance with his imagined soundscape as he moves quickly from one to the other. In doing so, Boiardo is telling us directly that this place is fictitious, and it both acts as an imagined listener, whilst also reflecting his emotional state.

This is connected to the common theme of the poet throwing his words to the wind—that is, abandoning his hope of them being heard by the beloved, and instead casting them into his imagined landscape. Through this gesture, the poet destabilises the relationship between his real and imagined soundscapes by suggesting the physical transference of sound from one to the other. Cariteo, for example, writes:

Amor con venenosi et aspri strali Non mi lassa posar sol una nocte: Anzi mi fa vegliare in fino al giorno. Poi ritornando lombra dela terra: Vo con gli altri animali: di bosco in bosco Spargendo le mie voci in vano al vento[56]	Love, with venomous and bitter blows, Lets me rest not a single night; Rather it keeps me awake till daylight. Then, returning to the shadows of the earth, I go with the other animals, from wood to wood Scattering my utterances in vain to the wind

Rather like Boiardo, Cariteo here establishes that, because of the pain caused to him by his beloved, he is forced to release his cries to his landscape. These words are thus in vain as, instead of being spoken aloud, they are thrown into the poet's internal world, where only he, alongside the woodland animals and trees he lists as visual elements, can hear them. Again, this directly connects the imagined landscape to the emotions of the poet, whilst also creating a strong resonance between the sounds contained within the landscape and the poet's own enunciation. In the sounding performance of Cariteo's verse, this direct

---

56 *Opera nova del Chariteo*, sig. [B iv] v.

connection actively destabilises the separation of these two worlds by integrating them one into the another.

Andrelini adds to the conceit of the poet's words scattered to the landscape an element of violence:

| Pande fores dixit pande corynna fores. | Open the doors, he says; open the doors. |
| At rapienda dabat celeri sua verba procellae:[57] | But he was giving his words, which ought to be seized, to the swift storm. |

As this verse exemplifies, the integration of the spoken word into the imagined landscape is not always a conscious or desired choice. Here the poet fights futilely to keep control of his utterance rather than giving it willingly, his words forcefully stolen by a storm, a landscape element which in itself reflects the emotional turmoil of their content. The landscape and the natural world here are given autonomous power and presented as characters, able to actively intervene in and interact with the author's spoken word.

The resounding of the landscapes of these poets entails, whether explicitly or implicitly, the collaboration of echo, without which the natural environment would lose its acoustic properties. Rather than being merely an acoustic device, in the world of both the neo-Latin and the lyric poets, Echo itself, or rather herself, is a character as well as a property of the landscape. We can see this duality already in her appearances in both Longus' *Daphnis and Chloe* and Ovid's *Metamorphoses*. Longus' Echo is recognised for her musical abilities during her lifetime, but is dismembered by a jealous Pan after rejecting his advances; Ovid's Echo carries more romantic connotations, as Echo wastes away to nothing but a repeating voice after being rejected by her love Narcissus.[58] In both versions of her tale, Echo's metamorphosis is not as simple as a complete dissolution, but rather leaves in place of her body the volume of space delineated by the reverberation of her sound; she is both anthropomorphic voice, and the environment that

---

57 Andrelini, *Amorum libri quattuor*, sig. [A iv] v.
58 For more on this, see Pauline A. LeVen, *Music and Metamorphosis in Graeco-Roman Thought* (Cambridge, UK: Cambridge University Press, 2020), 107–09.

voice inhabits.⁵⁹ This space is often the mountains and caves of her original mythology, but also becomes the forests, cliffs, and valleys of the poet's landscape, which create natural enclosures in which her resonating voice can exist. In harnessing this version of Echo, the poet is mobilising her as the force which reverberates the sound of his works around his imagined landscape, and as such, poetic invocations of Echo show an awareness of the space and its boundaries in both a real and an imagined manner, whilst also drawing on her as a sympathetic listener and comparator for the poet's plight.⁶⁰

Echo appears thus in the work of Andrelini, as the force prompting the poet's voice to echo in the trees and rocks of the landscape, weaving together the soundscape of nature with the poet's enunciation:

Quaeque cavos montes habitat penetrabilis eccho Ultima defecta verba remittet ope.⁶¹	Echo, which can penetrate everything, lives in the hollow mountains; She will send back the last words with weakened power.

Andrelini here addresses the power of Echo, as she reverberates his sound around the entirety of his imagined landscape. However, despite this great power, she is doomed to repeat only what she hears, and only the "last words" at that, filling her resonant space with fragments. This plays upon the tropes of "Echo poetry," inspired by the original Ovidian tale, such as Angelo Poliziano's famous *L'eco*, where Echo is able to form coherent replies in dialogue with Narcissus through the manipulation of his final questioning words.⁶² Andrelini also plays with Echo's acoustic

---

59 As LeVen notes, the key difference between these two versions of Echo is the contents of her echoing. While Longus' version imitates fragments of music, dance and song, it is Ovid's Echo that repeats words to her listener. LeVen, *Music and Metamorphosis*, 115. See also Judith Deitch, "The Girl He Left Behind: Ovidian imitatio and the Body of Echo in Spenser's 'Epithalamion'," in *Ovid and the Renaissance Body*, ed. Goran V. Stanivukovic (Toronto: University of Toronto Press, 2001), 224–38, at 226; Melissa A. Yinger, "Echo-Critical Poetic Narcissisms: Being Transformed in Petrarch, Ronsard, and Shakespeare" (PhD diss., University of California Santa Cruz, 2016), 14.
60 Ilic, "In Pursuit of Echo," 162.
61 Andrelini, *Amorum libri quattuor*, sig. E ii v.
62 Rispetto 36 in the online edition of Poliziano's *Rime*: http://www.bibliotecaitaliana. it/testo/bibit001113 (transcribed from Poliziano, *Rime*, ed. Daniela Delcorno

properties, drawing attention to the hollowness of her landscape and the weakening force of her reverberations.

Besides mountains, forests are also amenable settings for Echo's disembodied voice, as we read in Caiado:

| Nostris ut sylvae et praeruptaque saxa sonarent | So that the woods and the steep rocks would resound with our |
| Vocibus omniloquae non notis vocibus echi.[63] | Voices, and with the unknown voices of the many-tongued echo. |

Here Echo's multiple reverberations afford her multiple voices. The sounds being echoed are clearly identified as the voices of poets, but at the same time Echo is a character given a voice separate from the poet's own. It is this distinction that separates the resounding landscape more generally from the specific use of Echo. As we have seen, the utilisation of Echo in this way is common in contemporary pastoral verse and demonstrates the author's awareness of the imagined space their poetry inhabits.[64] But the addition of Echo to a landscape that is already understood as resounding serves to anthropomorphise it, giving it agency in its re-envoicing of the poet's words. The hollow landscape that Echo requires to resound is not just a reflective surface, it is what contains her, and she is made of both sound and the container in which she is heard.[65] Here there is a potential conflict with the poet's conception of his imagined landscape as an extension and representation of himself. It is perhaps for this reason that we do not see Echo featured in the work of Boiardo, despite (or rather, because of) the particular emphasis on landscape and nature elements in his soundscape more generally.

The use of Echo is not limited to the neo-Latin poets. She is named directly in the work of the lyric poets too, though her presence here is reflective of their self-focus, used in a similar manner to the other classical characters that populate their verse—that is, as a comparator to the authorial voice. Rather than her acoustic qualities, it is Echo's

---

Branca [Florence: Accademia della Crusca, 1986]).
63 Caiado, *Aeglogae et sylvae*, sig. B iiii r-v.
64 Ilic, "In Pursuit of Echo," 162.
65 Yinger, "Echo-Critical Poetic Narcissisms," 36–37; Marianne Shapiro, *From the Critic's Workbench: Essays in Literature and Semiotics*, ed. Michael Shapiro (New York: Peter Lang, 2005), 215.

unrequited love and cruel rejection from the Ovidian version of her tale that is the focus of the lyric poets. In Serafino's 1501 oeuvre, a reference to the story of Echo and Narcissus is used as the opening to a *strambotto*: "As Narcissus was cruel to Echo."[66] Serafino does not make use of the sonic element of the character of Echo, a logical omission because during her courtship of Narcissus she has not yet been reduced to mere voice; rather, she is an unrequited lover, just like the poet himself.

Sasso is the only lyric poet in our 1501 sample to make use of Echo in a manner that both mobilises her acoustic properties and focuses on Echo as a sympathetic and comparable character:

uno arbor senza ramo un troncho seccho	a tree without a branch, a dry trunk that longs to hear my laments, my sorrows,
chel mio lamento odir: el mio dolore	
desidera: ascolta el son dolente deccho[67]	listen to the sorrowful sound of Echo

The dead tree-trunk provides a resonant space for the sonic echo, but at the same time it emblematises the withering away of Echo as she turns to nothing but voice. Just as with the neo-Latin poets, Echo is not only her sound but also the environment that contains her. In Sasso this symbolism is particularly strategic. In this verse, her domain is reduced from the great scope of the poet's entire imagined landscape to a much narrower confinement. This helps Sasso to avoid a confusion between his greater resounding landscape, which he deploys as a reflection of the poet, and the closer boundaries of Echo's own resonant space. The "sorrowful sound" makes reference to both Echo's suffering at the hands of Narcissus, and her echoing of the poet's own suffering, as Echo is lacking in voice until she is given speech to repeat.

Birds are among the most abundant producers of natural sounds found across our 1501 poetic corpus.[68] They are often present as listeners,

---

66   "E come ad Eccho fu crudel Narciso." *Soneti del Seraphin*, sig. a [i] v.
67   Sasso, *Strambotti*, sig. a ii v.
68   On the presence of birds in sung verse more broadly, see, of course, Elizabeth Eva Leach, *Sung Birds: Music, Nature, and Poetry in the Later Middle Ages* (Ithaca, NY:

though—lacking in human emotion—they are not always sympathetic to the plight of the author; rather, their sweet, delicate singing offers a contrast to the tormented cries of the author.

In the work of Boiardo, birds are wildly abundant, in line with his focus on nature and landscape in his poetic soundscape. The little birds of his verse are called upon to sing with the poet in a variety of situations, and are present as one of the few distinct actors in the soundscape beyond the poet himself and his beloved. Notably, birds are most present in the first and second of the books into which his published poetry is separated—that is, the books which explore the initial joy, and the onset of despair in the course of Boiardo's imagined romance. In one of the first instances in which Boiardo refers to birds, they are present in a longer list of landscape elements:

Cantati mecho inamorati augelli	Come sing with me you little love-
Poi che vosco a cantare amor me invita	struck birds
E uvi bei rivi e snelli	Since love invites me now to sing with you
Per la piagia fiorita	And you, fair rapid streams
Tenete a le mie rime el tuon suave[69]	Accompany my verse With your sweet voice along your flowered banks[70]

Boiardo's birds are called to accompany him in his verse, as they do for the duration of this madrigal. The happy disposition of the birds is central to their character and is used in this instance to mirror the poet's own joy; the birds, like the poet, are cast as stricken by love. In these happy times, the flock of birds acts as a chorus to the voice of the poet, singing with him in expressing his joy.

However, this joyfulness on the part of the birds soon becomes a contrast for the unhappy sound of the author:

Cornell University Press, 2007).
69 Boiardo, *Sonetti e Canzone*, fol. 3r–v.
70 Boiardo, *Amorum Libri*, trans. di Tommaso, 39.

Cum que dolce conceto insieme accolti	With what sweet harmony those lovely birds
Se vano ad elbergar quei vagi ocelli	Fly off together to their place of rest
Vegiendo come lombra il mondo velli	Seeing how the shade has veiled the earth
E iragi del gran lume in mar involti	And the great sun's rays absorbed into the sea
Felici ocei, che de ogni cura sciolti	You happy birds, set free from every care
A riposar ne giti leiti e snelli	You cheerfully and swiftly find repose
Hor par chel mio dolor se rinovelli	Just now, it seems my painful song returns
Quando e la notte e non e chi lascolto[71]	When it is night and no one's here to listen[72]

Now, in the second book of Boiardo's verse, where the author is caught up in feelings of despair and sadness at the unrequited nature of his affection, the happy birds contrast with the poet's unhappy state both sonically, in their cheerful song, and temporally, referring back to a happier time in the past. The birds, in comparison to the poet, are free, a condition that we could interpret both practically (they can go where they please), and symbolically (their avian psychology leaves them free of such oppressive emotions). If the poet now finds himself alone in the shadowy night, the birds are connected to the bright light of day, an allegorical reference to the initial happiness of the poet's love.

Whilst Boiardo refers to birds in general terms, the most detailed and dedicated ornithologist among our 1501 poets is Panfilo Sasso. Several particular species of bird, with romantic connotations from the classical and natural worlds, are used to highlight different aspects of Sasso's heartbreak at the hands of his beloved in his verse, whilst adding to the pastoral character of his imagined soundscape. By using the sounds of birds as comparators to his own voice, Sasso deliberately and directly destabilises the distinction between the sound of his verse in performance and the sounds of the landscape setting constructed

---

71   Boiardo, *Sonetti e Canzone*, fol. 30v.
72   Boiardo, *Amorum Libri*, trans. di Tommaso, 177.

within his verse, creating a kind of performative soundscape that is highly characteristic of contemporary pastoral.

Among Sasso's poetic aviary, a popular comparator to the poet's voice is, of course, the swan:

como fa el tristo Cygno quando el more la lingua canta e dice le parole el cuor si struggle se lamenta e duole[73]	as the sad swan does when he dies, the tongue sings and says the words, the heart is torn, complains and grieves

The "swan song" was a popular poetic trope, deriving from an ancient Greek belief that the swan sings most beautifully at the point of their death, and the swan's musicianship won them a common association with the musical gods Apollo and Venus, visible in several contemporary images.[74] In the work of Sasso the swan comparison serves to convey the beauty of the poet's voice, and also to characterise the state of the author as being near death, only able to produce the music that he does because of his great anguish.

Sasso also makes extensive use of the turtledove, both as a comparator and as a distinct contributor to the soundscape:

La tortorella dolorosa e trista dapoi che ha perso la dolce compagna seletta va per boschi e per campagna fuggendo quanto po lhumana vista.[75]	The sorrowful and sad turtledove, since she has lost her sweet companion, wanders through woods and countryside fleeing as far as the human eye can see.

According to the medieval bestiary tradition, the turtledove was believed to mate for life, and at the loss of their mate, never ceased to mourn them.[76] As such it makes an ideal character, either as a sympathetic listener, or

---

73 Sasso, *Strambotti*, sig. [a i] v.
74 See Shephard et al., *Music in the Art of Renaissance Italy*, 142–43, 155, 229, 235, and 238.
75 Sasso, *Opera*, sig. [c iii] r.
76 See, for example, Richard Barber trans., *Bestiary* (Woodbridge: Boydell & Brewer, 1992), 163.

as a comparator to the poet's own lovesick state. The direct identification of the poet with the turtledove, implicit in the verses quoted above, is elsewhere made completely plain by Sasso, who opens one *strambotto*, "Crying, I go like the turtledove without a companion."[77]

The sisters Procne and Philomena, present in their respective forms as swallow and nightingale, can be found as distinct sonic actors in the lyric verse of Sasso, Tebaldeo, and Boiardo. In their final bird forms, the sisters are included in poetic soundscapes as sympathetic listeners who contribute their laments in counterpoint with those of the poet, in a similar manner to the birds already discussed. However, as humans transformed, they more deeply understand the plight of the poet, retaining some of their human attributes despite their metamorphosed state.

Much like with the nymph Echo, the form in which we usually find Procne and Philomena comes from the end of their Ovidian tale. However, in contrast with the case of Echo, the full story surrounding the sisters—that is, the events that lead them to be turned into birds—is largely ignored by the poets. Ann Rosalind Jones has observed that the sisters are often used by Renaissance poets without reference to their violent backstory; instead, their transformation into birds provides an opportunity to use them solely in a pastoral guise.[78] The general reluctance to face the violence of Procne and Philomena's story is certainly in evidence among the Italian poets printed in the early sixteenth century. For example, Petrarch makes explicit reference to the sisters in *canzone* 310, but in the 1503 commented edition of the *Canzoniere*, containing two commentaries from the late fifteenth century by Francesco Filelfo (1476) and Antonio da Tempo (1477), both commentators go no further than simply mentioning their presence.[79] In a later commentary by Giovanni Andrea Gesualdo (1533), upon mention of the sisters he remarks that "here I pass over the fable of Procne and Philomena in silence because it

---

77 "Piangendo vo como la tortorella/ senza compagno." Sasso, *Strambotti*, sig. [c iii] v.
78 Ann Rosalind Jones, "New Song for the Swallow: Ovid's Philomena in Tullia d'Aragona and Gaspara Stampa," in *Refiguring Woman: Perspectives on Gender and the Italian Renaissance*, ed. Marilyn Migiel and Juliana Schesari, (New York: Cornell University Press, 1991), 263–78, at 269–71.
79 Francesco Petrarca, *Petrarcha con doi commenti sopra li sonetti & canzone. El primo del ingeniosissimo misser Francesco Philelpho. Laltro del sapientissimo misser Antonio da Tempo, novamente addito. Ac etiam con lo commento del eximio misser Nicolo Peranzone, overo Riccio marchesiano sopra li Triumphi, con infinite nove acute et excellente expositione* (Venice: per Albertino da Lessona, 1503), fol. 100v.

is well known."[80] As William Kennedy has pointed out, Gesualdo's brief overview of the tale leaves out Tereus' silencing of Philomena and her subsequent communication with her sister.[81] These examples suggest the anxieties of commentators in dealing with the story, especially Tereus' silencing of Philomena. In line with this broader tendency, the vast majority of references to the sisters among our 1501 poets present them solely as beautifully singing birds.

The sisters are mentioned both by name, and also in the guise of their respective species, such that the distinction between bird and mythological character is often hazy. This is seen most frequently in references to nightingales and Philomena, as Philomena features often alone without her sister, and meanwhile the nightingale appears both with and without reference to the Philomena story. For example, in Petrarch's *canzone* 311, the nightingale in question seems unrelated to Philomena:

Quel rossigniuol; che si soave piange	The nightingale, that weeps so sweetly
Forse suoi figli, o sua cara consorte;	Perhaps for her sons, or her dear companion
Di dolcezza empie il cielo, et la campagne	With sweetness she fills the sky, and the fields
Con tante note si pietose et scorte;[82]	With so many piteous and bright notes.[83]

In this case, Petrarch introduces a nightingale whose nest has been pillaged, and the reference to her offspring and mate makes no sense in relation to Philomena's mythological tale. Alone, the nightingale is valued by poets for its beautiful song and as a bird of mourning; as Paul Alpers has noted, the nightingale is a bird very much at home in

---

80 "E taccio qui la favola di Progne and Philomena per esser notissima." Francesco Petrarca, *Il Petrarcha colla spositione di Misser Giovanni Andrea Gesualdo* (Venice: per Giovanni Antonio Nicolini da Sabbio & fratres, 1533), fol. 336r; translation found in William J. Kennedy, *Authorizing Petrarch* (New York: Cornell University Press, 1994), 180.
81 Kennedy, *Authorizing Petrarch*, 180.
82 Petrarca, *Le cose vulgari*, sig. p iiii v.
83 Adapted from Francesco Petrarca, *Canzoniere*, trans. J. G. Nichols (Manchester: Carcanet Press, 2002), 258.

pastoral poetry, associated with shepherds whose frustrated love has isolated them and whose pains are expressed in beautiful lament.[84]

Although in this case it seems that Philomena is not connoted by the bird, in many examples the boundaries are blurred, their identities overlapping. Often our 1501 poets refer to Philomena in ways that seem to disregard aspects of her backstory, as we have already noted above. For example, Boiardo writes:

Lhora del giorno che admar ce invita	That hour that invites us all to love
Dentro dal petto el cor mi raserena	Brings back to me a peace that calms my heart
Vegendo uscir Laurora colorita	Seeing the coloured dawn as it emerges
E ala dolce umbra cantar Philomena[85]	And the softly shadowed Philomena in song[86]

The first quatrain of this sonnet deploys imagery of the dawn, recalling the long poetic tradition of the *alba* (in which nightingales also feature). The poet's imagined landscape moves slowly from nighttime to the early morning, during which Venus is still visible in the sky, as the opening line suggests. This verse comes from Boiardo's first book, in which the poet is still focussed on his happiness and joy in the early stages of his imagined romance, his sweet song yet to turn to the bitter weeping that will shortly follow. As such, the mood of the overall work is one of peacefulness, though perhaps carrying the implication that the poet is aware that the happiness he feels will be fleeting. Philomena is not introduced as a character connoting loss or sadness, nor is her presence explained as a sympathetic listener to the plight of the poet. Instead, she softly sings as the poet's imagined landscape moves from night to dawn, her only contribution the nocturnal warbling of her nightingale song. In this respect, Boiardo's use of Philomena as bird rather than tragic princess is in line with his broader tendency not to populate his poetic landscape with classical characters.

---

84 Paul Alpers, *What is Pastoral?* (Chicago, IL: The University of Chicago Press, 1996), 56.
85 Boiardo, *Sonetti e Canzone*, fol. 7r.
86 Boiardo, *Amorum Libri*, trans. di Tommaso, 59.

In contrast, Philomena is one of the most prevalent classical characters in Sasso's verse, appearing well over a dozen times across the *Opera* and *Strambotti*. Here, she features as a sympathetic listener whose beautiful and mournful song can provide positive comparisons for the author to draw upon. At the beginning of a work she may feature to set a scene, giving a soundtrack to the dawn (as we saw in Boiardo): "When I rise and hear Philomena sing so sweet."[87] In this example, Philomena is an inspiring force, whose laments are characterised by their sweetness, prompting the author to sing beautifully of his own agony. Her presence at dawn keeps her firmly within the realm of nature, rather than mythology, connecting her with the nightingale as bird. A similar usage can be found at the close of a sonnet, where Philomena features as a comparator for the author: "and Philomena returns to her lament."[88] At this moment in the poem, all hope is gone, and Philomena's lament works as a comparator to Sasso's eternal suffering and his continuous cries and tears, as his imagined world is again shrouded in the darkness of night.

It is apparent that, of the two sisters, Philomena appears in the work of our 1501 lyric poets much more frequently than Procne. Whilst this could be explained by the poetic ubiquity of the nightingale, making Philomena a more popular trope to include generally, the anxieties displayed over the original story of the sisters suggest that matters may be more complex. Of the two sisters, the actions of Philomena do not transgress gender boundaries to the same extent as those of Procne; she is not a wife and does not commit infanticide. As a result, Philomena lends herself to being a more advantageous and sympathetic comparator.

Despite the general avoidance of the more violent dimensions of the sisters' story, some aspects of it are used by both Tebaldeo and Sasso. In Tebaldeo's verse, he makes direct reference to the cause of Procne and Philomena's lamentations:

---

87 "Quando me levo e sento philomena/ cantar si dolce." Sasso, *Opera*, sig. [q iii] v.
88 "et torna Philomena al suo lamento." Sasso, *Opera*, sig. [m iv] r.

> E progne: e Philomena che se
>   lagnano
> De lonta di Tereo a veder
>   vengono
> I pianti mei [...][89]

> And Procne and Philomena, who
>   lament
> Of the shame of Tereus, they come
>   to see
> My cries [...]

The sisters cry because of "the shame of Tereus;" that is, it is as a result of his actions that they have been turned to birds and now mourn their situation. Tebaldeo is the only 1501 poet to name Tereus, the husband of Procne, in his poetry. It seems unlikely the poet wishes to suggest the violence committed by Tereus could be comparable to the pain the beloved has caused him with her rejection. Instead, by putting the blame for their transformation on another, Tebaldeo makes the sisters more sympathetic characters, as their situation was out of their control, just as the poet has no control over his love or over the actions of his beloved that cause him pain. As characters who have been wronged and suffered as a result, presented here as distinct actors within the soundscape, we hear them lamenting their own pains, and they are present to hear the sound of the author, their sympathy implying that his sorrow is as great as theirs.

Sasso, in contrast, places the blame with the sisters themselves:

> con dolci versi Progne e
>   Philomena
> piange cantando la sua antiqua
>   poena[90]

> with sweet verses, Procne and
>   Philomena
> weep, singing of their ancient
>   punishment

Sasso does not mention Tereus, and so unlike Tebaldeo he does not suggest the sisters are characters who have been wronged. Instead, by asserting that the sisters sing as a result of their "ancient punishment," Sasso positions them as almost repentant, regretful of their prior actions, even though those actions are not directly described. It is perhaps also significant that Sasso calls the punishment "ancient;" though this could be taken to refer to the myth, it also suggests that the metamorphosis itself is old, and the sisters have existed as birds ever since. In general, in his use of the sisters, Sasso strikes a balance between utilising their

---

89 Tebaldeo, *Soneti, capituli et egloghe*, sig. [f iv] v.
90 Sasso, *Opera*, sig. [c iii] r.

mythology more fully, and adapting their story to his own benefit. Philomena is among the classical characters most often encountered in his verse, and, as we will later see, he tends to paint her in a sympathetic light so that he, as author, can transform into her and steal her beautiful singing voice to express his own pains.

The title given to this section, "landscape," with the implication of representations of natural sounds, is perhaps a little misleading, for, as we have seen in the lyric poets' manipulation of landscape elements, all these sonic contributors remain at the mercy of the poet—they are more artful than naturalistic. In the presence of Echo, we can see that in comparison to the neo-Latin poets, the vernacular lyric poets are careful not to invoke her in such a manner as to lose control of their environments, and as such do not mention her directly at all or relegate her to smaller spaces where her presence is more easily managed. Meanwhile, we have seen how birds can be harnessed as an audience to the poet in his landscape setting, or specific species used to feature as positive comparators to his sound. The landscape, and of course also its sonic aspects, are entirely fictitious, created by the lyric poet to stage his imagined romance; thus we are dealing with a landscape more comparable to a theatre set than a naturalist's sketch. Rather than imply a contemporary view of an idealised natural environment, this particular landscape reveals the purpose of the text in advancing the self-fashioning of the poet and the construction of his narrative.

2.3 The Beloved

Serafino Aquilano, *Soneti del Seraphin* (Brescia: per Bernardino Misinta, [1501])

Matteo Maria Boiardo, *Sonetti e Canzone del Poeta Clarissimo Matheo Maria Boiardo Conte di Scandiano* (Venice: per Giovanni Battista Sessa, 1501)

Benedetto Gareth, *Opera nova del Chariteo* (Venice: per Giorgio Rusconi, [1501–09])

Horace, *Horatius* (Venice: Aldo Manuzio, 1501)

Francesco Petrarca, *Le cose vulgari di messer Francesco Petrarcha* (Venice: Aldo Manuzio, 1501)

Panfilo Sasso, *Strambotti del clarissimo professore dele bone arte miser Sasso Modoneso* (Rome: per Johannem Besicken & Martinum de Amsterdam, 1501)

Panfilo Sasso, *Opera del praeclarissimo poeta miser Pamphilo Sasso modenese. Sonetti. CCCCVII. Capituli XXXVIII. Egloge V.* (Venice: Bernardino Viani, 1501)

Antonio Tebaldeo, *Soneti, capituli et egloghe* (Milan: per Giovanni Angelo Scinzenzeler, 1501)

The sound of the poet's beloved, the woman of his desires, features as the most widespread female actor in the soundscapes of the lyric poets. This beloved is most often an imagined character created in the mind of the poet, and as such she is presented to us as in an idealised form, constructed for the purposes of the verse rather than as a true reflection of a real-life person or series of events. Notably, like Petrarch's own Laura, the beloved as character is often named, such as Cariteo's Luna, or Tebaldeo's Flavia, and this name can be manipulated by the poet to different ends. A notable outlier in this is Boiardo, who represents a seemingly very real person as his beloved. In an acrostic across the first thirteen poems of Boiardo's printed works, and then again in another acrostic in the following sonnet, we are given the name "Antonia Caprara." As Andrea di Tommaso has noted, this name does not lend itself to the same manipulation nor carry the symbolism that Petrarch's Laura or the beloveds of the other poets do, and instead appears to be a reflection of a wholly real person, though still of course in the idealised form captured by the poet's mind and represented in his verse.[91]

The beloved's role in Petrarchan verse is as an embodiment of perfection. Central to her character is her unobtainability for the poet, separated from him by an impenetrable barrier, such as marriage or social class, that makes the imagined romance clearly unrequited from the beginning. Due to this distance, the poet worships her through his verse, and his role in recording and recounting her beauty is just as crucial as his own desire for her.[92] In the poet's verse, the beloved is elevated into an ideal, in both her physical beauty and her other qualities. Thanks to her embodiment of an ideal, her textual presence elevates the poet's verse, bringing him fame and recognition as writer and performer, whilst also turning his verse into a performance of his

---

91 See di Tommaso, "Introduction," in Boiardo, *Amorum Libri*, 8–9.
92 William J. Kennedy, *Jacopo Sannazaro and the Uses of Pastoral* (London: University Press of New England, 1983), 38.

neoplatonic contemplation of the divine beauty of the metaphysical world, as it is echoed in the material beauty of the beloved.[93]

The beloved's presence in lyric verse is entirely constructed by the poet: as Aileen Astorga Feng has observed, she sees herself converted from the idea of a person to an image, from image to possession, and from possession to projection.[94] Her sound, too, is idealised, as we will shortly see. However, at the same time, the poet enters into his relationship with the beloved passively, as one to whom love happens rather than one who seeks it out, and he must suffer its effects. This means that whilst the beloved is merely a construction of the author, she is granted a strange kind of agency in her great power over the poet.[95]

Across the lyric corpus, the voice of the beloved is characterised by "sweet" sounds, be it in laughter, speech, or song. As Sara Sturm-Maddox has noted, Petrarch's frequent references to Laura's sweet laughter and speech derive directly from Horace's praise of his own mistress in his *Odes*, who he describes as his "sweetly laughing, sweetly talking Lalage."[96] There are dozens of examples of the beloved's sweet voice in our 1501 poetry: Tebaldeo, for instance, speaks of the beloved's "sweet speech" that is both "gentle and pious."[97] The sweet quality of the beloved's voice is a component of her sweet nature overall, and is among the characteristics that bring the poet under her sway.

Sasso uses this feature extensively in constructing his textual beloved, surpassing even Petrarch in describing the sweetness of her sound. He mentions the sweetness of her various attributes—including her laughter, speech, and song—no less than sixty times across his *Opera*

---

93   On this vein in the Renaissance philosophy of love, see, among many others, Thomas Hyde, *The Poetic Theology of Love: Cupid in Renaissance Literature* (Newark, DE: University of Delaware Press, 1986), 92–110.
94   Aileen Astorga Feng, *Writing Beloveds: Humanist Petrarchism and the Politics of Gender* (Toronto: University of Toronto Press, 2017), 4.
95   Ross Knecht, "'Invaded by the World': Passion, Passivity, and the Object of Desire in Petrarch's *Rime sparse*," *Comparative Literature* 63.3 (2011), 235–52, at 237.
96   "Dulce ridentem Lalagen amabo,/ Dulce loquentem." *Horatius*, sig. b iiii v; Sara Sturm-Maddox, *Petrarch's Laurels* (Philadelphia: University of Pennsylvania Press, 1992), 47.
97   "e cum dolce parlar mansueto e pio." Tebaldeo, *Soneti, capituli et egloghe*, sig. l i r.

and *Strambotti*.⁹⁸ Indeed, the sweetness of her voice is frequently touted as a remedy by Sasso:

O parola suave et amorosa	Oh sweet and loving word
o medicina piena di dolceza	oh medicine full of sweetness
alla piagha crudel: e sanguinosa⁹⁹	to the cruel and bloody wound

This example is exceptional in the violence the beloved inflicts upon the lover in his pain; and yet it is the sweet sound of her voice that will heal the injury, creating the kind of contradiction that is typical of Petrarchan-inspired verse.

Boiardo, in contrast, links the sweetness of the beloved's sound with her angelic nature:

Io sento anchor nel spirto il dolcie thono	I hear still in my soul the sweet tones
De langelica voce e le parole	Of that angelic voice and the words are still
Formate dentro al cor anchor mi sono	Now being formed down deep within my heart.
Questo fra tanta zoglia sol mi dole	Just this amid such joy does cause me pain
Che tolto mha fortuna il revederle	That Fortune keeps me now from hearing them again
Quando vedro piu mai nel dolcie dire	When will I ever see in such sweet speech
Da quelle rose discoprir le perle¹⁰⁰	The pearls revealed again beneath those roses?¹⁰¹

Here we are given two examples of the beloved's sweetness in sound: she produces both angelic "tones" or "notes" (*thono*), and sweet speech (*dire*).

Boiardo describes the speech of the beloved in this example without giving her words—the beloved is talking, but her actual words evade description. Instead, they are transmuted into the beautiful sight of her

---

98 For example, respectively: "dolce riso," Sasso, *Opera*, sig. [g iv] r; "parlar dolce," sig. f ii v; "dolce canto," sig. [m iii] r.
99 Sasso, *Opera*, sig. g [i] r.
100 Boiardo, *Sonetti e Canzone*, fols. 40v–41r.
101 Boiardo, *Amorum Libri*, trans. di Tommaso, 229.

teeth and lips, pearls and roses, her sound viewed, rather than heard, through the male gaze. This mention of the beloved's words formed by pearls and roses derives from Petrarch, who describes Laura's speech in similar terms:

> Perle et rose vermiglie, ove l'accolto
> Dolor formava ardenti voci et belle;
> Fiamma i sospir; le lagrime cristallo.[102]

> Pearls and crimson roses where gathered Sorrow formed ardent beautiful words
> Her sighs a flame, her tears as though of crystal.[103]

By creating an image of the beloved in speech rather than reporting her words, she is almost caught in the moment before speech, her utterance serving not to generate meanings on her own account but only as a fragment of the image of her that the poet assembles piece by piece in his verse. Boiardo even tells us that he is speaking only of a memory conjured in his heart, for the cruelty of Fortune keeps them apart. But so sweet and angelic is her sound in his memory, that it escapes capture and transcription. This is the general pattern across our 1501 lyric corpus: the beloved is granted only this very narrow range of expression, existing as a perfected ideal, and we are given access to her voice only through the poet's recollection of her sound in snapshots, rarely appearing as any tangible utterance that would grant her greater autonomy.[104] By withholding her discourse, the beloved can be sonically painted as otherworldly, something that we will later see leads to more negative portrayals of her sound when she is once again restored to motion.

While most abundantly heard alone, the sound of the beloved is also frequently used in juxtaposition to the sound of the author, to highlight the depths of despair to which the poet has been sent. This is frequently presented within a series of comparisons involving both sound and other elements, as in this example from Sasso:

---

102 Petrarca, *Le cose vulgari*, sig. [i v] r.
103 Francesco Petrarca, *Petrarch: The Canzoniere, or Rerum Vulgarium Fragmenta*, trans. Mark Musa (Bloomington, IN: Indiana University Press, 1999), 249.
104 Ronald L. Martinez, "Mourning Laura in the Canzoniere: Lessons from Lamentations," *MLN* 118.1 (2003), 1–45, at 26.

> Tu voli col desio: io lale ho rotte
> tu canti in piaggia florida et amena
> io piango fra spelonche e cave grotte[105]

> You fly with desire, I have broken my wings,
> you sing on a blooming and pleasant hillside,
> I weep among caverns and caves.

Here we are presented with a dialogue of extremes, with the imagined location adding to the meaning of the sound being produced; the author's weeping will echo back only on him within his cave, whereas the beloved's song can fly through the imagined landscape and be heard by the poet still. The caverns and caves paint the poet in the role of Echo, a character who we have already seen as a sympathetic comparator and listener; and so the poet, like Echo, wastes away. Sasso's acoustic confinement within the cave serves to emphasise that the beloved is unaware of his plight, despite her profound effect on him.

In addition to her song, the beloved's laughter in particular is often used to suggest her indifference to the sound of the author and to highlight the one-sided nature of the relationship. Tebaldeo uses this trope when he says:

> Se or piango: ridi: sio mi golio e lagno
> tu canti: ahime glie cosa iniusta al danno
> pari non esser nui come al guadagno[106]

> If now I weep, you laugh, if I grieve and lament
> you sing, alas, it is an injustice that to us the harm is not equalled by the gain

This immediate contrast between the beloved laughing and the poet lamenting or crying is commonplace, and serves to convey the beloved's cruelty, sometimes even implying that she is laughing at the author in his plight. These are the very same audible qualities, laughter and song, that are elsewhere described as sweet: whether given a positive or a negative valence, the beloved's sonic interventions remain restricted to the same limited repertoire.

As Nancy Vickers argued in her classic article on the fragmentation of Petrarch's Laura, the beloved of the Petrarchan idiom is scattered throughout the verse, her "sweet" sound often heard alongside

---

[105] Sasso, *Opera*, sig. p ii v.
[106] Tebaldeo, *Soneti, capituli et egloghe*, sig. [h iii] r.

descriptions of her clear or angelic face, or her blonde hair, but never adding up to the sum of a whole person. Vickers writes: "When more than one part figures in a single poem, a sequential, inclusive ordering is never stressed—her textures are those of metals and stone, her image is that of a collection of exquisitely beautiful, disassociated objects."[107] As we have seen, the beloved's characterisation as a source of sweet sounds usually excludes the possibility of reporting actual speech, the imagined idea of her sound already separated from her words.[108] But in addition to this, the sounds of the beloved are fragmented into snippets, appearing in pieces as we hear her only as imagined by the poet; there is no continued sonic presence even in the description of her words, presenting us with a series of idealised sonic moments rather than a complete sonic image of any one scene.

For example, Cariteo presents fragments of the beloved's sound among a list of her other attributes:

Simile il vidi ala belta infinita	I saw her resembling the infinite
Dangelica natura: al chiaro viso	beauty
A la voce: al colore: al lieto riso	Of angelic nature, in the clear face
Ai capei biondi: et ala eta fiorita[109]	The voice, the colour, the joyful laughter
	The blond hair, the blooming age

This is one of very few instances where Cariteo refers to his beloved's sound—in general she is a far quieter character in Cariteo's soundscape in comparison to the other 1501 lyric poets. This may be because, like Petrarch's Laura, Cariteo gives his beloved a name: Luna.[110] As Luna, a name chosen (among other things) for its slippage with *l'una* (the one), Cariteo's beloved is immune to change, and commonly presented as a more distant figure, reducing her sonic influence. However, in this instance, Cariteo speaks of both hearing and seeing his beloved; she is angelic, with joyful laughter, and the visual description of her is separated into a few desirable characteristics. We gain a vague sketch

---

107 Nancy J. Vickers, "Diana Described: Scattered Woman and Scattered Rhymes," *Critical Inquiry* 8.2 (1981), 265–79, at 266.
108 Sturm-Maddox, *Petrarch's Laurels*, 48.
109 *Opera nova del Chariteo*, sig. [A iii] v.
110 Kennedy, "Citing Petrarch in Naples," 1205; and Kennedy, *The Site of Petrarchism*, 68–69.

of her hair, of her face, but what we are given fails to add up to a complete picture of her, and our view of her, including the sound of her voice, feels more like a perfected memory than a description of a real person. Her laughter is separated from her voice in a manner which reduces their feeling of audibility; they do not seem like descriptors of desirable sound, but rather descriptors of desirability more generally. The effect of the disjointed and frozen manner with which the beloved's sounds are intermingled with her physical attributes is to reduce their agency in the wider soundscape.

A similar example can be found in the verse of Sasso:

Le labre rosse: e le dolce parole	The red lips, and the sweet words
un canto ben soave: e misurato	a song, soft and measured
el riso un prato adorno de viole[111]	the laughter a meadow adorned with violets

Sasso's description is fragmented, separating both the sound and sight of his beloved into a list of idealised parts. Like Boiardo with his pearls and roses, Sasso moves between sound and sight, rendering his beloved's laughter as a flower-strewn meadow, converting the audible to the visible. The lyric poets, like Petrarch before them, have reduced their beloved to parts and scattered her throughout their verse. Her sound, which could threaten to escape such treatment, is reduced to image so that it too may be broken into parts; thus, an aspect of the beloved that could potentially eclipse the sound of the poet himself in its perfection is both celebrated and silenced.

The Homeric Sirens appear throughout our 1501 verse most commonly in association with the beloved. Indeed, they are among the most widespread classical characters used as comparators to the beloved within our corpus, featuring in the work of all the lyric poets apart from Cariteo.[112] With their terrifying ability to pull men and ships to their destruction, the Sirens make for an obvious reference point for the sound of the beloved, who in her imagined mistreatment of the poet

---

111 Sasso, *Opera*, sig. b [i] r.
112 As previously mentioned, Cariteo's Luna is a notably "quiet" beloved, and so her lack of a sonic comparator is not surprising.

dooms him to the same fate as those who hear the Sirens, pulled in by her sweet voice only to lose his life.[113]

We see this sonic attribute utilised in a wide range of manners, featuring both in quick references and also in much longer passages where the beloved as Siren appears in an imagined scene. At the more erudite end of the scale, Tebaldeo uses their classical tale as a whole to speak of the dangers of love when he says:

Fa che nel savio greco tu te spechi	Let yourself be mirrored in the wise Greek
che per fugir il suon dolce e fallace	who to escape the sweet and deceitful sound
de le Sirene a se chiuse lorechi[114]	of the Sirens closed his own ears

In literal terms, this is a reference to Odysseus, who in Homer's *Odyssey* had his crew stop their ears with wax so they would not fall victim to the Sirens' song as his ship passed by. However, it is also a clear implication of the passage that the beloved is cast in the role of Siren, the characteristic sweetness of her voice now turned against her, for though sweet, her sound is also deceitful. The wording of this passage is reminiscent of Petrarch's own reference to the same classical myth:

| [...] et di Sirene al suono Chiuder gliorecchi: et anchor non men'pento; | [...] and to Siren sounds I should have closed my ears; and yet I don't regret |
| Che di dolce veleno il cor trabocchi.[115] | That the heart overflows with such sweet poison.[116] |

Petrarch too speaks of how he should have "closed his ears," but follows this by asserting his lack of regret at his reckless actions, for the love he experienced as a result was worth the pain. Again, the sweetness of the beloved, though not described as audible in this case, becomes a toxic attribute. In these passages, both poets speak from an attitude

---

113 Elena Laura Calogero, "'Sweet alluring harmony': Heavenly and Earthly Sirens in Sixteenth- and Seventeenth-Century Literary and Visual Culture," in *Music of the Sirens*, ed. Linda Phyllis Austern and Inna Naroditskaya, (Bloomington, IN: Indiana University Press, 2006), 140–75, at 141.
114 Tebaldeo, *Soneti, capituli et egloghe*, sig. e [i] v.
115 Petrarca, *Le cose vulgari*, sig. l iii v.
116 Petrarca, *Petrarch: The Canzoniere*, trans. Musa, 305.

of reflection, a common theme in the use of the Sirens. Notably, it is implied that the poet had the option not to hear the Siren; in proposing their regret over their actions, the poets tell us that the result—their heartbreak and sorrow—was in fact an avoidable outcome.

In other cases, in contrast, the Sirens are used precisely to suggest the powerlessness of the poet against the pull of the beloved; there was no choice involved and no ability to resist. Sasso deploys the Sirens in this manner when he directly conflates the image of the beloved with the sound and sight of her as a Siren:

Che ascoltate? le sue dolce parole non ve acorgete? che glie una Sirena fara di voi: come de glialtri sole Non guardate la sua faccia serena che qual che locchio tien fermo nel sole perda la vista: e sente affanno e pena[117]	What do you hear? Her sweet words don't you realise? That she is a Siren she will do the same to you as the other sun, Do not look at her serene face for he who holds his eye still in the sun loses his sight, and feels distress and pain

The Siren is present here in her traditional form to serve as a warning, alluding to the sweet words and sounds of the beloved that only serve to hurt and destroy the author. In this case she is given both a visible and an audible dimension, with reference to both her sweet words and her serene face—something which also serves to fragment the Siren across the verse, as we have seen done with the beloved more generally.

In fact, the beloved rarely faces such fragmentation when in Siren guise, because the Sirens themselves are rarely fragmented. In giving her both sound and image, the Siren is established as a separate actor in the soundscape, suggesting that she is an entity outside of the author's control, and thus allowing him to be at her mercy. Indeed, when invoked, the Sirens are often given a landscape to inhabit, whilst retaining both the audible and visible dimensions seen in Sasso's usage. This use of the Sirens amplifies the imagined passivity of the author, who is not an active lover, but one to whom love happens and who must suffer its effects.[118] Serafino tells us that it is both his eyes and his ears that he

---

117 Sasso, *Opera*, sig. b [i] r.
118 Knecht, "Invaded by the World," 237.

must close to the call of his Siren when he says: "Flee my eyes from this siren,/ who with her voice submerges us towards the depths."[119] In this case the watery landscape of the Sirens also serves to tell us more of the author's emotions; the water refers to both the literal sinking of ships by the Sirens, and the depth of emotion to which the beloved sends the author. Additionally, the poet is taken from his traditional landscape of dry land and forests, in which he is established as in control, and forced out to sea to the imaginary landscape of the Sirens, within which he has no power.

The Siren's landscape is explored in more depth by Tebaldeo, who goes to great lengths to describe her setting before introducing her song:

Chio veggio da lontano in mare un scoglio	I see from afar in the sea a rock whence my star leads me directly,
ove la stella mia dritto me mena e di fortuna ognhor crese lorgoglio	and with fortune every hour my pride grows;
E sentovi cantare una syrena che per forza mi tira ove io non voglio	And I hear a siren singing there, who by force pulls me where I do not wish to go
tanto ho del suo bel son lorcchia piena[120]	so full is my ear of her beautiful sound

The Siren is given both an audible and a visible dimension by the poet, her setting sketched in, creating her as a distinct actor who exerts considerable control in her own habitat. Rather than presenting a snapshot as we saw often in the case of the beloved alone, there is the suggestion of the passing of time, and movement. The poet—as a character appearing in his own fiction—begins the scene a distance away from his Siren, and it is her image that he first encounters, perhaps too far away initially to hear her sound. The suggestion of being led by the stars and fortune, frequently invoked in lyric verse as markers of a turning point in the romance, indicates the inevitability of the meeting of the two characters within this imagined landscape, the poet powerless to prevent it. It is only after Tebaldeo has explored the detailed visual

---

119 "Fugite ochi mei questa syrena:/ Che con sua voce ci submerge al basso." *Soneti del Seraphin*, sig. [c iii] v.
120 Tebaldeo, *Soneti, capituli et egloghe*, sig. a ii r.

aspects of the encounter that we are presented with the sonic component of the Siren/beloved: her sweet singing voice pulling him towards her rock. By providing a landscape through which he can journey, Tebaldeo adds to the dimensions of his physical powerlessness to resist the allure of his Siren.

In all of these examples, the presence of the Siren in the soundscape as a stand-in for the beloved allows the author to show how helpless he is in the face of her sonic perfection, and their presence in the soundscape feels less regulated by the governing view of the author, as it is he who must present himself as at their mercy. By projecting the beloved into the image and sound of the Siren, the author is able to highlight his passivity in first entering into the romance. But, coming full circle, this trope also shows the poet's ability to reflect, at the end of his imagined romance, indicating that once separated from the moment and past the initial enchantment, he can rationally recognise the situation he was in. It was just that in the moment, the call, her sound, was irresistible, so great and so beautiful he had no choice but to listen and to fall for her. It is only in this form, which is as threatening as it is sonically perfect, that the beloved escapes the confines of sound reduced to image and fragmented across the verse.

2.4 The Author

Publio Fausto Andrelini, *Amorum libri quattuor* (Venice: per Bernardino Vitali, 1501)

Serafino Aquilano, *Soneti del Seraphin* (Brescia: per Bernardino Misinta, [1501])

Matteo Maria Boiardo, *Sonetti e Canzone del Poeta Clarissimo Matheo Maria Boiardo Conte di Scandiano* (Venice: per Giovanni Battista Sessa, 1501)

Henrique Caiado, *Aeglogae et sylvae et epigrammata Hermici* (Bologna: Benedetto Faelli, 1501)

Benedetto Gareth, *Opera nova del Chariteo* (Venice: per Giorgio Rusconi, [1501–09])

Ovid, *Ovidio Metamorphoseos vulgare* (Venice: per Cristoforo Pensi ad instantia de Lucantonio Giunta, 1501)

Francesco Petrarca, *Le cose vulgari di messer Francesco Petrarcha* (Venice: Aldo Manuzio, 1501)

Panfilo Sasso, *Strambotti del clarissimo professore dele bone arte miser Sasso Modoneso* (Rome: per Johannem Besicken & Martinum de Amsterdam, 1501)

Panfilo Sasso, *Opera del praeclarissimo poeta miser Pamphilo Sasso modenese. Sonetti. CCCCVII. Capituli XXXVIII. Egloge V.* (Venice: Bernardino Viani, 1501)

Antonio Tebaldeo, *Soneti, capituli et egloghe* (Milan: per Giovanni Angelo Scinzenzeler, 1501)

As the central protagonist of his own verse, it is not surprising that the most frequently "heard" element in our 1501 poetic corpus is the voice of the author. This strategy of audible self-construction is found principally in the shorter poetic forms, which are more commonly presented as first-person narrative accounts. In these works, the focus of the verse is the emotional experience of the author as he rides the highs and lows of his romance with his beloved. Even though the romance is imagined (albeit that it may reference real-life events), it is important that it is believable for the success of the verse. The poet creates for himself a poetic persona, which in the performance of his work he must be imagined to inhabit entirely. To do this, the poet has to create a consistent image of himself that works with the crossover between his fictional voice as a character in his own narrative, and his "real-life" sound in the performance of his verse. As a result, the sonic "image" he creates for himself is essential to the verse's success, allowing the poet to imbue his poetry with certain qualities to be related to the verse's sounding performance, but also providing structure to the narrative contained within the verse itself.

Sound and music are intrinsically tied to the main story of unrequited love that the poet, through his poetic persona, is aiming to create. When the poet first falls for his beloved, it is this great love that inspires him to sing and create his verse; later, the expressions of his pain help to distinguish a new chapter within the relationship—the poet has realised the hopelessness of his actions and that his love will remain unrequited, but the great emotion caused by his rejection leaves him with no option but to express his pain aloud in his verse. The "I" of this verse then represents both the poet (that is, the real-life executant of the verse), and the poetic persona fashioned within the verse; in performance these two personas, though distinct, had to become one and the same for a compelling and successful recital.

This interplay between the poet as character and the poet as performer can be seen in the use of singing in the verse. We have already noted how the expression of the verse as sung can be linked to its performance, relating to the audible nature of the verse in this form. In these cases, the singing is done by the poet in the present tense, it is happening in the moment, and can be understood as addressing both the real and imagined audience of the verse.[121] But the poet may also describe himself as singing when he expresses the emotions felt early in his imagined relationship; when the poet as a character is still hopeful that his feelings may be returned, he sings, and his song is characterised as sweet and joyful:

Cosi cantando me ne vo legiero	And so with a light heart singing I
Enon temo de colpi de fortuna[122]	am off
	Not fearing what the strokes of Fortune bring[123]

Here, Boiardo expresses a kind of carefree singing, yet to be weighed down by the pain and rejection that will follow. The threat of what fortune may bring looms ominously, both suggesting that this is the happy high point of the imagined romance, and also foreboding that the future can only bring less genial times.

Singing is often used as an expression of the joy felt by the poet in the early stages of his romance. It plays this role not only in the moment that those early stages take place, but also in recollections of them from later points in his narrative arc, creating a key sonic juxtaposition between the happiness of the past and the pain of the present. Cariteo, for instance, neatly describes how his past songs for his beloved have been twisted by the pain he feels as a result of his unrequited love:

---

121 Holmes, *Assembling the Lyric Self*, 174.
122 Boiardo, *Sonetti e Canzone*, fol. 6v.
123 Boiardo, *Amorum Libri*, trans. di Tommaso, 55.

Una volta cantai soavemente:	Once I sang sweetly
Et cantando ad amore il core apersi:	And singing, I opened my heart to love
Hor son noiosi et aspri li mei versi:	Now my verses are noisome and bitter
Hor crido lachrimando amaramente.	Now I cry out, weeping bitterly
Ne pianger posso tanto occoltamente[124]	Nor can I weep so secretly as once I did.

Whilst at the beginning his voice, and by extension his verse, was sweet, and he sang with an open heart, he has been forced to turn to bitter weeping; unable to sway his beloved with his once sweet verse, he is left with nothing but to sing of his pain. This pain is so great that his weeping cannot be disguised, and there is the suggestion that the character of the author even seeks out this suffering in order to experience the ennobling effects of love.[125] Singing in this case both connects the internal soundscape of the poetry to its real-world performance, and also refers back to an earlier point in the narrative of the poet's love, when he is still hopeful and his beloved acts as the inspiration for joyful and sweet performance. The changing sound of the authorial voice, from singing to weeping, serves a narrative function for the reader, articulating our progress through the imagined romance.

In Boiardo's verse, his neat separation of his work into three books structures the narrative in a more overt manner. If the first book is full of the poet's hopeful singing, at the opening to the second book, when Boiardo is newly grieving the hopelessness of his emotions, we can see the turn from sweet songs to bitter tears and laments:

---

124 *Opera nova del Chariteo*, sig. F [i] r–v.
125 For more on this specifically in the verse of Cariteo see Claudia Fanti, "L'elegia properziana nella lirica amorosa del Cariteo," *Italianistica* 14 (1985), 23–44, at 26.

Chi sia che ascolti el mio grave lamento	Who is there that will hear my grave lament
Miseri versi e doloroso stile	My wretched verses, and my doleful style
Con versi dal cantar dolce e gentile	Converted from a sweet and gentle song
A ragionar di poena e di tormento	To messages of torment and pain
Cangiato e in tuto il consueto accento	My usual tone has been completely changed
E le rime damore alte sutile	As have my love rhymes, once sublime and light
E son si fatto disdegnoso e vile	
Che sol nel lamentare mi so contento[126]	And I've become so bitter and so base
	I find contentment only in laments[127]

As in the example from Cariteo, Boiardo now refers to his hopeful singing as a past action. We are again presented with a host of contrasts: the controlled singing heard previously is established as the poet's "usual tone," meaning that the weeping and expressions of pain that are to follow are exceptional, only possible as a result of the new heights of negative emotion to which the poet has been sent, moving from an extreme of joy to an extreme of despair. It is this version of the authorial voice that is most prevalent in general. Indeed, it is this version of the poet that Petrarch presents in the opening of the *Canzoniere*—one of wretchedness in the present tense.[128]

The audibility of the poet's pain can also stretch beyond his lamenting, and we are occasionally presented with other audible expressions of pain that are not vocal in nature. In the case of Serafino, his whole body is forced to cry out:

El corpo lasso dal dolor suspinto	My body so tired from the pain,
Soccorso ad alta voce indarno chiama:[129]	In vain calls aloud for help.

---

126 Boiardo, *Sonetti e Canzone*, fols. 18v–19r.
127 Boiardo, *Amorum Libri*, trans. di Tommaso, 119.
128 Cynthia N. Nazarian, *Love's Wounds: Violence and the Politics of Poetry in Early Modern Europe* (New York: Cornell University Press, 2017), 12.
129 *Soneti del Seraphin*, sig. c ii v.

In doing this, Serafino introduces a separation between his voice and the physicality of his body, adding to the suggestion that his expression of pain is beyond his control. The pain caused by his unrequited love is so deep that the sounds he produces are untethered from his rational faculty; and even more than that, in his exhaustion from the constant state of lament in which he finds himself, his body has had to find new ways to express its pain. This separation also allows Serafino to comment on the hopelessness of his own body's expression of pain—he knows it cries in vain, and that there is no solution in view.

This state of exhaustion, the inevitable approach to the end as body and soul can take no more, is characteristic of the last of the three books into which Boiardo organises his verse. This third and final stage in his amorous journey is far quieter than the others, the poet both coming to terms with his grief and also having reached such a level of exhaustion and exertion that he is no longer capable of sound, only of the quiet acceptance of his fate:

Se in moriente voce ultimi pregi	If in a dying voice these final prayers
Han forza di pietade in alcun core	Can stir compassion in another's heart
Odi la voce de un che per te more	Do hear the voice of one who dies for you
Crudel che al fin anchor mercie mi negi[130]	Cruel lady, who denies me mercy at the end[131]

Now the authorial voice is characterised as dying, referring to both the death of the relationship and the end of the poet's weeping. As the hope of romantic fulfilment is the central reason for his existence, the poet as character must die; there is no longer any reason for him to live. The suggestion of mercy on the part of the poet's cruel lady reminds the audience that it is she who has caused the poet harm, and that the author's actions were beyond his own control. This quietness, much like the early singing, and dominant weeping, articulates the arc of the romance, telling us that the authorial voice is speaking to us from the end point of the narrative.

---

130 Boiardo, *Sonetti e Canzone*, fol. 37r.
131 Boiardo, *Amorum Libri*, trans. di Tommaso, 213.

The same final, quiet narrative phase can also be found in Sasso:

> de voce humana mha la doglia privo
> mi maraviglio pur como sia vivo[132]
>
> of human voice has my grief deprived me
> I marvel even that I am still alive

As with Boiardo, Sasso's end inspires ideas of death on the part of the poet as character: he does not understand how he can still be living. Again, the expressions of his pain have been so great as to rob him of his ability to vocalise it any longer; his grief, which once would not permit him to stop his weeping, has eventually deprived him of any voice at all. In this expression of pain, Sasso suggests a metamorphosis on the part of the author as he begins to lose human form—his voice is no longer human, suggesting that he may still be capable of producing sound in some other form. As we will later see, in fact Sasso transforms into a wide range of classical characters in his verse, relating to the wider themes of metamorphosis found throughout his oeuvre.

Whilst essential for creating moving and compelling verse, the sound of the poetic persona's moans, sighs, and cries are not the only way in which the author creates for himself an authorial identity through sound. Alongside, characters from classical mythology are frequently used to generate favourable comparisons to the author, both in the creation of himself as the great unrequited lover (adding to the believability of his wider narrative), and also alluding to the marvellous sound of the verse and its otherworldly qualities as experienced in real-world performance.

The imbuing of the verse with orphic powers is by far the most pervasive and popular trope in this vein. Orpheus rarely features as a distinct actor within the lyric soundscape, instead seen as a character in and of himself in the longer narrative works and in the neo-Latin poetry. For example, we see Orpheus present among a wide range of classical characters in the verse of Caiado:

---

[132] Sasso, *Strambotti*, sig. [a iv] r.

> [...] fidibusque canoris
> Parnasi dominas mulcet citharoedus apollo,
> Hoc modulante lyram: quaerebant orphea sylvae:
> Et curvo delphin portabat ariona dorso.[133]

> [...] and with melodious lyre,
> Apollo the citharodeus gently stirs the mistresses of Parnassus;
> As a result of the lyre playing, the forests were striving towards Orpheus,
> And the dolphin was carrying Arion on his curved back.

Here, Orpheus is present not so that Caiado can draw on him as a comparator, but to set the scene of Parnassus. Caiado's focus is on the power of lyre-playing in classical mythology, including both Orpheus' ability to move the landscape with the sound of his verse, and Arion's rescue by dolphins after attracting them to him through his song. The focus is not on a current performance, or contemporary times, but referring back to an ancient image of these characters, brought together in an imagined scene by the author. In general, when we see Orpheus named directly, it is in these more archaeological references to his mythology, and the purpose is not to suggest comparable qualities in the sound of the author's verse, but to allow the author to display his classical learning, or to set a classicising scene more generally.

In contrast, when he is used as a direct comparator to the authorial voice, Orpheus is rarely named; rather, the connotations carried by the orphic powers with which the poet imbues his verse require no explicit citation. This is something that can be seen right across our 1501 lyric corpus:

> Odeno lachrimando il mio dolore
> Homini et animali arbori et fronde.
> Ma riscaldar non posso il fredo core
> De questa che mascolta et non risponde.[134]

> They hear the crying of my pain
> Men and animals, trees, and foliage.
> But I cannot warm the cold heart
> Of this one, who listens, and does not respond.

In this passage from a *strambotto* by Cariteo, we can see how he expresses the power of his verse over others, as well as over animals and the very

---

133 Caiado, *Aeglogae et sylvae*, sig. [D viii] r.
134 *Opera nova del Chariteo*, sig. [G iv] v.

landscape; but despite the great power of his verse, and its otherworldly abilities, he is unable to sway the heart of his beloved, who hears his verse and is unaffected, choosing to ignore him. The orphic powers with which he imbues his verse are used to establish a stark contrast between the powerful and moving sound of the poet's verse, and its continuing inability to sway the feelings of the beloved, allowing the poet to suggest both his immense poetic and performative powers, and his status as an unrequited lover, feeding into the continuing narrative of his verse. This is one of the most popular applications of the orphic trope by the lyric poets, and through it, the poet is able to combine his creation of a believable narrative of unrequited love with his desire to achieve fame through his verse.[135]

This is not to say that in the frequent use of this trope poets lose their individuality in the creation of their authorial identity. Rather, we can see how the same central principle is executed with marvellous variety across numerous lyric poets. In the case of Boiardo, who, as we have already observed, largely avoids classical references and grounds his soundscape in his imagined landscape, the orphic references tend towards the same objective but are more carefully woven into the fabric of his landscape setting:

Farebe ad ascolatarmi a forza intento	I would oblige not only man to listen, But every beast apart from man as well,
Ogni animal da humanita diviso.	
E se mostrar potesse il dolcie riso,	And if I could describe her gracious smile,
Faria movere e sassi e star il vento[136]	I'd move the rocks and make the winds be still[137]

Whilst the author's sonic control over beasts, rocks and winds is implied, their inclusion focuses less on Boiardo's ability to sway them, and more on their presence within the landscape setting as auditors to his verse. At the same time, the gesture draws attention to the poet's act of sonic

---

135 Nicholas Mann, "From Laurel to Fig: Petrarch and the Structures of the Self," *Proceedings of the British Academy* 105 (2000), 17–42, at 33.
136 Boiardo, *Sonetti e Canzone*, fol. 10r.
137 Boiardo, *Amorum Libri*, trans. di Tommaso, 73.

authorship in singing the landscape and its inhabitants into being. We see something similar again in a later passage from Boiardo:

Ne sol gli ocei ma anchor le petre e londe	Not only the birds, but even rocks and waves
Hanno pieta del mio dolor insano	Have pity on me in my maddening pain
E il fiume apresso e il monte di lontano	And the nearby river and the distant hill
Come io soglio chiama cossi risponde[138]	Respond to me as I call out to them[139]

As before, the author quickly shifts the focus from animals (in this case birds) to landscape elements, creating evocative imagery and a detailed setting that gives a sense of the size and scope of the landscape. Boiardo even writes perspective into his scene—the nearby river, the distant hill—establishing a three-dimensional space within which his verse can acquire a size of its own by echoing to the very edges. As in the previous example, thus, the focus of this orphic moment is the landscape setting, more than the poet's bravura performance—this is Boiardo's distinctive spin on the common trope.

Perhaps the most intensive and impactful use of orphisms can be found in the work of Serafino, who, after his untimely death in 1500, was frequently remembered for his incredible abilities in verse performance.[140] An image of Serafino as an orphic poet, either as Apollo or Orpheus, was created by contemporaries in the years following his death, most notably in the *Vita di Serafino* by Vincenzo Calmeta, and the *Apologia* by Angelo Colocci. Colocci's *Apologia* was first published with the 1503 *Opera*, and Calmeta's *Vita* was first published with the 1504 *Collettanee*, a book containing only poems in praise of Serafino, before being published again with the 1505 edition of the *Opera*.[141] Far more

---

138 Boiardo, *Sonetti e Canzone*, fol. 33v.
139 Boiardo, *Amorum Libri*, trans. di Tommaso, 189.
140 For more on this, see Bortoletti, "Serafino Aquilano and the mask of *Poeta*," 140–42; Wilson, *Apollo Volgare*, 3–5 and 123–28.
141 *Collettanee grece, latine, e vulgari per diversi auctori moderni, nella morte de l'ardente Seraphino Aquilano per Gioanne Philoteo Achillino bolognese in uno corpo ridutte. E alla diva Helisabetta Feltria da Gonzaga duchessa di Urbino dicate* (Bologna: Caligola Bazalieri, 1504); Serafino Aquilano, *Opere del facundissimo Serafino Aquilano collette per Francesco Flauio Sonetti lxxxix Egloghe. iii Epistole yi Capitoli ix. Strasmmoti ccyi barzelette. X.* (Bologna: Girolamo Ruggeri, 1503).

than generic posthumous praise for his abilities in poetic performance, the image of Serafino as Orpheus is one that he created and maintained himself in his verse during his lifetime.[142] Even in the short selection of poetry featured in our 1501 edition of his *strambotti*, we see many examples of Serafino referring to the orphic qualities of his verse:

Se sol per canti humiliar serpenti	If with mere songs one can overcome serpents,
Voltar le stelle e linfernal furore:	Change the stars and the infernal fury,
Et io con i pianti in canti e gran lamenti	
A far humil costei non ho vigore[143]	Yet I, with tears in songs and great laments,
	Have not the strength to overcome her

Rather than provide a lengthy list of landscape elements and characters swayed by the poet's performance, in Serafino's verse we find the very specific use of snakes, making direct reference to the story of Orpheus and Eurydice and the snake that killed Orpheus' beloved. Whilst still playing into the common trope of contrasting the power of the verse to affect others with its impotence over the beloved, this reference to the original story of Orpheus creates a more concrete link between the ancient myth and Serafino's imagined narrative. Serafino and his verse do not just possess orphic powers; Serafino takes on the guise of Orpheus himself. We see this connection repeated in a later *strambotto*:

Ribomba il son de mei gravi lamenti	The sound of my sad laments resounds,
Si che ogni aspro animal con crudel tosto	so that every vicious animal with its cruel venom
Ha compassion de mei tanti tormenti:[144]	has compassion for my many torments

---

142 For a fuller discussion of Serafino and Orpheus, taking into account also the part of his oeuvre not printed in 1501, see Ciara O'Flaherty, "Performative Constructions of Authorship in Italian Vernacular Verse 1470–1550" (PhD diss., University of Sheffield, 2025), 100–05.
143 *Soneti del Seraphin*, sig. b ii r.
144 *Soneti del Seraphin*, sig. b [i] v.

Just as in the previous example, the "vicious animal" with "cruel venom" is clearly a snake; but this time Serafino goes further, suggesting that his song has the power to inspire compassion in the very animal that doomed Eurydice, implying that his abilities may even surpass those of Orpheus. Thus, Serafino creates for himself an image as Orpheus reborn, and the consistency with which he deploys this identity (which is also present in the later 1502 *Opera*) no doubt lent it a degree of authenticity.[145] In general, it is in Serafino's verse that we see the truest union of performed and imagined soundscape, crafting an image of himself within the verse that was fully concordant with the sound and sight of his verse in performance.

There is one of our lyric poets who notably avoids indulging in these orphic tropes. Sasso uses a much wider range of comparators for his authorial voice, in particular deploying a varied array of female classical characters, to construct a highly distinctive authorial identity which is unique among our 1501 lyric poets. As we have seen above, female classical characters most frequently feature among the inhabitants of the wider soundscape of the verse, finding their place either in the poet's imagined landscape, as in the case of the bird-sisters Procne and Philomena or the nymph Echo, or in connection to the beloved, as with the Sirens. In these roles they can be sympathetic listeners to the author, comparators to the sound of the beloved, or the narrative of their own stories can be used for favourable comparison to the plight of the author. However, in the work of Sasso, female classical characters break the boundaries of these roles. Sasso is an outlier in his pervasive and persistent use of female classical characters as comparators and metamorphic destinations for his authorial voice.

The first and perhaps least surprising of these female characters is Echo. We have already seen how this character is utilised by the lyric and neo-Latin poets both as an echoing force in the poets' imagined landscape, and as a sympathetic listener whose own narrative of doomed love makes for a favourable comparison to the author's plight. Sasso takes this one step further, showing us that he himself turns into Echo in a series of quick metamorphoses:

---

145 Serafino Aquilano, *Opere del facundissimo Seraphino Aquilano collette per Francesco Flavio. Sonetti. LXXXIX Egloghe. III Epistole. VI Capitoli IX Strammotti. CCVI Barzelette. X* (Venice: Manfredo Bonelli, 1502).

Hor salamadra son che in foco iace	Now am I a salamander, who is thrown in the fire
e presto aspetto tramutarme in Ecco	and soon I wait to be transformed into Echo
per non haver mai rispondendo pace[146]	that never finds peace in answering

Sasso states that he waits to become Echo, which suggests both his metamorphosis directly into the character, and also that he too, like the nymph, will waste away slowly at the rejection of his beloved until nothing is left but his voice. The final line makes for an interesting contrast with the orphic trope; rather than suggesting the innate power of his verse, the endless echoing of his voice as Echo emphasises its impotence. Although Sasso is unusual in his extensive use of cross-gender self-constructions, in fact this metamorphosis into Echo is not without precedent, as Petrarch too transforms into Echo in *canzone* 23:

[...] i nervi et l'ossa	[...] I felt my bones
Mi volse in dura selce: et cosi scossa	And sinew turn to flint: nothing remains
Voce rimasi de l'antiche some	Now but a voice shaken from my poor frame
Chiamando morte et lei sola per nome.[147]	Calling on death and calling out her name.[148]

In Petrarch, as in Sasso, this is one of many transformations; but unlike Sasso he does not name Echo directly, rather implying that his metamorphosis is the same as hers through the reduction of his body to nothing but voice. Sasso does name Echo, and this is likely in part because the transformation has not yet happened—he "waits to be transformed." By naming Echo, Sasso is able to draw more quickly on her story's wider narrative, and invoke the same sentiment as we find in Petrarch.

Like Echo, Philomena has already been noted, alongside her sister Procne, for her frequent presence in the wider landscape, found particularly in the verse of Tebaldeo and Boiardo in addition to Sasso's own. As we have seen, Philomena features frequently alone in Sasso's

---

146 Sasso, *Opera*, sig. i [i] r.
147 Petrarca, *Le cose vulgari*, sig. b ii r.
148 Petrarca, *Petrarch: The Canzoniere*, trans. Musa, 32–33.

verse, without her sister, and is one of the most prevalent classical characters, appearing well over a dozen times across the *Opera* and *Strambotti*. But she does not just feature prominently as a distinct character; like Echo, Philomena becomes a metamorphic destination for the voice of the author:

Sio potesse mutar in Philomena questo mio corpo afflitto: e lasso tanto cominciarei si doloroso pianto[149]	If I could change into Philomena this body of mine, so afflicted and weary, I would begin such sorrowful weeping

The connotations of Philomena after her metamorphosis into a nightingale, with her beautiful and sorrowful lament, provide an obvious positive comparator for the voice of the author.[150] This choice on Sasso's part, although in line with his use of female classical characters more generally, is interesting given that we have already seen him place the blame for the metamorphoses of Procne and Philomena with them—they "sing of their ancient punishment."[151] If Sasso suggests the sisters are repentant figures, then his transformation into Philomena implies a performative awareness that his own actions are, at least in part, to blame for his pain. From a narrative standpoint, this feels like a metamorphosis in which Sasso reflects on the romance from the final stage of acceptance, suggesting that in some ways he may be regretful of pursuing something that caused him so much pain. However, this metamorphosis also recognises that, as with Philomena, it is only as a result of this somewhat self-inflicted circumstance that Sasso has been able to produce beautiful "weeping," that is, his verse.

The final set of female classical characters utilised by Sasso, the Sirens, are perhaps the most surprising, and present the greatest contrast between their use by Sasso and their use more generally across the corpus. We have seen above that the Homeric Sirens, with their terrifying ability to pull men and ships to their deaths, make an obvious comparator to the

---

149 Sasso, *Opera*, sig. [h iv] v.
150 As LeVen has observed, in the Graeco-Roman traditions the nightingale represents "an ideal of vocal skills that a human musician can only wish to attain." LeVen, *Music and Metamorphosis*, 39.
151 "piange cantando la sua antiqua poena." Sasso, *Opera*, sig. [c iii] r.

sound of the beloved. But for Sasso, the sonic perfection suggested by the Siren can also generate a positive comparison to his own lamenting: "I come to sing as the Siren does/ when her cruel pain grows more and more."[152] As a comparator to the author and not the beloved, the Siren is forced to become a sympathetic character; she sings as she does for a reason, having been driven to it as a result of her own mistreatment as an unrequited lover. She is no longer singing for the purpose of deceitful allure, but as a result of circumstance. The visual element of the Siren is also stripped away in this example: she has become nothing but sound. With her bodily allure gone and her lamenting justified, the Siren becomes an ideal positive comparator to Sasso's own voice, for both the quality of his singing, and his power to enchant his audience. Such a use of the Sirens is not completely without precedent; at least in ancient usage, Sirens can be found as positive comparators for male oration, such as the presence of a Siren on the tomb of the ancient Greek orator Isocrates, or in descriptions of Greek writers such as Homer, Bacchylides, and Menander.[153] However, in Italian lyric verse around 1500, the use of the Sirens as a comparator to the male authorial voice is extremely rare, if not unique to Sasso.

2.5 Conclusions

The works in our 1501 poetic corpus present sonic elements that align with their differing purposes. From short histories describing real battles, to neo-Latin works and vernacular lyric, our oeuvre represents the full range of new conventional verse at the turn of the sixteenth century, and right across it we find sonic elements that are manipulated to some specific end by the poet-authors. In the short histories, we can hear the soundscapes of very real battles, described to make the narrative more vivid and lifelike; but we also begin to see how the performative nature of the work is represented strategically through sonic cues in its written and printed form. This can also be seen in the lyric poetry, to which the majority of this chapter has been dedicated. Here, there are a number

---

152 "vengho a cantar como fa la Serena/ quando piu cresce el so crudel dolore." Sasso, *Strambotti*, sig. [a i] v.
153 Leofranc Holford-Strevens, "Sirens in Antiquity and the Middle Ages," in *Music of the Sirens*, ed. Linda Phyllis Austern and Inna Naroditskaya (Bloomington, IN: Indiana University Press, 2006), 16–51, at 22.

of elements which work to connect the written word with its real-life performance, including audible openings, the conflation of writing and singing, and descriptions of the sound of the verse itself—elements that are representative of, or more fully realised in, the live performance of the verse, whether as song or as spoken recitation.

It is also in the lyric poetry, with its pervasive and self-conscious focus on the persona of the author, that we find ourselves exploring entire sonic worlds that are internal to the verse. Connected to the greater narrative of the poet as author are a whole host of sounding elements with which they can construct for themselves an imagined world where they may play out their story of unrequited love. In their imagined landscape, the author can demonstrate the scope of their poetic world through the sound of their verse resounding through it, creating an environment that stages their imagined romance, but also reflects their thoughts and emotions, as well as providing sympathetic listeners to their plight. In the sonic presence of the beloved, meanwhile, her existence as a construct of the poet and simultaneously as his narrative mistress requires, paradoxically, that she be both a perfected memory and also a force beyond the poet's control.

However, the most abundant sounds found in our 1501 verse are those of the poets themselves, and here we find further strong and pervasive links between the internal soundscape of the verse and its live performance. This is most evident in the orphic powers often attributed to the poet in describing his effect over his imagined world, but it is also heard more generally in the conflation of his sound within the verse with what may be heard in performance. These conflations are often fully integrated into the rhetoric and the narrative of the verse: we often read of the singing and the mournful cries of the poet, which connect to their role as a performer, but also act to articulate the narrative, helping the reader to follow the stages of the imagined romance. Thus, our 1501 corpus provides evidence of a whole host of sounding elements available for the poet's manipulation, and a very conscious decision on the part of the poet to use these sounds to shape the narrative, setting, and characters of their verse in pursuit of their own creative and professional ends. At the same time, these internal sounding elements have a clear and tangible connection to the author as a performer, not only as a writer, amounting to a sonic persona that aids the poet in the telling of his story whilst also deliberately commenting upon the live performance of his verse.

3. Scholarship

University students need textbooks and set works to study, and professors want to publish their scholarship—not to make money directly, of course (or at least, not usually), but to improve their reputation and status in ways that might advantage their careers, and to contribute to the advancement of the sciences and intellectual discourse. Thanks to these two fundamental factors, the universities had long fuelled the book trade.[1] Workshops attached to major European university centres, particularly from the thirteenth century on, copied the texts needed by students in large quantities using the *pecia* system.[2] Across the late fifteenth century in Italy, the universities rapidly began to exploit the new technology of print, and at the same time printers sought to take commercial advantage of the universities' voracious appetite for books. University professors quickly became involved in the production of printed books as editors, authors, and brokers of patronage, whilst printers and booksellers collaborated with staff and students to build distribution networks around university centres.[3]

Several categories of books associated with the universities are present in our 1501 corpus. There are set works of classical literature for discussion in grammar class, such as Virgil's *Aeneid* and Juvenal's *Satires*. There are classical works used as textbooks in teaching rhetoric, natural philosophy, law and medicine, such as Cicero's *De oratore*, Aristotle's

---

[1] An excellent overview of the close and intricate relationship between universities and books in this period, with a particular focus on the University of Bologna, can be found in David A. Lines, *The Dynamics of Learning in Early Modern Italy: Arts and Medicine at the University of Bologna* (Cambridge, MA: Harvard University Press, 2023), 137–68.

[2] Among many studies, for an overview see Barbara A. Shailor, *The Medieval Book* (Toronto: University of Toronto Press, 1991), 88–100.

[3] See, among others, Angela Nuovo, *The Book Trade in the Italian Renaissance*, trans. Lydia G. Cochrane (Leiden: Brill, 2013), 265–66.

De anima, and various sections of the *Corpus Juris Civilis*. And there are new works of scholarship and handbooks offering fresh treatments of the same subjects. The majority of our university-related books fit two of these categories at the same time: they present a set work of literature or an authoritative textbook, invariably very old, complete or in excerpts, together with both old and new commentaries, the majority by university professors. The commentaries—particularly the new ones (by which we mean those written in the fifteenth century)—can with reasonable confidence be taken to reflect the ways in which those works were taught in university lectures.[4]

By 1501, there were twelve universities in somewhat continuous operation in Italy.[5] Bologna and Padua were the oldest and the most famous, followed in prestige by Pavia; Siena, Rome, Perugia, Pisa, Florence, and Ferrara occupied a middling rank, followed by Naples and Turin, and then the smaller Catania.[6] Several other cities hired professors, in numbers and curricular dispositions amounting only to what Paul F. Grendler calls "incomplete universities," but nonetheless teaching the same set texts in the same manner as the universities proper. Moreover, some cities convened academic committees that examined candidates (with reference to the appropriate set texts) and awarded degrees even in the absence of a teaching university.[7]

The number of professors teaching at an Italian university ranged from fewer than 10 to more than 100, while the student enrollment ranged from a few dozen to more than 1000. The middle-ranking universities perhaps averaged around 20–40 professors and 200–400 students. Professors were usually laymen, commensurate with the orientation of Italian universities towards law and medicine rather than theology. Students usually attended university between the ages of eighteen and twenty-five, graduating with a doctoral rather than a bachelor's degree.

---

[4] On the relationship between commentaries and teaching, see Paul F. Grendler, *The Universities of the Italian Renaissance* (Baltimore, MD: Johns Hopkins University Press, 2002), 241–44.

[5] The following summary of the status of the Italian universities around 1501 is based closely on Grendler, *The Universities*, 3–108. Grendler (3–4) defines a university as an institution that is both authorised by charter to grant degrees, and actively running advanced classes in arts, law, and medicine. Only those institutions that Grendler considers to meet this definition are listed.

[6] On the reputation of the various universities see Grendler, *The Universities*, 165.

[7] Grendler, *The Universities*, 181.

The principal professors ("ordinary" professors) generally taught once a day, five days a week, in a fixed schedule of one- and two-hour lectures running from first thing in the morning until late afternoon, across an academic year stretching approximately from November to June, with breaks for Christmas, Carnival, and Easter. Professors also attended regular disputations in which students put themselves forward to debate particular topics—a crucial part of their intellectual training. A majority of staff and students were generally natives of their university town, but a significant proportion came from other Italian cities, or from outside of Italy; students from Germany were particularly common, but young men also came from France, Spain, Portugal, England, Greece and its islands, and other places, to study in Italy.

Universities needed professors to teach in several specific subject areas. The arts professorships covered several distinct topics and topic clusters: grammar, rhetoric, and poetry (the category into which the humanists inserted themselves, with differing success at different universities, across the fifteenth century); mathematics, astrology, and astronomy; logic; natural philosophy; metaphysics; and moral philosophy.[8] The medical professors were divided among medical theory, medical practice, and surgery. The law professors taught either canon law, or civil law, the latter split between junior professors lecturing on the elementary *Institutes*, and the main law professors teaching the *Digest* and *Codex* (all together comprising the *Corpus Juris Civilis*). Some universities also had their own professors of theology, but for the most part this subject was instead taught at, or in collaboration with, the local mendicant studium generale. At most of the universities, judging by the number of professors and their salaries, civil law, medical theory, and natural philosophy were the most important subjects.

Natural philosophy, logic, astrology, and moral philosophy were all considered preparatory or accessory to medical study, and for this reason arts and medicine were combined into one faculty, with law

---

8   In this chapter we use the noun "humanist" to refer to individuals closely involved in teaching and scholarship in the "studia humanitatis," corresponding roughly to what we now call the humanities (i.e., languages, literature, history, and philosophy), in the fifteenth and early sixteenth centuries. When used as an adjective, "humanist" refers to the scholarly activities and attitudes towards knowledge and learning that were shared, approximately and to an extent, among those individuals.

in another. Italian universities in 1501 only awarded doctoral degrees, usually in law (civil, canon, or both, but most often civil), arts, medicine, or arts and medicine. At Italian universities "arts" meant, primarily, Aristotle: the core texts in natural philosophy, logic, metaphysics, and moral philosophy were all supplied by Aristotle, and candidates for the doctorate in arts were examined on excerpts from his works. Thus, the traditional system of the seven Liberal Arts, which includes music and does not explicitly include natural or moral philosophy, is quite misleading with regard to the arts curriculum studied at Italian universities.

In her classic 1958 study of music in the medieval and Renaissance universities, Nan Cooke Carpenter gave a very optimistic assessment of the presence of music in Italian university curricula, encouraged especially by the residence of the important music theorists Marchetto da Padova and Prosdocimus de Beldemandis in Padua and their links with the city's university, and by the activities of the Spanish music theorist Bartolomé Ramos de Pareja who lectured publicly on music in Bologna (though not in association with the university) in the 1470s and 80s.[9] Claude V. Palisca, in his foundational study of musical humanism, was similarly confident that music found a place at the Italian universities, adding to Carpenter's list of potential music professors the hypothesis that Giorgio Anselmi may have taught the subject at the briefly-established University of Parma in the 1410s.[10] On the basis of a more cautious evaluation of the evidence, Grendler poured cold water on the case for music as a curricular subject in his magisterial study of the Italian Renaissance universities published in 2002, concluding that "There were no professors of music in Italian universities," and excluding music entirely from his overview of university subjects and studies.[11]

---

[9] Nan Cooke Carpenter, *Music in the Medieval and Renaissance Universities* (Norman, OK: University of Oklahoma Press, 1958), 32–46 and 128–39.

[10] Claude V. Palisca, *Humanism in Italian Renaissance Musical Thought* (New Haven, CT: Yale University Press, 1985), 7–8. The University of Parma opened in 1412, but closed again in 1420 owing to political problems, and was only conclusively established in 1601 (Grendler, *The Universities*, 126–28).

[11] Grendler, *The Universities*, 11 (note 22). Carpenter also makes this observation (*Music in the Medieval and Renaissance Universities*, 314), but gives it a very different emphasis.

Accepting that Grendler is correct so far as professors of music are concerned, our 1501 corpus nonetheless offers us an opportunity to approach the issue in a different way. What might a student have learned about music whilst attending lectures, not on music, but on natural philosophy, rhetoric, poetry, or law? In our corpus we have numerous texts that certainly were taught at Italian Renaissance universities, printed alongside commentaries by recent and contemporary university professors. With the help of these materials, in this chapter we investigate the ways and forms in which music must have snuck into the lecture room as a serious subject of academic study, thanks to short discussions or even mere mentions in well-established textbooks and set works that are principally concerned with another subject. The picture that emerges shows that, in fact, music was not absent from class.

3.1 Natural Philosophy

Aristotle, [*Opera*] (Venice: per Giovanni & Gregorio De Gregori impensa Paganino Paganini, 1501)

Aristotle et al., *Problemata Aristotelis cum duplici translatione antiqua & nova Theodori Gaze: cum expositione Petri Aponi. Tabula secundum Petrum de Tussignano Problemata Alexandri Aphrodisei. Problemata Plutarchi* (Venice: per Boneto Locatello haer. Ottaviano Scoto, 1501)

Aristotle et al., *Problemata Alexandri Aphrodisei. Georgio Valla interprete. Problemata Aristotelis. Theodorus Gaza e Graeco transtulit. Problemata Plutarchi per Ioannem Petrum Lucensem in Latinum conversa* (Venice: per Albertino da Lessona, 1501)

Walter Burley, *In Physicam Aristotelis expositio et questiones / Super octo libros phisicorum* (Venice: per Simone Lovere iussu Andrea Torresano, 1501—surviving with two alternative title pages)

John Duns Scotus, *Commentaria doctoris subtilis Ioannis Scoti in XII libros Metaphysice Aristotelis emendata & quottationibus concordantiis atque annotationibus decorata per fratrem Mauricium Hibernicum* (Venice: cura ac studio Boneto Locatello mandato & expensis haer. Ottaviano Scoto, 1501)

Giles of Rome, *Questiones methaphisicales clarissimi doctoris Egidii Romani Ordinis sancti Augustini* (Venice: per Simone da Lovere mandato Andrea Torresano, 1501)

Jean de Jandun, *Questiones Ioannis de Ianduno de physico auditu nouiter emendate* (Venice: Boneto Locatello mandato & expensis haer. Ottaviano Scoto, 1501)

Jean de Jandun, *Questiones Ioannis Iandoni de celo & mundo* (Venice: Boneto Locatello mandato & expensis haer. Ottaviano Scoto, 1501)

Jean de Jandun, *Questiones Ioannis Iandoni de anima* (Venice: per Boneto Locatello impendio haer. Ottaviano Scoto, 1501)

Gianfrancesco Pico della Mirandola, *Liber de imaginatione* (Venice: Aldo Manuzio, 1501)

Thomas Aquinas, *Divi Thome aquinatis in librum de anima Aristotelis expositio. Magistri Dominici de Flandria ordinis predicatorum in eundem librum acutissime questiones et annotationes* (Venice: per Pietro Quarengi, 1501)

That Aristotle remained centrally important to intellectual culture in Renaissance Italy is fully attested by our 1501 corpus.[12] Among our books associated with the universities, there is an approximate numerical balance between new humanist commentaries on classical literature, and old scholastic commentaries and treatises on Aristotelian philosophy. Upon reading through these books, the reason for their parallel value is easily apprehended: they deal with quite different aspects of the "arts" curriculum—the humanist commentaries with literature and history, or what we would now call the humanities; the Aristotelian commentaries with natural philosophy, or what we would now call the sciences. Both were considered preparatory and accessory to study of the more advanced and most important subjects, civil law and medicine, at the universities. Language and literature refined students' Latin and developed their eloquence, providing the essential foundation for all of their other studies; while natural philosophy was allied specifically with medicine, although it was also pursued on its own terms as an independent discipline.[13] It follows readily from this differentiation that it is in the science of the Aristotelian commentaries that we find the most detailed treatments available in our corpus of the physics of sound, the physiology of hearing, and the psychology of sensory cognition.

The protagonists of the Aristotelian revival pioneered at the universities of Paris and Oxford in the thirteenth and fourteenth centuries are richly represented in our 1501 corpus, as they are in print more broadly in the decades around 1500. The giants Thomas Aquinas,

---

12 The classic study of the importance of Aristotle in Renaissance thought is Charles B. Schmitt, *Aristotle and the Renaissance* (Cambridge, MA: Harvard University Press, 1983).

13 Grendler, *The Universities*, 268.

John Duns Scotus, and Giles of Rome are particularly prominent, as is Albertus Magnus, whose important (if probably misattributed) gynecological treatise *De secretis mulierum* is discussed above in Chapter 1.3. All four were bestselling authors in our period, represented by many dozens of editions printed in Italy between 1470 and 1520. Also numbering in the dozens, although on a different scale to the four superstars, are Walter Burley, Jean de Jandun, and Pietro d'Abano, all of whom comment on Aristotle's treatment of sound and hearing in 1501 editions. Although long-dead authorities dominated this discourse, prominent fifteenth-century Aristotelians are also to be found among our 1501 corpus, including Paolo da Pergola, Alessandro Achillini, and, most significantly for our purposes, Dominic of Flanders (Baldovino Lottin de Mervis), a Dominican and a dedicated Thomist who taught in Italy in the 1460s and 70s. His commentaries on several of Aristotle's works, and above all on *De anima*, entered print in Italy in the 1490s and were reissued throughout the sixteenth century.

Humanist commentary and scholastic commentary are highly distinctive in their differences, both of form and of content. For starters, the two look entirely different on the printed page. The humanist commentaries in our corpus present the main text, complete, in the middle of the page, often in a single column layout, and dispose the commentary around the outside, in smaller text. The Aristotelian commentaries follow a two-column layout, presenting a series of quotes from the main text (which may or may not add up to a complete statement thereof), each followed by commentary in smaller text. In humanist commentaries, the sign ℭ is sometimes used to draw the eye to the words and short phrases pulled out of the main text for comment; the commentary that follows is distinctly philological in orientation, focussing most often on linguistic and literary matters, such as the meaning and etymology of words, and assembles parallel passages quoted from other similar classical texts to contextualise unfamiliar ancient concepts and practices. In Aristotelian commentaries, the same sign ℭ is used instead to clarify the structure of the somewhat systematic ("scholastic") argumentation used by the commentator, which unpacks the relevant passage of Aristotle by first summarising his conclusions, then presenting possible objections, then offering clarifications and proofs that resolve the matter, usually in Aristotle's favour.

Both humanist and Aristotelian commentary share the tendency to completely overwhelm the commented text in terms of wordcount; but whereas humanist commentaries most often comprise many short comments on individual words and phrases, Aristotelian commentaries dwell at length on the substance of each of Aristotle's key points, often amounting to a series of somewhat original and independent treatises considerably extending and enriching Aristotle's own more concise deliberations. Thus, whereas in humanist commentaries the commented text generally remains the core of the book, in Aristotelian commentary it is the commentary itself that is the main event, a classic of philosophy in its own right. Accordingly, in some of our 1501 Aristotles there are in fact two layers of commentary, a "classic" medieval commentary, and a newer one which deals with both Aristotle's original text and its "classic" commentary—a commentary on a commentary, as it were, as is the case with Dominic of Flanders and Thomas' commentary on *De anima*.

Natural philosophy was strongly prioritised by the Italian universities throughout the fifteenth and sixteenth centuries, taught by comparatively numerous and well-paid professors.[14] The curriculum for students of natural philosophy was, very simply, Aristotle, with a particular and increasing focus on the *Physics* and *De anima*, and a secondary interest in the *De generatione et corruptione* and *De caelo et mundo*.[15] (The *Metaphysics*, meanwhile, was generally taught by a different professor as preparatory to theology.) In 1501, Aristotle was still read for the most part in medieval Latin translations, although interest in the original Greek texts was growing.[16]

Alongside a complete edition of Aristotle's *Opera* with the classic commentaries of Averroes (Ibn Rushd), several of Aristotle's individual works appear with commentary in our 1501 corpus. We have two editions of the *Physics*, one commentated by Jean de Jandun, the other by Walter Burley; and two of the *Metaphysics*, commented by Giles of Rome and "John Duns Scotus" (really his student Antonius Andreas). Music is mentioned quite frequently in both these works, and particularly in *Physics* 1.7, but mostly as part of a very detailed and methodical argument to parse the relationships among qualities or characteristics,

---

14 Grendler, *The Universities*, 267–68.
15 Grendler, *The Universities*, 269–71.
16 Grendler, *The Universities*, 271–79.

natures, and causes, in which "to be musical" is used as one of a handful of key examples of characteristics attaching themselves to a man which may be related in one or another way to themselves as such, to his other characteristics, to his nature as a man, and to his actions and their outcomes. The commentators respond by simply paraphrasing Aristotle in an effort to clarify his thinking, without remarking in any meaningful way on the musical component. In *Physics* 2.3, for example, Aristotle (in William of Moerbeke's Latin translation) analyses causation, introducing the example of the sculptor who may or may not be musical:

> Amplius autem secundum accidens et horum genera sicut statue et aliter policletus et aliter statuam faciens quoniam accidit statuam facienti policletum esse. Et continentes secundum accidens: ut si homo causa sit statue aut homo animal. Sunt autem accidentium alie alijs longius et propius: ut si albus et musicus causa dicuntur statue.[17]

> Another mode of causation is the incidental and its genera, e.g. in one way Polyclitus, in another a sculptor is the cause of a statue, because being Polyclitus and a sculptor are accidentally conjoined. Also the classes in which the accidental attribute is included; thus a man could be said to be the cause of a statue or, generally, a living creature. An accidental attribute too may be more or less remote, e.g. suppose that a pale man or a musical man were said to be the cause of the statue.[18]

Walter Burley gives the following explanation of the mention of the "musicus" at the end of this passage:

> Deinde narrat philosophus quod in illo qui est per accidens invenitur propinquum et remotum: quoniam causarum per accidens quidam sunt propinquiores quidam vero remotiores. verbi gratia. si faciens statuam sit albus et musicus tunc album et musicum sunt causare per accidens statue. sed album est causum remotior quem musicus: quare album est communis quem musicum: quare reperitur in alijs quem in homine: sed musicum non reperitur nisi in homine.[19]

> Then the Philosopher says that in that which is [caused] incidentally one finds the near and the remote, since among incidental causes some are

---

17 *In Physicam*, fol. 46v.
18 *The Complete Works of Aristotle: The Revised Oxford Translation*, ed. Jonathan Barnes, 2 vols. (Princeton, NJ: Princeton University Press, 1984), 1:333 (trans. R. P. Hardie and R. K. Gaye).
19 *In Physicam*, fol. 46v. On this commentary see, among others, Rega Wood, "Walter Burley's *Physics* Commentaries," *Franciscan Studies* 44 (1984), 275–327.

nearer and some more remote. For example, if the maker of a statue is white and musical, then white and musical are incidental causes of the statue. But white is a more remote cause than musical, because white is more common than musical, wherefore it is found in those other than man, whereas musical is not found except in man.

There are many other comments of this kind, but they do little to advance our objectives in the present study.

More productive than the *Physics* and *Metaphysics*, for our purposes, is the *De anima*, and specifically *De anima* 2.8, a passage that dominated and defined all scientific discussion of sound and hearing in the late Middle Ages.[20] We have two editions of *De anima* in our 1501 corpus: one containing Jean de Jandun's *questiones*, the other Thomas Aquinas' commentary partnered with a new commentary by Dominic of Flanders. Dominic's contribution is particularly valuable here, for it represents a reading of both Aristotle and Thomas originating from a natural philosophy professor at the universities of Bologna, Florence, and Pisa in the 1460s and 70s, thus it is as "new" as the humanist commentaries discussed in the following sections of this chapter.[21] Also, it had a lasting impact: although modern scholars consistently cite the commentary on the *Metaphysics* as Dominic's most important work, of the twenty-six known editions of his writings printed in Italy up to the end of the sixteenth century, eighteen featured the *De anima* commentary, whereas the *Metaphysics* commentary appeared only once (the balance is made up by the commentary on the *Posterior Analytics*). In all of these works, Dominic approaches Aristotle via Thomas; indeed, in the academic year 1473–74, perhaps responding specifically to a course of lectures on

---

20 For the broader picture, see Charles Burnett, "Sound and its Perception in the Middle Ages," in *The Second Sense: Studies in Hearing and Musical Judgement from Antiquity to the Seventeenth Century*, ed. Charles Burnett, Michael Fend, and Penelope M. Gouk (London: Warburg Institute, 1991), 43–69; and, on voice specifically, Elizabeth Eva Leach, *Sung Birds: Music, Nature and Poetry in the Later Middle Ages* (Ithaca, NY: Cornell University Press, 2007), 24–40.

21 The most recent review of Dominic's career is Luciano Cinelli, "Domenico di Fiandra: La carriera di un frate predicatore del quattrocento fra Bologna e Firenze," in *Università, teologia e studium domenicano dal 1360 alla fine del medioevo*, ed. Roberto Lambertini (Florence: Nerbini, 2014), 147–69. On Aquinas' commentary on *De anima* see, among others, the introduction to the most recent English translation: Thomas Aquinas, *A Commentary on Aristotle's* De anima, trans. Robert Pasnau (New Haven, CT: Yale University Press, 1999), xi–xxi.

De anima, students at the University of Pisa complained that Dominic taught Thomas rather than Aristotle.[22]

In *De anima* 2.8 we find Aristotle in the midst of discussing the senses one by one. Having dealt first with sight, he turns to hearing. In his lengthy commentary on this passage, Thomas breaks the discussion into three segments or "lectures," the first on sound itself, the second on hearing, and the third on voice; in his more concise summary of both Aristotle and Thomas' views, Dominic adopts the same structure (see Appendix, Excerpt 3.1 for the full passage). Following a scholastic process of argumentation, in addressing the first of these lectures Dominic identifies Aristotle's four key conclusions concerning sound, for each one stating the possible objections and then eliminating them with clarifications and counter-arguments. The nature of sound's existence is the most fundamental issue to be dealt with, which is problematic on account of sound's intangibility. First we must appreciate that sound can exist both in actuality and in potentiality, as is clear from a bell, which sometimes rings and sometimes does not, and when it does not it nonetheless retains the capacity to ring. Sound's existence in actuality is then thrown into question through various objections, which are overcome through careful differentiations of the nature of sound's actual existence built upon a comparison with sight. Whereas colour exists in actuality permanently, sound exists in actuality successively, its being lying not in its existence as such but in its production. And whereas colour has a material existence external to the eye and the medium through which it reaches the eye, sound is not manifested in the sounding object but rather in the ear and in the medium through which it reaches the ear—that is, the air. "For there is not any manifestation of sound in a sounding bell; rather, the manifestation is in the air and in the organ of hearing." Thus, whereas colour (and the other sensible qualities, odour and taste) have a permanent, material existence, sound exists only in its production, and only in the air and the ear.

---

22 Cinelli, "Domenico di Fiandra," 167; Grendler, *The Universities*, 282–83. On the continuing importance of Thomas Aquinas in Renaissance Italy see, among others, Paul Oskar Kristeller, "Thomism and the Italian Thought of the Renaissance," in Kristeller, *Medieval Aspects of Renaissance Learning: Three Essays by Paul Oskar Kristeller*, ed. and trans. Edward P. Mahoney, rev. edn. (New York: Columbia University Press, 1992), 29–94.

Next we turn to the generation of sound, for which three things are required: the thing striking, the thing struck, and the medium; because sound is a "breaking" or a motion of the air, which must arise from a "violent percussion." In order to sound well, the thing striking and the thing struck should be hard, light (as opposed to dense—e.g., lead does not sound well), and hollow (facilitating resonance), and they should be set in motion rapidly. Thus, a bronze bell will sound well, whereas wool (for example) will not. The medium must be "that which is easily dispersed and compressed, and through which sound can easily spread its manifestation to the organ of hearing;" therefore the most suitable medium is air, although water can also serve, albeit imperfectly. These considerations are relevant to the understanding of hearing (Aristotle's main topic in *De anima* 2.8) because, as we have learned already, sound exists as a motion produced in the air and the ear, and therefore the production and propagation of that motion are key to the mechanism by which sound moves the sense of hearing. In contrast, colour, which is "fixed and permanent," has as a result of its different form of existence a different means of moving the sense of sight.

Finally in the lecture on sound itself, we must investigate the manner in which sound propagates through the medium, in order to understand the phenomenon of reverberation or echo. Here, sound is understood through an analogy with ripples in water. When something is thrown into water,

> ripples occur in the vicinity of the strike, which are small with strong motion near the point of impact, but further away the ripples are larger and their motion weaker, until finally the motion fails completely and the ripples cease. But if, before the motion ceases, the ripples should find some obstacle, the ripples are set in motion in the opposite direction, and the more violently the nearer they are to the first impact.

Similarly, when the thing striking hits the thing struck, ripples are sent through the air in all directions, with a strong force close to the strike which weakens further away; and if those ripples hit a solid body before they disperse, they are sent back in the opposite direction and a reverberation is produced.

Next, Dominic moves on to summarise the lecture concerning hearing. Sound is able to move the sense of hearing because the ear itself contains air, retained by the eardrum, and thus the motion of the air that constitutes the manifestation of sound can transfer from the air outside the ear to the air inside the ear. In order for sensation to occur thus successfully, three conditions must be met. First, the air must be unified and continuous from the sounding object to the ear, so that the motion may reach the ear without interruption. Second, the eardrum must be whole and healthy. Third, the air inside the ear must be motionless, otherwise it will be unable to receive the motion of the external air. Impairments of hearing, such as deafness and tinnitus, occur when these last two conditions are not met. The ear is capable of differentiating high (*acutus*, lit. "sharp") and low (*gravis*, lit. "heavy") sounds. These differences of pitch arise because of differences of motion; high sounds result from rapid motion, low sounds from slower motion. (Thomas' own commentary adds the important clarification that it is the speed of oscillation that is key here, i.e., what we would now call frequency.) High and low sounds also differ in terms of intensity: "A high sound is one which in a short time moves the hearing a great deal; whereas a low sound is one which in a long time moves the hearing a little." Sounds can also be intermediate or wavering, of course, in which case they are a mixture of high and low, "just as middling colours are contained within the extremes"—Dominic cites Boethius' *De musica* on this point.

Finally, Dominic comes to the lecture on voice, which is a particular species of sound. Voice is the repercussion of breathed air, in the windpipe, by the soul, informed by the imagination. (Thomas unpacks this a little, noting that the motive power of the soul exists most forcefully in the heart, which is adjacent to the lungs; and that it requires "some imagination intending to signify something.")[23] It follows from this definition that animals that do not respire cannot have voice because they will lack the mechanism (breath in the windpipe); nor can inanimate objects, because they will lack both the motive force (soul) and the capacity for signification (imagination). Thus, musical instruments do not really have voice, even though they are commonly said to, because in themselves they lack breath, soul and imagination. Rather, they form "a similitude of voice" thanks to three features: continuity of sound,

---

23 "oportet enim ad hoc quod sit vox quod verberans aerem sit aliquid animatum: et cum imaginatione ad aliquid significandum." *Divi Thome*, sig. [e6]r. Thomas Aquinas, *A Commentary*, 247.

consonance, and interruption. Dominic's explanation of this point is so terse as to make the meaning obscure, so it is useful to turn to Thomas for the fuller version (Appendix, Excerpt 3.2). Voice and musical instruments both produce a continuous series of sounds (continuity); they both produce a variety of high and low sounds reflecting sentiment, which in music manifests as melody and harmony (consonance); and they both employ co-ordinated fragmentations of sound, which in voice produce words and syllables, and in music separate notes and articulations (interruption).

Sound emerges from this whole discourse as an enigma and a scientific problem—indeed, so difficult is it to conceive that Aristotle and his commentators repeatedly fall back on visual analogies to explain it. Sound is qualitatively different from other objects of sensation, such as colours and shapes, because its form of existence is inescapably ephemeral, lying in its production, propagation, and apprehension, and not in the tangible object that appears to produce it. This is the scientific basis for the critique of music's ephemerality that was developed by Leonardo da Vinci in his notebooks in the years around 1500.[24] Unlike paintings, which have a stable and permanent form, music comes and goes in an instant, existing only in the moment of the production and propagation of its sounds.

We read repeatedly that sound exists in the air and the ear. Thanks to its existence in the air, sound, unlike other sensible qualities, is expansively spatialised. Whereas the blueness of a block of blue colour on a canvas remains within the borders that circumscribe it there, sound propagates through air in all directions from its point of generation, until either it reaches the limits of its motive force or it reaches a reflective surface. Thus sound, unlike colour, defines its own dimensionality through propagation, filling out its environment and turning it into an acoustic space. Its existence in the ear, meanwhile, and its non-existence in the object that generates it, weights the system of acoustic sensation away from creation and towards reception, in a way that differs from the other senses.

High (*acutus*) sounds are by nature swift, vigorous and penetrating, having a powerful impact on the hearing; whereas low (*gravis*) sounds

---

24 Tim Shephard, Sanna Raninen, Serenella Sessini, and Laura Ştefănescu, *Music in the Art of Renaissance Italy 1420–1540* (London: Harvey Miller, 2020), 37–40.

are sluggish and weak, moving the hearing more feebly and slowly. *Acutus* and *gravis* are, as it were, the primary colours of sound; middling pitches are a mixture of the two, a mixture of sharpness and heaviness. The conception of pitch space operating here is quite different from that to which modern musicians are accustomed—indeed, it is not really a conception of pitch *space*, as such, at all. Rather than a simple directionality of up or down, pitch occupies three parallel and completely interrelated dimensions, namely height, intensity, and energy, which make of a rising or falling musical figure a semantic and emotional rather than simply a directional trajectory.

The voice is clearly established as the most important species of sound on account of its signification according to will. The voice is set in motion by the soul, generating sound-signs that represent concepts supplied by the imagination; without the signs, nothing would be signified in sound. This signification is made possible by the continuity of the voice, its articulation of sounds into words and syllables, and its variability of pitch and intensity to convey emotion. Instrumental music gives the illusion of vocal signification by imitating these three qualities, that is, through continuity (or one might say phrase), articulation, and melody or harmony. These three properties, which we might think of as generally musical, are according to Aristotelian science specifically *vocal*, and are the acoustic fingerprints of a soul in the act of making meanings audible. In this connection, it is obviously significant that the majority of the instrumental music played in Italy in our period was adapted from vocal music: instrumentalists imitated the voice in the most direct manner possible, that is, by playing songs.

Much of the analysis of sound and hearing found in *De anima* 2.8 turns up also in other books in our 1501 corpus—indeed, anywhere that a scientific discussion of sound and hearing is called for, this crucial passage makes itself felt. Another important example, and one that represents the parallel reception of Aristotle among medical (rather than philosophical-theological) authorities, is to be found in Pietro d'Abano's commentary on Aristotle's *Problemata*. Two very different editions of this work, whose attribution to Aristotle is now doubted, appeared in 1501. One (Venice: Albertino da Lessona) contains an elegant but very free Latin translation of the work completed in the 1450s by Teodoro Gaza; the other (Venice: Boneto Locatello) collates both this new translation, and the notoriously impenetrable thirteenth-century translation by Bartholomew of Messina, and Pietro d'Abano's very lengthy commentary completed in 1310.[25] The latter edition proved the more successful, being reissued in 1505, 1518 and 1519. It is clear from the book that this work was received primarily by physicians: Pietro d'Abano, the indexer Pietro Curialti, the editor Domenico Massaria, and the author of the dedicatory letter attached to the Gaza translation, Niccolò Gupalatino, were all medical experts.

Book 11 of the *Problemata*, containing problems relating to the voice, calls forth from Pietro d'Abano a detailed treatise on sound, voice and hearing, in which he presents and develops all of the points with which we are now familiar from the *De anima*.[26] As befits his profession, he inserts many more details concerning the anatomy of the voice and the ear, derived principally from Avicenna's *Canon of Medicine*. Thus, the air internal to the ear is located specifically between the stirrups, and the whole auditory assemblage is connected to the brain via the fifth pair of nerves. Meanwhile, the throat is crucial to the production of voice, for there are found the vocal folds which are the structures impelled by the soul, via adjacent muscles, in order to create the percussion of breathed air inside the windpipe; and for the purpose of forming speech, the tongue, teeth, lips and nose are also essential. (A complete edition of the *Canon of Medicine* was printed in Venice in five volumes by Bernardino Benalio between 1501–04, but the volume issued in 1501

---

25 On the translations of the *Problemata* see Iolanda Ventura, "Translating, Commenting, Retranslating: Some Considerations on the Latin Translations of the Pseudo-Aristotelian *Problemata* and their Readers," in *Science Translated: Latin and Vernacular Translations of Scientific Treatises in Medieval Europe*, ed. Michèle Goyens, Pieter de Leemans, and An Smets (Leuven: Leuven University Press, 2008), 123–54. On the printing history of the *Problemata* see Jill Kraye, "The Printing History of Aristotle in the Fifteenth Century: A Bibliographical Approach to Renaissance Philosophy," *Renaissance Studies* 9.2 (1995), 189–211.

26 The contents of Pietro d'Abano's comments on Book 11 are summarised very effectively in Charles Burnett, "Hearing and Music in Book XI of Pietro d'Abano's Expositio Problematum Aristotelis," in *Tradition and Ecstasy: The Agony of the Fourteenth Century*, ed. Nancy van Deusen (Ottawa: Institute of Medieval Music, 1997), 153–90. The commentary to Book 19 of the *Problemata* is in fact a detailed treatise on music: on this see especially Palisca, *Humanism*, 51–66; Pietro d'Abano, *Expositio Problematum (XIX)*, ed. Christian Meyer (Leuven: Leuven University Press, 2022); Tim Shephard and Charlotte Hancock, "Looking Up Music in Two 'Encyclopedias' Printed in 1501," *Renaissance Studies* 38.4 (2024), 564–95.

does not contain the relevant sections, so in themselves they fall outside the scope of our project.)

Prompted by the specific content of the problems upon which he is commenting, Pietro also applies the physics of sound found in *De anima* 2.8 to questions concerning the acoustics of buildings. Problem 7 posits that newly-plastered houses echo more, and proposes that this is because there is greater resonance owing to the smoothness and continuity of the surfaces. Pietro adds:

> Oportet similiter quod in talibus edificijs non sint aperture hostium fenestrarum vel rimarum: per quas aer egrediatur non refractus. Sed enim si forma eorum fuerit semisperalis non angulata multis angulis sintque alta satis et lata tunc optime resonant.[27]

> It is likewise necessary that in such buildings there should be no openings for windows or cracks through which air may escape rather than being refracted. Moreover, if their shape is hemispherical, not angular with many corners, and sufficiently high and wide, then they will resonate optimally.

In other words, a windowless apse of quite large dimensions, such as one might find behind the main altar of a church, or a cupola such as might sit atop the crossing, offers an ideal resonant space. Problem 8 then suggests that building jars, pots or other concavities into houses will further improve their resonance, for reasons that Pietro explains:

> Ostendit quare puteus et lacus magis resonant dicens: quia igitur puteus et lacus continent concavitatem habentem coangustationem in qua aer colligitur et retinetur: sunt causa maioris echo et resonantie: aer enim coadunatus in eis impulsione percussus: vehementius reverberatur.[28]

> He shows why jars and pots resonate more, saying that because jars and pots are hollow, enclosing a volume in which air is collected and retained, they are the cause of greater echo and resonance. For the air collected in them, struck by the impulse, reverberates more violently.

Musicologists are more familiar with the treatment of acoustic considerations such as these in Vitruvius' treatise *De architectura*, first printed under the editorship of Giovanni Sulpizio in 1486, which

---

27 *Problemata Aristotelis*, fol. 127r.
28 *Problemata Aristotelis*, fol. 127r.

describes the placement of resonant vases in theatres.²⁹ It is interesting to note that this technique of acoustic treatment was also familiar from another source, one whose circulation before the late fifteenth century was somewhat more extensive.

Like other authors dealing with these matters, Pietro draws comparisons with light and colour to explain sound. As we have already seen, the central role of visual analogies and comparisons between sight and hearing in the discourse on sound stemming from the *De anima* seems to arise because, thanks to its uncertain and insubstantial existence, secure knowledge of sound can only be acquired by approaching it through the greater fixity and materiality of visible things. The question of the differential capacity of hearing and vision as means of acquiring knowledge is thematised in the commentary on the *Metaphysics* by Giles of Rome. At the very beginning of the *Metaphysics*, Aristotle writes:

> Omnes homines natura scire desiderant. Signum autem est sensuum dilectio: preter enim utilitatem propter seipsos diliguntur et maxime aliorum qui est per ipsos oculos. non enim solum ut agamus: sed et nihil agere debentes: ipsum videre pre omnibus ut dicam aliis eligimus. causa autem est quia hic maxime sensuum congnoscere nos facit: et multas rerum differentias demonstrat. Animalia quidem igitur sensum habentia natura fiunt. ex sensibus autem quibusdam quidem ipsorum memoria non fit: quibusdam vero fit: et propter hoc alia quidem prudentia sunt: alia vero disciplinabiliora non potentibus memorari. Prudentia quidem sunt sine addiscere quecumque sonos audire non potentia sunt ut apes. et utique si aliquod aliud genus animalium huiusmodi est. addiscunt autem quecunque cum memoria: et hunc habent sensum.³⁰

> All men by nature desire to know. An indication of this is the delight we take in our senses; for even apart from their usefulness they are loved for themselves; and above all others the sense of sight. For not only with a view to action, but even when we are not going to do anything, we prefer sight to almost everything else. The reason is that this, most of all the senses, makes us know and brings to light many differences between

---

29 Vitruvius, *De architectura* ([Rome: Eucharius Silber, 1486]), fols. 41r–43r (*De architectura* 5.5). This passage is preceded by a chapter on harmonic theory, at fols. 40r–41r (*De architectura* 5.4), the mathematical principles of which should be taken into account when implementing the vases. On the reception of Vitruvius' treatise in Italian music theory of the sixteenth century, see Ann E. Moyer, *Musica Scientia: Musical Scholarship in the Italian Renaissance* (Ithaca, NY: Cornell University Press, 1992), 184–93.
30 Aristotle, [*Opera*], fol. 143r.

things. By nature animals are born with the faculty of sensation, and from sensation memory is produced in some of them, though not in others. And therefore the former are more intelligent and apt at learning than those which cannot remember; those which are incapable of hearing sounds are intelligent though they cannot be taught, e.g. the bee, and any other race of animals that may be like it; and those which besides memory have this sense of hearing, can be taught.[31]

This passage seems to claim that both sight and hearing are the primary means of accessing knowledge, to the extent that acquiring knowledge would seem to be the purpose of being taught. Giles takes a systematic approach to clarifying this ambiguity in his Question 17, which asks "Whether hearing is the only teachable sense" (Utrum solus auditus sit sensus disciplinabilis).[32] First he mentions four objections to Aristotle's position. 1. Sight is the primary means of acquiring knowledge, and acquiring knowledge is the main purpose of learning, therefore sight is the most teachable sense. 2. Bees cannot hear, but they can still be taught to recognise a sound. 3. According to Aristotle, the soul becomes wise by sitting and resting (i.e., by contemplation); hearing is to do with sound, which consists of motion of the air, therefore hearing is the sense most opposed to sitting and resting. 4. The deaf can be taught well using the sense of sight. The second of these is dealt with simply: if bees cannot hear, then they cannot respond to a sound, but may respond to vibration of the air, which they may perceive merely instinctively as a threat, thus they are not acquiring knowledge. The others require the introduction of some more detailed considerations. The senses occupy an intermediate position between the soul and the task of perceiving; the senses relate to the soul just like tools relate to craft. Hearing is the proper tool for learning; it is not the subject of the capacity to learn—that is the intellect—but rather a conduit for instruction. But one lacking hearing may still be able to learn by using a different tool which is not designed specifically for that purpose, such as sight, just as it is possible

---

31 *The Complete Works of Aristotle*, 2:1552 (trans. W. D. Ross). Although our 1501 Latin differs slightly from the accepted modern reading, the differences have no significant bearing on the translation.

32 *Questiones methaphisicales*, fol. 8r–v. On this text see, among others, Alessandro D. Conti, "Giles of Rome's Questions on the *Metaphysics*," in *A Companion to the Latin Medieval Commentaries on Aristotle's Metaphysics*, ed. Gabriele Galluzzo and Fabrizio Amerini (Leiden: Brill, 2013), 255–76.

to fetch water in a shoe even though the tool proper to the task is a bucket. However, to do so, that creature must have hearing as part of its universal (but not necessarily its particular) nature, because if the creature "is born to hear" (nata est habere auditum) then the soul will have the capacity for hearing even if the sense organ is lacking, and thus the capacity to be taught will remain although the proper conduit for instruction is absent. Creatures that are not born to hear are unable to be taught.

For the next episode in the story of the journey of sound into the sensory apparatus, concerning sensory perception and cognition, we are well served by another of our 1501 books that draws on the *De anima*, a short treatise *De imaginatione* by Gianfrancesco Pico della Mirandola, nephew of the famous neoplatonist Giovanni Pico.[33] Gianfrancesco Pico offers a particularly valuable summary for our purposes, being himself a reader of Aristotle in 1501 (he wrote a commentary on *De anima*, now lost), and one who balances a respect for Aristotelian thought and its medieval exponents (the "theologians of Paris," *Parisienses theologi*, as he calls them), with a characteristically humanist awe of Cicero and his stoic ethics, and an interest in the gleanings of fifteenth-century Platonic studies. To the great convenience of the reader, Pico does not follow Aristotle and his medieval commentators into all the tortured nuances of the subject, but rather offers an accessible summary, aimed specifically at Emperor Maximilian, the dedicatee.

Pico explains that perception and cognition involve several human faculties arranged into a distinct hierarchy.[34] At the bottom are the senses, belonging to the body and concerned with the material world. At the top, residing in the soul, are reason and intellect—the former concerned with the investigation and evaluation of the information supplied by the senses, and thus still tied up with the material world; the latter devoted to the apprehension of fundamental natures or forms, and held

---

33 On this work see especially the introductions to its modern English and Italian translations: Gianfrancesco Pico della Mirandola, *On the Imagination*, trans. Harry Caplan (New Haven, CT: Yale University Press, 1930), 1–10; and, in much greater detail, Gian Francesco Pico della Mirandola, *L'immaginazione*, ed. and trans. Francesco Molinarolo (Pisa: Edizioni della Normale, 2022), 7–168. For a broader view of concepts related to the perception of music in medieval Europe, see Leach, *Sung Birds*, 11–54.

34 This is the subject of the second and third chapters: *Liber de imaginatione*, fols. 6r–9r.

in common with the cognition of the angels. In between the body with its senses, and the soul with its reason, sits the imagination, mediating between the two: it receives the impressions of the senses and makes them available to reason for evaluation; it retains sensory impressions in memory for later recollection; and moreover it can generate sensory impressions even in the absence of provocations from the material world (i.e., what we now call imagination). In performing these operations, the imagination is influenced by the humours, and thus the sensory impressions that reach the reasoning faculty will be inflected by the humoural balance prevailing in the sensing body, rather than being an objective representation of material reality.[35] Pico—defaulting to a visual analogy—describes this as being similar to looking at an object through coloured and shaped glass, and receiving thereby a distorted image.[36] Inherited traits, and environmental factors such as the climate in a particular locale, will also have an impact.[37] Pico is absolutely clear that the imagination is biased toward sight as the chief of the senses; he points out that this is why it is called the image-ination.[38] Sound thus enters the Renaissance sensorium on the back foot, as it were, presenting itself to reason through an organ that is not specialised in its particular phenomenal modality.

The senses and the imagination, being of the body and thus earthly, tend toward evil, and are liable therefore to lead reason toward false opinions which arouse strong and unhelpful emotions, such as fear, anger, or lust.[39] A good deal of Pico's treatise is concerned with recommending remedies and countermeasures to this danger.[40] These include addressing humoural imbalance; avoiding negative sensory impressions; rigorously training the reasoning faculty; allowing time for reason to "catch up" before reacting to a sensory provocation; recalling core Christian precepts and contemplating Christ's example and those of the saints; and spending as much time as possible withdrawn to the

---

35 This is covered in Chapter 8: *Liber de imaginatione*, fols. 16r–20r.
36 *Liber de imaginatione*, fols. 17r–v.
37 *Liber de imaginatione*, fols. 17v–18v.
38 *Liber de imaginatione*, fols. 5v–6r.
39 This issue is first highlighted in chapter 7, "On the numerous evils which come from the imagination" (De Malis plurimis, quae de imaginatione prodeunt): *Liber de imaginatione*, fols. 13r–16r.
40 The ninth through twelfth chapters deal with this: *Liber de imaginatione*, fols. 20r–39v.

intellect, the human faculty that is closest to God and most remote from the evils of the mortal life.

It is against the backdrop of this particular model of sensory perception that the debate concerning the judgement of the ear versus that of reason played out in Renaissance music theory. The senses, being of the body, are shared by other animals; reason, being of the soul, is unique to man, and somewhat divine. However, because it is that faculty of the soul that investigates and evaluates the material world as reported by the senses, reason can be misled, and is liable to draw the soul into error and vice. This is why judgement (i.e., the evaluative function of reason) is urgently concerned with moral character. It is also why responses to sound based on the witness of hearing alone are bestial, in the specific sense that they make use only of the portion of man that is animal and not of the portion that is divine. For Pico, such a perceptual operation would constitute a betrayal of the basic aspiration always to ascend through the faculties toward that which is closest to God.[41]

According to Pico, it is the emotions stirred up by false opinions, reached by the reasoning faculty on the basis of dubious imaginings, that comprise the principal danger inherent in sensory cognition, because of the capacity of strong emotions to provoke rash actions.[42] Pico identifies pleasure and pain as the fundamental emotions, out of which all the others are mixed.[43] Music, of course, is routinely identified as a powerful sensory provocation to emotion. Across our 1501 corpus, love song and dance are often said to provoke lust, and the songs and sounds of war to inspire fear, both of which are (according to Pico's scheme) unhelpful emotions liable to prompt undesirable actions. On the other hand, music is also often said to generate joy (*gaudium*), a pathway that fulfils recreational, medical, and pious functions. Pico specifically recommends exposing children's impressionable imaginations to "choruses of angels chanting harmonious tunes" (psallentes Angelorum choros concinnas voces), among other visions of heavenly bliss, because the delight they inspire will encourage the young to obey Christian precepts.[44]

---

41 See especially *Liber de imaginatione*, fols. 13v–14r.
42 First introduced at *Liber de imaginatione*, fols. 14r–16r.
43 *Liber de imaginatione*, fol. 23v.
44 *Liber de imaginatione*, fol. 35r.

Pico implies a particular reading of the mechanism by which music might prompt joy when he refers to the Platonic doctrine of anamnesis or reminiscence. Aristotle argued that the soul enters the body as a blank canvas ("veluti nuda tabula, in qua nihil pictum, nihil delineatum est"), whereas according to Plato the soul retains knowledge from its residence in the divine realm, knowledge which the incarnated soul does not consciously remember, but which can be recollected thanks to a suitable sensory provocation.[45] Thus, for Plato music prompts joy because it generates a reminiscence of the harmony of the spheres—or of the music of the angels in heaven, if a more directly Christian reading is preferred—which had filled the disembodied soul with joy prior to its incarnation. (Here, though, a more determined Aristotelian could point out that the philosopher debunks the notion that the spheres generate tones comprising a harmony in *De caelo et mundo* 2.9, one of the Aristotelian works most commonly taught by professors of natural philosophy in Italy.)[46]

Thus, we can conclude that students attending lectures in natural philosophy at Italian universities in 1501 inevitably encountered musical and music-related topics, because Aristotle and his commentators discuss them in set works including *De anima*, *Physics*, *Metaphysics*, and *De caelo et mundo*. Students learned that sound is a passing disturbance of the air caused by the striking of a resonant object, giving it a more subtle and tenuous form of existence than other sensory provocations that took permanent material form. They heard that sound moves through the air like ripples in a pool, and that the speed and size of its ripples determine its pitch and intensity. No doubt students were able, like Pietro d'Abano, to apprehend in at least a general way the implications of these features for the acoustics of built spaces, such as churches and squares, and for the acoustics of sounding devices, such as lutes and bells. They further learned that voice, although formed by the same physical mechanism, differs from other forms of sound in that it allies sound to intention and meaning, turning motions of the soul into motions of the air, and giving acoustic shape to the memories and fantasies of the imagination. Music they came to understand as a discourse of meaningful sound built closely

---

45 *Liber de imaginatione*, fol. 12r.
46 Aristotle, [*Opera*], fols. 152r–v (misnumbered, actually 148r–v).

on the model of the voice, borrowing its dimensions of phrase, pitch, consonance, and rhythmic articulation directly from the soul's recipe for creating speech or song.

Hearing, students learned, worked thanks to a transference of the disturbance from the air outside to the air inside the ear, from whence it could be brought to the brain via the nerves. In the brain, sounds were received first by the imagination, which retained them in memory and made them available to the reasoning faculty for evaluation. The well-cultivated rational faculty would discern correctly between helpful and dangerous sounds, embracing the former and avoiding the latter; however, reason can be misled, resulting in false judgements. Students learned that the opinions formed by reason prompt emotions, which may be useful or destructive, and which motivate action; thus, a poorly cultivated rational faculty, mistakenly evaluating a dangerous sound as useful, will spur negative emotions, such as lust or anger, resulting in inappropriate actions. These are the ideas that lie behind the great concern with musical judgement, and especially the discernment of upright vs licentious music, found in many contemporary writers on music, among them Baldassare Castiglione, Paolo Cortesi, and Raffaello Brandolini (and as discussed in Chapter 1 above, particularly 1.2).[47]

Students surely understood that Aristotle's discussion of sound was obviously related to music, because his commentators (more, in fact, than Aristotle himself) integrate musical sound-producers (instruments, bells) and musical sound-elements (consonance, pitch) into their explanations—even to the extent of citing Boethius' *De musica*, as we have seen. Thus, university-educated Italians inevitably brought their scientific understanding of sound, hearing and sensory cognition along to the task of making, listening to, and talking about music. Much work remains to be done to tease out the implications of this fact for our readings of contemporary musical culture.

---

47 See, among others, Tim Shephard and Patrick McMahon, "Foolish Midas: Representing Musical Judgement and Moral Judgement in Italy c.1520," in *Music, Myth and Story in Medieval and Early Modern Culture*, ed. Katherine Butler and Samantha Bassler (Woodbridge: Boydell, 2019), 87–104.

3.2 Rhetoric

Gregorio Amaseo, *Gregorii Amasei Utinensis Oratoris Facuntissimi Oratio de laudibus studiorum humanitatis ac eloquentiae* (Venice: per Bernardino Benalio, 1501)

Bernardino Bornato, *Opusculum de laudibus matrimonii Et de immortalitate animae* (Brescia: per Bernardino Misinta, 1501)

François de Bourdon, *Oratio pro capessenda expeditione contra infideles habita in conspectu domini Alexandri divina providentia pape VI. Ex parte d. Petri Daubusson cardi sancti Adriani magni magistri Rhodi per fratrem Francisci de Bourdon decretorum doctorem ipsius reverendissimi domini cappellanum* (Rome: s.n., 1501)

Raffaello Brandolini, *Parentalis oratio de obitu Dominici Ruvere Sancti Clementis presbyteri cardinalis Romae in templo Sanctae Mariae de populo ad patres e populum habita MDI* (Rome: Euchario Silber, 1501)

Cicero, *Commentarii Philippicarum cum annotationibus Philippi Beroaldi* (Bologna: Benedetto Faelli, 1501)

Cicero, *Tullius De oratore cum commento et alia opera* (Venice: per Albertino da Lessona, 1501)

Erazm Ciolek, *Ad Alexandrum sextum pontificem maximum in prestita obedientia Romae habita oratio* (Rome: Johann Besicken, 1501)

Leonardo Commenduno, *Oratio d. Leonardi Comenduni Bergomatis ac militis Bergomatium legati congratulatoria ad serenissimum Venetorum principem dominum d. Leonardum Lauretanum* (Venice: per Bernardino Vitali, 1501)

Girolamo Donati, *Ad Christianiss. Ac invictiss. Gallorum Regem Oratio* (Venice: Aldo Manuzio, 1501)

Girolamo Donati, *Ad Caesarem pro re christiana* (Venice: per Bernardino Vitali, 1501)

Girolamo Donati, *La oration del magnifico & clarissimo misier Hieronymo Donado orator veneto, facta al sacra maiesta de re Maximiliano* (Venice: per Bernardino Vitali, 1501)

Pietro Pasqualigo, *Ad Hemanuelem Lusitaniae regem oratio* (Venice: per Bernardino Vitali, 1501)

Giovanni Battista Pio, *Praelectio in Titum Lucretium & Suetonium Tranquillum* (Bologna: s.n., 1501)

Girolamo Porcia, *In Turcos Porcia declamatio* (Rome: Johann Besicken, 1501)

Sallust, *Hoc in volumine haec continentur. Pomponii epistola ad Augustinum Maphaeum. C. Crispi Salustii bellum catilinarium cum commento Laurentii Vallae. Portii Latronis declamatio contra L. Catilinam. C. Crispi Salustii bellum iugurtinum cum commentariis preclarissimi fratris Ioannis chrysostomi Soldi brixiani. C. Crispi Salustii variae orationes ex libris eius dem historiarum exceptae. C. Crispi Salustii vita. Romae per Pomponium emendata: Mediolanique per Alexandrum Minutianum diligentissime revisa* (Milan: Alessandro Minuziano, 1501)

Among the core tasks of the humanities professors at an Italian university was the teaching of rhetoric. In studying rhetoric, students acquired the skills of persuasive speech in Latin, which (harnessed to their studies in logic) they practiced regularly in university disputations, and needed in order to pass their final oral examination.[48] Once graduated, it was hoped that students would use their rhetorical skills in future leadership roles in government, diplomacy and politics, soldiering, the church, or else in legal practice. They would also be useful for those aspiring to become university professors, who competed vigorously with one other for students when lecturing concurrently.

The centrality of oratory in Italian Renaissance society is amply represented in our 1501 corpus, among which there are at least twelve books presenting contemporary public speeches—either real speeches commemorated in print, or speeches planned or imagined that were never audibly delivered. Diplomatic and political oratory dominates, driven, logically enough, by Venetian diplomacy overseas, and overseas diplomacy at the Papal court. Girolamo Donati was appointed Venetian ambassador to the Holy Roman Empire in 1501, and is represented in our 1501 corpus by two speeches addressed to Maximilian I urging war against the Ottoman Empire, as well as an oration marking the French conquest of Naples which has the same objective in view. War against the Ottomans is also the aim for Pietro Pasqualigo, appointed Venetian ambassador to Portugal in the same year, in a speech delivered before Manuel I. Venetian politics at home is represented by a panegyric delivered to Leonardo Loredan marking his election as doge in 1501, by the Bergamasque patrician Leonardo Commenduno. Meanwhile, Pope Alexander VI is addressed by Vatican lawyer Girolamo Porcia, and François de Bourdon representing the Order of St John of Jerusalem, in separate speeches urging action to unite Christendom against the Ottomans; and by the Polish diplomat Erazm Ciolek advocating alliance

---

48 On the importance of Latin orality in Italian universities, including the topics of disputations and examinations, see Grendler, *The Universities*, 151–57.

between the papacy and the Lithuanian Orthodox Church to discourage aggression from Muscovy.

Also in our 1501 corpus is an anthology of wedding speeches (alongside other short works) by the Brescian lawyer and poet Bernardino Maccio Bornato, and a funeral oration for Cardinal Domenico della Rovere (d.23 April 1501) which was to have been delivered by Raffaello Brandolini but had to be cut from the funeral ceremonies because of time pressures. Finally, university oratory is represented by two inaugural lectures. One was delivered by the Udinese Gregorio Amaseo upon taking up a professorship in the Scuola di San Marco in Venice—a small institution of higher learning, one of Grendler's "incomplete universities," teaching humanities to future civil servants—left vacant by the death in 1501 of Giorgio Valla. The other was delivered by Giovanni Battista Pio upon his reappointment to a professorship in rhetoric at the University of Bologna in 1500, a post which he had previously occupied in 1495–96.

Political and legal speeches from antiquity are also present in some abundance in our 1501 corpus, furnishing models for students and practitioners of oratory. The most obvious example is Cicero's *Philippics*, a series of fourteen speeches delivered following the assassination of Julius Caesar through which he persuaded the senate to act against Mark Antony. Our 1501 edition is manifestly a university-related project, because it was instigated by Filippo Beroaldo, a prolific commentator and Professor of Rhetoric and Poetry at the University of Bologna from the 1470s to his death in 1505, together with his long-term printer-collaborator Benedetto Faelli, and includes commentaries by both Beroaldo and Francesco Maturanzio, Professor of Rhetoric at the University of Perugia. Several more Roman orations can be found in Sallust, including speeches by Julius Caesar and Cato the Younger in the *Bellum Catilinae*, and by M. Aemilius Lepidus and L. Marcius Philippus in the context of Aemilius' rebellion among the fragments of the *Histories*. Our 1501 Sallust was originally prepared for a 1490 Roman edition by Pomponius Leto, then corrected for our Milan edition by the printer-scholar Alessandro Minuziano; it includes commentaries by the itinerant humanities professor Lorenzo Valla and the obscure Giangrisostomo Soldi.

The key authority on rhetoric and oratory, as they were taught at the universities, was Cicero—particularly beloved of the fifteenth-century humanists for his elegant Latin style, his upright civic ethics, and above all for his marriage of literary eloquence with political eminence which substantiated their own claims to value and status within their communities.[49] Thanks to this reception, Cicero was perhaps the most extensively circulated classical author of the period: more than two hundred printed editions of his various works appeared in Italy between 1480 and 1520, around twice as many as Virgil and even exceeding Ovid by a comfortable margin. Among the statesman's many works on rhetoric, since the Middle Ages the standard textbook had been the *Rhetorica nova* (aka *Rhetorica ad Herennium*)—now no longer considered Cicero's work—in which music plays no role.[50] From the mid-fifteenth century on, Cicero's authentic mature works on the subject gained increasing traction, especially *De oratore*, facilitated by the rediscovery of its complete text in 1421 and then by its very early availability in print in Italy.[51] In contrast to the *Rhetorica vetus*, and indeed to all the other rhetorical treatises associated with Cicero, *De oratore* makes prominent mention of music, and establishes musical analogies as core to the conceptualisation of oratory. (The same can equally be said of the thoroughly Ciceronian *Institutio oratoria* of Quintilian, rediscovered complete in 1416 and also a hit in print, although it was not printed in 1501.)

Our 1501 edition of *De oratore*, a smart but rather austere folio volume, is in fact an anthology of Ciceronian texts on oratory. The *De oratore* itself takes up the lion's share of the space, but afterwards we also find the *Orator, Topica, De partitione oratio, De claris oratoribus* (aka *Brutus*), *De petitione consulatus* (supposedly by Cicero's brother, advising him on how to get elected consul), and *De optimo genere oratorum*. Also appended are the speeches for and against Ctesiphus by Aeschines

---

49 For an overview see David Marsh, "Cicero in the Renaissance," in *The Cambridge Companion to Cicero*, ed. Catherine Steel (Cambridge, UK: Cambridge University Press, 2013), 306–17.

50 Doubts about its authorship were raised already in the fifteenth century: see Grendler, *The Universities*, 200.

51 On the circulation of Cicero's rhetorical works and associated commentaries, see especially John O. Ward, "Renaissance Commentators on Ciceronian Rhetoric," in *Renaissance Eloquence: Studies in the Theory and Practice of Renaissance Rhetoric*, ed. James J. Murphy (Berkeley, CA: University of California Press, 1983), 126–73; Peter Mack, *A History of Renaissance Rhetoric* (Oxford: Oxford University Press, 2011), 13–32.

and Demosthenes, both giants of ancient Athenian oratory, translated into Latin by Leonardo Bruni. *De oratore* is commented by Ognibene Bonisoli, a student of Vittorino da Feltre, who for a short while took over his former master's school in Mantua, but spent the majority of his mid-fifteenth-century career teaching school-age grammar and rhetoric in Vicenza; most likely the commentary reflects the content of his own teaching. Thus, in this volume, the student in 1501 could find the standard textbook on rhetoric with a classroom-ready commentary, a selection of shorter Ciceronian works on the same subject, and also some examples of classical rhetoric in the form of the speeches of Aeschines and Demosthenes.

In the first book of *De oratore*, Cicero is concerned to define the nature of oratory as a discipline, and the fields of knowledge proper to it. This is tricky, because oratory is the art of speaking well, and in order to speak well one must have something worthwhile to say. As Cicero points out, "what can be more insane than the hollow sound of even the best and most distinguished words, if they are not based upon thought and knowledge?"[52] Thus, by implication, the orator must master not only speaking well, but also all of the subjects on which one might need to speak. Introducing the example of the sophist and polymath Hippias, Cicero observes that "the ancient teachers and masters of speaking regarded no type of discussion to be outside of their competence, and they always occupied themselves with speeches of every kind."[53] This places improbably wide limits on the scope of the orator's expertise, and risks bringing him into conflict with those who specialise in all of the individual sciences. As Cicero points out,

> Instaret academia quae quicquid dixisses: id teipsum negare cogeret. Stoici vero nostri disputationum suarum: atque interrogationum laqueis te irretitum tenerent. Peripatetici autem haec ipsa quae propria oratorum putas esse adiumenta atque ornamenta dicendi: a se peti dicerent oportere: ac non solum meliora sed etiam multo plura Aristotelem

---

[52] "quid est enim tam furiosum quam verborum vel optimorum atque ornatissimorum sonitus inanis nulla subiecta sententia nec scientia?" *Tullius De oratore*, fol. 10v. Cicero, *On the Ideal Orator*, trans. James M. May and Jakob Wisse (Oxford: Oxford University Press, 2001), 70 (1.51).

[53] "Namque illos veteres doctores auctoresque dicendi nullum genus disputationis a se alienum putasse accaepimus semperque esse in omni orationis ratione versatos." *Tullius De oratore*, fol. 127r. Cicero, *On the Ideal Orator*, 262 (3.126).

Theophrastum de his rebus: quam omnes dicendi magistros scripsisse ostenderent: missos facio mathematicos: grammaticos: quorum artibus vestra ista dicendi vis ne minima quidem societate coniungitur.[54]

The Academy would assail you, and would force you, whatever you had asserted, to deny it again. Certainly our Stoics would hold you ensnared in the nets of their debating and questioning. And the Peripatetic philosophers would succeed in proving that even these things you assume to be the exclusive property of orators, the tools and ornaments of speaking, should actually be obtained from them; and they would demonstrate that Aristotle and Theophrastus have written not only better, but even much more on such topics than all the teachers of rhetoric put together. And I won't even mention the mathematicians, the grammarians: with their fields, that oratorical faculty of yours hasn't even the slightest thing in common.[55]

Cicero deploys a few specific strategies in his efforts to think through these issues. At several points in *De oratore* he discusses the fundamental nature of the disciplines and the manner in which they arose, sometimes using the musical metaphor of harmony. Initially, he explains, the various components of each discipline were understood separately:

omnia fere quae sunt conclusa nunc artibus: dispersa et dissipata quondam fuerunt: ut in musicis: et numeri et voces et modi. In geometria lineamenta: formae: intervalla: magnitudines: in astrologia coeli conversio: ortus: obitus: motusque siderum: in grammaticis poetarum pertractatio: historiarum cognitio: verborum interpretatio. pronunciandi quidam sonus. in hac denique ipsa ratione dicendi. excogitare. ornare. disponere meminisse. agere. ignota quondam omnibus et diffusa late videbantur.[56]

Nearly all subjects that are nowadays covered by a systematic art were once disconnected and scattered, such as rhythms, notes, and tones in music; in mathematics, lines, figures, distances, and sizes; in astronomy, the revolutions of the heavens, the risings, settings, and movements of the heavenly bodies; in grammar, the examination of the poets, the investigation of the stories, the explanation of words, and the sounds that should be used in pronouncing them; and finally in our subject here (the

---

54 *Tullius De oratore*, fol. 9v. Modern editions give musicians in addition to mathematicians and grammarians in this passage, but musicians are absent from our 1501 text.
55 Cicero, *On the Ideal Orator*, 68 (1.43–44).
56 *Tullius De oratore*, fol. 26v.

theory of speaking), devising what to say, style, arrangement, memory, and delivery, were once, it seems, unknown and scattered far and wide.[57]

Bonisoli here accepts Cicero's invitation and comments on all the individual components of the arts listed in this passage. On music he writes:

> musica ex partibus vocum composita est atque mensura Voces. et numeri semper fuerunt. sed tametsi haec elementa fuerunt: tamen nisi vocis mensura cum numero vocis addita fuisset ars musica nunquam composita fuisset.[58]

> Music is composed from pitch-elements and measurement. Pitches and numbers have always been present, but although these elements were present, yet until the measurement of pitch had been added to the number of pitch, the art of music would never have been assembled.

This definition seems to refer clearly to two mathematical aspects of music, namely pitch and duration—a conventional account of the core elements of musical science in the period. However, its coherence is then destabilised when Bonisoli goes on to say that number refers to "well-turned rhythms" (rhythmimi concinitates), whilst pitch is identical with number, suggesting that it is not pitch as such but rather rhythm that is at stake. His reason for pivoting in this way immediately becomes clear: he wants to equate musical number with poetic meter ("nam numeros metra dixerunt"), a connection that will bear fruit much later in his commentary, when he discusses meter as "number" quite extensively in his remarks dealing with Cicero's passages on the musical qualities of oratorical delivery (on which more below).

According to Cicero, the disintegration of the arts persisted until some came along who, by mastering all the elements of a given discipline, were able to impose coherence upon them—for music he names Damon and Aristoxenus.[59] In addition to the coherence achieved within individual disciplines, coherence also characterises the academy as a whole. Cicero cites Plato as saying:

---

57 Cicero, *On the Ideal Orator*, 102 (1.187), slightly altered to match our 1501 Latin.
58 *Tullius De oratore*, fol. 26v.
59 *Tullius De oratore*, fol. 127v (3.132).

> omnem doctrinam harum ingenuarum et humanarum artium uno quodam societatis vinculo contineri. Ubi enim perspecta vis est orationis: eius quam causae rerum atque exitus cognoscuntur mirus quidam omnium quasi consensus doctrinarum concentusque reperitur.[60]
>
> that all the teachings of our noble and humane arts are held together by one common bond. Since, once it is perceived how forceful the method is on which the knowledge of causes and outcomes is based, there emerges, so to speak, an agreement and harmony between all disciplines that is quite extraordinary.[61]

The coherence of each science was borrowed from elsewhere—namely from philosophy, which Cicero thinks of as an inherently comprehensive discipline. As Bonisoli explains in his commentary on this passage, "every art which teaches the causes and effects of things is philosophy; and indeed every thing has some effect; therefore philosophy is the mother of all arts of whatever kind."[62] On the other hand, as Bonisoli observes in commenting on another passage comparing the arts, philosophy differs from the other disciplines in that it "concerns the precepts of living well;" or in other words (commenting on yet another similar passage), "the philosopher must know not only what it is to live, but what it is to live with virtue."[63] Elsewhere Bonisoli observes that the orator "cannot be ignorant of moral philosophy" if he is to conduct legal cases with good judgement, making out of ethics yet another affirming parallel between the orator and the philosopher.[64] The purpose of ethics, he implies in another comment, is to inform men's judgement such that they are useful to their communities, "For if each looks after his own affairs badly, he will not serve the whole city well."[65] Thus the ethical

---

60 *Tullius De oratore*, fol. 115v.
61 Cicero, *On the Ideal Orator*, 230 (3.21).
62 "omnis ars proficiscitur que causas et effectus rerum docet. Omnis enim res effectum aliquem habet. Ergo philosophia omnium artium cuiuscumque rei mater est." *Tullius De oratore*, fol. 115v.
63 "philosophia idest bene vivendi praecepta." *Tullius*, fol. 122r (commenting on *De oratore* 3.78-9). "et hoc ad philosophiam naturalem pertinet quia philosophi non solum est scire: quid sit vivere: sed est cum virtute vivere." *Tullius De oratore*, fol. 31r (commenting on 1.212).
64 "philosophiam moralem [...] nescire non potest." *Tullius De oratore*, fol. 11r (commenting on 1.51).
65 "Nam si male suam quisque rerum aegerit nec universam civitatem recte ministrabit." *Tullius De oratore*, fol. 115v (commenting on 3.20).

dimension of oratory, shared with philosophy, underpins its value as a tool of leadership and justice.

And yet, it is here in the comprehensive scope of philosophy—similar to that of oratory—that Cicero begins to find his strategies for limiting the scope of the orator's knowledge to realistic dimensions. For he argues that although philosophers (such as Plato) may have knowledge of geometry or music, it does not follow that geometry and music are integral to the discipline of philosophy (1.217). These subjects are, as it were, secondary, and more defined in their scope, compared to philosophy or oratory, with the result that they are easier to master:

> We all know how obscure the subjects handled by the so-called mathematicians are, and how abstruse, complex, and exact is the art with which they deal. Yet even in this area, so many geniuses have emerged that almost no one who has devoted his energies to mastering it appears to have been unsuccessful. As to the theory of music, and the study of language and literature so popular nowadays (the profession of the so-called grammarians)—has anyone really dedicated himself to them without managing to acquire enough knowledge to cover the complete, almost infinite range and material of those arts?[66]

Gaining a command of the whole territory of oratory, in contrast, is a near-impossible task, with the result that great orators are very rare compared to their preeminent counterparts in the other arts. This passage calls forth from Bonisoli one of his longest and most wide-ranging comments (see Excerpt 3.3 in the Appendix). His first gesture is to reinforce Cicero's basic point by re-stating it more fully:

> "Quis ignorat:" he continues, as before, to show that orators have always been rarer than men skilled in the other arts, and here he compares orators to mathematicians, whose art, although it may be obscure, speculative, and multifaceted, yet those who have studied it intensively seem to have attained their objectives, whereas those who have devoted themselves to the art of oratory have not achieved this outcome. For such is the breadth and depth of its knowledge, that few are found who can attain oratory.

Then, as if to demonstrate that the content of the other arts can indeed be compassed with relative ease, he proceeds to unpack the components of mathematics and grammar—with a particular emphasis

---

66   Cicero, *On the Ideal Orator*, 60 (1.10). For the Latin see Excerpt 3.3 in the Appendix.

on mathematics, which he clearly regards as an exceptionally obscure and difficult discipline. He twice lists the mathematical disciplines as arithmetic, geometry, and astrology, i.e., missing out music, although elsewhere he mentions in passing that music is a mathematical subject.[67] The mathematical disciplines are characterised by their certainty and their amenability to proof, whereas in contrast philosophy, grammar and rhetoric "are perceived not through the strongest demonstration [...] but through reason, study and inquiry." Despite their certainty, the mathematical disciplines are said to be "obscure," "secret," "subtle," and "hidden;" therefore they are "suited to a speculative talent." Bonisoli reviews the nature of number (perfect/imperfect; odd/even), associated with arithmetic, and of measure (continuous/discontinuous; length/width/height/depth), associated with geometry. Astrology, by implication, uses the tools of both arithmetic and geometry to study celestial phenomena. The components of Grammar, meanwhile, are said to be letters, syllables, words, and speeches, each furnishing the building blocks of the next.

Cicero argues that the newly coherent sciences were developed by the ancient Greeks without due consideration of their relative importance. Some of the ancients, finding themselves with excessive leisure, and having little interest in the affairs of their states, devoted themselves intemperately to subjects such as poetry, geometry, music, and logic, developing these—Cicero implies—well beyond what was strictly necessary and proper:

> sed ut homines labore assidio: et quotidiano assueti quum tempestatis causa opere prohibentur ad pilam se aut ad talos aut ad tesseras conferunt aut etiam novum sibiipsi aliquem excogitant in ocio ludum sic illi a negociis publicis tanquam ab opere. aut temporibus exclusi aut voluntate sua feriati totos se alii ad poetas alii ad geometras alii ad musicos contulerunt alii etiam ut dialectici novum sibiipsi studium ludumque pepererunt. atque in his artibus quae repertae sunt ut puerorum mentes ad humanitatem fingerentur: atque virtutem omnem tempus atque aetates suas consumpserunt.[68]

---

67 "Geometria enim et musica sunt mathesis." *Tullius De oratore*, fol. 127r (commenting on 3.127).
68 *Tullius De oratore*, fol. 119r–v.

> But when people who are used to uninterrupted, daily labor are prevented from work because of the weather, they often turn to ball games and dicing, or even think up some new game for themselves during their leisure time. Something similar happened to the people I mentioned. Being either shut out from the affairs of state, just as from work, by the stormy circumstances of the time, or having taken time off from these of their own accord, they transferred their attention entirely, some to the poets, some to mathematics, some to music; and others, such as the dialecticians, even produced a new game for themselves to pursue. And in these arts, which were devised to educate children's minds in humane culture and virtue, they spent all of their time—yes, their whole lives.[69]

Bonisoli lists "those arts which have been discovered to form the minds of youth to learning and to virtue" as grammar, rhetoric, dialectic (i.e., logic), music, arithmetic, geometry, and astrology, calling them the Liberal Arts and equating them directly with the *studia humanitatis*.[70] Cicero views these studies as praiseworthy when used as a curriculum for children, but as self-indulgent and purposeless when they become a life-long obsession. The same attitude, applied specifically to music, turns up elsewhere when Cicero contrasts a professional theatre musician—a man of low status in Cicero's social world, even if a celebrity—with a Roman patrician:

> Valerius quotidie cantabat. erat enim scaenicus. quid faceret aliud? At numerius furius noster familiaris. quum est commodum. cantat. est enim paterfamilias. est eques romanus puer didicit. quod discendum fuit.[71]

> Valerius used to sing every day; of course, since he was on the stage— what else was he to do? My friend Numerius Furius, by contrast, sings when it suits him, since he is the head of a household and a Roman *eques*; as a boy he learned what he had to learn about it.[72]

Thus, the orator, like the philosopher and the patrician, should not be ignorant of music, but need not pursue it as a specialist discipline. The point extends also to the other discrete scientific disciplines: the orator should study them in childhood to acquire sufficient expertise to be able

---

69 Cicero, *On the Ideal Orator*, 240–41 (3.58).
70 *Tullius De oratore*, fol. 119r.
71 *Tullius De oratore*, fol. 122v. Bonisoli explains that Valerius was compelled to sing daily in order to keep his voice in good order ("ut voce sibi obsequentiorem reddat").
72 Cicero, *On the Ideal Orator*, 251 (3.86–87), slightly altered to match our 1501 Latin.

to speak on them in a knowledgeable fashion, but he need not have the command of a specialist. His core concerns, instead, should be law and government.

So far, in Book 1 of *De oratore*, we have encountered music principally as a subject upon which the orator may be called to speak. In Book 3, music is once again to the fore, but now as an illuminating analogy in discussing different aspects of oratorical delivery. Music's most prominent role in Book 3 lies in several long passages discussing the musical qualities of language and speech. Cicero is clear that this is among the aspects of delivery that make a speech most compelling for the listener:

> In quoquo igitur homines exorrescunt. quem stupefacti dicentem intuentur in quo exclamant quem deum ut ita dicam inter homines putant qui distincte qui explicate qui abundanter qui illuminate et rebus et verbis dicunt et in ipsa oratione quasi quamdam numerum versumque conficiunt idest quod dico ornate[73]

> At whom do people stare in stunned amazement when he speaks? For whom do they cheer? Whom do they consider, if I may use the expression, a god among men? Certainly those whose speech is well shaped, is unfolded with clarity and abundance, and is brilliant, both in its content and in its words, and who, where the actual form of the speech is concerned, produce something resembling rhythm and verse—that is, those who practice what I call speaking with distinction.[74]

When he comes to discuss the matter in detail, from 3.173 on, Cicero explains that, in ancient times,

> Namque haec duo musici qui erant quondam iidem poete machinati ad voluptatem sunt versuum atque cantuum: ut et verborum numero: et vocum modo delectatione vocerent aurium satietatem. Haec igitur duo: vocis dico moderationem et verborum conclusionem. quo ad orationis severitas pati posset: a poetica ad eloquentiam traducenda esse duxerunt in quo illud est vel maximum[75]

> The musicians—who at one time were also poets—had devised two ways of giving pleasure, verse and song; they wanted to overcome satiety of the ears by giving delight, both through the rhythm of the words and the

---

73 *Tullius De oratore*, fol. 118v.
74 Cicero, *On the Ideal Orator*, 238–39 (3.53).
75 *Tullius De oratore*, fol. 132r.

cadence of the voice. And the ancients thought that these two things, I mean modulating the voice and rounding off a sentence rhythmically, should be transferred from poetry to eloquence, as far as the serious nature of oratory would permit.[76]

By "number" ("verborum numero"—the enumeration of words) Cicero means poetic meters and feet, as is made clear elsewhere in the same passage and also by Bonisoli in his commentary. When transferred to prose, in Cicero's conception, these become the judicious articulation of speech into sentences, clauses and phrases. Cicero says specifically that he is thinking of spoken rather than written text, but Bonisoli inverts the order of priorities, glossing this as primarily a matter of punctuation.

Cicero's evident desire to stress the proximity but at the same time the distance of music and poetry from oratory is matched by Bonisoli, who comments on this passage that "indeed, great poets and musicians discovered song and verse, so that the ears may be soothed with pleasure; but this is far from oratory."[77] In fact, the difference of the musicality of prose from the musicality of verse becomes a central tenet and a key theme of the discussion. Cicero is very clear that an orator cannot simply deliver a poem; as Bonisoli puts it, "It is a wonder that we want in a speech something of the form and manner of verse, and yet if it comes out simply as verse it is defective."[78] The reason for the difference is essentially one of genre—in verse one must follow the meter, in prose one must not, as Cicero explains:

> Neque vero haec tam acrem curam diligentiamque desiderant: quam est illa poetarum: quos necessitas cogit: et ipsi numeri ac modi: sic versu verba includere ut nihil sit ne spiritu quidem minimo brevius aut longius: quam necesse est. Liberior est oratio et plane: ut dicitur: sic est vere soluta. non ut fugiat tamen ut erret: sed ut sine vinculis sibi ipsa moderetur.[79]

> Certainly all this does not call for the painstaking care and diligence demanded of the poets. They are compelled by the constraints of their very rhythms and cadences to fit their words into the verse in such a

---

76 Cicero, *On the Ideal Orator*, 278 (3.174).
77 "Maiores poetae quidem: et musici cantum invenerunt et versum. ut aures delectatione mulcerent: sed hic ab oratorio distat." *Tullius De oratore*, fol. 131v.
78 "Mirumque quam in oratione volumus cuiusdam versus formam et modum ea tamen si in versum plane exierit viciosa sit." *Tullius De oratore*, fol. 131v.
79 *Tullius De oratore*, fol. 133r.

way that nothing is longer or shorter than required, even by the smallest breath. Prose speech is freer, and is indeed clearly unbound, as it is called—though not so much that it will slip away or wander about, but that, without being chained, it will set its own limits.[80]

Because of the greater freedom of prose, the orator must take something from the domains of poetry and music, but need not develop specialist expertise in either subject. Cicero states several times that the judgement of the ears is sufficient to the orator's purpose, and Bonisoli reinforces the point: "the feet are not followed exactly, rather speech is produced according to the judgement of the ears;" "he teaches that the use and choice of feet is not strict, but in accordance with the ready judgement of the ears of men."[81] To support this position, Cicero develops at some length the argument that a knowledge of poetics and music theory is necessary to the practice of those arts, but not to their judgement (3.195–98). As Bonisoli puts it:

> quaestioni respondet quae ratione fieri possit: ut indoctus et imperitus musicae possit in oratione deprehendere quid consonet: aut dissonet: quia videlicet in situs est hominibus tacitus quidam sensus: ut inquamque arte rectum pepereramque diiudicent. Illud concinnum vel congruum.[82]

> He answers the question, how can it be that those uneducated and inexpert in music can detect in a speech that which is harmonious or discordant? Because it is evident that there is a certain innate sense within man, which allows them to judge what in art is rightly created, what is elegant and fitting.

Cicero observes that people exercise such judgement in their reactions to the visual arts; and (in Bonisoli's words) "if this is so in other arts, it is much more so in numbers and voice, the consonance and dissonance of which are naturally accessible to us."[83] Indeed, according to Cicero, "nothing is, in fact, so akin to our natural feelings as rhythms and the sounds of voices: they rouse and inflame us, calm and sooth us, and

---

80 Cicero, *On the Ideal Orator*, 281 (3.184).
81 "quia non lege certa pedum: sed aurium iudicio conficitur oratio." "docet usum et rationem pedum non esse admodum difficilem: sed concinnitatem auribus hominum facillime iudicari." Both *Tullius De oratore*, fol. 133r.
82 *Tullius De oratore*, fol. 134r (in relation to 3.195).
83 "Si in aliis artibus hoc sit: multo magis in numeris ac voce: quorum consonantia se nobis: ac dissonantia naturaliter offert." *Tullius De oratore*, fol. 134r.

often lead us to joy or sadness."[84] As further evidence for the natural basis of musical judgement, he observes that when an actor or a musician makes a mistake, the audience will raise a cry and throw them out of the theatre.

The other major role for music in Book 3 of *De oratore* is as a source of analogies emphasising the importance of variety in oratorical delivery, often in parallel with analogies to the visual arts. At 3.25, Cicero locates the fundamental mechanism of the pleasure of variety in the capacity of the senses of hearing and sight to find similar value in dissimilar provocations:

> Natura nulla est ut mihi videtur quae non habeat in suo genere res conpluris dissimiles inter se quae tamen consimili laude dignentur. nam et auribus multa percipimus quae et si nos vocibus delectant tamen ita sunt varia saepe ut id quod proximum audias iocundissimum esse videatur: et oculis conliguntur pene innumerabiles voluptates quae nos ita capiunt ut unum sensum dissimili genere delectent: et reliquos sensus voluptates oblectent dispares ut sit difficile iudicium excellentis maxime[85]

> It seems to me that every category of natural phenomena includes many things that are different from one another but are nevertheless equally highly valued. For instance, all of the many delightful sounds caught by our ears consist of tones, but they are often so varied that what you have heard last seems most pleasant. The number of pleasing sensations gathered by our eyes is almost infinite, but the manner in which they captivate us is such that they delight this one sense in different ways. Each of the other senses is also charmed by dissimilar pleasures, so that it is always difficult to judge which experience is most agreeable.[86]

At 3.98, Cicero adds a nuance to this position, explaining that upon repetition pleasant sensory provocations dull and tire, by implication requiring variation, whereas more austere sounds and images have more lasting appeal:

> difficile enim dictu est: quae nam causa sit: cur ea quae maxime sensus nostros impellunt voluptateque et specie prima acerrime commovent

---

84 "Nihil est autem tam cognatum mentibus nostris quam numeri atque voces quibus et excitamur. et incendimur et lenimur et languescimus et ad hilaritatem et tristiciam saepe deducimur." *Tullius De oratore*, fol. 134r. Cicero, *On the Ideal Orator*, 285 (3.197).
85 *Tullius De oratore*, fol. 115v.
86 Cicero, *On the Ideal Orator*, 232 (3.25).

et ab iis celerrime fastidio quodam et satietate ab alienemur: quanto colorum pulcritudine: et varietate floridiora sunt in picturis novis pleraque quam in veteribus: quae tamen etiam si primo aspectu nos ceperunt diutius non delectant quum iidem nos in antiquis tabulis illo ipso horrido obsoletoque teneamur quanto moliores sunt: et delicatiores in cantu: flexiones ac false voculae: quam certe et severae quibus tamen non modo austeri: sed si saepius fiunt multitudo ipsa reclamat[87]

It is difficult to say why the very things that most stir our senses with pleasure and rouse them most strongly when we first encounter them are also the quickest to give us feelings of aversion and satiety, and thus to alienate us. How much brighter than old paintings are most of the modern ones, with their beauty and variety of color! Yet, even if they captivate us at first glance, they do not delight us much longer, whereas, on the contrary, our attention is held precisely by the roughness and fainter color of ancient paintings. In singing, how much softer and more delicate are the wandering and deceitful tones than those that are strict and true! Yet, not only people of more austere tastes dislike them, but even the crowd shouts its disapproval if they are heard too often.[88]

Bonisoli intervenes to clarify the nature of these "flexiones ac false voculae" in contrast with those that are "certe et severae." "Flexiones," he explains, "means suppleness of voice, high, low, and middling," whilst "false" indicates "not truths, but falsehoods, which are issued by a servile rather than an upright spirit."[89] Cicero's opinion of these meandering and misleading melodies is clearly justified, "because they change, and are therefore uncertain, and they do not so much delight," whereas the "certe et severae" are "said more strictly, as if following the truth."[90] This mingling of ethics and musical style is highly characteristic of contemporary accounts of musical judgement, and echoes the tendency in some classicising circles to favour a plain style of heroic recitation over more lyrical love-song.[91]

---

87   *Tullius De oratore*, fol. 124r.
88   Cicero, *On the Ideal Orator*, 253 (3.98), slightly altered.
89   "Flexiones: mollitudinem vocis acutae gravis: mediae significat. False: non proprie: sed fictae quae submisso spiritum et non proprio emittuntur." *Tullius De oratore*, fol. 124r.
90   "Certe ad id quod dixit flexiones: quia illae mutantur: ideo incertae: et non tantum delectant. [...] Nam severius dicitur quasi sequens verum." *Tullius De oratore*, fol. 124r.
91   On the mingling of musical and moral judgement see, among others, Tim Shephard and Patrick McMahon, "Foolish Midas: Representing Musical

Much later, as *De oratore* reaches its closing passages and deals most directly with audible aspects of delivery, Cicero describes the shifting emotions required of great oratory and the mechanisms by which they are produced:

> Omnis enim motus animi suum quaedam a natura habet vultum et sonum: et gestum: corpusque totum hominis: et eius omnis vultus omnesque voces ut nervi in fidibus ita sonant ut a motu animi quoque sunt pulsae. Nam voces ut chordae sunt intentae: quae ad quemque tactum respondeant acuta gravis: cita: tarda: magna: parva: quas tamen inter omnis est. suo quoque in genere mediocris. Atque etiam illa sunt ab his delapsa plura genera lene asperum contractum diffusum continenti spiritu intermisso factum scissum flexo sono attenuatum inflatum.[92]

> For by nature, every emotion has its own facial expression, tone of voice, and gesture. The entire body of a human being, all the facial expression and all the utterances of the voice, like the strings on a lyre, "sound" exactly in the way they are struck by each emotion. The voice is stretched taut like the strings of an instrument, to respond to each and every touch, to sound high, low, fast, slow, loud, and soft. And apart from each of these extremes, there is also, in each category, a middle between the extremes. Moreover, from these kinds of sounds are also derived others: smooth and rough, restrained and wide-ranging, sustained and staccato, hoarse and cracked, and with crescendo and diminuendo and a changing of pitch.[93]

The concept of variety provides the governing principle here: the different facial expressions, tone colours and gestures are "available for the actor, as colours for the painter, to secure variety."[94] The nature of the palette is clarified by Bonisoli, whose commentary on this passage

---

Judgement and Moral Judgement in Italy ca.1520," in *Music, Myth and Story in Medieval and Early Modern Europe*, ed. Katherine Butler and Samantha Bassler (Woodbridge: Boydell, 2019), 87–104. On the style of humanist recitation see most recently Blake Wilson, *Singing to the Lyre in Renaissance Italy* (Cambridge, UK: Cambridge University Press, 2020).

92 *Tullius De oratore*, fol. 130[/2]v (3.216). The foliation at this point in our 1501 copy begins to repeat numbers in error; this quote appears at the second instance of fol. 130.

93 Cicero, *On the Ideal Orator*, 292 (3.216). Note, though, the refinements to the reading of Cicero's music-theoretical vocabulary defined by Bonisoli and discussed in the next paragraph.

94 "Hi sunt actori ut pictori expositi ad variandum colores." *Tullius De oratore*, fol. 130[/2]v. Cicero, *On the Orator: Book 3. On Fate. Stoic Paradoxes. Divisions of Oratory*, trans. H. Rackham, Loeb Classical Library 349 (Cambridge, MA: Harvard

is particularly dense. The various emotions are enumerated as "anger, wretchedness, indignation, gentleness, meekness."[95] Their natural appearance is revealed "because if you are quickened to indignation, nature gives warning through a terrible countenance; if to wretchedness, [through a] sorrowful [countenance], and so on, according to the quality of each affection [...] the movement of the whole body will be wonderfully apt: gentle, violent, or humble."[96] Cicero's phrase "nervi in fidibus" uses a term for the strings of an instrument, *fides*, to refer to the lyre itself, a common poetic substitution; Bonisoli builds from this a kind of ethical resonance to anchor the notion that "men's voices are like the strings of a cithara; now, 'fides' refers to a kind of cithara, according to Festus [*De verborum significatione*], because its strings are attuned to each other, like good faith among men."[97] Bonisoli then glosses Cicero's terms for the different qualities of voice arising from different emotions: "cita" is "velox" (swift); the opposites "acuta" and "gravis" are respectively "intensa et acra" (intense and sharp) and "remissa: et plena se veritatis" (relaxed and straightforward); and the opposites "magna" and "parva" are "vox canora: magna et altitona" (a voice sounding loud and thunderous) and "modici toni" (small tones).[98] He goes on to summarise these points as follows: "gentle requires a small voice, and serious requires a loud and piercing voice, and so on for the rest. And thus it seems that all kinds of speech are divided into three, and all the species of voice are likewise threefold: intense, relaxed, and in-between."[99]

University Press, 1942), 173 (3.217), adapted. (The Loeb translation of this passage is closer to the Latin than the Oxford one.)

95 "irae misericordiae: indignationis: lenitatis. mansuetudinis." *Tullius De oratore*, fol. 130[/2]v.

96 "quia. si ad indignationem concites natura monet: ut terribilem vultum si ad misericordiam. flebilem et sic de caeteris per cuiusque affectus qualitate. [...] totius corporis motum mirabundum placabundum: lenem vehementem summissum." *Tullius De oratore*, fol. 130[/2]v.

97 "quia voces in homine sunt quaedam quasi chordae in cithara. Est autem fides citharae genus sic dicta ut Festo placet quod ita eius chordae inter se conveniant: sicut fides inter homines." *Tullius De oratore*, fol. 130[/2]v.

98 *Tullius De oratore*, fol. 130[/2]v.

99 "Nam lene parvam et gravem vocem asperum magnam et accutam desiderat: et sic de caeteris. Et sic apparet omnia genera orationis in tria derivari: et species vocis item omnes in tres: intentam: remissam: mediocrem." *Tullius De oratore*, fol. 131[/2]r.

The final advice on delivery given by Cicero in *De oratore* concerns the care of the voice by avoiding extremes of pitch; and here, again, variety is desirable. Cicero's key example in this passage is the 2nd century BCE politician and soldier Caius Gracchus, who reportedly had a piper concealed behind him when giving a speech, whose job was to play so as to call the orator back from extremes of excitement or langour. Cicero disapproves of the mechanism ("you will leave the piper at home"—"fistulatorem domi relinquetis"), but agrees with its objective, for reasons that he clearly outlines:

> Quid ad auris nostras et actionis suavitatem: quid est vicissitudine et varietate et commutatione aptius [...] In omni voce inquit Crassus est quiddam medium: sed suum cuique voci: hinc gradatim ascendere vocem utile et suave est. nam a principio clamare agreste quiddam est et illud idem ad firmandam est voci salutari: deinde est quiddam contentionis extremum: quod tamen interius: est quam acutissimus clamor quo te fistula progredi non sinet et tamen ab ipsa contentione revocabit. Est item contra quiddam in remissione gravissimum quoque tanquam sonorum gradibus descenditur. Haec varietas: et hic per omnes sonos vocis cursus et se tuebitur: et orationi deferet suavitatem:[100]

> And indeed, what is more suitable for a pleasing delivery than alternation, variety, and change? [...] "There is," replied Crassus, "a middle range in every voice (though this is different in every individual case). Raising the voice gradually from this level is useful as well as pleasing, since shouting right from the start is a coarse thing to do, and this gradual approach is at the same time salutary, as it will strengthen the voice. Moreover, there is a certain limit to raising the voice (which is still below the level of shouting at the highest pitch). Beyond this the pipe will not allow you to go, while it will also call you back when you are actually reaching this limit. Likewise, at the other end of the scale, when you are dropping your voice there is also a lowest sound, and this you reach step by step, descending from pitch to pitch. By this variation, and by thus running through all the pitches, the voice will both preserve itself and make the delivery pleasing.[101]

Cicero hesitates to discuss the care of the voice because it is only tangentially connected to the subject of oratory; Bonisoli clarifies that it is really a matter for "physicians and sophists" (quia medicorum est et

---

100 *Tullius De oratore*, fols. 131[/2]v–132[/2]r.
101 Cicero, *On the Ideal Orator*, 296 (3.225–27).

sophistarum—on this see Chapter 1.3).[102] Nonetheless, Cicero implies here (and Bonisoli clarifies), and he states explicitly at 3.190, that the orator must practice the delivery of speeches in order to keep his voice in fine fettle.

In sum, students taking classes on Cicero's *De oratore* learned to connect music with rhetoric in three quite distinct ways. First, they encountered music as a topic on which a good orator ought to be able to say something intelligent and reasonably well-informed. In this respect, music is one of a group of specialised subjects that sit towards the periphery of the orator's sphere of expertise (the centre of which is, essentially, moral philosophy), but are not excluded from it. There is no need for the orator (or, by implication, the student of rhetoric at an Italian university) to gain a professional mastery of the details of musical science—doing so would be either a waste of time or an admission of low status. Nonetheless, "sufficient" musical knowledge is both necessary and desirable. It is interesting to note that the discussions of music found in the writings of fifteenth-century Italian literati tend to follow these precepts rather closely, in that they say enough to demonstrate a general understanding of musical concepts and ideas, and then they stop.[103]

Second, students encountered music as a valuable analogy when thinking about rhetorical *pronuntiatio* (the delivery of speeches). They learned that the musicality of verse is defined by number, that is, by its adherence to the rules of metrics—which, as explained in Chapter 1.1 above, is the meeting point of poetics and music theory. Good oratory has a musicality similar to that of verse, which it acquires by borrowing something from metrics, but applying it more freely, according to the musical judgement of the ear rather than through strict adherence to particular metrical and rhythmic schemes. Thus, oratory may have a musical quality, but it is not music. Once again, issues of status are caught up in this position. The poet and the musician must have a professional mastery of the precise forms that govern their disciplines, and that professional expertise in itself marks them as servile. The orator,

---

102 *Tullius De oratore*, fol. 131[/2]v.
103 A case in point is Leonardo Bruni, on whose brief discussion of music see Evan MacCarthy, "'This is another and greater subject': Leonardo Bruni on Music," in *Renaissance Then and Now: Danza, musica e teatra per un nuovo Rinascimento*, ed. Stefano U. Baldassari (Pisa: Edizioni ETS, 2014), 101–09.

in contrast, is literally "free" (*liber*) of those constraints, and does not need such professional expertise, relying instead on his well-cultivated judgement; those features mark his practice as liberal.

Third, students learned to describe and implement the aesthetic principle of variety in oratory, partly through musical analogies. In Cicero's discussion, variety is found across several distinct axes of musical experience. There is variety among musical performances or compositions: musical works may be quite different from one another, and yet be judged equally charming. Then there is variety as a necessary remedy for satiety—although here we must differentiate between musical styles: sounds that give the most pleasure also tire the quickest, whereas those that are more austere have more lasting appeal. Cicero's discussion of this point sets up a dichotomy between elaborate melodies issuing from a servile spirit and associated with falsehood, and restrained melodies that are upright and truthful. Finally, there is the variety of pitch and rhythm that makes voice and music possible as communicative tools. Students learned from Cicero to recognise the variation of sound across three spectra—fast/slow, intense/relaxed, and loud/small—within which a sound may occupy the extremes or a middling position. Among these, the spectrum from intense to relaxed could be considered to encompass the other two.

It seems clear that these precepts drawn from the third book of *De oratore* share a great deal with the aesthetics undergirding the practice of *cantare ad lyram* in late fifteenth- and early sixteenth-century Italy. The insistence on being musical but not quite music, the concern to differentiate the elaborate and wanton songs of servile professionals which will be but a passing fashion from the restrained and upright songs of noble orators which will win lasting fame, the assertion that theoretical expertise is not necessary to sound musical judgement, the emphasis placed on variety—all of these resonate deeply with the perspectives adopted by those working at the intersection of musical with humanist literary culture around 1500. It could be that the growing importance of *De oratore* as a rhetorical textbook in Italy in the second half of the fifteenth century, replacing the music-free *Rhetorica ad Herennium*, was instrumental in bringing their practice and its supporting ideologies into being.

3.3 Literature

Apuleius, *Commentarii a Philippo Beroaldo conditi in Asinum aureum Lucii Apuleii* (Venice: per Simone Bevilacqua, 1501)

Claudian, *Commentarius primus in Raptum Proserpinae Cl. Claudiani* (Milan: in aedibus Lucio Cotta dexteritate Guillame Le Signerre, 1501)

Juvenal, *Argumenta Satyrarum Iuvenalis per Antonium Mancinellum. Cum quattuor commentariis* (Venice: per Giovanni Tacuino, 1501)

Juvenal, *Argumenta satyrarum Iuvenalis per Antonium Mancinellum. Cum quattuor commentariis Sebastianus Ducius recensuit* (Milan: per Giovanni Angelo Scinzenzeler sub impensis Giovanni da Legnano, 1501)

Juvenal, *Commentarii Ioannis Britannici in Iuuenalem, cum gratia a ducali dominio Venetiarum nequis alius eos intra decennium imprimat* (Brescia: ab Angelo & Giacomo Britannico, 1501)

Ovid, *Epistolae Heroides Ouidii cum commentariis Antonii Volsci et Ubertini Clerici Crescentinatis* (Venice: per Giovanni Luigi Varisio, 1501)

Niccolò Perotti, *Cornucopie nuper emendatum a domino Benedicto Brugnolo: ac mirifice concinnatum cum tabula prioribus aliis copiosiori: utiliori: faciliorique* (Venice: per Giovanni Tacuino, 1501)

Persius, *Aulus Flaccus Persius cum glosis Scipionis Ferrarii Georgii filii de Monte Ferrato artium et medicine doctoris* (Venice: Giacomo Penzio, after 1501)

Pliny the Elder, *Libro de l'historia naturale* (Venice: per Albertino da Lessona, 1501)

Pliny the Younger, *Quae in isto continentur opusculo. C. Plinii iunioris epistolae per Philippum beroaldum emendatae: et unus est adiunctus liber: qui in aliis super impressis minime continebatur. Etiam eiusdem auctoris panegaerycus in laudem Trayani imperatoris: et de iuris illustribus libellus* (Venice: per Albertino da Lessona, 1501)

Terence, *Terentius cum tribus commentis. Videlicet Donati Guidonis [et] Calphurnii* (Milan: per Giovanni Angelo Scinzenzeler [et] Giovanni da Legnano, 1501)

Giovanni Tortelli, *Orthographia. Ioannis Tortelii Lima quaedam per Georgium Vallam tractatum de orthographia* (Venice: per Bartolomeo Zani, 1501)

Giorgio Valla, *De expetendis et fugiendis rebus opus* (Venice: in aedibus Aldo Manuzio impensa ac studio Giampietro Valla, 1501)

Virgil, *Vergilius cum commentariis quinque, videlicet Servii, Landini, Ant. Mancinelli, Donati, Domitii* (Venice: s.n., 1501)

As well as teaching grammar and rhetoric, the humanities professors at Italian universities were responsible for offering lectures on the most canonical and morally uplifting of the Roman poets. First among these was Virgil, and especially his *Aeneid* which, on account of its heroic theme, offered a model of both Latin style and ethical conduct. Horace was also an oft-taught author, partly because his *Ars poetica* remained until later in the sixteenth century the principal surviving ancient work of poetics. The satirical Juvenal, Persius, and Martial were favoured despite their scandalous subject matter; Ovid, though, was viewed with suspicion, although his popularity with readers made him impossible to ignore entirely. Among classical dramatists, the evergreen Terence was widely taught. All of these authors were printed in 1501, in some cases several times, as well as a few others whose position in the literature curriculum was less well established.

Much of the classical literature in our 1501 corpus is printed in large editions equipped with one or more commentaries. Many of the commentaries were written by professors of rhetoric and poetry active at Italian universities from the mid-fifteenth century on. From the university of Rome we have the professors Domizio Calderini, Antonio Mancinelli, Antonio Volsco, and Bartolomeo della Fonte (whose commentary on Persius appears in our 1501 corpus under the name of a plagiarist, Scipione Ferrari).[104] Della Fonte also taught at the University of Florence, as did Cristoforo Landino. Bologna is represented by Niccolò Perotti and Filippo Beroaldo, and Padua by Giovanni Calfurnio. From Pavia we have both Giorgio Valla and Ubertino Clerico. Other commentators on literature published in 1501 include teachers at private schools, and professors appointed by cities without a university; indeed, some of our university professors also took on these roles at different times in their careers.

These men were employed to offer courses of lectures upon specific set texts—*viva voce* commentaries, as it were—which showed students how to read, understand, and make meaning out of classical literature. It seems clear that a close relationship can be assumed between their published commentaries and their lecture plans. Moreover, in their teaching professors were expected to critique the insights of previous

---

104 On the authorship of the plagiarised commentary see Paolo Rosso, "La politica culturale dei Paleologi fra Quattro e Cinquecento e i suoi riflessi nell'editoria del marchesato," in *Trino e l'arte tipografica nel XVI secolo*, ed. Magda Balboni (Novara: Interlinea, 2014), 71–90, at 75.

commentators, accumulating layers of competitive interpretation that could grow thick and sometimes bitter. This too is very evident in their published commentaries. Our 1501 commented classics can therefore give us quite rich insights into how students were encouraged by their professors to approach the musical words, phrases and topics that pepper classical verse, both in print and in class. Students took this understanding with them into later life, informing their more leisurely enjoyment of classical literature as a morally uplifting pastime.

The Roman satirist Juvenal furnishes an excellent case study through which to introduce the key features of new commentaries on the classics, and the ways in which they deal with matters musical. Juvenal's *Satires* were printed more than seventy times in Italy in the period 1469–1520, most often with commentary or commentaries but also sometimes without. In 1501 alone they were issued five times: three times with accompanying commentary, once anthologised with the *Satires* of Persius, and once alone.

The oldest Juvenal commentary printed in 1501 is that of Domizio Calderini of 1475 (in which Calderini continually contends with a commentary completed the year before by his colleague in Rome, Angelo Sabino). Next came Giorgio Merula, best known for the *Historia Vicecomitum*, a history of the Visconti family, whose career encompassed teaching posts in Venice, Pavia, and Milan; his commentary on the *Satires* was first published in 1478. The contribution of Giorgio Valla appeared in 1485; and in 1492 we see the first edition of a commentary by Antonio Mancinelli. The most recent Juvenal commentary printed in 1501 is that of Giovanni Britannico, who taught rhetoric and grammar in Brescia. Among these many options, Calderini's commentary dominated in print before 1500, and from 1501 it was eclipsed by that of Britannico.

These five commentaries are disposed across three 1501 editions. In the *Argumenta Satyrarum Juvenalis per Antonium Mancinellum. Cum quattuor commentariis*, issued identically by different printers in Milan and Venice, we find represented, in addition to the headliner Mancinelli, Calderini, Merula, and Valla. The *Comentarii Ioannis Britannici in Iuvenalem*, meanwhile, is the first edition of Britannico's commentary, issued by his brothers, Giacomo and Angelo, who were among Brescia's most important printers.

As the *Satires* wittily attack elements of everyday life in ancient Rome, the topic of music appears frequently in different social and occasional contexts, making it is easy to see how the moral treatment of music is broadly integrated with the overall moral tenor of the work. In Satire 3, for example, which is concerned with the growing internationalisation of Rome, Juvenal uses musicians and instruments to illustrate the "pollution" of Roman culture by foreign others. In Satire 14, fear at the sound of brass instruments, specifically the *litus* and *cornu*, is used to suggest shrinking away from military life, within the broader context of the undermining of child-parent relations which forms the main topic of the satire.[105] But it is in the sixth satire, the longest of Juvenal's and addressing the morality of Roman wives, that instruments, instrumentalists, and playing practices feature most prominently.

Juvenal's objective in his sixth satire is to persuade the addressee, Postumus, not to marry, by drawing attention to the promiscuity of rich wives, and by reflecting on men who have married for money and then allowed their wives to do as they wish. Music is central to his argument, for it is professional musicians who the wives seduce and with whom they sleep. Early on in this satire, in a passage dealing with women's behaviour in the theatre, we encounter named theatre musicians of several kinds:

> Solvitur his magno comoedi fibula: sunt quae
> Chrysogonum cantare vetent: hispulla tragoedo
> Gaudet: an expectas ut quintilianus ametur:
> Accipis uxorem de qua cytharoedus echion
> Aut glaphyrus fiat pater: ambrosiusque choraules.[106]

> These women pay a lot to get a comic actor's fibula undone. There are women who stop Chrysogonus from singing. Hispulla is crazy for a tragic actor. Or would you expect them to fall for a Quintilian? You're marrying a wife who'll make the singer-citharist Echion or Glaphyrus or the *choraules* Ambrosius a father.[107]

---

105 See Alan M. Corn, "'Thus Nature Ordains': Juvenal's Fourteenth Satire," *Illinois classical studies* 17.2 (1992), 309–22, at 310.

106 Satires 6.73–77 as given in *Comentarii Ioannis Britannici*, fol. xlvii r. The text of Juvenal given in this edition does not differ from modern editions except in the smallest details; that in *Argumenta Satyrarum Juvenalis* differs a little more.

107 English translation slightly adapted from *Juvenal and Persius*, ed. and trans. Susanna Morton Braund, Loeb Classical Library 91 (Cambridge, MA: Harvard

In dealing with this passage, the first objective of all our commentators except Valla is to explain the purpose of the *fibula* (buckle) of the comedic actor or musician, and in so doing they seem largely derivative of one another. In the *Argumenta Satyrarum Juvenalis* the fullest explanation is given by Merula:

> SOLvitur his magno comoedi fibula: sensus magna persoluta pecunia refibulari vident comoedum: quem vocis servandae gratia Celso tradente infubulare consueverunt: De huiusmodi infibulatione est Martialis distichon. Dic mihi simpliciter comoedis et citharoedis Fibula quid praestas: carius ut futuant. Et rursum de refibulato adolescente idem ait. Occurrit aliquis. inter ista draucus. Et iam pedagogo liberatus Et cuius refibulavit turgidum faber penem. Adolescentulos autem infibulabant interdum vocis: interdum valitudinis causa: quae infibulatio fiebat perforata utrinque a lateribus cute: quae super glandem extenditur atque superadita fibula. id quod idem Celsus pluribus verbis in medicinae libris explicat. Set quod fibula circulus sit aeneus Columella de bobus loquens significat. ait enim aenea fibula pars auriculae latissima circumscribitur: ita ut manante sanguine tanquam o litterae ductus appareat.

"Pay a lot to get a comic actor's fibula undone:" the sense is that large sums are paid to see the comedian de-infibulated, which is done [i.e., the infibulation is done] in order to preserve his voice, as Celsus says, and they [i.e., the wives] subvert the infibulation in order to have sex. Martial's distich [*Epigrams* 14.215] concerns this kind of infibulation: "Tell me candidly, fibula, what is it you do for comic actors and singers? 'Get them a higher price for their fucking.'" And again he says something similar about a young man who was de-infibulated [*Epigrams* 9.27]: "If, as this goes on, some young athlete comes your way, now freed from tutelage, whose swollen penis has been unpinned by the smith." Moreover, youths were infibulated sometimes for the sake of their voice, sometimes for the sake of their health, the which infibulation was made by piercing holes in both sides of the skin, which extends over the glans and is raised by a clasp; this is what Celsus explains at length in his *De medicina* [7.25]. And that the buckle is a circle of bronze is explained by Columella in *De bobus* [= *De re rustica* 6.5.4], for he says that "A line is

---

University Press, 2004), 240–41. The term *citharoedus* refers specifically to a singer who accompanies himself on a cithara. A *choraules* is a musician who plays the aulos (a double-reed instrument) to accompany a theatrical chorus. The commentaries on this passage appear at: *Argumenta Satyrarum Juvenalis*, fols. LXXVIr–v; *Comentarii Ioannis Britannici*, fol. xlvii r.

drawn round the widest part of the ear-lap with brazen pin in such a way that a figure resembling the letter O appears where the blood flows."[108]

All the texts cited here had received several printed editions by 1501—in fact, Celsus was the first medical textbook ever to appear in print, in a Florentine edition of 1478. Britannico introduces a refinement by noting that the fibula covering Menophilus' penis seems to be a garment, whereas the fibula described by Celsus is a wire tether attached to the foreskin. He concludes, applying common sense in a manner that often eludes the other commentators, that "more is known about this type of fibula than about the garment, since this serves better to preserve the voice than a garment, something that can easily be loosened and removed."[109] All the commentators briefly note the reason why the fibula is necessary: sex makes the voice hoarse, something that is clearly detrimental for those who plan to "sell their voice in the recitation of plays" (vocem suam vendant in recitatione fabularum) as Britannico puts it. Valla, who evidently blushes to discuss the fibula, has a particularly elegant way of putting this:

> SUNT quae chrysogonum cantare vetent: epheborum enim vox per veneris usum solet immutari. Causamque philosophi plaerique tradunt et ipse in primis Alexander Aphrodiseus in libro problematon: quae nos latina olim fecimus.

> "There are women who stop Chrysogonus from singing:" the voice of youths is usually changed by the practice of Venus. This is explained by most of the philosophers, and first among them Alexander of Aphrodisias in his *Problemata*, which we once translated into Latin.

Two things seem clear from the comments on the start of our excerpt. The first is that readers in 1501 were expected to be unfamiliar with infibulation; the second is that the negative impact of sex on the voice is

---

108 Translations of Martial from *Epigrams, Vol. 3: Books 11–14*, ed. and trans. D. R. Shackleton Bailey, Loeb Classical Library 480 (Cambridge, MA: Harvard University Press, 1993), 321; and *Epigrams, Vol. 2: Books 6–10*, ed. and trans. D. R. Shackleton Bailey, Loeb Classical Library 95 (Cambridge, MA: Harvard University Press, 1993), 249–51. Translation of Columella from *On Agriculture, Vol. 2: Books 5–9*, ed. and trans. E. S. Forster and Edward H. Heffner, Loeb Classical Library 407 (Cambridge, MA: Harvard University Press, 1954), 147.

109 "Placet magis intelligamus de hoc genere fibulae quem de indumento: hoc enim modo vox magis servari potest quem per indumentum: quiddam facile et solvi et deponi potest."

taken to be axiomatic, something known from several authoritative texts (on this see also Chapter 1.3 above).

The next priority for the commentators is to deal with the named musicians: explaining that they are named musicians, where possible establishing them as historical personages through cross-references in other texts, and explaining the etymologies of their names. All other than Valla have similar comments on these points; Mancinelli can stand for the group:

> ECHIon. hic citharoedi nomen. In metamorphosi. vero cadmi socius in construendis thebis. GLAphyrus: citharoedi nomen: interpretatur autem festiuus iucundus astutus ornatus politus. Martialis libro quarto ait: Plaudere nec cano plaudere nec Glaphyro. [...] AMBrosius choraules: Ambrosius viri proprium: sed interpretatur divinus aut immortalis.

> "Echion:" this is the name of a singer-citharist. But in the *Metamorphoses* [of Ovid, 3.125–30] he was Cadmus' associate in building Thebes. "Glaphyrus:" the name of a singer-citharist, translating [i.e., from the Greek γλαφυρός (*glaphyros*)] as festive, pleasant, intelligent, adorned, polished. Martial, *Epigrams* 4[.5] says: "nor clap for Canus, nor clap for Glaphyrus." [...] "The *choraules* Ambrosius:" Ambrosius is a man's name, but it means "divine" or "immortal."

Calderini strikes a note of skepticism concerning the identity of Juvenal's Echion with Ovid's Echion, given that one is a singer-citharist and the other an action hero. Valla is extremely terse on these matters, using the formula "ECHion: proprium" ("Echion:" a proper name).

Finally, prompted by Ambrosius, all the commentators explain at some length what a *choraules* is. All five are excited to show their Greek erudition by explaining that the word *choraules* is a compound of χορός (*choros*), meaning the ancient Greek theatrical chorus, and αὐλός (*aulos*), a wind instrument, thus a *choraules* is a wind player involved in theatrical performances with the chorus. Calderini gives the fullest account, contextualising with the help of the popular biographies of Greek and Roman celebrities written by Suetonius and Plutarch:

> CHOraules: choraule a graecis a nostris Tibicines appellantur χορός [*choros*] enim chorum significat et αὐλός [*aulos*] tibiam magna olim estimatione et mensis principum grati. Tranquillus de Galba. Cano inquit choraulae mite placenti super coenam denarios quinque donavit. Idem Plutarchus in Galba in hoc genere claruerunt Ismenias. Dionysiodorus:

> Nicomachus: Ambrosiae autem dapes principum dicebantur quibus exhilarandis quem adhibebatur choraules.

> *Choraules*: the Greek *choraulae* are called by us "pipers." For χορός [*choros*] means "chorus," and αὐλός [*aulos*] [means] *tibia*, [an instrument] once held in great esteem and welcome at the tables of princes. Suetonius, *Life of Galba* [12.3]: "when the *choraules* Canus greatly pleased him at dinner, he [i.e., Galba] presented him with five denarii." Similarly Plutarch, *Life of Galba* [16.1]. In this category were celebrated Ismenias, Dionysiodorus, Nicomachus. Moreover, the banquets of princes at which a *choraules* was employed to enliven the proceedings were called *ambrosiae*.[110]

The reason for his extra detail soon becomes clear: he wants to show that his rival in Juvenal commentary, Angelo Sabino, who he refers to as "Fidentini," is wrong in his reading of this passage.

> Quam turpiter errat praeceptor Fidentini quam pueriliter insanit bone deus: ait enim choraulem accipi pro proprio nomine: idque affirmat Tranquilli testimonio in Nerone: qui scribit eum novisse se proditurum: hoc est se exhibiturum hydraulem et choraulem et utricularium hic invertens legit periturum: idest necaturum choraulem quem accipio pro nomine proprio.

> Good God, how shamefully master Fidentini errs, how childishly he raves, for he says that *choraulem* should be taken as a proper name. And he confirms this interpretation with the testimony of Suetonius in the *Life of Nero* [54], who writes that "he [i.e., Nero] announced that he would present himself"—that is, that he would perform—"as a player on the water-organ, the aulos, and the bagpipes." Here, turning the passage upside-down, he reads "going to perish" [*periturum*, instead of "going to appear," *proditurum*]—that is, "going to murder" [someone named] Choraules, which he takes to be a proper name.[111]

Valla is able to add further nuance, having found a more detailed account of the performance practices associated with ancient theatre in a different source:

---

110 Translation of Suetonius adapted from *Lives of the Caesars, vol. 2*, ed. and trans. J. C. Rolfe, Loeb Classical Library 38 (Cambridge, MA: Harvard University Press, 1914), 203. In fact it is Plutarch who mentions that the performance took place at dinner, not Suetonius. *Tibia* was the Latin term for the Greek *aulos*.

111 Translation of Suetonius adapted from *Lives of the Caesars, Vol. 2*, ed. and trans. Rolfe, 177.

Choraules a choro et αυλοσ [*aulos*] tibia: nam ut Diomedes refert pantomimus et pyraules [sic: pythaules] et choraules in comoedia canebant. item quando inquit chorus canebat choricis tibiis: idest choraulicis artifex concinebat in canticis autem pyraulices [sic: pythaulicis] responsabat: cum igitur comoediarum membra sint tria: di verbium: canticum: chorus a choro et tibiis choraules dicti.

Choraules [is derived] from *choro* and αυλοσ [*aulos*], *tibia*; for, as Diomedes [Grammaticus, in *Ars grammatica*] relates, "pantomimes and Pythian pipers (*pythaules*) and chorus pipers (*choraules*) performed in comedy;" and also when he says: "the chorus performed with the choric pipes, that is, the *choraules* accompanied the singing and the *pythaules* responded;" thus the parts of comedy are three: speaking, singing, and the chorus; and *choraules* is derived from *choro* and *tibiis* (pipes).

Britannico clarifies in addition that the chorus is a group of performers who both dance and sing ("nam χορός dicitur tripudium: coetus: chorus").

What is evident in the commentators' treatment of these named musicians is something like an archaeological interest to establish the historicity of both the individuals and their manner of performance, something that characterises the humanist commentary on music in our 1501 corpus more generally. Even the disreputable behaviour of the musicians, which drives the moral of the story in this excerpt, is investigated historically, rather than ethically, reconstructing the practice of infibulation. The commentators are certainly not impervious to the ethical dimension: in some way they all briefly acknowledge that Juvenal wants us to see the transaction between the women and the musicians as wicked, as when Britannico writes "He notes another vice in women. They are captured, he says, by the love of singers" (casually assigning blame to the women, as Juvenal clearly intends).[112] This is obvious to the reader without explanation, however: the concern that professional musicians may be sexual predators who might endanger the chastity of high-status women was shared by Italian readers in 1501.[113]

---

112 "Aliud vitium notat in mulieribus. Capiuntur inquit amore scaenicorum cantantium."

113 See, for example, Flora Dennis, "Unlocking the Gates of Chastity: Music and the Erotic in the Domestic Sphere in Fifteenth- and Sixteenth-Century Italy," in *Erotic Cultures of Renaissance Italy*, ed. Sara F. Matthews-Grieco (Farnham: Ashgate, 2010), 223–45, at 234; and for the broader association of music with seduction, Shephard et al., *Music in the Art of Renaissance Italy*, 223–44.

As the sixth satire continues, Juvenal turns to the religious ceremony of the Bona Dea to focus on the depravity of Roman women. This celebration was held once a year in December at the magistrate's house; every male inhabitant, including animals and images, had to leave the premises, and it was one of the few occasions on which Roman women were permitted to drink wine.[114] This is not the first time that the rites of the Bona Dea are mentioned in the *Satires*: we encounter them also in Satire 2.86–99. However, the focus of the reference in Satire 2 is on men dressing as women so as to gain entry to the ceremony, so the commentators ignore the musical elements (Juvenal mentions the absence of a "music girl with her *tibia*") and take note instead of the crossing of gender boundaries.[115]

In Satire 6, the rites of the Bona Dea are used to pass comment on the women, who are crazed with lust and drink in celebration, conflicting with the normative view that they should be chaste and sober. Sound plays a key role in Juvenal's description: music is a component of the rites, including horns (*cornu*) and wind instruments (*tibia*) that are driving the women to their frenzied state, alongside the wine. The beginning of the section is where we find the references to sounds and music:

> Nota bonae secreta deae: cum tibia lumbos
> Incitat: et cornu pariter vinoque feruntur
> Attonitae: crinemque rotant ululante priapo
> Maenades:[116]

> Everyone knows the secret rites of the Good Goddess, when the pipe excites the loins and, crazed by horn and wine alike, the maenads whirl their hair as Priapus howls.[117]

Music is integral to the commentators' basic characterisation of the rite of the Bona Dea, which is drawn from Macrobius' *Saturnalia* and Plutarch's *Life of Caesar*. Among the commentators of the *Argumenta Satyrarum*

---

114 H. S. Versnel, "The Festival for Bona Dea and the Thesmophoria," *Greece and Rome* 39.1 (1992), 31–55, at 32.

115 *Comentarii Ioannis Britannici*, fol. XVIIr; *Argumenta Satyrarum Juvenalis*, fol. xxvi v.

116 Satires 6.314–17 as given in *Comentarii Ioannis Britannici*, fol. lv (mislabelled xlix in our copy, with a handwritten correction) r.

117 English translation from *Juvenal and Persius*, ed. and trans. Braund, 260-261, amended. The commentaries on this excerpt are at *Argumenta Satyrarum Juvenalis*, fols. LXXXVIIIr–v; *Comentarii Ioannis Britannici*, fol. lv (mislabelled xlix in our copy, with a handwritten correction) r.

Juvenalis, Mancinelli gives the fullest presentation of his sources, quoting from Guarino da Verona's Latin translation of Plutarch's Greek:

> Secreta deae: scribit Macro[bius] horum sacrorum ritum occultiora fuisse: dumque deae ipsi sacra celebrarentur: ut Plutar[chus] scribsit in caesare: neque eo virum accedere neque domi adesse fas erat. In eis sacrificiis ipse inter se mulieres multa orphicis consentanea facere tradebantur: ibi maxima sacrorum pars noctu peragebatur: promiscua sonis et cantibus ioca longas quae exercebant vigilias.

> "The secret rites of the Bona Dea:" Macrobius [*Saturnalia* 1.21–29] writes that the sacred rites that accompanied the celebration of the goddess were most secret, and Plutarch writes in the *Life of Caesar* [9–10]: "It is not lawful for a man to attend, nor even to be in the house. The women, apart by themselves, are said to perform many rites during their sacred service which are Orphic in their character. There, the greatest part of the rites is celebrated by night, jocund activities, intermixed with [instrumental] sounds and songs, that they enjoy through long sleepless hours."[118]

Having established the general character of the rite (either here in Satire 6, or earlier in Satire 2 in the case of some of the commentators), all of our commentators in both 1501 editions note specifically the erotic nature of its musical component, glossing the line "cum tibia lumbos incitat" (when the pipe excites the loins). Mancinelli and Britannico both enlist an intertext here in the shape of a line from Persius' Satire 1: "as the song enters the loins" (Quum carmina lumbum intrant), a striking phrase which neatly emphasises the direct effect of music (or poetry— "carmina" could be translated either way) upon lust. Britannico, who tends to be fuller and more nuanced than our other commentators in the way he summarises what he has learned from his sources, adds: "For lust is greatly excited by lascivious singing and playing of musical instruments."[119] It is interesting to note that, whereas the descriptions of the rite itself are historical in character, this comment seems more like a general statement of truth; readers in 1501 would have had no difficulty in accepting it as such, given that the erotic charge of music had the status of an axiom in Italian culture at this period.[120]

---

118 Translation of Plutarch adapted from *Lives*, Vol. 7, trans. Bernadotte Perrin, Loeb Classical Library 99 (Cambridge, MA: Harvard University Press, 1919), 463.
119 "Nam lascivo cantu et sono libido maxime excitatur."
120 See, among many others, Dennis, "Unlocking the Gates of Chastity;" Shephard et al., *Music in the Art of Renaissance Italy*, 223–44.

When the Bona Dea comes up in Satire 2, several of our commentators expend considerable energy in setting out the close links between her cult and the Bacchanalia, delving into the details of the religions of the ancient Mediterranean and their syncretic interrelationships. Our excerpt from Satire 6 strongly reinforces the connection by referring to the devotees of the goddess as "maenads." Valla, who often chooses a different point of emphasis from the other commentators in the compilated edition, takes this as an invitation to paraphrase Livy's sensational description of Bacchic rites in *Decades* 39.9–10, giving particular attention to the violent initiation rite masked by loud music:

> CUm tybia lumbos incitat: nam non sacrorum casus sed concubitus convenerunt: veterem tangit morem quae postea abolitus fuit: bacchanalia enim romae celebrari mente prorsus insana coeperunt: in quibus omnis generis flagitii fuerat licentia: ut quidquam ad omnem explendam libidinem paratam haberet voluptatem: nec enim unum genus noxae tantum fuit: sed stupra promiscua ingenuorum et foeminarum: tum inter se: tum cum maribus falsi testes falsa signa etiam et testimonia ac falsa iudicia ex illa exibant officina. venena quoque et intestinae caedes ita ut et corpora iam sepulta e sepulchris ad incantamenta eruerentur: cuius mali labes ex hetruria in urbem convecta est in contagionis morem. Nemo ad haec sacra statu maior annis viginti admittebatur: qui introducebatur et velut victima sacerdotibus tradebatur: introductus autem a sacerdotibus priapi et cybelles producebatur in locum qui ululatibus circumsonabat multorum quae cymbalorum et tympanorum et huiusmodi musicorum modulatores instrumentorum in penitiora eius loci agebantur ne quaeritantis vox cum per vim stuprum inferebatur posset exaudiri: quod cum multis palam actum fuisset: idque novum et inusitatum sceleris genus per mulierem hispanam nomine fescenninam et adolescentem ebucium ad senatum delatum et expositum est: in quos morum subversores bonorum a posthumio consule animadversum est ex quibus alii fugientes compraehensi neci dati sunt: alii sibi mortem consciverunt. erant autem virorum ac foeminarum supra decem milia.

> "When the pipe excites the loins:" for they had assembled not for sacred purposes but for sex. This refers to an old custom which was afterward abolished. For the Bacchanalia began to be celebrated in Rome with complete insanity, in which every kind of debauchery was allowed, such that anyone might have any pleasure satisfied and every lust provided for; nor was there only one kind of crime, but a promiscuous defilement of youths and women, and with each other, and false testimony, forged seals and wills, and false judgements, emerging from the same workshop;

likewise poisonings, and murders within families, such that bodies already buried were exhumed from their graves with incantations, the which evils were brought into the city from Etruria in the manner of a contagion. No one over the age of twenty was admitted to these sacred rites; initiates were handed over to the priests as victims, and having been led in by the priests of Priapus and Cybele, he was brought forth into a place resounding with the howls of a multitude, which players of cymbals, drums, and [other] musical instruments of that kind were inciting within its confines so as to drown out the cries of the victim as he was forced to undergo some act of debauchery, which had been done with many [and] in plain view. And this new and unprecedented kind of crime was reported to the senate and exposed by a Spanish woman named Fescenna and a youth, Ebucius. The consul, Posthumius, turned his attention to these corruptors of good morals, some of whom, captured as they fled, were put to death, while others, conscious of their crime, killed themselves—and there were more than ten thousand men and women.

Valla, for whom at this point the Bona Dea has turned entirely into Bacchus, does not cite his source. Livy enjoyed a robust print transmission in Italy around 1501 both in Latin and in Italian translation, and was a treasure trove for Latinists looking for historical information on Roman musical customs—particularly those associated with religious rites, whose inception Livy generally records. Britannico, who gives a more concise paraphrase of the same points, does cite Livy; and he is also careful to explain why he is pivoting from one sacred cult (Bona Dea) to another (Bacchus), glossing the phrase "ululante priapo Maenades" (howling maenads of Priapus) by explaining that "the poet wants to show that in the cult of the Bona Dea women perform rites which are usually associated with the Bacchanalia."[121]

The final substantive musical reference in the sixth satire takes the form of a long passage concerning wives having sexual relations with musicians and committing adultery. The opening of this passage in particular draws extensive parallels between the anatomy of the lyre and that of the human body, and uses the physical gestures involved in playing an instrument and the skill of coaxing sound to refer to the skills required for intercourse:

---

121 "vult omnino ostendere poeta in sacris bonae deae: omoina fere fieri a mulieribus quae fieri consueverant in Bacchanalibus."

> Si gaudet cantu: nullius fibula durat
> Vocem vendentis praetoribus: organa semper
> In manibus: densi radiant testudine tota
> Sardonices: crispo numerantur pectine chordae
> Quo tener hedymeles operam dedit: hunc tenet: hoc se
> Solatur: gratoque indulget basia plectro.[122]

> If she enjoys singing, no one who sells his voice to the praetors will hang onto his buckle/clasp. She's forever handling musical instruments, her thicket of sardonyx rings sparkling all over the tortoise shell lyre, and she strikes the strings rhythmically with the quivering quill used by tender Hedymeles in his performances. This she hugs, this is her consolation, and she lavishes kisses upon the beloved plectrum.[123]

In the *Argumenta Satyrarum Juvenalis*, the primary focus of the commentators is upon providing definitions for the Latin words that are most likely to be unfamiliar to the contemporary reader. Mancinelli explains that "testudine" refers to the tortoise-shell lyre, and "pectinem" is the plectrum "with which the strings were struck," adding that this was said to have been invented by Sappho.[124] Similar clarifications are also given by Merula and Valla. All of our commentators save Merula, whose comments on this passage are rather terse, note that Hedymeles is a made-up name, compounded from ἡδύ (*hedu*: "sweet") and μέλος (*melos*: "song").

Calderini's commentary on this passage extends beyond these basic points, taking the opportunity to deploy several ancient musical factoids pertaining to the "inventors" of music derived from Pliny:

> CANTui: idest citharoedo: canere cum cithara docuit amphion: vel ut alii aiunt Livius auctore Plinio.

> "singing:" that is, [of] the singer-citharist. Amphion taught how to sing to the harp; or as others say, Livius [= Linus], according to Pliny [*Naturalis historia*, 7.56].

---

122 Satire 6.380–85, as given in *Comentarii Ioannis Britannici*, fols. lvi v–lvii r.
123 English translation from *Juvenal and Persius*, ed. and trans. Braund, 270–71, slightly emended. The commentaries on this excerpt are found at: *Argumenta Satyrarum Juvenalis*, fols. XCr–v; *Comentarii Ioannis Britannici*, fols. lvi v–lvii r.
124 "Testudine: cheli cithara"; "Plectro. ωληττο (πλήττω; *pletto*; strike) percutio significat: Inde plectrum quo quidem chordae percutiuntur. Id vero Sapho dicitur invenisse."

> SARdonices: [...] Tibicines autem et citharoedos gemmis uti primus docuit ismenias choraules et dionisiodorus aequalis eius et aemulus et vicomachus eodem tempore auctor Plinio.
>
> "Sardonyx rings:" [...] Tibia-players and singer-citharists were first taught the use of gems by the *choraules* Ismenias, and Dionysiadorus his equal and rival, and Vicomachus [= Nicomachus] around the same time, according to Pliny [*Naturalis historia*, 37.3].

Pliny's *Naturalis historia*—also printed in 1501, in a vernacular translation by Cristoforo Landino—contained a wealth of musical information, and was often raided by commentators for concise and clear explanations of musicians, musical instruments, and musical practices in the ancient world. In Italian editions of the period, *Naturalis historia* 7.56 is helpfully entitled "Quae quis invenerit in vita" ("What anyone invented in their life"), or "Inventori delle chose" ("The inventors of things") in Landino's translation, making it an obvious place to look for this kind of information. From the frequency with which this passage is used by the commentators, it seems likely that it was widely memorised or excerpted in commonplace books. *Naturalis historia* 37.3, on the other hand, is about gemstones, so probably Calderini found his information on Ismenias—a piper with expensive and luxurious tastes—serendipidously while looking for material on sardonyx. Britannico follows Calderini's lead in inserting a reference to musical inventors, but cites a much less obvious source:

> Testudine: idest Cithara quam Mercurius primus Teste Eratosthene ex Testudine fecit: quamquae postea Orpheo: sive ut alii volunt Apollini tradidit: quum ab eo contra dono Caduceum accepisset.
>
> "Tortoise:" that is, the cithara, which Mercury first made (as Eratosthenes testifies) from the tortoise-shell; and afterwards given to Orpheus, or, as others say, Apollo, after receiving the caduceus from him as a gift.

The ultimate source here is a work known in Italy at this date as the *Poetica astronomica* (aka *De Astronomica*; *Poeticon Astronomicon*), a short handbook on the constellations, then attributed to Hyginus, which was (and remains) the principal surviving summary of Eratosthenes' lost *Catasterisms*. Although now rather obscure, an attractive edition of the work replete with diagrams, illustrations and decorative initials was printed several times in our period. It seems that, seeking information on the cithara, Britannico has looked up the constellation "Lyra" (lyre), and given a close paraphrase of what he has found. The idea was perhaps not his, however, for Giovanni Tortelli does exactly the same in the entry on "lyra" (lyre) in his *Orthographia*—also printed in 1501—, an authoritative Latin dictionary focussed on Greek etymologies, completed probably in 1452, which was extensively plundered by the commentators.[125] Britannico's paraphrase includes points from Hyginus that are not mentioned by Tortelli, though, indicating that, whilst he may have borrowed the reference from Tortelli, he probably consulted the source direct.

Valla, meanwhile, ever the odd one out, glosses "organa" with a description of a contemporary church organ, vividly recalling the majesty of the instrument's sound, evidently from personal experience; only afterward does he note that classical authors used the term to refer to string instruments:

> ORGana semper in manibus. per excellentiam dicta musica instrumenta quod multis meatibus quasi cicutis imparibus: unum vox erumpat consurgant et concentum cum bombulo emittant. Veteres tamen organa fidibus obtensa dicitur voluerunt: at ut hic Iuvenalis ita Lucretius. Constare elementis levibus aeque. ac musaea mele per chordas organicique. Nobilibus digitis expergefacta figurant.

> "Forever handling musical instruments:" on account of [its] excellence, it [i.e., the organ] is called "musical instruments" because a single sound bursts forth from many pipes [acting] as passageways; they arise together and send forth harmony with a deep, hollow sound. The ancients, however, applied the name to instruments with strings stretched across them, as here Juvenal, and also Lucretius [*De rerum natura* 2.411–13]: "Consists of elements as delicate, as the melodies of the Muses from the strings and instruments, which noble fingers awaken and shape."[126]

---

125 *Orthographia*, fol. 103r.
126 Translation of Lucretius adapted from *On the Nature of Things*, trans. W. H. D. Rouse, rev. Martin F. Smith, Loeb Classical Library 181 (Cambridge, MA: Harvard University Press, 1924), 127. Note that the variant reading "per chordas organicique," which with its "and" implies two separate categories of instrument, complicates the usual "per chordas organici" (from the strings of instruments). Valla seems to have had a special interest in music: the lengthy section on ancient music theory included in his encyclopedic summary of philosophical disciplines, *De expetendis et fugiendis rebus opus*, printed in 1501, has been extensively studied by musicologists—see Palisca, *Humanism*, 67–87; Moyer, *Musica Scientia*, 92–100.

Valla's initial gloss here implicitly invites the reader to think of "handling musical instruments" in terms of fingering a keyboard, something which inverts Juvenal's intention, circling the musical *double entendre* back away from sex and into the practicalities of playing an instrument. This interpretative strategy seems particularly apt for Valla, who is certainly the most prudish of our five Juvenal commentators. Valla is also attentive to the nature of the tortoise-shell lyre: whereas Braund, the modern translator of Juvenal, reads the passage "densi radiant testudine tota sardoniches" as referring to sardonyx rings worn by the woman as she handles the instrument, both Valla and Britannico (the only commentators who take a view on this point) read it as referring to a "cithara sparkling with jewels" (citharae gemmis fulgent), as Valla puts it.

Among the contributors to the *Argumenta Satyrarum Juvenalis*, only Calderini registers the central role of the woman in the satirical economy of the passage, glossing the phrase "Si gaudet cantu" by noting that "he writes of women who desperately love singer-citharists" (hoc notat in mulieribus qui citharoedos perdite ament). However, he takes the mention of singer-citharists as an excuse for an immediate switch back to music-historical matters, noting that the emperor Domitian instituted contests for musicians, as described by Suetonius in his *Life of Domitian*.[127] Britannico writes more extensively about the dynamic between the woman and the singer-citharist, but he does so in order to present an unexpected interpretation of the whole passage. He begins his remarks with the phrase "Si gaudet cantu," but already bearing in mind the word "durat" (endure) from the end of the line:

> Si gaudet cantu: Varia mulierum studia percurrit poeta earum semper flagellans impudicitiam: si mulier inquit cytharedis et cantoribus delectatur nullus est qui durare possit: ita defatigantur continuo cantu.

"If she enjoys singing:" The poet runs through the various pursuits of women, always condemning their indecency, and says that if a woman delights in citharists and singers, there is none can that can endure, that is, they are exhausted by continuous singing.

---

127 "SI Gaudet cantu hoc notat in mulieribus qui citharoedos perdite ament: quorum certamina instituit Domitianus, ut scribit Tranquillus: victoresque corona quaterna donabantur."

In case the reader assumes that when he writes of "singing" he is still working within Juvenal's rather obvious *double entendre*, he immediately clarifies his position:

> Nullius fibula durat id est nullus adolescens infibulatus potest tam diutinum canendi laborem perferre.

> "No fibula can endure:" that is, no infibulated youth can endure such a long labour of singing.

He is evidently aware that reading this passage as referring straightforwardly to musical performance, rather than via musical performance to sex, will strike his readers as counter-intuitive. Thus, after explaining the fibula (in exactly the same way as the other commentators had in relation to the earlier excerpt discussed above), he presents his argument in the clearest possible terms:

> Alii interpraetantur que mulieres praetio corrumpant cytharedos et cantores ad coitum et sic fibulam solvere cogantur: quod falsum est: nam non amat eos mulier ut coeat: sed ut voluptatem capiat ex cantu: nam in sequentibus ait: sed cantet potius quam totam peruolet urbem Supra vero taxavitalias mulieres quae cytharedos amarent ad coitum: Solvitur is magno comoedi fibula sint quae Chrysogonum cantare vetent: Ergo poeta notat hic mulierem quae studio Citharedorum canentium teneretur.

> Others interpret this as meaning that the women bribe the citharists and singers for sex, and thus they are compelled to loosen their fibulas, but this is wrong, for the woman does not love them for sex, but to take pleasure in [their] singing, for later on he says [Satire 6.398]: "But it's better for her to be musical than to go all over the city." Previously, indeed, he condemned other women who love singer-citharists for sex [Satire 6.73-4]: "These women pay a lot to get a comic actor's fibula undone. There are women who stop Chrysogonus from singing." Therefore, here the poet mentions a woman who was captivated by the pursuit of singer-citharists singing.[128]

So Britannico finds in Juvenal a hierarchy of women's musical vices, in which having sex with singers is the worst offence, and showing an unseemly love for song the less severe.

---

128 Translations of Juvenal adapted from *Juvenal and Persius*, ed. and trans. Braund, 273 and 241.

Britannico's reading here is creative, but it is deliberately contrary. In fact, the musical eroticism of this passage was probably quite obvious to Italian readers in 1501: sexualised analogies between musical instruments and human bodies, and between playing techniques and erotic gestures, were familiar from numerous contemporary texts and practices, as well as being encoded into instrument decoration and visual representations of music-making.[129] Sexualised readings of women's musicianship were also common currency, and increasingly so thanks to the emerging discourse of the musical courtesan.[130] In the judgement of the other commentators, it was not these aspects that readers would want explaining, but rather the poetical obscurity of Juvenal's musical terminology—*testudo*, usually meaning tortoise, and *pecten*, usually meaning comb.

As educators and as scholars, our five Juvenal commentators were interested above all in classical language and classical history, and it was in teaching classical language and classical history that their commentaries were destined most often to be used. This perspective is evident in their approach to unpacking Juvenal's musical mentions: they want to investigate the etymology of musical terms, and they want to give a coherent historical account of the classical musical practice, instrument, or musician to which Juvenal is referring. The archaeological process employed in their music-historical investigations is to assemble intertexts until there is sufficient information on the table to write a coherent summary, leaning principally on a canon of well-known classical sources: the historians Suetonius, Plutarch and Livy, the poets Martial, Ovid and Persius, the philosophers Macrobius and Lucretius, and the encyclopedist Pliny the Elder, among others. As the examples we have reviewed amply demonstrate, their work is strikingly intertextual, each author building on and contending with the efforts of those that went before, amounting to a collaborative—albeit often grumpy—effort to elaborate and refine a shared understanding of ancient musical practices and their purposes. This general characterisation applies substantially to all the other humanist commentaries in our 1501

---

129 Dennis, "Unlocking the Gates of Chastity," 226–27.
130 William F. Prizer, "Cardinals and Courtesans: Secular Music in Rome, 1500–1520," in *Italy and the European Powers: The Impact of War, 1500–1530*, ed. Christine Shaw (Boston: Brill, 2006), 253–78, at 272.

corpus, and represents a distinct approach and discourse in the study of music that was evidently widespread in the period, although modern musicology has largely overlooked it.

Among the most musically productive individual commentaries in our 1501 corpus is Filippo Beroaldo's compendious notes on Apuleius' *Asinus aureus* (also known as the *Metamorphoses*). A lighthearted and irreverent prose novel, the only such surviving from Roman antiquity, the *Asinus aureus* was of interest to the humanist educators on that account, but was not particularly suitable as a classroom text. The initial Apuleius *Opera* volume, edited by Giovanni Andrea Bussi and printed in Rome in 1469, was reprinted in 1488, 1493, and 1497—a much more modest circulation than that enjoyed by Juvenal over the same period. Beroaldo's new edition with commentary first appeared in 1500 and remained the standard version for nearly two decades, acquiring illustrations from 1510. In 1518, though, an Italian translation of the *Asinus aureus* by Matteo Maria Boiardo was printed, and the work was principally read in that form through the rest of the century, reflecting the fact that it was enjoyed for its entertainment value, rather than for its pure Latin style or its Stoic ethics (both of which it lacks). Nonetheless, Beroaldo's commentary—the only one produced in the period—had an exceptionally long life: it can still be found in some nineteenth-century editions of the Latin text. Whereas our five Juvenal commentaries offer the opportunity to compare how several expert readers responded to the same musical passages, in reviewing Beroaldo's comments on the *Asinus aureus* we can evaluate the range of musical material produced by a single commentator, observing how his treatment of music relates to his wider style and preoccupations in approaching Apuleius' text.

Beroaldo's basic method is made particularly clear when he finds it necessary to comment on the "chorus" no fewer than four times within about thirty folios, spanning books 4–6 of the *Asinus aureus*. It seems that in his notes Beroaldo has three principal excerpts mentioning the chorus—nearly identical quotations from Seneca (*Epistles* 84.9–10) and Macrobius (*Saturnalia* preface), and a passage from Plato (*Laws*, Book 2)—and in three of the four instances he uses all of them, but varies his comments by elaborating one or another in a different way. Thus, at *Asinus aureus* 4.31, when he needs to explain what is the "choral song" (chorum canentes) sung by the daughters of Nereus, first he paraphrases Seneca/Macrobius—"The chorus is composed of many voices, such that out of many it is rendered one, and concord is made out of dissonance"—and then he paraphrases Plato—"'Chorum' is thought to come from 'chara,' which is 'joy,' as Plato says in *Laws*, Book 2. Moreover, 'chorea' means to dance and sing together at the same time."[131] At 5.3, he wants to clarify the meaning of "conferta vox," referring to a choir that is invisible but unmistakable from its sound, and deploys the same two references, but this time he quotes Seneca/Macrobius direct (or rather, strictly speaking, he quotes Macrobius, for the final clause is absent from Seneca):

> Conferta vox: Chorum intelligit: de quo seneca. et macrobius sic referunt. non vides quam multorum vocibus chorus constet: unus tamen ex omnibus sonus redditur: aliqua illic acuta est aliqua gravis aliqua media: accedunt viris foeminae interponuntur tibiae: singulorum illic latent voces omnium apparent. fit concentus ex dissonis.[132]

> "Conferta vox:" by this we understand "chorus," on which Seneca and Macrobius say this: "You know how a chorus consists of many people's voices, and yet they all produce a single sound. One voice is high-pitched, another low, another in the middle, men are joined by women, a pipe is added to the mix: individual voices disappear while the voices of all are revealed, and the disparate tones produce a harmony."

A few pages later, at 5.15, Beroaldo gives his most abbreviated paraphrase of these same points—"'Choros canere': which from many different voices make harmony and concord."[133] The brevity here is required by the context, for he has several different musical terms to deal with in a single sentence of Apuleius. Finally, in response to a particularly evocative musical passage at 6.24, we get the most extended version of this material. This time he places the Plato paraphrase first, extending it with a note about Spartan choruses based on Plutarch's *Life of Lycurgus* 21:

---

131 "Multorum vocibus constat chorus. ita nt ex plurimis una reddatur fiatque concentus ex dissonis: auctores Seneca et Macrobius. chorum a chara id est leticia dici autumat plato. libro secundo de legibus: Chorea vero tripudium simul et concentus significatur." *Commentarii a Philippo Beroaldo*, fol. 78r.

132 *Commentarii a Philippo Beroaldo*, fol. 82r.

133 "CHOros canere: qui ex multorum vocibus dissonis symphoniam faciunt atque concentum." *Commentarii a Philippo Beroaldo*, fol. 86r.

Chorum canerent: A chara id est laeticia chorum nominaverunt. ut interpretatur Plato. qui tres choros fieri percipit videlicet puerilem. Iuvenilem et senilem. quod ex instituto laconico sumptum videtur: Namque apud Lacedemonio ex disciplina Lycurgi tres chori constituti sunt: unus senum. qui sic canebat: nos olim fuimus robustius venes. Alter iuvenum. qui succinebat. nos autem sumus. qui si velis periculum facito. tertius vero puerorum. a quo illud cantabatur. ημεσ εσομεθα πολλα καρρομεσ id est nos erimus multo meliores.[134]

"Chorum canerent:" "Chorum" is named from "chara," that is, joy, as Plato explains, who notes the creation of three choruses, namely of children, youths, and elders, which seems to have been taken from the constitution of Sparta. For among the Spartans three choruses were established, according to the principles of Lycurgus: one of the elders, who sang thus: "in times past we were solid and strong;" another of youths, who accompanied with: "and now we are; if you would test us, risk it;" and a third of children, by whom it was sung: ημείς εσομεθα πολλω καρρονες, that is, "we will be much better."

Then he gives the full quotation from Seneca/Macrobius once again, this time appending a further detail on ancient choral performance practice: "'Mesochorum' is the name for the modulator [i.e., regulator, time-beater] who sings in the middle of the chorus, which is a term used by Pliny the Younger [*Epistulae* 2.14] and Sidonius [*Epistulae* 2.15]."[135]

The Latin text of the *Asinus aureus* was understood by Renaissance philologists to survive in a rather corrupt state, which accounts in part for the particular length of Beroaldo's commentary and also its utility to readers. Beroaldo was particularly well respected among his contemporaries as a philologist, and sometimes suggests alternative readings, some of which remain in place in modern editions of the text.[136] Two cases in point involve musical passages. At *Asinus aureus* 5.25, Pan is found making music; the text in the 1501 edition reads "Tunc forte pan deus rusticus iuxta supercilium amnis sedebat, complexus hic humo

---

134 *Commentarii a Philippo Beroaldo*, fol. 107v.
135 "Mesochorum vocant modulatorem. qui in medio canit choro. qua dictione Plinius minor et Sidonius utuntur." *Commentarii a Philippo Beroaldo*, fol. 107v.
136 On Beroaldo's philological style and abilities, see especially the introduction to the modern edition of his 1488 *Annotationes centum*, an anthology of 104 emendations and interpretations of passages from Latin authors and a landmark in Renaissance philology: Filippo Beroaldo the Elder, *Annotationes Centum*, ed. Lucia A. Ciapponi (Binghampton, NY: Centre for Medieval and Early Renaissance Studies, 1995), 1–30.

cannam deam: eamque voculas omnimodas edocens retinere," whereas Loeb reads "Tunc forte Pan deus rusticus iuxta supercilium amnis sedebat, complexus *Echo montanam* deam eamque voculas omnimodas edocens *recinere*" (our emphasis).[137] Beroaldo quite reasonably takes "cannam" (reed) to refer to the nymph Syrinx, thus he begins his comment by summarising the story of Pan and Syrinx, then notes with Pliny (*Naturalis historia* 16.66.165) that the Greeks called the reed considered most suitable for musical pipes "auleticon" (or "tibialem" in Latin). However, he casts doubt on "retinere," noting that "a more convenient reading is 'recinere canna',"—i.e., "echoing back" rather than "restraining"—"for the piper echoing, that is, playing, produces all kinds of notes."[138]

Beroaldo's proposed solution to another problematic reading, at *Asinus aureus* 10.31, draws him into a virtuoso demonstration of music-antiquarian geekery. First he glosses the established reading, "hormum canebat bellicosum," noting that "the Greek word ὁρμάω (hormao) means 'to set in motion,' and ὁρμή (horme) attack and commotion; thus 'hormum canticum' means impetuous and well-adapted to the fervour of war."[139] Then he introduces an alternative reading: "In fact, I personally think that the reading is 'orthrium'," from the Greek ὄρθϊος (órthios), meaning high-pitched, and the name of one of the ancient Greek nomoi (melodic types). To substantiate this claim and ground the new reading in the context of the passage (i.e., as relevant to warlike song), he turns first to Dion of Prusa (now usually called Dio Chrysostom), whose *De regno* (comprising *Discourses* 1–4) had been translated into Latin by Gregorio Tifernate and printed in 1471; an identical second edition was published in Beroaldo's Bologna in 1493. The *De regno* opens with an anecdote concerning the ancient musician Timotheus, who performs for Alexander the Great in a manner described as "orchum qui palladis carminem dicitur" ("the high-pitched strain which is called the song

---

137 *Commentarii a Philippo Beroaldo*, fol. 89v; *Metamorphoses* (*The Golden Ass*), Volume I: Books 1–6, ed. and trans. J. Arthur Hanson, Loeb Classical Library 44 (Cambridge, MA: Harvard University Press, 1996), 244.

138 "REtinere: Commodior lectio est recinere canna enim fistularis recinit hoc est canendo reddit voces omnimodas. ad marem Recanunt dicit Plinio de perdicibus scribens." *Commentarii a Philippo Beroaldo*, fol. 89v.

139 "ορμαω verbo graeco diciter impetum facio. et ορμη impetus. et perturbatio: inde hormum canticum dictum impetuosum: et alacritati bellicae accommodatum." *Commentarii a Philippo Beroaldo*, fol. 205r.

of Pallas"), prompting the king to leap to arms.[140] Thus, Beroaldo paraphrases:

> est autem orthrium ut docet Dion carmen palladis bellici ardoris incentivum. Quod Timotheus arte musica celebratus cum aliquando perite admodum modularentur, ferunt Alexandrum magnum tanquam numine quodam correptum mox ad arma posiluisse. adeo regem illum musici cantus vehementia concitaverat.

> "orthrium" is, as Dion explains, a song of Pallas inciting a passion for war. Whereby of Timotheus, celebrated in the art of music, when at times his modulations were expertly attuned, it is said that Alexander the Great, as if seized by a divine power, immediately leapt to arms, so vehemently did this musician's song incite the king.

Next he traces the usage in Herodotus (*Histories* 1.24.5: "νόμον τὸν ὄρθιον" [nómon tón órthion]) and Aulus Gellius (*Noctes Atticae* 16.19.14: "carmen quod 'orthium' dicitur"). Both of these authors link the orthian nomos with the mythological musician Arion and his miraculous escape from pirates, and Beroaldo follows suit:

> quidem et olim arion quoque voce sublatissima cantavit: cantuque peracto sese procul in profundum eiaculavit. Ubi adelphine exceptus evasit incolumis.

> Indeed, once upon a time Arion too sang with a very high voice, and when he had finished singing, he threw himself into the depths, where he was caught by a dolphin and escaped unharmed.

Finally he turns to the Suda, a medieval Byzantine lexicon that served as an encyclopedia of the ancient Greek world and was printed for the first time in Italy in 1499, for a more direct explanation of the ὄρθιος νόμος (orthios nomos):

> apud suidam lego. ορθίος esse νομος κιθαρῳδικος id est legem citharedicam: a quo etiam memoratur. ορθίος νομος κιθαρῳδικος της αμονιας itaque orthrium et orthium pro cantico et lege citharedicae armoniae.

> In the Suda [at Adler omicron,574] I read that ορθίος (orthios) is a νομος κιθαρῳδικος (nomos kitharodikos), that is, a law of the citharist; the same author also mentions ορθίος νομος κιθαρῳδικος της α[ρ]μονιας

---

140 *Dion de Regno* (Bologna: Franciscus de Benedictis, 1493), sig. a ii v.

(orthios nomos kitharodos tis armonias), and thus "orthrium" and "orthium" for song and the law of citharedic harmony.

Whilst this all seems on the face of it quite learned, it is certainly possible that Beroaldo has assembled these citations with the help of a dictionary, or a commentary on ορθιος found in another text. Indeed, like most contemporary commentators, Beroaldo makes use of shortcuts to learning and serendipitous discoveries as often as he presents focussed primary research. These pragmatic methods are richly on display in his commentary on the phrase "TIbiae multiforabiles" (many-holed tibias) at 10.32, appearing in a passage where pipers accompany a sensuous dance performed by the goddess Venus. Beroaldo's first destination here is Horace's *Ars poetica* 203–04, but in looking up the relevant passage he has evidently noticed how the early scholia on Horace—in the period considered the work of Helenius Acron—deal with the tibia, referring to a lost work by Marcus Terentius Varro. Beroaldo inverts the order of discovery, and borrows the comment with a citation to Varro, omitting all mention of Helenius Acron:

> A multitudine et numero foraminum multiforatilis tibia dicta. apud antiquos tibia tenuis fuit quartuor tamen foraminibus distincta: tales in templo videsset se se refert M. Varro de hac tibia intelligit Oratius in arte poetica. tenuis simplexque foramine pauco aspirare et adesse choris erat utilis.[141]

> Concerning the multitude and number of holes in a many-holed tibia, it is said among the ancients that the slender tibia was distinguished by having just four holes; it is such a tibia that Marcus Varro mentions having seen in the temple. Of this tibia Horace observes in *De arte poetica* [that it was] "slight and simple, with few holes, [and] was once of use to lead and aid the chorus."

Next he digs further into this vein of plagiarism by lifting remarks from Servius' commentary on the phrase "biforem dat tibia cantum" in *Aeneid* 9.618. First, paraphrasing Servius' own words: "Moreover, tibias which are equal and have equal holes are called Serranan, whereas those that are unequal and have unequal holes are called Phrygian."[142] Next, exactly

---

141 *Commentarii a Philippo Beroaldo*, fol. 205v.
142 "praeterea tibiae aut seranae dicuntur. quae sunt pares et aequales habent cavernas. aut phrygiae: quae sunt impares inaequalibusque foraminibus."

copying material attributed by Servius to Varro: "The Phrygian tibia has one hole on the right and two holes on the left; one produces a high sound and the other a low one."[143] Then Beroaldo pauses in his plunder of Roman grammarians to turn to Pliny, whose *Naturalis historia* offers quite detailed comments on the materials and manufacture of tibias:

> tibiae sacrificae ex buxo fiunt. ut docet plinus ludicrae vero ex loto ossibusque asininis. et argento. tibialem calamum auleticon vocant graece enim αυλη tibia est.

> "Tibias used in sacrifices are made of boxwood," as Pliny teaches [*Naturalis historia* 16.66.172], "while tibias for the theatre are made of lotus-wood and asses' bones and silver." The reed for making tibias is called "auleticon" in Greek [*Naturalis historia* 16.66.165], thus αυλη [aule; evidently αὐλός (aulos) is intended] is tibia.

The next target is Solinus' *Polyhistor* (5.19), a well-known geographical work Beroaldo's own edition of which was first published by the same printer in the same year as his *Asinus aureus* commentary. We are given a paraphrase of a passage differentiating varieties of tibia, without citation:

> inter genera tibiarum sunt praecentoriae: quibus in sacrificiis praecinunt ad pulvinaria: sunt et puellatoriae. quibus a sono clariore vocamen datur quasdam vescas vocant: quae multiforatiles sunt Gigrinae nominantur. quae exiguae licet sint subtilioribus tamen modis insonant

> Among the varieties of tibia are "praecentoriae," which are played before sacrifices at the sanctuaries of the gods; "puellatoriae," which are so-called because of their clear sound, called by some "vescas;" those that are many-holed are called "Gigrinae," which, although they are short, nevertheless produce a finer sound.

"Gigrinae" evidently struck Beroaldo as an odd term in need of further explanation, so he adds that "By the ancients a tibia-player was called 'gigeriator' and 'subulo'" (a priscis tibicen dicebatur gigeriator et subulo), a comment most likely based on looking these terms up in Festus' *De verborum significatione* (at Müller p95 "Gingriator" and p308 "Subulo"), a much-printed Latin dictionary. Beroaldo then concludes

---

143 "tibia phrygia dextra unum habet foramen sinistra duo quorum unum acutum reddit sonum alterum gravem."

his remarks with a note on the inventors of the tibia; Pliny is cited here, and is indeed the ultimate source, but Beroaldo has actually paraphrased this passage from Apuleius' *Florida* (3.1–5), included in the older *Opera* printed editions of Apuleius and cited quite regularly in our commentary:

> ante hiagnim marsiae tibicinis patrem rudibus adhuc musicae seculis in usu fuit simplex tibia hic primus duas tibias uno spiritu animavit quamvis plinius marsiam dicat geminas tibias invenisse. primus multiforatili tibia sinistris et dextris foraminibus distincta acutis gravibus sonis concentum musicum miscuit.

> Before Hyagnis, the father of the tibia-player Marsyas, in the age in which music was as yet unrefined, the single pipe was in use; he was the first to fill two tibias with one breath—although Pliny [*Naturalis historia* 7.56] says that Marsyas invented the double tibia; the multi-holed pipe, with different holes on the left and the right, first mixed musical harmony from high and low sounds.

Thus, in building his commentary on the tibia, Beroaldo has looked up the uses of the word in Horace and Virgil to borrow from their classic Roman commentaries, consulted the Latin dictionaries of Festus and (via other sources) Varro, cribbed from Solinus which he happened to be editing around the same time, and drawn upon Apuleius' other writings which he has evidently read carefully in support of his work on this edition of the *Asinus aureus*—as well as using the ubiquitous Pliny, the commentators' favourite encyclopedia of the ancient world. Although the end result is actually quite detailed and well-informed, this resembles a jumble of shortcuts and happy coincidences much more than it does a rigorous research process, and the almost complete lack of citations (unusual in this commentary) makes Beroaldo look a little sheepish about it.[144]

Like Britannico, Beroaldo is one of those commentators who sometimes breaks from the endless procession of quotes, paraphrases and etymologies to write from his own point of view. This makes him engaging and rewarding for readers of a modern sensibility, and perhaps it is among the features that made him popular with early

---

[144] Indeed, the shortcuts may have been shorter still, as many of the same points and references could be found in the commentary on the last line of Martial's *De spectaculis*, epigram 5, in Perotti's *Cornucopiae*, particularly cols. 625 and 626.

sixteenth-century readers too. At 6.24, Beroaldo becomes quite animated in his discussion of the cithara, in response to the consecutive phrases "Musae quoque canora personabant" ("The Muses also performed melodiously") and "Apollo cantavit ad citharam" ("Apollo sang to the cithara") in Apuleius' text. First he establishes the musical connection between the Muses and Apollo by paraphrasing *Iliad* 1.601–04: "Homer, in the *Iliad*, Book 1, writes [that] the Muses sang to the cithara of Apollo at the banquet of the gods, with sweet voice and melodious song."[145] The presence of music at fancy banquets in the ancient world is a point sometimes used by commentators to suggest music's importance and high status, and next Beroaldo leans further into this reading by paraphrasing from the key discussion of music in Aristotle's *Politics* (specifically, at 8.3.22-32): "Aristotle, in *Politics*, Book 8, argues that music should be used for pleasure; and on the authority of Homer, the cithara should be performed at convivial delights, which soothes all, for then the guests, filled with joy, gladly listen to the cithara."[146] At this point Beroaldo departs from his scholarly methodology momentarily to praise the cithara in a more rhapsodic vein:

> denique per cithare dicam artem Orpheus plurimum potuit. hanc procul dubio Philosophi graves et prudentes amant: hanc diligunt musae: quibus tradentibus in usum hominum venit. haec in agonibus. hoc est sacris certaminibus coronatur: Denique constat musicam inter honestas professiones numerari: quam Plato et Aristoteles in primus discendam esse percipiunt.

> Moreover, I will say that Orpheus was able to do a great deal by the art of the cithara. This without doubt is beloved of serious and prudent philosophers; it is esteemed by the Muses, through whom it comes to the use of men; it is crowned in competitions, that is in sacred contests. Finally, it is agreed that music is counted among the honorable professions, which Plato and Aristotle take to be in the first phase of education.

---

145 "Homerus in primo iliados scribit musas in convivio deorum. suavissima voce et modulato cantu cencinisse apolline citharizante." *Commentarii a Philippo Beroaldo*, fol. 107r.

146 "Aristoteles in octavo politicorum auctor est musicam adhibendam esse rebus voluptariis. et ex auctoritate homerica citharedum delitiis convivalibus exhibendum qui omnes demulceat. tunc enim leticia convivae perfusi libenter audiunt citharedum." *Commentarii a Philippo Beroaldo*, fol. 107r.

Following this brief *laus musicae*, Beroaldo turns to the phrase "Apollo cantavit ad citharam," and proceeds with a direct but uncredited quote from Pliny (*Naturalis historia* 7.56): "The cithara was played without voice by Thamyras; with song [by] Amphion. Terpander published songs composed on the cithara."[147] He then interposes Apollo into Pliny's scheme: "Truly Apollo is the inventor of the cithara and its music, who was contending with Marsyas."[148] This prompts him to summarise the contest of Apollo and Marsyas: "First he used the cithara without voice, then when it seemed that Marsyas had beaten him, to the melody of the cithara he added the sweetness of the voice, and was judged the victor for singing to the cithara."[149] His source for the story is probably Diodorus Siculus (*Bibliothecae historicae* 3.59.2-3), because the other sources that specify a second round to the contest (including Apuleius' own *Florida* 3) have Apollo turn his instrument upside down rather than singing along to it.

Beroaldo is not the only commentator in our 1501 corpus to show a particular interest in the cithara—indeed, among the humanist commentaries we have reviewed for our project it is probably the leading musical topic.[150] This is hardly surprising, given the centrality of the cithara, and of its divine practitioners Apollo and Orpheus, to humanist poetics in this period.[151] Across our 1501 corpus, the most elaborate and developed statement of that poetics is to be found in the proemium to Cristoforo Landino's commentary on Virgil's *Aeneid*, first published

---

147 "Cithara sine voce cecinit Thamyras. cum cantu amphion. cithara edita carmina composuit terpander." *Commentarii a Philippo Beroaldo*, fol. 107v.
148 "apollinem vero citharae eiusque musicae inventorem ferunt. qui cum marsia certans." *Commentarii a Philippo Beroaldo*, fol. 107v.
149 "primum cithara sine voce usus est: mox cum videretur a marsia superari. ad citharae modulationem addidit vocis quoque suavitatem: ad citharamque cantilans victor est iudicatus." *Commentarii a Philippo Beroaldo*, fol. 107v.
150 There is no attempt made in the commentators' remarks to differentiate lyre from cithara; indeed, Tortelli's entry on the cithara simply reads "a musical instrument which is called 'lyre'" (instrumentum est musicum: quidem est ilyra dicitur), *Orthographia*, fol. 59r. Other musical matters of particular interest to our 1501 commentators include the Corybantes—e.g., *Commentarius primus in Raptum Proserpinae*, sig. C ii r (commenting on Claudian, *De raptu Proserpinae* 1.210)—and the wedding hymn—e.g., *Terentius cum tribus commentis*, fol. clxvi v (commenting on *Adelphoe* 905).
151 See, among others, Concetta Carestia Greenfield, *Humanist and Scholastic Poetics, 1250-1500* (London: Associated University Presses, 1981); Wilson, *Singing to the Lyre*; and Shephard et al., *Music in the Art of Renaissance Italy*, 171–89.

in 1481 and thereafter a staple of commentated Virgils—which in themselves were among the most-printed texts from the 1480s to the early 1500s in Italy, with several editions per year.[152] With an enormous debt to Marsilio Ficino and his neoplatonism, Landino wants to explain how the inspired poet captures an echo of the harmony of the spheres in his verse, but to do so he must first detach this Pythagorean doctrine from music itself:

> Neque enim ut musici qui quoniam aurium dumtaxat sensum suavioribus voculis demulcent: a Platone tanquam vulgares levioresque contemnuntur: sed graviori ac firmiori iudicio divinam harmoniam imitatus poeta: altos intimosque mentis sensus eleganti carmine exprimit et divino illo furore de quo plurima maximaque idem Plato scribit afflatus: ac parcitus res saepenumero adeo admirandas adeo supra humanas vires constitutas grandiori quodam spiritu profertur. ut paulo post ubi furor ille iam referbuerit ac resederit: seipsum admiretur atque obtupescat.[153]

> And indeed not musicians, who because they merely please the ear with sweet tones are despised by Plato as vulgar and trifling, but rather the poet imitates divine harmony with more serious and firm judgement, expresses the profound and intimate sentiments of the mind in elegant verses, and, inspired to the most copious and the greatest by that divine frenzy of which Plato writes, is provoked repeatedly to utter things astonishing and beyond human strength with a certain grander spirit, so that a little later, when the frenzy has bubbled over and subsided, he marvels at and is astonished by himself.

Shortly after, Landino expands on the nature of the harmony of the spheres. Poetic inspiration is said to come from the Muses, of course, but:

> Musas autem ipsas nihil aliud quam caelestes cantus intelligunt. Quamobrem musis: idest caelestibus numinibus ac cantibus divini illi viri concitati ad eorum imitationem poeticos numeros meditantur: ac fingunt. Plato enim libro de repub. cum celerrimam illam spherarum volubilitatem describeret: singulas serenas singulis orbibus insidere dixit

---

[152] On the printing of Virgil and commentaries thereupon in this period see Craig Kallendorf, *Printing Virgil: The Transformation of the Classics in the Renaissance* (Leiden: Brill, 2020), esp. 16–53.

[153] *Vergilius cum commentariis quinque*, fol. cxi v.

motum spherarum: quae assiduo cantu deo gloriam exhibent significans: cum ςύρειν deo canere sit.¹⁵⁴

> By the Muses themselves, however, understand nothing other than the songs of the heavens. Wherefore those men, impelled by the Muses—that is, by the heavenly divinities and the divine songs—, in imitation of them devise and fashion measured verses. For Plato, in his book *De republica* [Book 10], when he describes the swift motion of the spheres, says that on each orb sits a Siren in motion with the spheres, meaning that they give glory to God through constant singing, for ςύρειν (syrein) is singing to God.

In other words, to say that the poet is inspired by the Muses who are sent by Jupiter, is the same as to say that the poet hears the harmony of the spheres which are set in motion by Plato's demiurge. The strings of the lyre, of course, numbered seven in imitation of the mobile spheres, so that the lyre itself could be seen as a metaphor for the harmony of the spheres; one could even say that "Jupiter holds the sky like a lyre and creates celestial harmony" (Iuppiter [...] caelum veluti cytheram tenens caelestem efficit harmoniam).¹⁵⁵ Landino's views on these matters could also be found in his earlier work of Virgil interpretation, the *Disputationes Camaldulenses*, in his lectures on the *Aeneid* at the University of Florence, and in the *proemio* to his commentary on Dante's *Commedia* (first printed in 1488) where very similar passages appear in Italian.¹⁵⁶

Landino's account of poetic theology must have been quite widely disseminated. Nonetheless, it is important to acknowledge that in the depth of its neoplatonism, and in its theological subtlety, it is unusual in our 1501 corpus. For the other commentators represented in our sample, as we have seen above with Beroaldo, it was perfectly possible to be strongly invested in the association of poetry with music, and in the rich symbolism of the lyre, without disappearing off into the resounding heavens to look for Plato's world soul. Another case in point

---

154 *Vergilius cum commentariis quinque*, fol. cxi v.
155 *Vergilius cum commentariis quinque*, fol. cxi v.
156 On the relationships among the surviving examples of Landino's *Aeneid* criticism see, among others, Craig Kallendorf, "Cristoforo Landino's *Aeneid* and the Humanist Critical Tradition," *Renaissance Quarterly* 36.4 (1983), 519–46. For the parallel passage in Landino's Dante commentary, see Tim Shephard, "Musical Classicisms in Italy Before the Madrigal," *Music & Letters* 101.4 (2020), 690–712, at 699.

is presented by our 1501 edition of Ovid's *Heroides*, a series of imaginary letters written by and to various classical heroes and notables, printed in Venice by Giovanni Luigi Varisio. The principal commentators here are Antonio Volsco and Ubertino Clerico, both widely published pedagogues. Volsco studied privately in Naples, where he associated with the circle of Panormita, and in Rome, where he associated with Pomponio Leto's academy and embarked on a career as professor of rhetoric and poetry at the university (where he lectured on the *Heroides*, among other texts). Clerico, from Crescentino near Turin, taught rhetoric at the University of Pavia in the 1460s and 70s, before moving on to teaching posts in Casale Monferrato then Chivasso. Neither commented on every letter in the *Heroides*, however, in particular missing out the letter from Sappho to Phaon, so printers usually added notes from another author—either Giorgio Merula, or more commonly (as in our edition) Domizio Calderini. The *Heroides* were popular on a scale comparable to Juvenal: printed most often in Latin but sometimes in the vernacular, they account for around seventy of the nearly two hundred Ovid editions issued in Italy between 1480 and 1520. More than half of those contain either one or both of our main commentaries.

The *Heroides* is not an especially musical work, but lyres and citharas turn up in connection with Achilles and Sappho, both of whom were important to the rhetorical strategies underpinning elite musical identities in Italy around 1501—the former for his combination of musical skill with martial prowess (proving that musicians need not be wimps), the latter as an exemplar asserting the legitimacy and quality of women's musical and poetic creativity.[157] Upon encountering the mention of music in Briseis' letter to Achilles, however, we immediately find ourselves in a tangle thanks to a careless compositor. Our 1501 edition says this:

> Pugna nocet: citharae noxque ventusque iuvant.
> Tutius est iacuisse toro. tenuisse puellam.

---

157 On Achilles see, for example, Vergerio's *De ingenuis moribus*, in *Humanist Educational Treatises*, ed. and trans. Craig Kallendorf, I Tatti Renaissance Library 5 (Cambridge, MA: Harvard University Press, 2002), 84/85–86/87. On Sappho, see Tim Shephard, *Echoing Helicon: Music, Art and Identity in the Este Studioli* (Oxford: Oxford University Press, 2014), 81–83.

Threiciam digitis increpuisse tyram.¹⁵⁸

But what it should say is this:

> Pugna nocet: citharae *voxque venusque* iuvant.
> Tutius est iacuisse toro. tenuisse puellam.
> Threiciam digitis increpuisse *lyram*.
>
> Because the fight brings danger; while the cithara, and song, and Venus, bring delight. Safer is it to lie on the couch, to clasp a sweetheart in your arms, to tinkle with your fingers the Thracian lyre.¹⁵⁹

These are definitely typos rather than misreadings, because when the keywords are called out in the commentary they are given correctly— meaning, of course, that it is possible for an attentive reader (or one who already knows Ovid's text) to extract a correct reading from the page, but equally possible for a cursory reader to end up confused. In the commentaries, Clerico explains that "cithara" refers to "the song of the cithara which brings delight" (cantus cithare qui delectaris), and both Clerico and Volsco note that Achilles had been taught to play by the centaur Chiron.¹⁶⁰ When they come to the "Threiciam [...] lyram," both explain that this refers to Orpheus, who came from Thrace and was known for his skill on the lyre.¹⁶¹ Volsco extends this point with material credited to Eratosthenes, a strategy we have already seen deployed by both Tortelli and Britannico:

> Threiciam lyram: qualem in thracia Orpheum personasse tradunt: quam a Mercurio in Cyllene monte arcadiae inventam illi musas tradidisse scribit Eratosthenes.
>
> "Thracian lyre:" which Orpheus is said to have played in Thrace, which was invented by Mercury on Mount Cyllene in Arcadia and given to him [i.e., to Orpheus] by the Muses, according to Eratosthenes.

---

158 *Epistolae Heroides Ouidii*, sig. [c iiii] v. The commentaries relating to this passage appear on the same page.

159 *Heroides. Amores*, trans. Grant Showerman, rev. G. P. Goold, Loeb Classical Library 41 (Cambridge, MA: Harvard University Press, 1914), 40/41 (*Heroides* 3.116–18).

160 Volsco: "quibus a chirone instructus est;" Clerico: "nam achilles optimus citharedus fuit a chirone centauro canendi artem edoctus."

161 Clerico: "Lyram threiciam: idest orphei qui Trax fuit et lyra optime cecinit."

In this case the reason for turning to Hyginus' treatise on the constellations is much clearer: his entry on the constellation Lyra is among the key sources for the Orpheus myth.

In Sappho's letter to Phaon the cithara is mentioned twice in quick succession, but indirectly, by reference to its strings. This is precisely the sort of allusive language that the commentators aim to clarify to assist readers. Calderini steps up to the plate:

> Nec mihi dipositis nervis: concinatae cytharae in qua olim quattuor erant nervi. Sed terpander lesbis septem composuit. Octavam symonides: nonam tymotheus.[162]

> "Nor can I arrange [...] strings:" the well-made cithara on which there were once four strings. But Terpander of Lesbos made it seven; Simonides eight; Timotheus nine.

We have seen this material before: it is drawn (without citation on this occasion) from Pliny's *Naturalis historia* 7.56. Calderini will continue in his Plinian groove in a moment, but at this point he steps out briefly to mention a fragment of Terpander's verse preserved in Strabo's *Geography* (13.4) that is primary evidence for his innovation in the stringing of the lyre. The correct quotation, from the Latin translation of Strabo by Guarino da Verona and Gregorio Tifernate that appears in contemporary printed editions, runs "Nos tibi mutato chordarum quattuor usu: Iam nova per septem modulamur carmina nervos" ("I having changed your usage from four strings,/ Already you play new songs on seven strings").[163] However, the rogue compositor of our 1501 edition confuses and runs together "usu: Iam" to produce the very unfortunate misreading "*Hos* tibi *mutari* chordarum quattour *vulvam*. nova per septem modulamur carmina nervos" (our emphasis). Next, Calderini turns to another word from the same line, "iungam," which he takes to mean "join" or "unite" the lyre with song. This gives him an excellent excuse to return to the same passage of Pliny, explaining that "Amphion is said to have been the first to introduce the practice of singing with the cithara; previously Thamyras [played it] without the

---

162 *Epistolae Heroides Ouidii*, sig. o iii v. The commentary relating to this passage appears on the same page.

163 Strabo, *Geographia, libri XVI* ([Venice]: Johannes Rubeus, 1495), fol. ciiii r.

voice."[164] Finally, satisfying his fascination with Latin itself, he notes that "those who sing together with the cithara are called 'psallocithariste'."[165]

A few lines later in the *Heroides*, the strings of the cithara are again invoked using a different word, "fidem." Calderini explains that this also means "cithara;" "In fact, 'fides' literally means the strings of a cithara, but [here] it is taken for [the] cithara [itself], as also in Statius [*Silvae* 4.7.27–28]: 'essays with daring string (*fide*) the joys of Mantuan fame'."[166] Then, in an unexpected twist, he notes that the similar term "fidicula" is used in Suetonius' *Life of Tiberius* 62.2 to refer to strings used in torture, specifically for tying up the penis so that it is impossible to urinate.[167] Finally, he turns to music-mythological matters with a quote from Horace:

> Apollo autem lyram a Mercurio accepit unde etiam ad amphionem pervenit. Horati. Mercurii nam te docilis magistro movit amphion lapides canendo.[168]

> Furthermore, Apollo received the lyre from Mercury, from whence it came to Amphion. Horace [*Odes* 3.11]: "Mercury—for, thanks to your teaching, Amphion learned how to move blocks of stone by his song."[169]

As this passage exemplifies, when discussing the cithara we are never far from the myths concerning Orpheus, Amphion and Arion. All three are mentioned in Virgil's *Eclogues*—among the most pervasively

---

164 "Amphion autem primus cum cantu cythara usus dicitur: antea thamiras sine voce."
165 "Qui autem simul canunt cum cythara psallocitariste dicuntur."
166 "Fidem idest cytharam. Fides autem proprie cytharae nervos significat. sed pro cythara accipitur. ut etiam a papi. Tentat audaci fide Mantuanae gaudia famae." *Epistolae Heroides Ouidii*, sig. o iii v. Translation of Statius adapted from *Silvae*, ed. and trans. D. R. Shackleton Bailey, rev. Christopher A. Parrott, Loeb Classical Library 206 (Cambridge, MA: Harvard University Press, 2015), 277.
167 "Fidicula. item nervus est. sed proprie quo ad tormenta utebantur. Pro nervo simpliciter tranquillus in tyberio. Veretris deligatis fidicularum simul utinaeque [= urinaeque] tormento distenderet. Eam enim colligationem. Tiberius ad supplicii acerbitatem excogitaverat." *Epistolae Heroides Ouidii*, sigs. o iii v–[o iv] r.
168 *Epistolae Heroides Ouidii*, sig. [o iv] r. Further comments on lyres and citharas in our 1501 corpus can be found at *Aulus Flaccus Persius*, fol. 86v (commenting on *Satires* 6.2); *Commentarius primus in Raptum Proserpinae*, sigs. [C v] v–[C vi] v (commenting on several aspects of the opening of Claudian, *De raptu Proserpinae*, 2, preface); *Terentius cum tribus commentis*, fol. lii r (commenting on *Eunuchus*, 133)—this is not an exhaustive list.
169 Translation of Horace from *Odes and Epodes*, ed. and trans. Niall Rudd, Loeb Classical Library 33 (Cambridge, MA: Harvard University Press, 2004), 173.

musical of all classical verse, thanks to their *mise-en-scene* involving herdsmen and their musical contests, and in the decades around 1500 riding a wave of popularity thanks to a vigorous fashion for the eclogue form and the pastoral mode.[170] On account of these qualities, indeed, it is Landino's commentaries on the *Eclogues*, rather than his notes on the *Aeneid*, that are his most musically productive. We meet Amphion first, at Eclogue 2.24, and reading Landino's commentary we are initially a little disappointed, because his focus seems to be upon the myths involving the twin brothers Amphion and Zethus together with their mother Antiope, with no mention of his musical skill. Then Landino introduces Plutarch's *De musica*, a work not available in print until the publication of Carlo Valgulio's Latin translation in 1507, giving a close paraphrase:[171]

> Plutarchus in libro de musica refert Herclide autore Amphionem thebanum: quem Antiope Iovi peperit primum a iove patre cithareticam poesim cleotum fuisse. Idque probat ex iis quae in syrione de sacris argivorum et poetis et musicis scripta sunt: Plinius autem ubi de rerum inventoribus tribuit musice inventionem et lydios modulos Amphioni tribuit.[172]

> Plutarch, in his book *De Musica* [3], says that according to Heraclides [Ponticus] Amphion was a Theban, whom Antiope bore to Jove, and was the first to make poetry to the cithara, from his father Jove. And this is attested by what is written in Syrion [= Sicyon] about the mysteries of the Argives and poets and musicians. Moreover, Pliny [*Naturalis historia* 7.56], in his passage on the inventors of things, attributes the invention of music and of Lydian modes to Amphion.

---

170 See, among many others, Giuseppe Gerbino, *Music and the Myth of Arcadia in Renaissance Italy* (Cambridge, UK: Cambridge University Press, 2009), 21–34; Shephard et al., *Music in the Art of Renaissance Italy*, 260–86.

171 *Musica Plutarchi a Charolo Valgulio Brixiano Versa in latinum*, published together with his *Prooemium in Musicam Plutarchi* (Brescia: Angelo Britannico, 1507). Valgulio's translation was completed in the 1470s, during which decade he spent some time in Florence associating with Ficino's circle, but Landino's paraphrase here is entirely independent of Valgulio's rendering. On Valgulio's translation see recently, among many others, Angelo Meriani, "Notes on the *Prooemium in Musicam Plutarchi ad Titum Pyrrhynum* by Carlo Valgulio (Brescia 1507)," *Greek and Roman Musical Studies* 3 (2015), 116–36; and, of course, Palisca, *Humanism*, 88–110.

172 *Vergilius cum commentariis quinque*, fol. 6r.

Landino concludes with Pliny's passage on inventors, which attributes to Amphion (among other contenders) both music as a whole and the Lydian mode. So, in fact, here he misses out the usual story of Amphion building the walls of Thebes with his lyre, although he does mention it in passing in his proemium to the *Aeneid* commentary.

In Eclogue 8 we find mention of Arion, and Landino's first gesture is to refer the reader back to Servius' brief summary of the dolphin story, although this is immediately followed by Landino's own more detailed summary of the same myth, paraphrased quite closely from Herodotus (*Histories*, 1.23–24):

> Addit tamen Herodo. hunc virum Metimneum fuisse ac omnes cytharedos superasse et a Periandro corynthiorum tyranno: abeuntem in Italiam venisse ac multas adeptus opes: ex suo artificio navem quorundam corynthiorum qua ad periandrum rediret consendisse: et animadversis insidiis impetravit a nautis: ut aliquantulum canere cythara sinerent: atque νόμόν ορθιοH cecinisse mox se in mare precepitasse ac delphino susceptum in insulam tenaron incolumen delatum esset. atque inde ad periandrum redisse et nautas qui illum in Italiam esse mentiti fuerant ita arguisse: scelus fateri cogerentur.[173]

> Herodotus adds, moreover, that he was a man of Methymna and surpassed all citharists, and leaving Periander the tyrant of Corinth, and proceeding to arrive in Italy he acquired great wealth, by his art; he planned to return to Periander on a ship belonging to some Corinthians, who conspired together, and an evil plot was accomplished by the sailors, and they allowed him to sing a little to the cithara, and singing the *nomos orthios* he immediately threw himself into the sea, was caught up by a dolphin and taken safely to the island of Taenarus. And thence he returned to Periander, and denounced the sailors, who had pretended that he was in Italy; they were compelled to admit their crime.

More detailed and involved by far, though, are Landino's comments on Orpheus and Linus called up by their mention in Eclogue 4 (see Appendix, Excerpt 3.4). These split roughly into two halves, the first more freeform and strongly Ficinian, the second more conventional in style albeit with a clear leaning towards sources that were important to Ficino. At the outset Landino states clearly that his concern is with

---

[173] *Vergilius cum commentariis quinque*, fol. 25v. Servius' commentary on the passage can be found on fol. 25r.

"Orpheus Theologus," the "ancient theologian" (priscae theologiae), and he immediately presents a genealogy of this pre-Platonic theology that is essentially quoted from Ficino's preface to his Latin translation of the *Corpus Hermeticum*, prepared in 1463 and first printed in 1471: from Hermes Trismegistus, to Orpheus, to Aglaophemus, to Pythagoras, to Philolaus, to Plato.[174] Next, Landino notes that the Orphic mysteries were imported to Greece from Egypt, another key principle of Ficino's *prisca theologia*, and furthermore that the rites of Dionysus (the "Theban Bacchus") made the same journey. These comments lean upon a long passage in Diodorus Siculus' *Bibliothecae historicae* (1.96) that describes everything the Greeks were said to have learned from the Egyptians. Then Landino makes reference to the supposed power of Orpheus' eloquence (associated with *poetica*, not *musica*) to move not only men but also beasts and rocks, interpreted as referring to his work as a priest or prophet to move men beyond the barbarities of primitive religious practice—a long-standing component of Orpheus' mythography that was already present in ancient sources (e.g., Horace, *Ars poetica* 391–92).[175] Next we read that Orpheus the Argonaut sang his shipmates clear of a terrible storm, an episode of the saga of the Argonauts that only appears in the version attributed to Orpheus himself, the *Argonautica Orphica*, a very obscure text of which Ficino made a Latin translation for private use.[176] This initial, more profoundly neoplatonic phase of Landino's remarks then concludes with the comment that Mount Cithaeron took its name from Orpheus' cithara, because he often contributed to the rites of Dionysus that were celebrated there, an etymology drawn from another of Ficino's well-loved sources, Lactantius' *Institutiones Divinae* (Book 1).[177]

---

174 For the relevant passage from Ficino, see Brian P. Copenhaver and C. Schmitt, *Renaissance Philosophy* (Oxford: Oxford University Press, 1992), 147. On the reception of Orpheus Theologus among Ficino's circle, see D. P. Walker, "Orpheus the Theologian and Renaissance Platonists," *Journal of the Warburg and Courtauld Institutes* 16.1–2 (1953), 100–20.

175 See further John Block Friedman, *Orpheus in the Middle Ages* (Cambridge, MA: Harvard University Press, 1970).

176 John Warden, "Orpheus and Ficino," in *Orpheus: The Metamorphoses of a Myth*, ed. John Warden (Toronto: University of Toronto Press, 1982), 85–110, at 91 (note 36). The *Argonautica Orphica* was printed, in Greek, in Florence in 1500.

177 Of course, Lactantius was widely read, not only by Ficino and his associates, and was regularly printed. Tortelli cites the same source when presenting this etymology in his entry on Cithaeron in the *Orthographia*, fol. 59v.

Landino's comments then shift into a more conventional style with a citation of Pliny's passage on inventors, where Orpheus is credited with advances in augury. Next we turn to Diogenes Laertius' *Vitae philosophorum*, a work of wide interest, printed in Latin several times through the 1470s, 80s and 90s, then in Italian translation in the 1500s. Drawing on the Prologue, Landino presents two contrasting accounts of Orpheus' death, one at the hands of the maenads and the other struck by Zeus' lightning. Diogenes is a useful source for Landino because he deals with Linus, who Landino must also cover, earlier in the same passage; thus next we stay with Diogenes to reveal that Linus was born of Mercury and Urania, died when struck by an arrow of Apollo, and wrote a poem presenting an account of cosmogony, astronomy, and natural history. To clarify the musical connection, we then turn to Plutarch's *De musica* 3, where Linus is said to have sung dirges, and once again Pliny on inventors, where Linus is among the candidates for the inventor of the cithara.

Landino is in a conflicted position among the commentators in our corpus. On the one hand, his remarks are extremely unusual in their dedicated neoplatonism, even to the extent of drawing on a quite different roster of classical sources—none of our other commentators have used the *Corpus Hermeticum*, *Argonautica Orphica*, Plutarch's *De musica*, the *Institutiones Divinae*, or even the *Vitae philosophorum* in their comments on music. In this respect, he is unrepresentative of our 1501 sample. On the other hand, Landino was a prominent professor whose commentaries immediately joined the canon of Virgil scholarship, becoming widely available in print, and this makes his contributions—however idiosyncratic—difficult to overlook.

The case of Landino gives us an important reminder that our 1501 corpus does not always speak with a single voice regarding the significance of music in classical literature. Nonetheless, on the whole our 1501 commentaries seem to offer a window onto a project shared among the fifteenth-century educators and scholars who prepared them, one of reconstructing ancient musical culture and making it comprehensible to students as they read their set texts at school and university. This constitutes a significant vein of musical scholarship in the period, albeit one nested within the larger sweep of topics that were dealt with by the commentators using similar methods. Very likely, because of its exposure via university teaching and the printed book, it touched many more lives than the more specialised discourse that we now call Renaissance music theory.

The contrast between these two approaches to musical study is instructive. Specialist writers on music in this period approached their subject through a distinctive classical music-theoretical canon: Boethius, Isidore, Plato and Aristotle were foundational; Quintilian and Cicero had been newly added; they were in the process of assimilating Ovid and Virgil (for their accounts of mythological musicians), particularly for the introductory gestures of their treatises; and by 1501 excitement over Vitruvius was sending some forging bravely forward into the territory of ancient Greek music theory (Ptolemy, Cleonedes, Aristides Quintilianus, etc.). Our university commentators had a historical interest in the pragmatic and social—rather than the philosophical and technical—dimensions of ancient musical practice, and that motivation sent them in search of different kinds of information in different sources from those beloved of the music theorists.

What we see as a result is two quite different classicising reading lists, amounting to two quite different ways to pursue an interest in music that might loosely be called "humanist" around 1501. From a musicological perspective, it is of course tempting to see the classical library of the music theorists as normative for musical understanding in the period, and that of the literature professors as secondary or peripheral. But in fact Boethius' *De musica* and Isidore's *Etymologiae* were hard to find in an Italian bookshop in 1501, at least among the print matter, whereas our commentators' bookshelves were stacked with bestsellers, several of which were required reading for university students.[178] For our commentators, and for their readers and students, knowing the difference between a citharist and a choraules, being able to differentiate the musical components of different religious rites across the ancient Mediterranean, knowing which musicians made which contributions in ancient theatre performances, knowing which Roman emperors had instituted which musical competitions, and other similar

---

178 Boethius' *De consolatione philosophiae* was a print bestseller; but his *De musica* was only available in print within the two *Opera* editions of 1491–92 and 1497–99. By 1501, Isidore's *Etymologiae* had appeared in just two print editions in Italy, in 1483 and 1493.

things, represented legitimate, relevant and interesting ways to know things about music in 1501. In reconstructing the history of musical knowledge in the period, we should attend to their opinion.

3.4 History

Francesco Maria Grapaldi, *De partibus aedium libellus cum additamentis emendatissimus* (Parma: Angelo Ugoleto, 1501)

Horace, *Horatius* (Venice: apud Aldo Manuzio, 1501)

Livy, *Titi Livii Decadis* (Venice: per Giorgio Rusconi, 1501)

Martial, *Martialis* (Venice: in aedibus Aldo Manuzio, 1501)

Pomponius Mela, *De situ orbis Hermolai Barbari fideliter emendatus* (Venice: Giovanni Battista Sessa, 1501)

Niccolò Perotti, *Cornucopie nuper emendatum a domino Benedicto Brugnolo: ac mirifice concinnatum cum tabula prioribus aliis copiosiori: utiliori: faciliorique* (Venice: per Giovanni Tacuino, 1501)

Philostratus of Athens, *De vita Apollonii Tyanei scriptor luculentus a Philippo Beroaldo castigatus* (Bologna: Benedetto Faelli, 1501)

Giovanni Battista Pio, *Prælectio in Titum Lucretium & Suetonium Tranquillum* (Bologna: s.n., 1501)

Pliny the Elder, *Libro de l'historia naturale* (Venice: per Albertino da Lessona, 1501)

Giovanni Sulpizio, *Regulae Sulpitij* ([Venice: s.n., 1501–09])

Dario Tiberti, *Epithome Plutarchi* (Ferrara: Lorenzo Rossi, 1501)

Giovanni Tortelli, *Orthographia. Ioannis Tortelii Lima quaedam per Georgium Vallam tractatum de orthographia* (Venice: per Bartolomeo Zani, 1501)

Valerius Flaccus, *Argonautica diligenter accurateque emendata & suo nitori reddita in hoc volumine continentur* (Venice: per Cristoforo Pensi, 1501)

Virgil, *Vergilius* (Venice: ex aedibus Aldo Manuzio, 1501)

Xenophon, *Opera* (Milan: Alessandro Minuziano, c.1501–02)

The commentators' methodology gives us a model to follow in approaching the classical texts on ancient Greek and Roman history printed in 1501. In this section we bring to the fore a selection of the texts routinely plundered by commentators for "archaeological" information on classical civilisations, and attempt to read them as a university professor or student might have read them in 1501, had they been seeking information on ancient musicians, musical practices, and musical customs. Here we are mimicking a different reading practice from that undertaken in the previous section, although one that is no less historically apposite. Rather than reading a set text under the guidance of a professor, now we are searching through a range of key texts to find useful and significant information on a specific topic—information that we will excerpt under a suitable heading in our commonplace book, and if possible memorise for use in future discussion and debate.[179]

Italian educators of the fifteenth and early sixteenth centuries pursued this reading practice with lofty aims in view. In his *De ingenuis moribus ac liberalibus studiis,* printed in around two dozen editions between 1480 and 1520, Pier Paolo Vergerio explains the ethical and practical objectives behind the distinctive interleaving of rhetoric, history and moral philosophy in the humanist curriculum. These three disciplines are particularly valuable to "those who are obligated to involve themselves in public affairs and human communities," because:

> Per philosophiam quidem possumus recte sentire quod est in omni re primum; per eloquentiam grativer ornateque dicere qua una re maxime concilantur multitudinis animi; per historiam vero in utrumque iuvamur. Nam si senes idcirco prudentiores iudicamus eosque libenter audimus quod per longam vitam et in se multa experti sunt et in aliis pleraque viderunt atque audierunt, quid de his est iuducandum qui multorum saeculorum res cognitu dignas memoriter norunt et ab omnem casum proferre illustre aliquod exemplum possunt?[180]

> Through philosophy we can acquire correct views, which is of first importance in everything; through eloquence we can speak with weight and polish, which is the one skill that most effectively wins over the minds of the masses; but history helps us with both. For if we consider old people wiser and listen to them gladly because they have found out

---

179 On this reading practice, see, among others, Ann Blair, "Reading Strategies for Coping with Information Overload ca.1550–1700," *Journal of the History of Ideas* 64.1 (2003), 11–28.
180 *Humanist Educational Treatises*, ed. and trans. Kallendorf, 48.

many things in the course of their long lives both through their own experience and through the other people they have seen and heard, how much ought we to esteem those who have memorized things worth knowing from many centuries and are able to produce an example to illuminate every situation?[181]

Commentaries, whether written or explained *viva voce* in a lecture, are nothing if not magnificent demonstrations of the ability to cite an example to illuminate every situation presented by a given text. As such they are exercises modelling and teaching a skill that students will later use to construct their authority and sound judgement beyond the classroom, as politicians, lawyers, doctors, astrologers, and prelates. By filling their memories with factoids from classical history—at least in theory—students could learn to speak eloquently on any subject, and at the same time would be inspired by historical examples "to act as well as possible." We can see precisely how musical knowledge might be deployed within this framework by reading the passages on music in Castiglione's *Il libro del Cortegiano* and Cortesi's *De cardinalatu*, or the opening chapters of the music treatises by Florentius de Faxolis or Franchino Gafori, which collate musical facts and citations from classical history in order to present, in stylish fashion, an ethical argument for the utility of music and its proper practice in the present day.

The commentator's bookshelf, as characterised in the previous section, is well represented in our 1501 corpus. Livy's *Ab urbe condita*, commonly known in the period as the *Decades*, and Pliny the Elder's *Naturalis historia*, were the standard encyclopedias of the ancient Roman world, then as now. (Pliny's was not a historical work *per se*, of course, but as we have seen in Chapter 3.3 it was widely used as a source of historical information.) Both were printed in translation quite early, in 1476. Between 1480 and 1520 in Italy, Livy appeared in more than a dozen Latin and around half a dozen Italian language editions from printers in Venice, Milan, and Treviso; some editions were illustrated.[182] In the same period, Pliny was printed

---

181 *Humanist Educational Treatises*, ed. and trans. Kallendorf, 49.
182 The reception of Livy in Renaissance Italy is adeptly summarised in Jillian Curry Robbins, "The Art of History: Livy's Ab Urbe Condita and the Visual Arts of the Early Italian Renaissance" (PhD diss., Florida State University, 2004), 25-49.

in Italy a dozen times in Latin and four times in Italian in Venice, Parma, and Brescia, the last of the Italian language editions having illustrations; moreover, several editions also appeared of a compilation of the medical information given by Pliny.[183]

Our 1501 Livy, its austere title page notwithstanding, is a smart folio printed in Roman type with a single-column layout and clear navigational apparatus, opening with a dedicatory letter addressed to Pope Paul II by Giovanni Andrea Bussi, Bishop of Aleria and Vatican librarian, who edited the *editio princeps* of 1469. Livy, of course, is extremely long, and for the convenience of the reader this edition includes two summaries which could serve either as abridged versions of the text or as detailed tables of contents: the ancient summary known as the *Periochae*, here entitled as an epitome, and a newer one by Marco Antonio Sabellico, a teacher of rhetoric in the second half of the fifteenth century who served as public historian in Venice and curator of the Greek manuscripts in the doge's palace.

Our 1501 Pliny is another stylish folio, this time in two columns but otherwise similar in its practical features to the Livy. Rather than Pliny's Latin, it presents a direct and faithful Italian translation prepared by Cristoforo Landino at the request of King Ferdinand I of Naples, to whom the dedication in our volume is addressed. Related to Pliny both topically and textually is Pomponius Mela's *De situ orbis*, the earliest surviving work of Roman geography, sometimes called the *Cosmographia* in the Renaissance. Printed in eight editions through our period and only in Latin, this work is mercifully much shorter than Pliny, and our 1501 quarto, edited by the Venetian politician and scholar Ermolao Barbaro, is an easy read with clear Roman typography. The copy consulted for our project (Munich, Bayerische Staatsbibliothek, Res/4 A.lat.b. 371 m) has evidently been intensively used, with fragile page edges, stains, and extensive period annotations (most of them corrections to the Latin).

---

183 For an overview see Andrea Rizzi, "Editing and Translating Pliny in Renaissance Italy: Agency, Collaboration and Visibility," in *Issues in Translation Then and Now: Renaissance Theories and Translation Studies Today*, ed. Annet den Haan, Brenda Hosington, Marianne Pade, and Anne Wegener (*Renaessanceforum* 14, 2018), 117–38.

Biography was an important historical genre, playing neatly into the objective of setting examples of praiseworthy behaviour from the ancient world before the minds of young leaders-in-training.[184] Particularly successful was Suetonius' *Vitae XII Caesarum*, which appeared in around two dozen editions in our period—none of them was printed in 1501, but Suetonius has a foot in the door of our project nonetheless, thanks to the printed edition of an inaugural lecture given by Giovanni Battista Pio on the occasion of his reappointment to the professorship in rhetoric at the University of Bologna in 1500, which takes the form of a preface to a course of lectures on Lucretius and Suetonius.

Second to Suetonius among the ancient biographers was Plutarch, whose *Parallel Lives*, printed under various titles but most often as the *Vitae illustrium virorum*, ran through around a dozen editions in our period. As a Greek author whose works were printed in Latin or Italian versions, and were often excerpted and anthologised alongside those of other authors, Plutarch's Renaissance print reception was rather more complex than that of the Romans Livy, Pliny, Pomponius Mela, and Suetonius. His other major work, the compilation known as the *Moralia*, rarely appeared as a whole, its various sections on different topics pursuing their own independent and distinctive trajectories. The *De liberis educandis* (*Moralia* 1), for example, was often anthologised alongside works on education by St Jerome, Pier Paolo Vergerio, and other authors; the *De musica* (*Moralia* 78) printed in Brescia in 1507 is another such excerpt finding its own way in the world. The standard Latin edition of the *Vitae illustrium virorum* in our period brought together unabridged and relatively direct translations of the various lives from the Greek by a roster of fifteenth-century Italian *literati*, including Leonardo Giustiniani, Francesco Filelfo, Guarino da Verona, and more, curated by the professor of rhetoric, bishop, and Vatican administrator Giovanni Antonio Campano for an *editio princeps* in 1470. Our 1501 Plutarch is not this one, however, but rather a Latin epitome prepared from the Campano edition at the beginning of the 1490s by Dario Tiburti, a nobleman of Cesena—a rather crude

---

184 Overview, including discussion of the classical precedents, in Martin McLaughlin, "Biography and Autobiography in the Italian Renaissance," in *Mapping Lives: The Uses of Biography*, ed. Peter France and William St. Clair (Oxford: Oxford University Press, 2002), 37–65.

abridgement, but certainly much more efficient to read. A full-page image facing the opening of the first life (that of Theseus) presents Plutarch sat beneath a tree writing, a *lira da braccio* hanging above him from a branch (Figure 3.1).

Fig. 3.1 Dario Tiberti, *Epithome Plutarchi* (Ferrara: Lorenzo Rossi, 1501), fol. [iii] v. Augsburg, Staats- und Stadtbibliothek, 4 Bio 1139, urn:nbn:de:bvb:12-bsb11210570-1. Image © Bayerische Staatsbibliothek.

Much more obscure, at least in print, are our other two Greek biographers, Xenophon and Philostratus of Athens, whose fates at the press were very similar in our period. Xenophon's nearest approach to a bestseller was his *Hiero*, also known as *De tyrannide*, a dialogue on happiness between a ruler and a poet which was sometimes included in anthologies focussed on education, alongside works by Vergerio and Plutarch. Complete Latin *Opera* editions appeared in Milan and Bologna nearly simultaneously in 1501–02, the latter edited by Filippo Beroaldo, followed by Manuzio's edition of the Greek in 1503. Ours is the Milan printing, in which an unnamed editor has brought together Latin translations of Xenophon's works by several fifteenth-century Italian luminaries, by far the longest and most significant of which is the *Paedia Cyri Persarum regis* (now known as the *Cyropaedia*), a biography of the Persian king Cyrus, translated by Francesco Filelfo. Philostratus of Athens' biography of the first-century Neopythagorean philosopher Apollonius of Tyana, the *De vita Apollonii Tyanei* (now *Vita Apollonii*), was translated into Latin in the 1470s by the Florentine scholar and politician Alamanno Rinuccini, and first printed under Beroaldo's editorship in Bologna in 1501, with a second edition appearing in Venice in 1502; Manuzio's edition of the Greek was published that same year. Our copy of the 1501 Bolognese edition (Rome, Biblioteca Casanatense, CCC O.IV 8), a smart folio printed in a single column with generous margins, has been extensively annotated in a few passages, with manicules, wavy lines, and callouts drawing the reader's attention to key points in the text.

As we have seen in the previous section, the commentators drew historical insights from the poets just as readily as they did from prose histories. In this section our imaginary professor will follow suit, drawing uncommented 1501 editions of Horace, Martial, and Virgil into the scope of his investigation, all of them pocket-sized octavos from Manuzio printed in attractive italics.[185] All three poets are treated in similar fashion by the printing press in our period—albeit that the roughly two dozen editions each of Horace and Martial are dwarfed by the hundred-or-so printed Virgils issued in Italy between 1480 and 1520. All three are printed almost exclusively in complete *Opera* editions, variously entitled *Opera* (for Horace and Virgil), *Epigrammata* (for Martial), or simply *Horatius*, *Vergilius*, *Martialis*. In contrast to our relatively compact and user-friendly 1501 poetry anthologies, a majority of editions are dense folios including commentaries: for Horace these are generally the early scholia attributed to Helenius Acron and

---

185 On the Renaisance reception of these poets see, respectively: Giacomo Comiati, "Horace in the Italian Renaissance" (PhD diss., University of Warwick, 2015); J. P. Sullivan, *Martial: The Unexpected Classic* (Cambridge, UK: Cambridge University Press, 1991), 262-9; Kallendorf, *Printing Virgil*, among many others.

Pomponius Porphyrio, plus new commentaries by Antonio Mancinelli and Cristoforo Landino; for Martial, fifteenth-century commentaries by Domizio Calderini and Giorgio Merula; and for Virgil, the late-classical Servius and Donatus alongside new efforts by Calderini, Mancinelli, and Landino. To these behemoths of classical verse our professor will add the *Argonautica* of Valerius Flaccus, a work of very modest circulation, in a 1501 quarto with a title page printed in striking red, the last in a small family of editions descended from the Bolognese bookseller and publisher Benedetto Faelli's 1498 issue and preserving his dedication to the lawyer and patrician Anton Galeazzo Bentivoglio.

Pliny the Elder offers our professor an obvious starting point in his investigation, with a touchstone passage on the inventors of music, part of a longer chapter entitled "Inventori delle chose" ("Inventors of things"):

> La musica Amphione. El zufolo pan. Monavolo trovo merchurio. El piffero torto Myda in phrygia. E pifferi dopoi Marsia. Le melodie lydie Amphione. Le dorie Thamira di Tracia. Le phrygie Marsya di phrygia. La Cithera trovo Amphione. Altri dicono Orpheo. altri lino. Con septe chorde Terpandro. Loctava aggiunse Simonide: la nona. Thimotheo. Sonare la Cithara senza cantare uso Thamyra. Colcanto Amphione: overo lino. Trovata la Cithera Terpandro fece versi. Dardano troezenio comincio acantare in supifferi El ballo armato trovorono e Cureti & quello che e decto pyrrhice. pyrrho. luno & laltro in Creta cioe candia.[186]

> Music Amphion. The recorder Pan. The single pipe was discovered by Mercury. The bent pipe Midas in Phrygia. And the double pipes Marsyas. The Lydian melodies Amphion. The Dorian Thamyris of Thrace. The Phrygian Marsyas of Phrygia. The cithara was discovered by Amphion. Others say Orpheus, others Linus. With seven strings Terpander. The eighth was added by Simonides, the ninth Timotheus. Playing the cithara without singing was the use of Thamyris. With singing Amphion, or Linus. Terpander first made verses for the cithara. Dardanus the Troezenian first began to sing above the pipe. The armed dance was discovered by the Curetes, and that which is called Pyrrhic, Phyrrhus, the one and the other in Crete, that is, Candia.

This material will be useful to our professor in framing the general topic of music—it is used in this way, for example, by Pietro d'Abano in his

---

186 *Libro de l'historia naturale*, fol. 57v (*Naturalis historia* 7.56). Note that there are several divergences from the accepted modern reading of Pliny's Latin in this passage, which we can assume would have been noticed by some but not all readers in 1501.

commentary on Aristotle's *Problemata*, mentioned above in Chapter 3.1. It will also be valuable in establishing the genealogy of the cithara or lyre, and we have seen it used in this way many times in the commentaries examined in Chapter 3.3.

The biographies of several of these mythological and semi-mythological musicians are easily fleshed out further using our 1501 corpus. Orpheus, especially, was the musical hero *par excellence*, featuring not only in the stories told by Ovid and the *Eclogues* of Virgil, but also, in more properly heroic guise, as one of the Argonauts and an important mystic. In Valerius Flaccus' *Argonautica*, his music keeps the oarsmen in time, and moreover he performs a full range of bardic functions: his songs tell the stories of the regions through which the crew travels, celebrate their daring deeds, comfort his companions in grief, and communicate with the shades of departed heroes.[187] From the *De situ orbis* of Pomponius Mela our professor learns further that Orpheus instituted the rites of the maenads in the mountains of Thrace, and in Horace he reads that "While men still roamed the woods, Orpheus, the holy prophet of the gods, made them shrink from bloodshed and brutal living," an interpretation that configures the power of his song to move even beasts, rocks, and trees as an allegory of the civilising influence of his eloquence upon primitive humanity.[188] Horace also gives him several datapoints on Amphion, mentioning that he learned music from Mercury, used it to build the walls of Thebes, and had a twin brother named Zethus who disapproved of his musicianship.[189]

However, with its mixture of mythological and historical individuals, and its extreme concision, Pliny's list of inventors is of limited value in extending commentary on classical music history beyond introductory gestures. Fortunately, our 1501 corpus is replete with numerous brief but entertaining anecdotes and comments concerning celebrated musical

---

187 Respectively: *Argonautica*, sig. B [i] v (*Argonautica* 1.470–72); sig. [A vi] v (*Argonautica* 1.77ff) and sig. [F v] r–v (*Argonautica* 4.344ff); sig. [F v] r (*Argonautica* 4.342–43); sig. F [i] r (*Argonautica* 4.85-7); sig. [G vi] r (*Argonautica* 5.98–100).

188 *De situ orbis*, fol. 13v (*De situ orbis* 2.17). "Sylvestres homines sacer, interpresque deorum/ Caedibus, et victu foedo deterruit Orpheus." *Horatius*, sig. [k vii] v (*Ars poetica* 391–92). Translation of Horace from *Satires. Epistles. The Art of Poetry*, trans. H. Rushton Fairclough, Loeb Classical Library 194 (Cambridge, MA: Harvard University Press, 1926), 483.

189 Respectively: *Horatius*, sig. [e v] v (*Carmina* 3.11.1–2); sig. [k vii] v (*Ars poetica* 394-6); sig. [m viii] r (*Epistulae* 1.18.41–44).

personalities of the ancient world, who at least appear to have a stronger claim to historicity. Pliny himself is a valuable source: at the beginning of Book 37, having found little to report on the subject of famous jewels, he resorts to a cautionary tale about the luxurious tastes of famous pipers:

> si trova apresso de gli auctori excepto di ismena cantore & sonatore di piffero elquale uso molto risplendenti gemme onde nacque favola da la sua vanita perche posto al pregio in Cyppri a uno smeraldo di cento denarii doro nel quale era intaglata Amymone lui di subito fece numerare la pecunia & essendoglene riportati in drieto due denarii per diminutione del pregio: dixe che lui era stato mal governato stimando che per quello fussi tolta essa riputatione alla gemma. Costui pare che ordinassi che tutti quelli dellarte musica fussino giudicati da questa ostentatione come Dionysiodoro suo equale e emolo: accioche anchora lui paressi pari & scrivesi che Nycomacho il quale in quelli tempi fu el terza tra emusici hebbe molte gemme.[190]

> We only find mentioned by the authors Ismenias the singer and player of the pipe, who used many resplendent gems, from which arose a fable of his vanity, because, an emerald on which was engraved Amymone being put up for sale on Cyprus for 100 golden denari, he immediately offered the money, and being sent back 2 denari because of a fall in the price, he said that he had been badly done by, considering that by this the renown of the gem had been taken away. By him it seems that it was established that all those in the art of music should be judged by this ostentation, such as Dionysiodorus his equal and emulator, so that he would still seem his equal, and it is written that Nicomachus, who in those times was the third among musicians, had many gems. But not chosen with any skill, but by chance.

Pliny explains that he has presented this example as a warning to those who, for love of jewels, "become puffed up like the vainglory of pipers" (che loro gonfieno per vana gloria da pifferi). This is not the only anecdote concerning Ismenias to be found in our 1501 corpus. Philostratus has his protagonist, the sage Apollonius of Tyana, discourse with Emperor Vespasian about how best to deal with the unfortunate legacy of his predecessors following the disastrous Year of the Four Emperors. To help the emperor find a positive view of the situation, Apollonius reaches for a musical analogy: "There was once a great piper who sent his sagest disciples to hear the most foolish pipers, so that from them they might

---

190 *Libro de l'historia naturale*, fol. 250v (*Naturalis historia* 37.1).

learn how not to play."[191] Although Philostratus does not name the piper, Plutarch attaches this anecdote to Ismenias in his *Life of Demetrius* (1.6); unfortunately the passage is elided in Tiburti's epitome, the only version of Plutarch issued in 1501. An early owner of the copy of Philostratus consulted for our project, using what could easily be a sixteenth-century hand, has highlighted this passage vigorously in the margin, adding a miniature drawing of a shawm as a pointing device (see Figure 3.2).

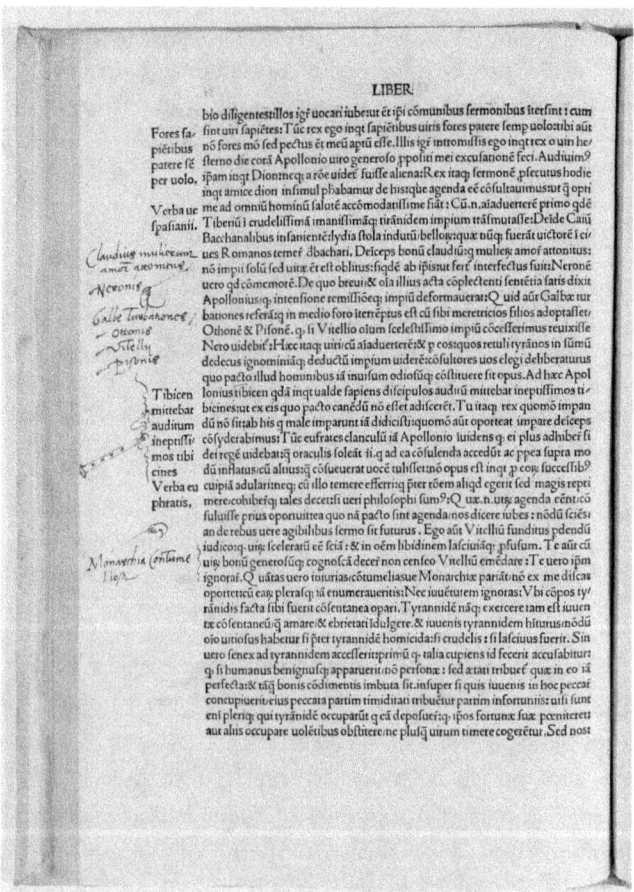

Fig. 3.2 Philostratus of Athens, *De vita Apollonii Tyanei* (Bologna: Benedetto Faelli, 1501), fol. 51v, with marginal annotations. Rome, Biblioteca Casanatense, CCC O.IV 8. By permission of the Biblioteca Casanatense, Rome, MiC.

---

191 "tibicen quondam inquit valde sapiens discipulos auditum mittebat ineptissimos tibicines: ut ex eis quo pacto canendum non esset adisceret." *De vita Apollonii Tyanei*, fol. 51v (*Vita Apollonii* 5.32).

Elsewhere in the *Vita Apollonii*, Philostratus has his protagonist enter into a lengthy exchange with the celebrated piper Canius in Rhodes, in which the technique and aesthetic of piping is explored in astonishing detail (see Appendix, Excerpt 3.5). In response to Apollonius' playfully superior interrogation, Canius explains that his listeners turn to his music because it can "save the mournful from their mourning, and moreover increase the cheerfulness of the joyful, and the ardour of lovers, and cause the religious to be more seized by divine power and better prepared to praise the gods." These effects are achieved, Canius continues, because "music, and modulations, and the mingling of harmonies, and their alteration, according to the requirements of different styles," serve to "move the audience, and, leading their souls in various ways, the piper brings them to the state that they wish for." Apollonius adds that these effects rely on the technical skills of the player, namely "his blowing, and his good breath, and fitness of mouth, and a certain dexterity of the hands," giving details of each element. He further notes that the pipe itself may be "made of gold or silver, or the shin of a deer or an ass." Our professor—an avid reader of Virgil's *Eclogues*, in which pipes are ubiquitous—is here reminded of a contrasting and more detailed discussion of pipe materials and manufacture in Pliny (see Appendix, Excerpt 3.6), where we read that the best instruments are made from reeds cut in particular locations, at a specific time of year, aged, and then carefully crafted and blown in.

Our professor will find the names of several more ancient musicians in our 1501 corpus. Horace's *Satires* aim several barbs at a famous and very rich Sardinian singer named Tigellius Hermogenes, who would never sing when asked, but if not asked wouldn't shut up, and after his death was mourned by "the Syrian singing-girls' guilds, the drug-quacks, beggars, actresses, buffoons, and all that breed."[192] From Pliny our professor learns that "Xenophilus the musician lived 205 years without bodily discomfort," referring to the Pythagorean philosopher Xenophilus of Chalcidice.[193] This example is picked up by

---

192 "Ambubaiarum collegia pharmacopolae/ Mendici, mimae, balatrones, hoc genus omne." *Horatius*, sig. [o v] r (*Satirae* 1.2.1–2). Translation adapted from *Satires. Epistles. The Art of Poetry*, trans. Fairclough, 19. Also *Horatius*, sig. [o vii] r–v (*Satirae* 1.3.1–8); sig. p [i] v (*Satirae* 1.3.76); sig. p iii r (*Satirae* 1.4.71–78).

193 "Xenophilo musico vixe ccv anni senza alchuno incomodo di corpo." *Libro de l'historia naturale*, fol. 54v (*Naturalis historia* 7.50, where the claim is a mere 105

Francesco Maria Grapaldi—another magpie, like the commentators, with a particular taste for Pliny—in his *De partibus aedium*, which also features in our 1501 corpus.[194] Although Ismenias is lost from Tiberti's abridged Latin version of Plutarch's *Parallel Lives*, a few other named musicians are preserved. In the *Life of Themistocles*, the young and as yet unknown Themistocles "asked Epicles the citharist to practise his art in his presence, in order that he might be noted and frequented by all."[195] In the *Life of Demetrius*, our professor reads of a woman musician, described in a vein similar to a Renaissance courtesan, who was won by Demetrius as booty following his victory over Ptolemy I in the Battle of Salamis:

> Erat enim inter hasce mulieres lamia omnium suae aetatis tum forma: tum tibiarum modulatione: et cantus suavitate excellentissima: quae uti apud quoscumque sibi gratiam conciliavit: sic demetrium allexit: ut eam prae caeteris admaret.[196]

> There was among the women Lamia, most excellent of her age, both in beauty, and in the music of her pipes and the sweetness of her singing, which she used to win favour with whoever she was with; thus she enticed Demetrius, so that he loved her above all others.

Indeed, women musicians are mentioned often, both individually and as a distinct professional group. In Philostratus our professor learns of Damophyle, "the Pamphylian woman who is said to have had intimacy with Sappho, and is held to have composed the hymns, which in these times they sing in honor of Diana of Perga; indeed it is said she produced these following the Aeolian and Pamphylian modes."[197] Apollonius adds that Damophyle "gathered about herself similar virgins, and composed poems, some amorous, some in praise of modest Diana."[198] In Xenophon's

---
years).
194 *De partibus aedium*, fol. 108r.
195 "Epyclem citharaedum rogasse. Ut apud se artem exerceret: ut ab omnibus dignosceretur: frequentareturque." *Epithome Plutarchi*, fol. 26r (*Themistocles* 5.2).
196 *Epithome Plutarchi*, fol. 133r (*Demetrius* 16.3).
197 "uxor Pamphili vocata fuerit quae cum sapho familiaritatem habuisse, et composuisse perhibetur hymnos: que est his temporibus in honorem Pergeae dianae cantantur: eos vero eoliae pamphiliaeque modum secuta dicitur edidisse." *De vita Apollonii Tyanei*, fol. 9r (*Vita Apollonii* 1.30).
198 "quae aequales sibi virgines congregasse: et poemata composuisse partis amatoria: partis dianae laudes continentia." *De vita Apollonii Tyanei*, fol. 9v (*Vita Apollonii* 1.30).

Cyropedia our professor encounters "citharistrias duas optimas" ("two of the best female citharists"), highly valued entertainers, mentioned at the end of Book 4 and again at the beginning of Book 5; later in Book 5, "unaque citharistrias" ("one of the female citharists")—a different individual from the two mentioned before, and the next in ability—is allotted to the king of the Medes for his tent when visiting Cyrus' camp.[199] Among the commentators, Niccolò Perotti, author of the enormous Martial commentary known as the *Cornucopiae*, is particularly attentive to these feminine forms of the Latin terms for musicians—albeit most likely from a sense of grammatical propriety rather than a commitment to social justice—highlighting *citharistria* as well as *psaltria* and *fidicina*; Tortelli says that these are all synonyms ("Psaltria fidicina citharistria dicitur idem").[200] As in the case of Lamia, the social and ethical situation of these women is generally dubious. Horace mentions musical prostitutes twice, referring to a "piping courtesan" ("meretrix tibicina") in his *Epistulae*, and in his *Carmina* asking "Who will entice Lyde, that discreet prostitute, from her house? Go on; tell her to grab her ivory lyre and hurry up."[201] Livy records that "female lyre-players and harpists" ("psaltriae sambucistriaeque") were first introduced to Roman dinner-parties by soldiers returning from campaigns in Asia, regarding them as an unwelcome exotic import and a sign of declining moral standards.[202]

Now armed with several names and distinct categories of musician, our professor will be keen to add to this an understanding of the roles they played in ancient societies. The *Epithome Plutarchi* records that Numa was responsible for first organising the pipers of Rome into a distinct profession, as a part of a wider scheme to bring order to the faction-riven city by creating trade groups and assigning them religious rites and privileges.[203] The importance of pipers to the religious life of the city, and

---

199 Xenophon, *Opera*, sig. f ii v (*Cyropedia* 4.6.11 and 5.1.1), and sig. [g iiii] r (*Cyropedia* 5.5.2).
200 *Cornucopie*, cols. 621 (*citharistria*), 630 (*psaltria, fidicina*), and 1206 (*citharistria*); *Orthographia*, fol. 22r. On musical comments in Perotti's *Cornucopiae*, see Shephard and Hancock, "Looking Up Music in Two 'Encyclopedias'."
201 Respectively: *Horatius*, sig. m iii v (*Epistulae* 1.14.25). "Quis devium scortum eliciet domo/ Lyden? eburna dic age cum lyra/ Maturet." *Horatius*, sig. [c viii] r (*Carmina* 2.11.21–23). Translation from *Satires. Epistles. The Art of Poetry*, trans. Fairclough, 117–19.
202 *Titi Livii Decadis*, fol. 217v (*Decades* 39.6).
203 *Epithome Plutarchi*, fol. 11r (*Life of Numa* 17.1–3).

the importance of their religious privileges to the pipers as a professional group, is vividly illustrated in a dispute described by Livy:

> tibicines quia prohibiti a proximis censoribus erant in aede Iovis vesci: quod traditum antiquitus erat: aegre passi Tybur uno agmine abierunt: adeo ut nemo in urbe esset: qui sacrificiis praecineret.

> The pipers, angry at having been forbidden by the last censors to hold their feast, according to old custom, in the temple of Jupiter, went off to Tibur in a body, so that there was no one in the city to pipe at sacrifices.

Concerned by the religious dimension of what (in Livy's view) would otherwise have been an inconsequential occurrence, the senate sent emissaries to the Tiburtines asking for their help in returning the pipers to Rome. Finding that the musicians could not be persuaded by reasoned arguments, the Tiburtines resorted to a ruse:

> die festo alii alios per speciem celebrandarum cantu epularum causa invitant: et vino: cuius avidum ferme genus est: oneratos sopiunt: atque in plaustra somno victos coniiciunt: ac Romam deportant

> On a holiday various citizens invited parties of the pipers to their houses, on the pretext of celebrating the feast with music. There they plied them with wine, which people of that profession are generally greedy of, until they got them stupefied. In this condition they threw them, fast asleep, into waggons and carried them away to Rome.

The pipers then awaking, hung over, the citizens of Rome immediately prevailed upon them to return to their occupation, in exchange affording them renewed privileges:

> datum ut triduum quotannis ornati cum cantu atque hac: quae nunc solemnis est licentia per urbem vagarentur: restitutumque in aede vescendi ius iis: qui sacris praecinerent.[204]

> They were permitted on three days in every year to roam the City in festal robes, making music and enjoying the licence that is now customary, and to such as should play at sacrifices was given again the privilege of banqueting in the temple.[205]

---

204 *Titi Livii Decadis*, fol. 73v. The episode is also mentioned very briefly in *Quae in isto continentur opusculo. C. Plinii iunioris epistolae*, sig. [m vi] r (Sextus Aurelius Victor, *De Viris Illustribus Romae* 34.1).

205 Livy, *History of Rome, Volume IV: Books 8–10*, trans. B. O. Foster, Loeb Classical Library 191 (Cambridge, MA: Harvard University Press, 1926), 279–81 (*Decades*

As this example indicates, Livy is particularly conscientious in recording the history of Roman religious customs, and that entails describing musical practices which, by themselves, would not in his view merit notice. The hymns and dancing of the Salii in honour of Mars Gradivus are described in Book 1; young girls singing hymns to Juno in procession in Book 27; and the terrifying percussion accompanying Bacchic initiation, which we found mentioned by Giorgio Valla in his commentary on Juvenal, is heard in Book 39.[206] The poets Horace, Martial, and Virgil, meanwhile, make quite frequent mention of the Corybantes and the worship of Cybele, accompanied by the rite's characteristic cymbals (*cymbala, aera*), hand-drums (*tympana*), and pipe (*cornu*).[207]

Religious considerations also prompt Livy's account of the inception of Roman theatre, a practice that he regards as antithetical to the warlike character of the early Roman citizenry, but necessary to appease the gods in a time a pestilence:

> sine certamine ullo: sine imitandorum carminum actu: ludiones ex Ethruria acciti ad tibicinis modos saltantes haud indecoros motus more tusco dabant: imitari deinde eos iuventus simul inconditis inter se iocularia fundentes versibus coepere: nec absoni a voce motus erant. Accepta itaque res saepiusque usurpando excitata vernaculis artificibus: quia hister tusco verbo ludio vocabatur nomen histrionibus Iditum: qui non sicut ante fescenino versu similem incompositum temere ac rudem alternis iaciebant: sed impletas modis satyras descripto iam ad tibicinem cantu motuque congruenti peragebant.[208]

> Without any singing, without imitating the action of singers, players who had been brought in from Etruria danced to the strains of the piper and performed not ungraceful evolutions in the Tuscan fashion. Next the young Romans began to imitate them, at the same time exchanging jests in uncouth verses, and bringing their movements into a certain harmony with the words. And so the amusement was adopted, and frequent use kept it alive. The native professional actors were called *histriones*, from *ister*, the Tuscan word for player; they no longer—as before—alternately

---

9.30).

206 *Titi Livii Decadis*, fols. 3v (*Decades* 1.20), 142r (*Decades* 27.37), and 218r–v (*Decades* 39.10) respectively.

207 *Horatius*, sig. b ii r (*Carmina* 1.16.7–8—*aera*); sig. b iii r (*Carmina* 1.18.13–14—*cornu, tympana*); *Martialis*, sig. [& vi] r (*Epigrammata* 14.204—*cymbala, aera*); *Vergilius*, sig. [D v] v (*Aeneid* 3.111—*aera*).

208 *Titi Livii Decadis*, fol. 54v.

threw off rude lines hastily improvised, like the Fescennines, but performed medleys, full of musical measures, to melodies which were now written out to go with the pipe, and with appropriate gesticulation.[209]

Livy goes on to explain that the roles of actor and singer were later separated from each other, with the actor responsible for dialogue and gesticulation, and a professional singer performing the songs, still to the accompaniment of a piper. In Horace's opinion the later history of Roman theatre was marked by a trajectory of decline, resulting from greater popularity and therefore vulgarity, visible in the arrogance and luxury of pipers also remarked upon by Pliny.[210]

The ancient Greek festivals and their musical contests are mentioned by several authors. Philostratus is particularly valuable to our professor here, as his protagonist, Apollonius of Tyana, spends much of his time in the Hellenic world. In Book 8, in an episode set in Olympia in which Apollonius discourses with a man from Thessaly, the philosopher itemises the characteristic components of a Greek festival:

> nam in panegyris templa sunt, et deorum cellae, et stadia ad currendum: tum vero scenae et gentes plurimae partim ex finitimis, partim ex transmarinis regionibus venientes: ex multis insuper artibus et sophismatibus panegyris ex vera quoque sapientia et poetica ex consultativis etiam, et disputativis orationibus, et musicis cantibus.[211]

> For in a festival there are temples, and sanctuaries of the gods, and racecourses for running, and of course theatres, and many people, some coming from neighbouring regions and some from overseas; moreover, a festival is made from many arts and sophistries, from true wisdom and poetry, from orations of advice and debate, and musical songs.

Elsewhere we learn that those arriving at the Pythian festival are "invited in by pipes and songs and lyres, indeed they are called to comedies and tragedies," whereas "those who preside over the Olympian [festival] have dismissed these as useless and not at all suited to the place."[212]

---

209 Livy, *History of Rome, Volume III: Books 5–7*, trans. B. O. Foster, Loeb Classical Library 172 (Cambridge, MA: Harvard University Press, 1924), 361 (*Decades* 7.2).
210 "Sic priscae motum, et luxuriam addidit arti/ Tibicen, traxitque vagus per pulpita vestem." *Horatius*, sig. k iiii v (*Ars poetica* 214–15).
211 *De vita Apollonii Tyanei*, fol. 90r (*Vita Apollonii* 8.18).
212 "tibiis et cantibus ac psalmis invitantur: quippe qui ad comoedias tragoediasque vocentur: spectaculumque tandem similium rerum illis proponitur. Qui vero

Meanwhile, at the Panathanaic festival, dedicated to Pallas, "the praises of Harmodius and Aristogeiton"—founding heroes of Athenian democracy—"are sung."[213] When visiting Athens, Apollonius is shocked at the improper musical celebration of the festival of Dionysus: instead of "simple songs, or melodies [...] such as are usually sung in comedies and tragedies," he finds the Athenians "dancing to the sound of the pipe."[214]

Among the Greek cities, a particular wealth of information is available on the musical customs of ancient Sparta, an example often adduced in Renaissance apologiae for music as proof of the heroic quality of the artform. Amid the 1501 corpus, our professor finds that Xenophon is the most useful authority. In the *De re publica Lacedaemoniorum* we learn that Lycurgus, the founding figure of Spartan society, placed a great value on concision in speech, preferring silence to prolixity. He required adolescents, whose age was prey to insolence and desire, to walk in silence in the street, keeping their hands hidden and their eyes fixed on the ground; and "when they have taken their seat at mealtime, it will be enough that they answer your questions."[215] The importance of silence is a precept encountered regularly in classical literature, often in connection with Pythagoras' requirement that his students keep silence for five years. It is very likely a precept that our professor will wholeheartedly endorse: in the dedication preceding his address to his students at the University of Bologna, Pio notes that Pythagoras "valuably taught that silence is the fortress and so to speak the asylum of the uneducated," and in a classroom scene illustrated at the beginning of the grammatical *Regulae* of Giovanni Sulpizio, Professor of Grammar at the University of

---

olympiis praesunt, haec tanquam inutilia locoqiue minime accommodata posthabent." *De vita Apollonii Tyanei*, fol. 57v (*Vita Apollonii* 6.10).

213 "ubi harmodii et aristogitonis laudes cantabantur." *De vita Apollonii Tyanei*, fol. 69v (*Vita Apollonii* 7.4).

214 "simplices cantus: aut modulationes [...] quales comediarum, tragediarumque cantus esse solent [...] ad sonum tibiae illos saltare." *De vita Apollonii Tyanei*, fol. 38v (*Vita Apollonii* 4.21).

215 "Ad haec volens quasi naturalem his pudorem vehementer conciliare imperavit ut in viis manus intra pallium haberent: silentioque incederent: ac nusquam circumspicerent sed humi defixos oculos tenerent. [...] ac posteaquam in convivium venerint: satis profecto sit si vel ad interrogata respondeant." Xenophon, *Opera*, sig. [b v] r (*Lacedaemonion Politeia* 3.5).

Rome in the later fifteenth century, the instructor is flanked by the word "SILENTIUM" (see Figure 3.3).[216]

Fig. 3.3 Giovanni Sulpizio, *Regulae Sulpitij* ([Venice: s.n., 1501–09]), sig. a ii r. Padua, Biblioteca Universitaria, SEC.XV.524.1.

Xenophon also describes the distinctive and much-cited piping of the Spartan army, part of a larger practice of celebratory and cheerful campaigning, contrasting with the discipline and self-imposed hardship of everyday life for the Lacedaemonian elite. On campaign, the king's

---

216 "Pytagoras samius [...] salutariter edocuit munimentum, et quodam veluti asylum indoctis esse taciturnitatem." *Prælectio*, sig. A 1 r. Grendler notes that classroom conduct often failed to live up to this standard (*The Universities*, 163).

personal staff comprises "seers and doctors and pipers and military commanders, and those who attach themselves additionally;" once the enemy is within sight, a goat is sacrificed, and "the rule is that all pipers present should use their pipes, and none of the Lacedaemonians should be without a wreath."[217] In Xenophon's *Agesilaus* we read that the Spartan king once returned home from military campaigns at the time of the Hyacinthia festival, so he "took the place assigned by the leader of the chorus, at once performing the hymn to Apollo."[218]

The life of Lycurgus in the *Epithome Plutarchi* adds that music was integral to the educational program followed by Spartan children. Lycurgus had the girls train in wrestling, throwing the discus, and throwing javelins; and "no less than these he accustomed the children to sing and dance," sometimes watched by the male youths, who competed among themselves to see who could best master his base urges.[219] In fact Plutarch's original text contains a great deal more than this, giving further details of music education, describing the practice of Spartan festival choruses, mentioning marching songs and military piping, and explaining how Spartan bachelors were forced to sing songs of self-mockery in view of their failure to marry and procreate. Plutarch also describes how the Helots, an enslaved group within Spartan society, were forced to get drunk and sing bawdy songs to provide a counter-example for elite Spartan youths. It is striking that Tiburti omits almost all of this from his epitome; indeed, in his effort to reduce Plutarch's sometimes quite lengthy biographies to a pretty regular six pages each of printed Latin, music is often left out in favour of a focus on the protagonist's virtues, and his achievements in war and government.

---

217 "Hi vero sunt quotquot eiusdem ordinis simul convivatur et vates et medici et tibicines ac exercitus principes: et si qui ultro assuerint [...] Nam cum intuentibus iam hostibus capra iuguletur: lex est omnes astantes tybicines tybiis uti ac neminem lacedaemoniorum sine corona esse." Xenophon, *Opera*, sig. C [i] r (*Lacedaemonion Politeia* 13.7-8); also mentioned at sig. [C v] r (*Agesilaus* 2.15).
218 "ac patefactis peloponessi ianuis ita domum rediens ad hyacintia ubi a chori principe consitutum fuerat paeanem Apollini simul perfecit." Xenophon, *Opera*, sig. [C v] r (*Agesilaus* 2.17).
219 "Quas et assuefecit non minus quaque pueros canere saltare. Quibusdam insacris nudas versari inspectantibus iuvenibus: et interdum omne probitatis genus invicem exercentibus: et repugnantibus: ad maiorem vincentis gloriam." *Epithome Plutarchi*, fol. 7v (*Lycurgus* 14.2-3).

As the Spartan military pipers neatly exemplify, our professor will certainly notice that in these 1501 history books music is encountered most often in a military context. Several pieces of evidence suggest that contemporary readers recognised this fact, and that they found the information available on ancient military sound both interesting and valuable. Rhetorical defenses of music, such as that found in Castiglione's *Libro del Cortegiano*, routinely point to the ways in which ancient military commanders—especially Achilles—valued and used the art. Meanwhile, Roberto Valturio's *De re militari*, printed in Italy in 1472 and 1483, gives a whole book to music, running to seven pages. To prepare his chapter, Valturio (who spent a decade as a rhetoric professor at the University of Bologna) has undertaken precisely the type of reading we are imitating here, namely collating and summarising relevant excerpts from the classics; the table of contents in the Italian printed editions even lists his sources, which do not overlap entirely with our 1501 historical literature but are certainly of the same ilk.

A majority of military musical mentions in our 1501 histories involve Roman brass trumpets—usually either the straight *tuba* or the curving *cornu*—played to signal muster, charge, and retreat. In his passage on inventors, Pliny lists the trumpet among military equipment, separately from the musical innovations, naming Pisaeus the Tuscan ("Piseo thoscano") as its originator.[220] In both these respects—that is, the military uses of the trumpet, and the identification of trumpeters with soldiers rather than musicians—our professor will observe ancient and contemporary practice to be identical. The ubiquity of the military trumpet resulted in its recruitment to ingenious schemes and devices of ancient military strategy, of which Livy records several. During the Roman-Volscian wars, for example, the consul Titus Quinctius used his trumpeters and pipers to keep the enemy up all night whilst the Roman soldiers got a full night's sleep:

> Quinctius sedato tumultu: quem terror subitus exciverat: cum manere in tentoriis quietum militem iussisset: hernicorum cohortem in stationem educit cornicines tibicinesque in equos impositos canere ante vallum iubet: sollicitumque hostem ad lucem tenere: reliquum noctis adeo tranquilla omnia in castris fuere: ut somni quoque romanis copia esset.

---

220 *Libro de l'historia naturale*, fol. 56r (*Naturalis historia* 7.202).

Volscos species armatorum peditum quos et plures esse: et romanos putabant: fremitus hinnitusque equorum: qui et insueto sedente equite: et insuper aures agitante sonitu saeviebant: intentos velut ad impetum hostium tenuit:[221]

Quinctius stilled the tumult which the sudden alarm had raised, and bidding the soldiers remain quietly in their tents, led out a cohort of Hernici to an outpost, and mounting the cornu-players and pipers upon horses, ordered them to blow their instruments in front of the rampart and keep the enemy in suspense till daybreak. For the remainder of the night all was so peaceful in camp that the Romans were even able to sleep. But the Volsci, beholding armed foot-soldiers, whom they supposed to be more numerous than they were, and to be Romans; and hearing the stamping and neighing of the horses, which were infuriated not only at finding unaccustomed riders on their backs, but also by the blare of the players, were kept on the alert in anticipation of an attack.[222]

Enemies of Rome also made use of trumpet tactics. During his unexpected midnight occupation of the Greek colony of Tarentum in southern Italy, Hannibal confused the Roman garrison by capturing one of their trumpets and having a Greek play signals on it from the theatre.[223] The success of the ruse flowed not only from the misleading signals, but from the disorienting combination of a Roman instrument and a Greek performance practice (described by Livy as "ignorant"—"inscienter a graeco inflata"). Strikingly, inventive strategies such as these are themselves characterised through a musical analogy by Xenophon, in a long section of Book 1 of the *Cyropedia* where Cyrus receives advice on military matters from his father Cambyses:

Est igitur inquit opus: ubi haec omnia studiose didiceris: non his solum utaris sed tuo quoque ingenio alia adversus hostis moliare: quemadmodum musici non his utuntur duntaxat: quod didicere. sed alios novos modulos facere student. Ac sicuti in musicis quoque nova et florida habentur plurimum in precio: sic in rebus bellicis nova inventa existimantur longe illustriora: quoniam haec magis queunt hostis decipere.[224]

---

221 *Titi Livii Decadis*, fol. 19r (*Decades* 2.64).
222 Livy, *History of Rome, Volume I: Books 1–2*, trans. B. O. Foster, Loeb Classical Library 114 (Cambridge, MA: Harvard University Press, 1919), 431.
223 *Titi Livii Decadis*, fol. 119v (*Decades* 25.10).
224 Xenophon, *Opera*, sig. [b iv] v (*Cyropedia* 1.6.38).

"For this reason," said he, "since you are learning all these things diligently, not only should you use those things, but also use your ingenuity to devise other things against the enemy, just as musicians do not only use those things they have learned, but aim to make other new melodies. And just as in music whatever is new and florid is held in greater esteem, so in matters of war new inventions are considered far more distinguished, since these are more likely to deceive the enemy."

Trumpets are not the only sonic components of warfare described in our 1501 histories. In Valerius Flaccus' *Argonautica*—another 1501 book bristling with ancient war-trumpets—among the peoples mobilised by Perses in his war against Aeetes for control of Colchis are the Corallians, who do not use the *cornu* but instead "sing of their native chiefs and the deeds of their ancestors and the praises of heroes of old to stir their men to valour."[225] Livy, meanwhile, is particularly attentive to war-cries, and their significance emerges with great clarity in his description of another conflict with the Volsci:

> clamor indicium primum fuit: quo res inclinatura esset: excitatior crebriorque ab hoste sublatus: ab romanis dissonus: impar: segnis: saepe iteratus incerto clamore prodidit pavorem animorum:[226]

> The battle-cries were the first intimation of how the affair was likely to go; for the enemy's was louder and fuller, that of the Romans dissonant and uneven and, dragging more with each repetition, betrayed the faintness of their hearts.[227]

The true virtuosi of the war-cry, judging from Livy's descriptions, were the Gauls. During the Romans' fateful conflict with the Gallic tribe of the Senones under their chieftain Brennus, the enemy's "wild songs and discordant shouts filled all the air with a hideous noise" (cantu clamoribusque variis horrendo cuncta compleverat sono), and, as they threatened the very city of Rome, their "dissonant howls and songs"

---

225 "Praelia nec rauco curant incendere cornu: / Indigenas sed rite duces et prisca suorum / Fata canunt: verumque viris hortamina laudes." *Argonautica*, sig. I (i) v. Valerius Flaccus, *Argonautica*, trans. J. H. Mozley, Loeb Classical Library 286 (Cambridge, MA: Harvard University Press, 1934), 307 (*Argonautica* 6.92–94).
226 *Titi Livii Decadis*, fol. 35r.
227 Livy, *History of Rome, Volume II: Books 3–4*, trans. B. O. Foster, Loeb Classical Library 133 (Cambridge, MA: Harvard University Press, 1922), 379 (*Decades* 4.37).

(ululatus cantusque dissonos) terrified the populace within the walls.[228] Memories of this disastrous defeat echo in Livy's account of the much later war against the Galacians, another Gallic tribe settled in Anatolia. Livy vividly describes their warlike aspect:

> procera corpora: promissae et rutilatae comae: vasta scuta: praelongi gladii: ad hoc inchoantium proelium cantus et ululatus et tripudia: et quatientium scuta in patrium quendam modum horrendus armorum crepitus: omnia de industria composita ad terrorem.[229]

> They have tall frames and long, red-dyed hair, huge shields and long swords. In addition there are their chants as they go into battle, their yells and war dances, and the frightening clash of arms as they strike their shields following some ancestral custom—all deliberately contrived to instill terror.[230]

By this time, however, the Romans have had enough experience of the Gauls to dismiss these displays as bluster ("vanitates").

If Roman trumpets and Spartan piping connoted a manly and virtuous musicianship, our professor will not be surprised to find that classical historians associated some other musical practices with licence and vice. The *Epitome Plutarchi*, in which (as we have observed above) musical details found in Plutarch's original Greek are often missed out, luxuriates in the musical leisure of Mark Antony, who is subjected to a straightforward character assassination. Tiburti stays quite close to Plutarch in describing Antony's mode of life as a Triumvir and ruler of the eastern portion of the Roman Empire:

> Antonius in graeciam profectus cum facilitate: tum liberalitate omnibus magnificum se praebuit. Postque in asiam concessit: ad quem cum reges undique confluerent: donisque concertarent: Reginae etiam ornatu contendentes se se: formamque suam antonio offerebant. Corruptus itaque antonius his illecebris et consuetudinibus in pristinum recidit incontinentiae morbum. Qualiter inter mimmos: cytharedos: saltatores:

---

228 *Titi Livii Decadis*, fol. 44v–45r. Livy, *History of Rome, Volume III*, 129 (*Decades* 5.37–39).
229 *Titi Livii Decadis*, fol. 210r.
230 Livy, *History of Rome, Volume XI: Books 38–40*, ed. and trans. J. C. Yardley, Loeb Classical Library 313 (Cambridge, MA: Harvard University Press, 2018), 55 (*Decades* 38.17).

cantus et odores versans: unguenta et flagrantia serta tractabat. Suavissimis undique redolens odoribus.²³¹

> Antonius went into Greece willingly, and through liberality showed himself magnificent to all. And afterwards he went to Asia, to which kings from every quarter flocked, and competed with each other in gifts. Accordingly, corrupted by these allurements and convivialities, Antony relapsed into his former disease of incontinence. Thus among mimes, singers to the lyre, dancers, turning to song and scents, he handled perfumed and passionate garlands, smelling the sweetest scents on every side.

It is at this moment that Antony's famous romance with Cleopatra begins, and in describing her journey to meet him, Tiburti gives full rein to sensory delight:

> Et propterea in credibili pompa et ornatu se accingens dona parat Reginae quadrantia: Et per Cydnum amnem navigans: pupi aurea: purpureo exculta velo residebat: remi argentei ad fistularum, tibiarumque concentum agitabantur. Ipsa autem subaureo requescens tentorio: persimilem veneri teddebat aspectum.²³²

> And therefore, preparing herself with incredible pomp and adornment, and gifts and coin fitting a queen, along the river Cydnus she progressed, amid gilded stern and fine purple sail, the silver oars pulled to the music of pipes and tibias. And she herself, reclining beneath a golden tent, strove to look exactly like Venus.

If listening to music could indicate incontinence and effeminate luxury, for an elite Roman man playing it was certainly worse, because although successful musicians and actors could become famous and wealthy—Martial calls performance on the cithara and pipe "lucrative arts" ("artes [...] pecuniosas")—the social standing of their profession was relatively low.²³³ Nero's musicianship especially is widely mocked in our 1501 histories, most pungently of all by Philostratus, whose protagonist, Apollonius of Tyana, deliberately maintains extremely tense relations with the much-despised emperor. Apollonius accuses Nero of "living in the manner of female lyre-players and pipers," and notes that the philhellenic emperor "came to Greece submitting himself to the heralds

---

231 *Epithome Plutarchi*, fol. 137v (*Life of Antony*, 24.1–2).
232 *Epithome Plutarchi*, fol. 138r (*Life of Antony*, 26.1).
233 "Artes discere vult pecuniosas/ Fac, discat cithareodos, aut choraulas." *Martialis*, sig. [H v] v (*Epigrammata* 5.56.8–9).

of the Olympic and Pythian festivals, [...] and his victories were in the contests for singers to the cithara and heralds."[234] For Apollonius, it is a disgrace for an emperor to practice ignoble trades, and even more so to perform in the hope of pleasing a crowd of his inferiors, as he explains in a dialogue concerning imperial pastimes:

> Cui autem studio inquit Apollonius o philolae vacat imperator. Publice inquit ille velut auriga quadrigam regit: cantatque in Romanorum theatris et cum gladiatoribus vivit: ipse quoque munere fungens gladiatorio homines iugulat: Ad ea respondens Apollonius, Vir inquit egregie an maius aliquid spectaculum erudito homini esse censes: quam regem impudentem videre: Dei namque ludibrium homo est: iuxta Platonis sententiam: Rex autem hominum ludibrium factus, suumque pudorem, ut plaebi gratificetur negligens, quos et quales philosophantibus praebebit sermones.[235]

> "Then which hobby," said Apollonius, "O Philolaus, does the emperor pursue?" "For example," said he, "in public he steers the quadriga of a charioteer, and sings in the theatres of Rome, and lives with gladiators, and also performs the role of a gladiator, killing men." To this Apollonius said in response, "My good man, do you think that there is a greater spectacle for a learned man than to see a king without shame? For if indeed man is the sport of the gods, as per the opinion of Plato, and the king is made the sport of men, neglecting his dignity that he may please the silly masses, which and what kinds of themes for discourse will he provide to philosophers?"

Moreover, by devoting so much time to trifles, Nero neglected his duties as a ruler. "Indeed, he has degenerated so far from his own dignity and that of the Romans," Apollonius remarks, "that instead of safeguarding the laws as he should, he prefers to sing, and to philosophise like an actor, outside the palace in which he should be seated as king, passing judgement as he is consulted on the most important matters of land and sea."[236] Asked by Vespasian to sum up his view of Nero's reign, Apollonius

---

234 "psaltriae fidicinaeque more viventem." *De vita Apollonii Tyanei*, fol. 69r (*Vita Apollonii* 7.4). "in graeciam venit preconiis olimpiis pythiisque se subiiciens: [...] erant autem eius victoriae citharedorum et preconii." *De vita Apollonii Tyanei*, fol. 39r (*Vita Apollonii* 4.24).
235 *De vita Apollonii Tyanei*, fol. 42r–v (*Vita Apollonii* 4.36).
236 "A sua vero ac romanorum dignitate tantum degeneravit, ut pro conditore legum: quas ferre oportebat cantare, et in hystrionica philosophari, extra urbem

replies: "Nero perhaps knew how to tune a cithara, but he disgraced the empire by over-tightening and over-slackening [its strings]."[237]

By this time our hypothetical professor has certainly found enough information to explain the musical terms and characters encountered in Roman poetry to his students and readers with a reasonable degree of confidence. He has some general information on the origins and inventors of music to use as opening gestures on the subject. He has references that will help him flesh out the named historical musicians he comes across, and to differentiate among various particular kinds of ancient musician—from the singer-citharists to the theatre pipers, and from the female lyre-players to the noisy Corybantes, as well as many others. Information on the design of particular instruments and their playing techniques could come in useful when they are mentioned by Virgil or Martial. He has excerpts that will help him summarise the nature of the music used at the principal ancient religious rites, and for the famous Greek festivals. He has taken note of the endless procession of war trumpets, and can formulate assertions about the prominent role of music among the warlike Spartans, if the need arises to compose a concise *laus musicae*. When he finds Juvenal or Persius satirising musical pastimes, he will readily explain the role of music in *luxuria*, according to Roman ethics, giving other similar examples.

In short, our professor's findings are quite consonant with the musical remarks we found in our 1501 commented classics in the previous section—and that is hardly a surprise. The exercise that we have allowed to play out in this section has been somewhat contrived, of course, not least because our professor's library has been artificially limited to those classical texts that happened to be printed in Italy in 1501. But it seems inevitable that some version of the operation we have modelled here was the bread and butter of music history research for humanities professors and students at Italian universities around 1501, to the extent that such research was necessary to their complete understanding of classical literature. Clearly, music was not the professor's primary concern, whether in class or in print, but neither was it ignored; and his efforts

---

malit: in qua sedendo debuit, ut rex de maximis terrae marisque rebus consultus responderer." *De vita Apollonii Tyanei*, fol. 46r (*Vita Apollonii* 5.7).

237 "Nero forsan inquit cytharam aptare novit: imperium vero contentone remissioneque dedecoravit." *De vita Apollonii Tyanei*, fol. 50v (*Vita Apollonii* 5.28).

to elucidate musical mentions in the classics constitute a distinctive and quite widespread strand of Renaissance musical scholarship.

3.5 Law

Bartolo da Sassoferrato, *Consilia questiones & tractatus cum additionibus novis* (Venice: per Giovanni & Gregorio De Gregori, 1501)

Pietro Boattieri and Rolandino de Passaggeri, *Commentaria seu expositio in summa notarie Rolandini* (Milan: per Giovanni Angelo Scinzenzeler ad impensas Giovanni da Legnano, 1501)

Digestum novum de Tortis (Venice: per Battista Torti, 1501)

Digestum vetus de Tortis (Venice: per Battista Torti, 1501)

Guillaume Durand, *Speculum judiciale* (Venice: Baptista de Tortis, [1501])

Statuta magnifice communitatis regii (Reggio Emilia: Vincenzo Bertocchi impressit, 1501)

Alessandro Tartagni, *Alexander de imola super secunda veteris cum apostilis noviter editis* (Venice: per Battista Torti, 1501)

Law books in 1501 present a rather limited view of music, of acoustic understanding and sound cultures. People, individual artists, performers, composers, are entirely missing from the picture; instead, dusty shadows of ancient Roman jurists stand solemnly in the background, while, in the foreground, their Renaissance interpreters decorate the age-old statutes with definitions, explanations, and reiterations. The *Corpus Juris Civilis* (CJC), a title only applied a thousand years after its completion, refers to the system of Roman law as gathered and organised for Emperor Justinian in the sixth century.[238] In addition to the *Codex* of laws actually in use during the 520s and 30s, Justinian ordered the creation of an encyclopedia—the *Digest*—of relevant historic laws, such as those recorded by the Roman jurists Ulpian and Gaius, allowing its compilers to add their own interpretations, comments and opinions, and to clear out all overlapping or irrelevant material. As this work turned out to be rather mammoth, Justinian ordered a condensed version of this

---

238 From among an enormous literature, a useful starting point is Wolfgang Kunkel, *An Introduction to Roman Legal and Constitutional History*, trans. J. M. Kelly (Oxford: Clarendon Press, 1966).

enormous encyclopedia—a more digestible work for law students, confusingly known as the *Institutes*. Finally, to keep track of all new laws passed during Justinian's reign, the *Novallae* were created. Following its rediscovery in the eleventh century, the CJC came to dominate legal scholarship across Europe, supplying a substratum of legal principles and precedents known as the *ius commune* that could anchor and inform the operation and development of *ius proprium*, that is, the laws made and observed by a particular city or territory.[239]

Inevitably there is a close relationship between the structure and character of university legal studies, and the roster of legal books in our 1501 corpus. Italian universities offered lectures and awarded degrees in both civil (i.e., secular) and canon (i.e., church) law, but over the course of the fifteenth and sixteenth centuries civil law came overwhelmingly to dominate, and the CJC was its set text.[240] The teaching of civil law at Italian universities began with the *Institutes*, as preparatory to study of the *Digest*—the main event—and then the *Codex*. Our 1501 corpus includes two books on the Institutes, and nine dealing with different sections of the *Digest*, usually incorporating the *Glossa ordinaria* of Accorso da Bagnolo (Accursius), an authoritative thirteenth-century compilation of the comments of the "glossators." The other principal genres of legal scholarly writing are also represented, including several anthologies of *consilia* (advisory legal opinions) and a number of *repetitiones* (treatises on specific passages and concepts from the CJC). These volumes on the *ius commune* inevitably give much space to the fourteenth-century "commentators," chief among them Bartolo da Sassoferrato and Baldo degli Ubaldi; but also present are some fifteenth-century legal luminaries, such as Alessandro Tartagni whose mid-century career encompassed the universities of Pavia, Padua, Ferrara, and Bologna. A few of our 1501 books, meanwhile, fall into the category of *ius proprium*, presenting and commenting upon statutory

---

239 Manilo Bellomo, *The Common Legal Past of Europe, 1000–1800*, trans. Lydia Cochrane (Washington, DC: The Catholic University of America Press, 1995), xi. See also, among many others, Susan Reynolds, "Medieval Law," in *The Medieval World*, ed. Peter Linehan and Janet L. Nelson (New York: Routledge, 2001), 485–502; and Andrea Zorzi, "Justice," in *The Italian Renaissance State*, ed. Andrea Gamberini and Isabella Lazzarini (Cambridge, UK: Cambridge University Press, 2012), 490–514.

240 On the teaching of law at Italian Renaissance universities, see especially Grendler, *The Universities*, 430–43; on the decline of canon law, 443–47.

law; for example, there is a volume compiling the statutes of the city of Reggio Emilia. Also present are some of the standard handbooks on legal practice, such as Guillaume Durand's *Speculum judiciale* on court procedure, and Rolandino de Passaggeri's *Summa totius artis notariae* on notarial practice, both dating from the thirteenth century.

Sound enters into the CJC principally via the inconvenience of its absence. Numerous opinions and deliberations attempt to set out whether and how the deaf and the non-verbal can operate within a legal arena that relies heavily on making and comprehending *viva voce* verbal statements—considering, for example, whether such individuals can enter into a contract, serve as witness, present an appeal, make a will, receive an inheritance, or be appointed as guardian to a minor. These points are duly picked out for comment in Accursius' *Glossa ordinaria*. For example, in *Digest* 2.14.4 the question arises as to whether a non-verbal individual (*mutus*) can enter into a pact, such as an agreement regarding a marriage. The Roman jurist Julius Paulus is quoted as concluding that, because consent can be indicated in ways other than through a verbal statement, "even a mute can make a pact" (et mutus pacisci potest). Accursius confirms that the main issue is whether the individual can show their consent, which might be done "either by a nod of the head or the shoulders or another sign" (si enim annuit vel capite vel humeris vel aliis signis), thus the non-verbal do have sufficient capacity in this legal situation.[241] In *Digest* 3.1.1, meanwhile, the issue is whether a deaf person can make an appeal to a praetor; the Roman jurist Ulpian is quoted explaining that this should not be allowed, because the appellant would not be able to hear the praetor's reply. In his gloss on this passage, Accursius notes that not only would this be indecorous for the praetor, but it would also disadvantage the appellant, because, having not heard the praetor's ruling, they might inadvertently break it.[242] There are many other similar examples throughout the *Digest*. It seems inevitable that questions regarding legal capacity connected with acoustic disabilities must also have arisen in real legal practice in 1501.

Music itself plays little role in the CJC, as one might expect, but it is not entirely absent. Roman law on slander encompassed a wide range of

---

[241] *Digestum vetus de Tortis*, fol. 38r.
[242] *Digestum vetus de Tortis*, fol. 49v.

defamatory actions, among which singing is specifically mentioned. In *Digest* 47.10.15.27 Ulpian is quoted as recording that:

> Generaliter autem vetuit pretor quid ad infamiam alicuius fieri. Proinde quodcumque quis fecerit: vel dixerit: ut alium infamet: erit actio iniuriarum. Hec autem fere sunt que ad infamiam alicuius fiunt. Utputa si quamvis ad invidiam alicuius veste lugubri utitur: aut squalida: aut si barbam demittat: vel capillos submittat: aut si carmen conscribat: vel proponat: vel cantet aliquod quod pudorem alicuius ledat.[243]

> The praetor bans generally anything which would be to another's disrepute. And so whatever one do or say to bring another into disrepute gives rise to the action for insult. Here are instances of conduct to another's disrepute: to lower another's reputation, one wears mourning or filthy garments or lets one's beard grow or lets one's hair down or writes a lampoon or issues or sings something detrimental to another's honor.[244]

Accursius' brief gloss on the passage from "carmen [...]" notes that the principle derives from the *lex Cornelia de iniuriis*, written by Sulla in the first century BCE, in which (among other things) it was established that an injury could be done to a person through the creation and circulation (in written or unwritten form) of a literary composition.

This aspect of ancient slander law was certainly of immediate relevance to lawyers training in 1501, because closely related provisions formed part of the statutory law of several Italian cities.[245] A detailed case study can be found among our 1501 books. In the statutes of Reggio Emilia, confirmed by Duke Ercole I d'Este in 1480 and printed in 1501, a law concerning slanderous speech establishes that if an individual defames another in court before a judge then a fine of £20 can be immediately levied, summarily and without the need for legal process.[246] If the offence is committed outside of court but still before a

---

243 *Digestum novum de Tortis*, fol. 218r.
244 *The Digest of Justinian*, vol. 4, trans. Alan Watson (Philadelphia, PN: University of Pennsylvania Press, 1985), 292.
245 Of course, the key study of the regulation of sound in the public spaces of an Italian Renaissance city is Niall Atkinson, *The Noisy Renaissance: Sound, Architecture, and Florentine Urban Life* (University Park, PA: Penn State University Press, 2016). Several specific examples similar to that discussed in the present paragraphs can be found in Christiane Klapisch-Zuber, *Women, Family and Ritual in Renaissance Italy* (Chicago, IL: University of Chicago Press, 1985), 261–85.
246 *Statuta magnifice communitatis regii*, fol. 23v.

judge, the fine is halved. Examples of slander falling within scope are given: calling someone a liar, forger, traitor, swindler, pimp, murderer, or assassin; insulting someone's dead relatives; and calling a woman a prostitute, procuress, or slut. Next the law deals with slanderous accusations brought into public circulation by other means, that is, not in court and not before a judge:

> faciens vero libellum: carmen: vel cantilenam ad infamiam alicuius vel fieri faciens: puniatur in libris centum: et in quattuor ictus funis: quas si non solverit infra mensem amputetur ei manus:[247]

> Moreover, whoever makes a pamphlet, poem or song slandering someone, or causes such to be made, shall be punished with [a fine of] £100 and four strokes of the lash, which if he does not satisfy within a month, his hand will be cut off.

The amputation of a hand had a long legal history in Europe as a punitive measure, of course, but in this specific instance it seems to speak rather directly to the act of authoring a slanderous "pamphlet, poem or song"—and moreover, for musicians, to the task of accompanying such a song on an instrument.

Another law that is evidently related deals with the practice of nuisance music- and noise-making known as "matutinata" (i.e., mattinata).[248] In Reggio, it is absolutely forbidden to perform mattinatas at any time of the night, "with any sound, or instrument of any kind, or voice, or in any other way, before the house, or the doors of anyone, under penalty of £5," and the confiscation of the instruments.[249] If the offence concerns those mattinatas "that are customarily performed for the elderly who marry, and widows," then the fine is doubled.[250] Mattinata comes up once again in the midst of a series of offences relating to the *clausura* of nuns:

---

247 *Statuta magnifice communitatis regii*, fol. 23v.
248 On mattinata see, among others, Klapisch-Zuber, *Women, Family and Ritual*, 261–85; Flora Dennis, "Sound and Domestic Space in Fifteenth- and Sixteenth-Century Italy," *Studies in the Decorative Arts* 16.1 (2008–09), 7–19, at 13–15; and Dennis, "Unlocking the Gates of Chastity", 235–37.
249 "cum aliquo sono sive instrumento cuiuscunque generis vel cum voce: aut aliter: ante domum: vel fores alicuius: sub pena librarum quinque." *Statuta magnifice communitatis regii*, fol. 102v.
250 "in illis matutinatis: que senibus nubentibus: et viduis fieri consuevere" *Statuta magnifice communitatis regii*, fol. 102v.

> Prohibemus insuper hoc presenti statuto maitinatas et seu cantilenas fieri aut aliquod instrumentum pulsari de nocte ante et sive prope aliquod monasterium claustrale monialium sive sororum pena contrafacienti librarum vigintiquinque monete currentis pro quolibet et qualibet vice applicandarum ut supra quam penam incurrat ipso facto contra faciens.[251]
>
> Furthermore, by this present statute we prohibit mattinatas or songs from being performed or any instrument from being played at night before or near any cloistered monastery of nuns or sisters, with a penalty of £25 in the prevailing currency to be applied to the offender on each and every occasion.

Here, aside from the simple nuisance and offence, the concern is presumably that music—widely viewed as effective in seduction—might offer a means to overcome both the security of the convent wall and the spiritual armaments of the sisters.

The statutes of Reggio Emilia also reveal a practical role for music in the transaction of the law. The city trumpeters, whose roles and responsibilities are set out in the section concerning officers of the state, are mentioned dozens of times across the statutes, managing the interface between legal process and the public sphere.[252] Whenever any aspect of legal action must be made public—for example, when an individual must be summoned, or denounced in the sight of their community—a city trumpeter is required, acting essentially as the city's broadcast media.

Thus, professors and students of civil law at Italian universities in 1501 certainly were not scholars of acoustics and music history, as were their counterparts studying natural philosophy and the humanities; and yet music and sound cannot have been entirely absent from their lectures. In a legal culture that was deeply concerned with what is said and heard in the public sphere, whether as part of legal process or as the target of legal sanction, saying (or singing) and hearing were "performative" acts in the sense originally intended by J. L. Austin, that is, they constituted powerful interventions in a social world—the social world which legal codes set out to structure and control.[253] The force

---

[251] *Statuta magnifice communitatis regii*, fol. 103r.
[252] The duties and remuneration of the trumpeters are set out in two places especially: *Statuta magnifice communitatis regii*, fols. 29r–v and 174r.
[253] We refer to Austin's classic study *How to Do Things with Words* (Oxford: Oxford University Press, 1962). More recently the term "performative" has come to be

allotted to the oral and the aural in a legal and public context, in a way, provided foundational conditions that were further elaborated in the discourse surrounding the persuasive power of song, verse, and oratory developed by those studying ancient literature and rhetoric. Music could indeed move rocks and trees; and moving the wrong rocks and trees with music was legally actionable.

---

used in a rather broader sense among musicologists.

4. Conclusions to Volume 1: A Musical Life in Italy c.1501

Our findings from the books in our 1501 corpus that we have categorised under the approximate headings of "lifestyle," "poetry," and "scholarship" are, not surprisingly, bewilderingly heterogeneous. There is no clear epistemological thread, no coherent total understanding; instead what we have generated is the raw materials for a collage, a set of diverse and overlapping fragments that have yet to be arranged into a recognisable picture. Drawing succinct and satisfying conclusions from such materials is a daunting task, but perhaps not beyond hope. The books in our 1501 corpus find coherence not in their combined content, but in their use. They weave in and out of a Renaissance life following the logic of lived experience rather than that of knowledge systems. 1501 readers used schoolbooks when attending or teaching at a school; they interacted with medical literature when consulting a physician or taking steps to improve their health through diet and regimen; they read or sang lyric verse as young men and women caught up in asserting identities and developing emotional understanding. Perhaps by following the thread of a life in 1501, tracing the ways in which readers at different ages and stages encountered our books and their musical contents, we can find in practice the coherence that is so obviously lacking in theory. In other words, the picture that emerges when we assemble our collage is the rough sketch of a musical life.

Astrology was integral to the normative worldview in Italy in 1501, inflecting the musical as well as every other domain of activity, but not in the ways musicologists have tended to assume. Rather than discussing the harmony of the spheres, our 1501 astrology textbooks reveal how elements of musicianship are governed by different specific spheres, as raw data for generating horoscopes predicting the characteristics and skills of individuals born under particular celestial conjunctions. Professional astrologers understood that the ability to make music that was beautiful and pleasant was a result of Venus' influence, whilst Mercury could confer technical skill or virtuosity; meanwhile, to make music of moving profundity, the more elevated contribution of Jupiter was essential. Receiving these influences in different combinations could predispose an individual to different kinds of music-making. Of course, most Italians in 1501 were not professional astrologers; but many consulted astrologers for horoscopes and when making important life decisions. The notion that specific, predictable musical abilities were acquired at birth through particular planetary influences was probably commonplace.

In grammar class, although music-making as such seems to have been little in evidence, children learned to use and manipulate Latin terms for musicians, instruments, and musical practices, developing a parallel classicising vocabulary to describe their musical experiences. Once the fundaments of Latin were mastered, children might move on to study metrics, or the rhythms and cadences of verse, which they learned to view as a territory held in common between poetics and music theory, encapsulating the music of language. Meanwhile, children were vigorously drilled in the skills of literary composition and memory that could later serve them well in improvising songs.

Attitudes towards musical leisure encountered in the school classroom in 1501 were rigidly differentiated according to both social status and gender. Schoolboys from ordinary families engaged in artisan or commercial work were routinely discouraged from pursuing music and dance, which were seen as distractions from study and invitations to vice. At least, this is what is implied by our 1501 corpus; no doubt such precepts, where individual teachers did endorse them, were only partially followed. The same advice was given to parents of girls, who were more often educated within the home. The clear implication of both the early conduct books for girls, and the popular grammar textbooks, is that if song is to feature in the lives of children it should take the form of prayers and psalms. For the children of the elite, in contrast, secular musical pastimes were an acceptable form of recreation, provided they were practiced in private as a well-earned rest from the labour of study. In that context, a marked preference for voices, strings and keyboards is evident, whereas wind instruments were regarded as servile and therefore beneath the dignity of the high-born.

Whether schoolkids of the artisan class or aristocratic children in the care of private tutors, all learners in Italy in 1501 encountered stern precepts on the use of the voice. Speech should be concise, measured, calm, and controlled, adopting a middling and pleasant tone; verbosity, crudeness, and violent passions must be avoided at all costs. Such care is required because a well-managed voice is a primary sonic indicator of upright character and well-cultivated judgement. The voice is a sonic domain that encompasses song but is not limited to it; thus, it seems reasonable to suppose that attitudes towards the voice may have influenced views on song in a fundamental way. When we read Brandolini contrasting the restrained style of humanist recitation with the more sensuous idiom of the popular singer-songwriters, or Castiglione contrasting the sweet simplicity of Marchetto Cara's singing with the vehemence of Bidon's, perhaps we are not only reading about melodic styles, or melodic ethos, or the decorum of poetic genre (e.g., heroic vs lyric). Perhaps, at the same time, and even more fundamentally, we are seeing how views on the decorum of voice itself inflected judgements about music.

Like music, the practice of poetry, and particularly the performative culture of lyric verse, were routinely associated with the condition of being young and beautiful. It is certainly intentional that the first Latin word that is introduced as an example to manipulate in the grammar known now as the *Ianua*, printed at the start of our 1501 edition of the classroom grammatical anthology *Donatus Melior*, is "poet," followed immediately by "Muse." As seems apt to the condition of youth, the lyric verse printed in 1501 is overwhelmingly caught up in the task of identity construction, exploring extremes of emotion, and expressing the technicolor experience of desire, all the while dancing lightly along the ambiguous boundary between performativity as literary conceit and performance as audible practice. These are precisely the kinds of vice-ridden songs that daughters, and the sons of artisans, were warned against; and it is clear that they were very popular.

Our 1501 lyric offers a kind of theatrical staging of and through the singing voice. The poet's singing voice is carefully characterised, through description (for example, as sweet or bitter), and also through comparison—to Orpheus or Apollo, Echo or the Sirens, each with different implications. The voice itself unfolds a landscape setting that gives it physical size and scope (echoing off distant mountains), reflects its emotional valence, and supplies listeners whose reactions can communicate its affective power (for example, by moving beasts and rocks). The character of the poet's singing voice is unstable, changing in ways that serve to articulate the stages of the narrative: from sweet and cheerful beginnings, to cries and tears, to quiet acceptance or even death. In all of this there is a clear intention on the part of our 1501 lyric poets, several of whom can also be documented as singers of their own verse, to build a close equivalence between their textual voice and their audible voice. In the case of professional singer-songwriters like Serafino Aquilano and Panfilo Sasso, that equivalence was evidently a central element in their efforts to develop a distinctive "brand" or personal style as a performer.

The soundscape of our 1501 lyric verse speaks not only of the individual but of the community. Through a shared sense of the rhetorical and narrative construction of the emotional journey through love, and a shared vocabulary of sonic inflections and metaphors through which to convey the twists and turns of that journey, lyric verse effectively built an emotional community that was strongly attuned to the affective potential of sounds and voices. The song of Philomela or Orpheus, the gentle tinkle of a stream, or the voice broken by sobs—among many other sonic motifs—evoked settings and conjured subjectivities in similar ways for different readers or singers.

For youths possessed of a secondary education and eager to advance their status through professional training, a developing interest in poetry ran alongside study at a university. Although students at Italian universities were not required to attend classes on music as a separate subject of study, music and closely allied topics turned up in their lectures on natural philosophy, rhetoric, literature, and law. Our 1501 library provides a selection of the textbooks and set works through which music found its way into class.

From the professor lecturing on Aristotle's *De anima*, students learned that sound differed fundamentally from other sensory provocations in its ephemeral nature, existing only momentarily in its production, and only as a kind of disturbance or motion, propagating through the air like ripples through water. In voice, they learned to hear the physics of sound harnessed to intention and meaning by the intervention of the soul, manipulating phrase, pitch, consonance and rhythm to effect communication. Music acquired its appearance of meaningfulness by imitating these same communicative strategies. The cognition of sound students learned to understand as taking place at the meeting point of the sensory capacities of the physical body, and the rational capacities of the soul, which sought to evaluate sounds according to whether they were helpful or unhelpful, and thereby to moderate emotional response. Whilst attending the classes on the *De caelo et mundo*, meanwhile, students learned that the notion of the harmony of the spheres was beautiful, but wrong.

Students taking the lecture course on Cicero's *De oratore* found themselves grappling in more detail with the musical qualities of voice, learning that they must get a feel for the manipulation of pitch and rhythm in poetry and music, and aim to achieve similar effects (though less rigorously) in their spoken prose, so as to captivate their audience. The way students learned these principles, moreover, was threaded through with issues of status. Students learned that undue technical expertise and professional proficiency in music are evidence of a time-waster and a servile spirit. For the man of liberal rank, it is sufficient to know "enough," and to rely on the judgement of the ear rather than specialist understanding.

A mastery of oratory could be valuable, among other career paths, if a student went on to teach as a humanities lecturer. In that role, professors took responsibility for guiding students as they learned to make sense of and enjoy Roman poetry, both as an exercise in stylish Latin and as a window onto the customs and morals of a much-admired ancient culture. In order to elucidate the many mentions of music in classical verse, professors of poetry turned themselves into music historians, assembling a patchwork of excerpts and citations that together could flesh out the religious and social roles of musicians and musical instruments in the ancient world. Students receiving classroom instruction reflecting the content of the commentaries on Virgil, Juvenal, Martial, Terence, and other authors printed in 1501, learned about the origins and inventors of the lyre and pipe, the place of music in Roman theatre, the measures required to prevent star singers from having sex, the essential role of the pipers in sacrifices, the noisy music accompanying the rites of Bacchus and Cybele, the role of trumpets and war-cries in stirring the courage of Roman soldiers, and many other musical features of the classical world. Indeed, it seems likely that the poetry class was the principal source of formal instruction in music history in Italy in 1501. This information, though historical, was not redundant: it helped students to fulfil the requirement, learned during the lectures on *De oratore*, that they have something—*something*, though not much—well-informed and morally uplifting to say when circumstances required them to speak on the subject of music.

As well as encountering music in the classroom, we know that university students enjoyed making music as a pastime, in ways that were closely linked to their developing poetic tastes—whether for austere Latin epic or sensuous lyric. According to the medical books printed in 1501, it would be wise to maintain musical hobbies throughout one's life, because of their potentially beneficial effect on health and wellbeing. The physicians printed in 1501 considered listening to or making music to be warming activities, and thus apt to counterbalance any excessive frigidity in a person's complexion, a complaint associated with both aging and studious pursuits. Moreover, music promoted *gaudium*, a quality of sensory enjoyment that effectively remedied the stress and anxiety which were both caused by and a cause of illness. However, the timing and proper measure of musical pastimes were important to their beneficial effects: making music too soon after eating might divert necessary heat from the stomach and harm digestion, while too much music could over-heat the complexion thereby becoming a cause of imbalance and disease.

Meanwhile, the professional musician consulting the physicians represented in our 1501 corpus—whether through reading, or indirectly, during a *viva voce* consultation with a local medic—could also learn much to their advantage. For a singer, certain imbalances in their complexion could actually be beneficial. A somewhat hot and dry brain, for example, could confer sharp hearing, and hot and dry lungs a clear, projecting voice. The throat, meanwhile, had better be somewhat moist to avoid hoarseness, but not such that phlegm becomes excessive; and the size of the throat will determine the vocal range, high or low. There is plenty of advice among our 1501 books on how to affect changes that might correct or reinforce these aspects of complexion, much of it dietary. Leeks, for example, were heating and drying, and acted upon the throat, making them very suitable for clearing phlegm, while rosemary had a similar effect upon the lungs. On the other hand, the singer had better avoid nuts, which make the voice hoarse.

Musicians—both professionals and amateurs—should concern themselves not only with their means of vocal production, but also and urgently with the setting and content of their performance. Following an ancient Roman precedent, Italian cities legislated to control music- and sound-making intended to cause insult, imposing heavy penalties on offenders. The attention paid to the public circulation of sound in our 1501 law books bespeaks a fundamental role for the oral and the aural in comprising the public sphere and its discourse, which forms an essential backdrop to favoured contemporary notions about the power and efficacy of music and oratory, as crystallised for example in the figure of Orpheus. Lying behind the popular image of Orpheus moving even trees, rocks, and wild beasts with his affective song, we can discern a piazza filled with well-ordered citizens, brought into audible accord through their shared observance of prudent laws governing the public circulation of sound.

Do these fragments from a musical life add up to the "everyday musical knowledge" that we set out to document through our project? Somewhat, at least. Clearly not every musicking individual in Italy in 1501 had encountered and retained all of this information; and some must have possessed other kinds of musical knowledge that have not turned up in our 1501 sample. Nonetheless, what our 1501 findings seem quite compellingly to do is to trace the weave of musical threads into the fabric of everyday life—a topic that has long caught the attention of scholars of modern musical culture, but has yet to be explored by musicologists working on the period around 1500. As we set out in the Introduction, this assertion does not rely on a bogus claim of universal literacy, or Latinity, because much of what we read in these printed books could also be encountered orally—at first, second, or third hand—from the schoolmasters, astrologers, physicians, lawyers, orators, performers, and university professors whose attitudes, creative products, and technical expertise or competencies our 1501 books encode. (Preachers, confessors, exorcists, and other clerical professionals will also join this list, once the dimension of religious experience is added more fully to our analysis in Volume 2.)

An obvious and fascinating question arising from these conclusions concerns the specificity of the 1501 musical worldview that is revealed in our findings. Would we arrive at a substantially different picture if we undertook a similar exercise in Italy in 1451, or in 1551? What about 1401 or 1601? As we have repeatedly observed, many of the texts printed in 1501 were not new, but ancient or medieval, and of long-standing cultural and intellectual influence. So, perhaps some things would be the same, at least within a fifty-year span either side of our date—but certainly not everything. For example, most of the humanist commentaries on classical literature discussed in Chapter 3 were yet to be written in 1451, their underlying epistemological and cultural attitudes not yet fully established at the Italian universities. At the same time, by 1551 some of the medical theories and practices present in our 1501 books and discussed in Chapter 1 would have seemed old-fashioned, as physicians' reliance on the medieval Arabic reception of Aristotle and Galen was replaced with new analyses taken straight from the Greek, as well as new empirical work on human anatomy. Much of the poetry discussed in Chapter 2, meanwhile, would already have sounded out of style by the 1530s, as Pietro Bembo's new theories began to influence vernacular literature. The transformation of knowledge (musical and otherwise) in Italy across the fifteenth and sixteenth centuries was a complex and shifting mixture of changes and continuities, as much kaleidoscopic as linear. No doubt a comparison of the Italian musical worldview in 1501 with that current in 1451 or 1551 would reveal both similarities and fundamental differences. In the final analysis, though, such a comparison lies outside the scope of our project; it would require new campaigns of research focussed on different samples of literature. Perhaps other researchers will eventually take up the challenge.

Appendix: 1501 Excerpts

Excerpts from our 1501 books that are too long to place within the main text are given here.

Excerpt 3.1: Dominic of Flanders summarises Thomas Aquinas' commentary on Aristotle's *De anima* 2.8

> Sequitur in textu. (Nunc autem primo de sono et olfatu etc.) Hec est lectio decimasexta eiusdem libri: et in commento sancti Thome.
>   Istud est decimum caputulum presentis tractatus in quo philosophus determinando de generatione soni ponit quattuor conclusiones. Quarum prima est quod sonus quandoque est in actu quandoque in potentia. hec conclusio probatur tali ratione elicitive secundum phylosopum. Illud quod quandoque est et quandoque non est aliquando est in actu: aliquando est in potentia: sed sonus quandoque est et quandoque non est ut patet de campana que quandoque sonat quandoque non: ergo sonus quandoque est in actu quandoque in potentia. ❡ Contra hanc conclusionem arguitur. Illud quod non est non est in actu: sed sonus non est: ergo sonus non est in actu. probatio maioris [actually, minoris]: quia quod fit non est: sed sonus solum habet esse in fieri: ergo sonus non est. Preterea illud quod est sensibile in actu habet propriam speciem in re sensibili per quam actu potest percipi: sed sonus non habet propriam speciem in re sonante: ergo non est actu. ❡ Pro declaratione horum considerandum est primo quod corpora sonantia sunt in quadruplici differentia: nam quedam sunt secundum actum bene sonantia ut campana dum actu pulsat: quedam vero sunt bene sonantia secundum potentiam: utputa de campana que non actu sonat: sed tamen habet potentiam bene sonare. Alia sunt que non sunt bene sonantia nec in actu nec in potentia: apta tamen nata esse sonantia: ut patet de lana et similibus. Alia sunt que non sunt apta nata bene sonare. nec sonare aliquo modo ut aer. ❡ Considerandum est secundo quod aliquid dicitur in actu dupliciter: uno modo in actu permanente. et isto modo color habet esse in actu. Alio modo in esse successivo: et isto modo sonus habet esse in actu. et per hoc patet solutio ad primum argumentum quia illa auctoritas. Illud quod fit etc. habet intelligi de permanentibus et non de successivis:

permanentia enim dum fiunt non sunt: successiva vero dum fiunt sunt et dum facta sunt non sunt. ⁋ Considerandum est tertio quod aliquid dicitur esse sensibile in actu dupliciter. Uno modo quia habet speciem per quam sentitur extra medium et sensum: videlicet in re exteriori: et isto modo color odor sapor sunt in actu et non sonus. Alio modo quia habet speciem per quam actu sentitur in medio vel organo: et isto modo sonus dicitur esse in actu: non est enim aliqua species soni in campana sonante: formatur tamen species in aere et in organo auditus: et per hoc patet solutio ad secundum. ⁋ Secunda conclusio est: tria requiruntur ad generationem soni: videlicet percutiens: percussum et medium. hac conclusio probatur tali ratione quae elicitur ex dictis phylosophi. nam sonus causatur ex fractione aeris quae sit ex vehementi percussione sed in omni percussione requiritur percutiens et percussum: et requiritur etiam tertio ictus percutientis qui non potest fieri sine motu locali: motus vero localis non potest fieri sine medio: ergo in generatione soni requiritur percutiens percussum et medium: unde phylosophus dicit in littera quod sonus est semper alicuius idest percutientis ad aliquid idest percussum et in aliquo idest in medio. ⁋ Pro huius conclusionis declaratione est advertendum secundum phylosophum quod ad hoc quod predicta faciant sonum: presertim bonum quattuor conditiones requiruntur. quarum prima est: quod talia corpora sint dura: secunda est quod sint levia. tertia est quod sint concava: quarta quod sint velociter mota: ita quod motus percutientis preveniat divisionem aeris. ⁋ Contra predictam conclusionem sic arguitur. et primo contra suppositum. nam phylosophus non determinat hic de generatione soni coloris: ergo non habet determinare hic de generatione. ⁋ Preterea ad generationem soni requiruntur motus localis et ictus verberantis: ergo non sufficiunt predicta tria. ⁋ Ad primum dicendum negando consequentiam quia non est similis ratio de sono et colore et odore et sapore: nam color odor et sapor et alie qualitates tangibiles (ut dicit hic doctor sanctus) habent esse fixum et permanens in suo subiecto: unde est alia ratio illorum sensibilium secundum se et secundum quod immutat sensum: sed sonus cum causetur a motu non habet fixum et quietum in subiecto: sed in quadam immutatione consistit. ideo cum phylosophus in hoc libro intendat determinare de sensibilibus secundum quod habent immutare sensum: ideo simul et semel determinat de immutatione soni et generatione eius. ⁋ Ad secundum dicendum quod ictus percutientis et motus localis comprehenduntur sub percutiente et percussio concomitative. Tertia conclusio. Aer est proprium medium soni: aqua vero minus proprium: hec conclusio probatur tali ratione. Illud est proprium medium soni quod faciliter rarefit et condensatur: et per quod sonus faciliter potest diffundere suas species ad organum auditus: sed aer est huiusmodi: ergo etc. Ex hac conclusione sequitur quod aer non est corpus sonans. quia si esset corpus sonans non susciperet sonum: cum intus existens prohibeat extraneum. ℭ Contra hanc conclusionem sic arguitur. Aeris ad sonum nulla est resistentia: ergo si aer sit proprium medium sequitur quod sonus fiat in instanti. nam ratio quare visio fiat in instanti est: quia aeris ad lumen nulla est resistentia: cum aer sit dispositus ultima dispositione ad susceptionem luminis: consequens est falsum. ergo etc. ℭ Preterea illud quod est subiectum alicuius quantitatis sensibilis non est medium eius: sed aer est subiectum soni: ergo aer non est medium soni. ℭ Preterea quantitas sensibilis habet esse intentionale in suo medio: sed sonus habet esse reale in aere: cum nullibi habeat esse nisi in aere: ergo idem ut supra. ℭ Ad primum dicendum quod licet aeris ad sonum nulla sit resistentia: quia tamen sonus non potest fieri sine motu locali: ideo non oportet quod sonus fiat in instanti: quia contradictionem implicat motum localem esse in instanti. ℭ Ad secundum dicendum quod sonus est in aere propinquo corpori sonanti subiective in aere vero magis distanti est tanquam in medio in quo habet esse intentionale. et per hoc patet solutio ad tertium. ℭ Quarta conclusio in omni sonatione fit repercussio soni a corpore opposito corpori sonanti. hec conclusio probatur tali ratione. In omni illuminatione fit repercussio luminis: ergo a fortiori in omni sonatione fit repercussio soni. Sed si arguatur contra hanc conclusionem: si in omni sonatione esset repercussio soni: sequeretur quod in omni sonatione causaretur sonus echon: consequens est falsum: et contra omnem experientiam. ergo etc. ℭ Dicendum quod in omni reverberatione soni causatur sonus echon: sed talis sonus non semper est manifestus. oportet enim ad hoc quod fiat manifestus ut dicit hic doctor sanctus quod repercussio soni fiat ad corpus concavum in quo natus est multiplicari sonus: si autem fiat talis reverberatio ad alia corpora que non sunt apta nata multiplicare sonum fiat quidem sonus echon sed non manifestus. ℭ Pro ampliori declaratione huius soni echon. considerandum est secundum doctorem sanctum quod cum generatio soni sequatur motum aeris: sic contingit de immutatione aeris apud generationem soni: sicut de immutatione aque cum aliquid in aqua proiicitur: manifestum est autem quod fiunt quedam regenerationes in circuitu aque percusse que circa locum percussionis sunt parve et motus est fortis: ubi autem sunt maiores regenerationes et motus debilior: tandem motus totaliter deficit et regenerationes cessant si autem antequam motus cesset regirationes ille aliquod obstaculum invenirent: fit motus et regiratio in contrarium: et tanto vehementius quanto propinquius fuerint prime percussioni: pariformiter intelligendum est quod ad percussionem corporum sonantium: aer in quodam giro movetur: et sonus diffunditur circulariter et in propinquo ille generationes sunt minores et motus est fortior: in remoto autem girationes sunt maiores et motus est debilior. Si autem nunquam deficiant huiusmodi girationes: fiat reverberatio ad aliquod corpus ille regirationes revertuntur in contrarium et auditum sonus: quasi ex adverso qui dicitur echon.

Sequitur in textu. (Vacuum autem recte dicimus proprium audiendi etc.) Hec est lectio decimaseptima eiusdem libri: et in commento sancti Thome.

Istud est undecumum capitulum presentis secundi tractatus in quo phylosophus determinans de immutatione auditus a sono. ponit tres conditiones que requiruntur ad hoc quod auditus possit immutari a sono. Quarum prima est quod ibi sit unitas et continuitas aeris et continuus motus ab aliquo corpore solido et firmo. ❡ Secunda conditio est quod in organo sit aer intraneus inclusus in quadam pelicula. ❡ Tertia condictio est quod talis aer sit immobilis. Et his conditionibus eliciuntur tria impedimenta et opposito per que impeditur talis immutatio. Primum quod est quando ille aer in organo corrumpitur. Secundum est quando illa pellicula circundans illum aerem corrumpitur vel leditur. Tertium est quando talis aer est mobilis. ❡ Considerandum est ulterius secundum phylosophum in littera quod due sunt differentie soni: videlicet grave et acutum. Sonus enim acutus est qui in pauco tempore multum movet auditum. sed sonus gravis est qui in multo tempore parum movet auditum. Et si dicatur est aliquis sonus moderatus et circumflexus: ergo predicte differentie non bene assignantur. ❡ Dicendum quod sonus circumflexus et sonus moderatus continentur sub predictis: sicut medij colores sub externis: quia participant aliquid de sono acuto: et de sono gravi: ut patet in musica Boetij. ❡ Si dicatur ulterius sonus acutus et sonus gravis sunt species soni: ergo acutum et grave non sunt differentie eius. ❡ Dicendum quod grave et acutum possunt accipi dupliciter. Uno modo formaliter sic sunt differentie soni. Alio modo materialiter pro ipso sono qui est acutus vel pro illo sono qui est gravis sic sunt species soni. ❡ Considerandum ulterius quod acutum et grave non sunt idem quod tardum et velox quia sonus non est idem quod motus: ergo differentie soni non sunt eedem cum differentijs motus: sed acutum et grave sunt differentie soni: ut ex dictis patet: et tardum et velox sunt differentie motus. ergo etc. Verumtamen quia sonus causatur a motu: ideo acutum et grave in sono causantur a velocitate et tarditate motus. ❡ Circa predicta dubitatur primo utrum tam percutiens quam percussum sint causa activa soni: et videtur quod non. ❡ Nam illud quod est causa activa non est causa passiva respectu eiusdem: sed corpus percussum est causa passiva: ergo non videtur quod sit causum activa soni. ❡ In contrarium arguitur per phylosophum in littera. ❡ Dicendum quod tam percutiens quam percussum est causa activa soni: cuius ratio phylosophi est. quia sonus generatur ex fractione aeris: sed corpus percutiens est causa activa huius fractionis. ergo corpus percutiens concurrit active ad generationem soni. Et quia ad talem fractionem aeris requiritur quod corpus percussum sit durum et firmum: ideo facit illum aerem resilire: ad quam resilitionem corpus percussum concurrit active: ideo corpus percussum active ad generationem soni concurrit. ℂ Ad rationem dubij dicendum quod licet corpus percussum passive concurrat ad fractionem aeris: active tamen concurrit ad predictam resilitionem que ad generationem soni concurrit. ℂ Dubitatur secundo verum sonus sit proprium obiectum auditus et videtur quod non. ℂ Nam nullum sensibile commune est proprium obiectum alicuius sensus: sed sonus est sensibile commune. ergo etc. Probatio maioris [really, minoris]. quia motus est sensibile commune: sed sonus non est nisi quidam motus aeris (ut hic concedit phylosophus) ergo sonus est sensibile commune. ℂ Preterea illud quod immutat auditum est obiectum auditus: sed corpus percutiens sive sonans immutat auditum: ergo corpus percutiens sive sonans est obiectum auditus: et per consequens non sonus. cum tamen unius potentie sit unum obiectum. ℂ Dicendum quod sonus est proprium et per se obiectum auditus: quod sic patet: nam illud est proprium et per se obiectum alicuius potentie sub cuius ratione formali omnia sensitiva illius potentie apprehenduntur ab illa potentia: sed sonus est huiusmodi. ergo etc. ℂ Ad primam rationem dubij dicendum quod sonus non est motus essentialiter sed effective solum: quia causatur a motu et consequitur ipsum. ℂ Ad secundum dicendum quod corpus sonans immutat per accidens auditum et non per se: unde ratio nulla.

Sequitur in textu. (Vox autem est sonus quidam animati etc.) Hic incipit lectio decimaoctava eiusdem libri: et in commento sancti Thome.
 Istud est duodecimum capitulum predicti tractatus in quo phylosophus determinando de quadam specie soni: videlicet de voce: ponit unam conclusionem: videlicet quod vox est repercussio aeris respirati ab anima secundum imaginationem que est in his partibus ad arteriam vocalem. Hec conclusio probatur quantum ad singulas partes: et primo quod vox sit reverberatio aeris. ℂ Nam omnis sonus est reverberatio aeris idest ex reverberatione aeris causatur: sed omnis vox est sonus: ergo omnis vox est ex reverberatione aeris. Quod autem vox sit reverberatio aeris respirati: probat phylosophus duobus signis quorum primum est. ℂ Nam non potest formare vocem nisi aspirando vel respirando nisi retineat aerem: ergo signum est quod vox est reverberatio aeris respirati. ℂ Secundum signum est. quia animalia non respirantia non possunt formare vocem. ergo etc. Quod autem vox sit reverberatio aeris respirati ab anima ad arteriam vocalem patet. Nam sicut in sono ita in voce reperitur corpus percussum: sed vocalis arteria videtur corpus percussum in generatione vocis. ergo etc. Ex hac conclusione infertur quod inanimata non possunt formare vocem. ℂ Infertur secundo quod animalia non respirantia non possunt formare vocem. et per consequens pisces non possunt formare vocem. ℂ Infertur tertio quod his animalia

carentia sanguine non possunt etiam formare vocem. ⁋ Considerandum est secundum phylosophum in littera. Primo quod aer respiratus est medium vocis: cuius respirationis organum est vocalis arteria que est quedam vena procedens a pulmone ad guttur. ⁋ Contra predictam conclusionem sic arguitur breviter. ⁋ Reverberatio est quidam motus: sed vox non est motus: ergo vox non est reverberatio aeris. ⁋ Preterea si vox esset reverberatio aeris ab anima: sequeretur quod instrumenta musicalia non formarent vocem: consequens est falsum: et contra communem modum loquendi. ergo etc. ⁋ Preterea respiratio est naturalis animalium: ergo si vox esset reverberatio aeris respirati sequeretur quod quelibet vox esset naturalis significativa naturaliter. ⁋ Ad primum dicendum quod dum dicitur vox est reverberatio aeris est predicatio casualis et non essentialis. ⁋ Ad secundum dicendum quod instrumenta musicalia et alia inanimata dicuntur formare vocem similitudinarie: tum primo propter continuitatem soni. tum secundo propter consonantiam. tum tertio. propter interemptionem: non tamen dicuntur formare vocem proprie ⁋ Ad tertium dicendum quod licet formare vocem in communi sit naturale animali conditionibus predictis reservatis: tamen formare hanc vel illam vocem non est naturale animali: unde non oportet quod quelibet vox sit naturalis animali.

Thomas Aquinas, *Divi Thome aquinatis in librum de anima Aristotelis expositio. Magistri Dominici de Flandria ordinis predicatorum in eundem librum acutissime questiones et annotationes* (Venice: per Pietro Quarengi, 1501), sigs. [15] v–[16] v

There follows in the text: "Nunc autem primo de sono et olfatu etc." Here begins the sixteenth lecture in the same book, and in the commentary of St Thomas.

This is the tenth chapter of the present treatise, in which the Philosopher, in determining the generation of sound, sets forth four conclusions. The first of which is that sound is sometimes in actuality and sometimes in potential. This conclusion is proved by the following reasoning, according to the Philosopher. That which sometimes is, and sometimes is not, exists sometimes in actuality, sometimes it exists in potential; and sound sometimes exists, and sometimes not, as is clear from the bell, which sometimes rings and sometimes does not; therefore sound sometimes exists in actuality and sometimes in potential. ⁋ Against this conclusion it is argued: that which is not, does not exist in actuality; but sound is not, therefore sound does not exist in actuality. Proof of the major [premise]: that which is in the process of coming to be, does not exist; but sound only has being in becoming [i.e., in being produced], therefore sound is not. Moreover, that which is sensible in actuality has its proper manifestation in the sensible thing through which it can be actually perceived; but sound has not its proper manifestation in the thing that sounds, therefore it does not exist in actuality. ❧ For the clarification of these points, we must first consider that sounding bodies are differentiated fourfold. For some are sounding well in actuality, as a bell when it actually rings; while some are sounding well in potentiality, as a bell which does not actually sound, but nevertheless has the capacity to sound well. There are others that are not well-sounding, neither in actuality nor in potentiality; for some are born apt for sounding, whereas it is clear from wool and the like that others are not born apt for sounding well, nor [even] to sound at all as with the air. ❧ Secondly, we must consider that something is said to exist in actuality in two ways. In one way, in actuality permanently, and this is the way in which colour has its being in actuality. In another way, in successive existence, and this is the way that sound has being in actuality. And from this the solution to the first argument is clear, because the passage "Illud quod sit etc." should be understood as referring to the permanent and not to the successive, for the permanent do not have their being in the act of their production, whereas the successive have their being in their production and not in their existence. ❧ Thirdly, it must be considered that something is said to be sensible in actuality in two ways. In one way because it has a manifestation through which it is felt outside the medium and the sense [organ]—that is to say, in an external substance—and this is the way in which colour, smell, and taste exist in actuality, but not sound. In another way, because it has a manifestation through which in actuality it is felt within the medium or the [sense] organ, and this is the way in which sound is said to exist in actuality. For there is not any manifestation of sound in a sounding bell; rather, the manifestation is in the air and in the organ of hearing. And through this the solution to the second question is clear. ❧ The second conclusion is that three things are required for the generation of sound: the thing striking, the thing struck, and the medium. This conclusion is supported by the reasons that are put forward by the Philosopher, for sound is caused by a breaking of the air, which is due to a violent percussion, and in every percussion a thing striking and a thing struck are required; and thirdly the blow of the striker is required, which cannot take place without a local movement, and local movement cannot take place without a medium. Therefore, in the generation of sound, the thing striking, the thing struck, and the medium are required. Whence the Philosopher says in the book that sound is always of something, i.e., the thing striking, at something, i.e., the thing struck, and in something, i.e., the medium. ❧ For the clarification of this conclusion, it is necessary to note, following the Philosopher, that what was said above concerning making sound, especially a good [sound], requires four conditions. The first of which is that the bodies are hard; the second is that they are light; the third is that they are hollow; the fourth is that they are moved rapidly, so that the movement of the thing striking prevents the division of the air [i.e., it is too fast for the air to get out of the way]. ⁋ It is argued against this conclusion, firstly that it is beside the point, because the philosopher is not dealing here with the generation of sounds and colours, therefore he does not have to determine here [the nature of its] generation. ⁋ Moreover, for the generation of sound, a local movement and a beating stroke are required; therefore the aforementioned three [i.e., thing striking, thing struck, medium] are not sufficient. ⁋ To answer the first by denying the reasoning: there is no similar reason for sound and colour and odour and taste. For colour, odour and taste and other tangible qualities (as the Doctor Sanctus [i.e., Thomas] says) have to be fixed and permanent in their subject, whence there is another explanation for their sensation, according to themselves [i.e., their own nature], and according to how they move the sense. Whereas sound, with motion as its cause, is not fixed and at rest in its subject, but consists in a kind of change. Therefore, in this book where the Philosopher intends to investigate sensible things in terms of their ability to move the sense, he thus deals at one and the same time with the motion of sound and its generation. ⁋ To the second the response is that a percussive blow and local movement are included under the thing striking and the thing struck concomitantly. [⁋] The third conclusion: air is the proper medium of sound, and water the less proper medium. This conclusion is proved by this reason: the proper medium of sound is that which is easily dispersed and compressed, and through which sound can easily spread its manifestation to the organ of hearing; and air is of this kind, therefore etc. From this conclusion it follows that air is not a sounding body, for if it were a sounding body it would not receive the sound, the internal existence prohibiting the external. ⁋ Against this conclusion it is argued as follows. Air has no resistance to sound; therefore, if air is a proper medium, it follows that sound is produced instantaneously; for the reason why vision is made in an instant is because air has no resistance to light, since air is arranged in the ideal disposition for the reception of light; it follows that it is false, therefore etc. ⁋ Moreover, that which is the subject of a sensible quantity is not its medium; but air is the subject of sound, therefore air is not the medium of sound. ⁋ Moreover, sensible quantity has intentional existence in its medium; but sound has real existence in air, whereas it has no existence anywhere but in the air; therefore as above. ⁋ To the first the response is that although air has no resistance to sound, since sound cannot be produced without local motion, therefore it is not necessary that the sound be made in an instant, because that a local motion [take place] in an instant implies a contradiction. ⁋ To the second the response is that the sound exists subjectively in the air close to the sounding body, but in the air more distant it is as if it exists in the medium intentionally. And from this the solution to the third is [also] clear. ⁋ The fourth conclusion is that in all sounding there is a reflection of the sound from the body opposite to the sounding body. This conclusion is proved by reasoning thus: in every illumination there is a reflection of light; therefore, in every sounding there should be a reflection of sound. [⁋] But if it be argued against this conclusion [that] if there were a reflection of sound in every sounding, it would follow that in every sounding an echo would be caused, the implications are false, and against all experience; therefore, etc. ⁋ It is said that every reverberation of sound causes an echo, but the sound of that echo is not always manifest. For in order for it to become manifest, as the Doctor Sanctus says, it is necessary that the reverberation of the sound should propagate within a hollow body, which is of a nature to multiply sound. But if such a reverberation be propagated within other bodies which are not of a nature apt to multiply the sound, the sound would indeed be an echo, but not manifest. ⁋ For a more detailed explanation of this echo of sound, it is to be considered, according to the Doctorem Sanctum, that upon the generation of sound there follows the motion of the air. The disturbance of the air upon the generation of sound is just as the disturbance of water when something is thrown into water. It is evident that certain ripples occur in the vicinity of the strike, which are small with strong motion near the point of impact, but further away the ripples are larger and their motion weaker, until finally the motion fails completely and the ripples cease. But if, before the motion ceases, the ripples should find some obstacle, the ripples are set in motion in the opposite direction, and the more violently the nearer they are to the first impact. It must be understood similarly that upon the striking of sounding bodies, the air is moved in ripples, and the sound is diffused in all directions, and nearby the ripples are smaller and the motion is stronger, but at a distance the ripples are larger and the motion is weaker. But if, before these ripples run out, they reverberate off some body, those ripples return in the opposite direction, and sound is heard as if from the opposite direction, which is called echo.

There follows in the text: "Vacuum autem recte dicimus proprium audiendi etc." Here begins the seventeenth lecture in the same book, and in the commentary of St Thomas.

This is the eleventh chapter of the present second treatise in which the Philosopher determines how sound moves [the sense of] hearing. He states three conditions which are required in order that sound move hearing. Of which the first is that there be unity and continuity of air, and continuous motion from some solid and hard body. ⁋ The second condition is that the air internal to the organ [of hearing] should be enclosed by a certain little skin [i.e., the eardrum]. ⁋ The third condition is that this [internal] air be motionless. And from these conditions are brought forth three impediments and opposites by which the movement [of the sense of hearing] is hindered. The first of which is when the air in the organ [of hearing] is corrupted. The second is when the skin enclosing that air is corrupted or damaged. The third is when that air is in motion. ℂ We must also take into account, according to the Philosopher in the book, that sound has a twofold differentiation, namely low and high. A high sound is one which in a short time moves the hearing a great deal; whereas a low sound is one which in a long time moves the hearing a little. And if it be said that a certain sound is in-between and wavering, and that therefore it cannot be properly categorised according to this differentiation, ℂ it can be said that the wavering sound and the in-between sound are contained within the aforementioned [differentiation] just as middling colours are contained within the extremes, because they share something of the high sound, and of the low sound, as is clear from Boethius' *De musica*. ℂ If it is further said that if a high sound and a low sound are species of sound, then high and low are not differentials [of sound], ℂ it should be said that low and high can be taken in two ways: one way in terms of form they are differentials of sound; and another way materially, for the sound that is low and the sound that is high are species of sound. ℂ Let us further consider that high and low are not the same as slow and fast, because sound is not the same as motion, so differentials of sound are not the same as differentials of motion, but rather high and low are differentials of sound, as is clear from what has been said, and slow and fast are differentials of movement; therefore etc. Nevertheless, since sound is caused by motion, therefore the high and low in sound are caused by the fastness and slowness of motion. ℂ Regarding the aforesaid, the first doubt concerns whether both the thing striking and the thing struck are the active cause of sound; and it seems that they are not. ℂ For that which is an active cause is not a passive cause at the same time; but the thing struck is a passive cause, therefore it does not seem that it is the active cause of the sound. ℂ The opposite is argued by the Philosopher in the book. ℂ It must be said that both the thing striking and the thing struck are the active cause of the sound, for which the following reason is given by the Philosopher. Sound is generated by the breaking of the air; and the thing striking is the active cause of this breaking, therefore the thing striking conspires actively in the generation of sound. And because for such a breaking of the air it is necessary that the thing struck be hard and firm, so that it causes the air to rebound, in which rebounding the thing struck actively participates, therefore the thing struck actively participates in the generation of sound. ℂ To settle the doubts, let us say that although the thing struck passively conspires to break the air, it nevertheless conspires actively to the aforementioned repulsion [of the air], which corresponds to the generation of sound. ⁋ Secondly it is doubted whether sound is in truth the proper object of hearing, and it seems that it is not. ⁋ For nothing common to the sensible is the proper object of any sense; but sound is common to the sensible, therefore etc. Proof of the major [premise]: because motion is common to the sensible, and sound is nothing but a certain motion of the air (as the Philosopher here admits), therefore sound is common to the sensible. ⁋ Moreover, that which moves the hearing is the object of hearing, but a struck body, or rather a sounding body, moves the hearing, therefore a struck or rather sounding body is the object of hearing, and in consequence not a sound; when there is one capacity there is one object. ⁋ It must be said that sound is in itself the proper object of hearing, which is clear thus: for that is in itself the proper object of that capacity under whose rational form all things with power of sensation apprehend by that power; and sound is of this kind, therefore etc. ⁋ To the first doubt the reason is stated that sound is not essentially motion but is an effect of motion, because it is caused by motion and results from it. ⁋ To the second, the reply is that the sounding body moves the hearing accidentally and not in itself, thus the reasoning is negated.

There follows in the text: "Vox autem est sonus quidam animati etc." Here begins the eighteenth lecture in the same book, and in the commentary of St Thomas.

This is the twelfth chapter of the aforesaid treatise, in which the Philosopher, in investigating a particular species of sound, namely the voice, puts forward one conclusion, namely that voice is the repercussion of the breathed air by the soul, following the imagination which is a part of it, in the vocal artery (i.e., the windpipe). And also the conclusion is proven in its individual parts; and first, that voice is the reverberation of air. ⁋ For all sound is the reverberation of air, that is, it is caused by the reverberation of air; and all voice is sound; therefore all voice is reverberation of air. Now, that voice is the reverberation of breathed air the Philosopher proves by two signs, the first of which is: ⁋ For it is impossible to form voice except by breathing in and out, and only when the air is retained; therefore this is a sign that voice is the reverberation of breathed air. ⁋ The second sign is: because non-breathing animals cannot form voice; therefore etc. Now, that voice is the reverberation of breathed air by the soul in the vocal artery is evident. For just as in sound, so in voice is found the thing struck; and the vocal artery seems to be the thing struck in the generation of voice; therefore, etc. From this conclusion it follows that inanimate things cannot form voice. ⁋ It is inferred, secondly, that non-breathing animals cannot form voice; and consequently fish cannot form voice. ⁋ Thirdly, it is inferred that those animals lacking blood also cannot form voice. ⁋ It is to be considered, according to the

Philosopher in the book, first that breathed air is the medium of voice, the organ of which respiration is the vocal artery, which is a certain vein leading from the lungs to the throat. ⁋ Against the aforesaid conclusion it is argued briefly: ⁋ reverberation is a kind of motion; but voice is not motion; therefore voice is not the reverberation of air. ⁋ Moreover, if voice were the reverberation of air by the soul, it would follow that musical instruments do not form voice, the which consequence is false, and contrary to the common way of speaking; therefore, etc. ⁋ Moreover, breathing is natural to animals; therefore, if voice were reverberation of breathed air, it would follow that is naturally significative of nature. ⁋ To the first the reply is that while voice is reverberation of air, the predication is casual and not essential. ⁋ To the second it must be said that musical instruments and other inanimates are said to form a similitude of voice, which is first because of the continuity of sound, second because of consonance, and third because of interruption; yet they are not said to form voice proper. ⁋ To the third it must be said that although it is natural for an animal to form voice in general under the aforesaid conditions, nonetheless to form voice is not in the nature of animals, hence it is not necessary that every voice should be in the nature of an animal.

Excerpt 3.2: Thomas Aquinas explains why musical instruments produce a similitude of voice but not voice itself

Nullum autem inanimatum habet vocem: et si aliquando aliquod eorum dicatur habere vocem: hoc est secundum similitudinem: sicut tibia et lyra et huiusmodi instrumenta dicuntur habere vocem. Habent enim tria eorum soni in quibus assimilantur voci. Quorum primum est extensio. manifestum est enim quod in corporibus inanimatis ex simplici percussione causatur sonus. unde cum percussio statim transeat: sonus etiam cito transit et non contineatur. Sed vox causatur ex percussione aeris ad vocalem arteriam: ut post dicetur: quae quidem percussio continuatur secundum appetitum animae: et ideo vox extendi potest et continuari. Illa igitur instrumenta de quibus dictum est ex hoc ipso quod habent quamdam continuitatem in suo sono: habent similitudinem vocis. ⁋ Secundum autem in quo assimilantur voci est melos idest consonantia. Sonus enim corporis inanimati cum ex simplici percussione proveniat uniformis est non habens in se diversitatem gravis et acuti. unde in eo non est consonantia quae ex eorum proportione causatur: sed vox diversificatur secundum grave et acutum: eo quod percussio quae causat vocem diversimode fit secundum appetitum animalis vocem emittentis. unde cum in praedictis instrumentis distinctio sit gravis et acuti in sono: eorum sonus est cum quadam melodia ad similitudinem vocis. ⁋ Tertium in quo sonus horum instrumentorum habet similitudinem vocis est locutio idest interpretatio sonorum ad similitudinem locutionis.

manifestum est enim quod humana locutio non est continua. unde et in libro praedicamentorum: oratio quae in voce profertur ponitur species quantitatis discrete. distinguitur enim oratio per dictiones: et dictio per syllabas: et hoc accidit propter diversas percussiones aeris ab anima. et similiter sonus praedictorum instrumentorum distinguitur secundum diversas percussiones: utpote diversarum chordarum: vel diversorum flatuum aut aliquorum huiusmodi.

> Thomas Aquinas, *Divi Thome aquinatis in librum de anima Aristotelis expositio. Magistri Dominici de Flandria ordinis predicatorum in eundem librum acutissime questiones et annotationes* (Venice: per Pietro Quarengi, 1501), sig. [e 5] v

Nothing without soul makes vocal sounds, however. And if sometimes one of those things is said to make a vocal sound, this is in virtue of a likeness—as when the tibia and the lyre and instruments of that sort are said to make vocal sounds. For their sounds have three [respects] in which they are likened to vocal sound. The first of these is extension. For it is clear that sound is caused in bodies without souls by a simple striking. Hence, when this striking passes at once, the sound also passes soon and is not continued. But vocal sound is caused by air's being struck against the windpipe, as will be said later. This striking is continued according to the soul's appetite, and in this way vocal sounds can be extended and continued. Therefore these instruments of which we have been speaking, by the mere fact that they have some kind of continuousness in their sound, have a likeness to vocal sound.

The second [respect] in which [these instruments] are likened to vocal sound is melody–that is, a pleasing combination of sounds. For the sound of a body without soul, when it comes from a simple striking, is uniform: in itself it does not have any variety of low and high [pitch]. So in it there is no pleasing combination of sounds, which is caused by the balance of these [low and high pitches]. Vocal sound, however, is varied by low and high [pitch], because the striking that causes the vocal sound occurs differently according to the appetite of the animal issuing the vocal sound. So because in the case of the above instruments there is a variety of low and high pitches, their sound occurs with a certain melodiousness, which makes it like a vocal sound.

The third [respect] in which the sound of these instruments bears a likeness to vocal sound is speech—i.e., the breaking up of sounds, likening it to speech. For it is clear that human speech is not continuous. (For this reason, too, the *Categories* [4b22–23] presents discourse pronounced in vocal sounds as a species of discrete quantity. For discourse is split up into words, and words into syllables.) This occurs because of the soul's striking air [against the windpipe] in various ways. And the sound of the above-mentioned instruments is likewise varied in virtue of being variously struck—that is, the strings, or the breathings, or things of this sort.

> Thomas Aquinas, *A Commentary on Aristotle's De anima*, trans. Robert Pasnau (New Haven, CT: Yale University Press, 1999), 243–44

Excerpt 3.3: Cicero's reflections on the knowledge required of the orator (*De oratore* 1.10) prompt Ognibene Bonisoli to summarise the natures of the sciences

Cicero:

Quis ignorat: ii qui mathematici vocantur quanta in obscuritate rerum: et quam recondita in arte: et multiplici subtilique versentur? Quo tamen in genere ita multi perfecti homines extiterunt: ut nemo forte studuisse ei scientiae vehementius videatur: quin quod voluerit consecutus sit. Quis musicis? Quis huic studio litterarum quod profitentur ii: qui grammatici vocantur: penitus se dedit: quin omnium illarum artium pene infinitam vim et materiem scientia et cognitione comprehenderit?

> Cicero, *Tullius De oratore cum commento et alia opera* (Venice: per Albertino da Lessona, 1501), fols. 4v–5r

We all know how obscure the subjects handled by the so-called mathematicians are, and how abstruse, complex, and exact is the art with which they deal. Yet even in this area, so many geniuses have emerged that almost no one who has devoted his energies to mastering it appears to have been unsuccessful. As to the theory of music, and the study of language and literature so popular nowadays (the profession of the so-called grammarians)—has anyone really dedicated himself to them without managing to acquire enough knowledge to cover the complete, almost infinite range and material of those arts?

> Cicero, *On the Ideal Orator*, trans. James M. May and Jakob Wisse (Oxford: Oxford University Press, 2001), 60

Bonisoli:

"Quis ignorat:" pergit facere: quod coeperat: ut ostendat rariores semper extitisse oratores quam caeterarum artium periti viri: et hic oratores comparat mathematicis: quorum ars quanquam? sit obscurissima: speculativa: atque multiplex: tamen qui illi vehementius studuerint. videntur id quod optarunt consecuti: sed non hunc assequuntur effectum qui oratoriae arti se dederunt. Nam tanta est ipsius scientiae magnitudo et profunditas: ut vix pauci tolerabiles inveniri possint oratore. "Mathematici:" sunt qui in arithmetica: Geometria et Astrologia versantur. Nam mathesis graece latine appellatur disciplina:

Appendix: 1501 Excerpts   325

sed haec scientiae disciplinae dicuntur: eo quod discantur plane et per demonstrationem quandam percipiantur. Sed philosophia: Grammatica atque Rhetorica non disciplinae dicuntur: quia non firmissima demonstratione: ut illae: sed ratione quadam et studii investigatione percipiuntur. In quanta obscuritatem vero habent: quia versantur in numeris atque mensuris: quibus nihil potest esse obscurius. propterea quod de his cuncta dimetiuntur. Sed numerus est: alius perfectus alius imperfectus. Perfectus numerus dicitur qui ex suis partibus constat: et in suas partes resolvitur: ita ut ad unitatem reducatur ut ternarius numerus. Imperfectus dicitur numerus qui ita resolvi non potest: sed aliquid habet superfluum: ut quaternarius. nam in numeris est paritas et imparitas. Imparitas: ut unus. Paritas ut duo. In mesuris vero consideratur quantitas continua: et quantitas discreta. In quantitate discreta est perfectio et imperfectio. Sed in quantitate continua consideratur Longitudo: Latitudo: Altitudo et profunditas. Per altitudinem consideramus aetherea et res coelestes. Per latitudinem consideramus aerea et res aeris. Per longitudinem res terrenas: et per profunditatem aquas consideramus. Quarum rerum rationem numerus arithmeticus complectitur: quae res obscurissima est: et speculativo indiget ingenio. "Recondita arte:" in occulta arte et speculativa: nam res speculativae reconditae dicuntur. "Multiplici:" quia in arithmetica: qua numerum agit: in geometria: ubi de mensuris et astrologia versantur mathematici: sic multiplex est mathematica. "Subtilique:" Hac tres profecto sunt subtiles: et speculativis accommodantur ingeniis sed tamen harum subtilius est astrologia. "Multi perfecti homines:" ut Nicomachus in arithmetica: Euclides in geometria. Ptolomeus in astrologia. Plures alii fuere: sed hi principatuum tenet. "Quis musicis dedit se:" coepti specialiter probare in omni arte plures inveniri prestantes viros: quam in arte dicendi: ac de philosophis quidem superius: et de mathematicis dixit. nunc idem de musicis: et grammaticis intendit. "Pene infinitam vim et materiem." nam siquis varietates vocum et numerorum comprehendere voluerit: illud vix conficere poterit Pari ratione siquis omnem artis grammaticae materiam complecti voluerit illud vix consequi poterit. Materia enim artis grammaticae sunt litterae: syllabae. dictiones et orationes. Nam elementa ipsae litterae sunt ex quibus syllabae conficiuntur. ex syllabis dictiones. ex dictionibus orationes componuntur. Quae omnia siquis complexti voluerit. inveniet laborem pene infinitum et inexuperabilem.

"Quis ignorat:" he continues, as before, to show that orators have always been rarer than men skilled in the other arts, and here he compares orators to mathematicians, whose art, although it may be obscure, speculative, and multifaceted, yet those who have studied it intensively seem to have attained their objectives, whereas those who have devoted themselves to the art of oratory have not achieved this outcome. For such is the breadth and depth of its knowledge, that few are found who can attain oratory. "Mathematici" are those who are versed in arithmetic, geometry, and astrology. For "mathesis" (μάθημα [mathema]) in Greek is called "discipline" in Latin, moreover these sciences are called disciplines because they are learned clearly and are perceived through a kind of demonstration. Whereas philosophy, grammar and rhetoric are not called disciplines, because they are perceived not through the strongest demonstration, as are the others, but through reason, study and inquiry. Their [i.e., the mathematical disciplines'] considerable intricacy arises because they are engaged with number and measure, than which nothing can be more complex, because everything is quantified with these. And among numbers, some are perfect and others imperfect. A number is called perfect which is equal to its own parts, and can be divided into its own parts, so that it can be reduced to unity, as with a ternary number. A number is called imperfect which cannot be thus resolved, but has something superfluous, such as a quaternary number. Also in numbers there is even and odd: odd as in one, even as in two. Measurement, moreover, considers continuous and discontinuous quantities. In discontinuous quantities there is perfect and imperfect. Whereas length, width, hight and depth are considered as continuous quantities. By means of hight we examine the sky and celestial things. By means of width we examine the air and aerial things. By means of length, earthly things; and by means of depth, we examine waters. The matter of rational number is comprehended by arithmetic, which is a most obscure thing, and requires a speculative talent. "Recondita arte:" in secret and speculative art, for speculative things are said to be hidden. "Multiplici:" that is, mathematicians attend to arithmetic, which deals with number; geometry, which deals with measurement; and astrology; thus, mathematics is multiplex. "Subtilique:" These three are certainly subtle, and suited to speculative talents, but nonetheless the most subtle is astrology. "Multi perfecti homines:" such as Nicomachus in arithmetic, Euclid in geometry, Ptolemy in astrology. There were many others, but these hold the first places. "Quis musicis dedit se:" continuing to show specifically that in every art there are to be found more outstanding men than in the art of speaking, as he said above of philosophers and mathematicians. "Pene infinitam vim et materiem." for if he wishes to understand the varieties of words and numbers, he will scarcely be able to accomplish it. Similarly, if he wished to comprehend all the matter of the art of grammar, he would hardly be able to achieve it. The matter of the art of grammar is letters, syllables, words, and speeches. For the elements are the letters, from which the syllables are made; from syllables, words; and from words, speeches are composed. He intends to show that these things are complex, and that one will find the work almost infinite and inexhaustible.

Excerpt 3.4: Cristoforo Landino comments on Orpheus and Linus in Virgil's Eclogue 4.55–57

Orphaeus Theologus priscae theologiae fuit: quam quidem rem hymni sui iudicant: Huius theologiae princeps fuit Mercurius trimegistrus: Mercurii vero sectator fuit Orphaeus: Orphaei sacris imitatus est aglaophaenus: aglaophaeni Pythagoras. Pythagorae auditor: fuit Philolaus. Philolaum autem audivit Plato: Sed redeo ad Orphaea. Hic enim orgya ab aegyptiis accepta ad graecos transtulit: quae ab eo Orphica dicta sunt: et fretus obscuritate antiquitatis omnia quae de Baccho thebano ex thebae aegyptiaca ferebantur: quoniam Cadmeis amicus esset ad Bacchum thebanum ex boetia transtulit. Cuius cum tanta vis in poetica fuisset. ut aut effrenatos: aut stolidos stupidosque homines ad mitiorem cultum traduceret: dictus est tygres leonesque demulcere potuisse: et sylvas movisse. Extant ergo ut diximus hymni eius profunda primae theologiae doctrina refecti: et mira suavitate gravitateque insignes. Dicunt fuisse unum ex argonautis: et atrocem tempestatem in quam inciderant suis sacris avertisse. Volunt Cytheronem Boetiae montem: quoniam ibi in sacris crebrius caneret: a sua cythara nomen sumpsisse: Scribit Plinius auguria quae prius ex avibus tantum sumerentur: ex reliquis quoque animantibus sumi posse orphaeum demonstrasse: Verum cum in thracia instituisset: ut in sacris bacchi viri a mulieribus abstinerent: ratae illae id in earum contemptum esse institutum facto agmine hominem nil tale timentem invasere atque laceravere. Plerique tamen teste Laertio Diogene illum fulmine ictum perisse affirmarunt: quidem est epigramma in dio macedone sculptum testatur: quidem est huiusmodi θρηικα χρυσολυρην τηδ ορφεα μούσαι εθυχαν ον κτανεν υζιμελον ζευς χολοιντι βελει. qui sic latine dicemus: Orphea chrysoliram musae hic posuere poetam: Fulmine quem stravit Iuppiter alta regens. Linus autem thebanus poeta fuit Apollinis secundum eos: quos nunc poeta sequitur filius. Diogenes vero refert illum a Mercurio ex Urania nympha genitum fuisse: et ab apolline sagitta transfixum perisse cum iam mundi generationem et solis lunaeque cursum et animantium fructuumque originemque scripsisset. hic in principio poematis dixit omnia simul fuisse: quem secutus Anaxagoras omnia simul nata esse dixit Plutar. in li. de musica cum dixisset artem cytharedicam primum Amphionem a Iove didicisse: addit eodem tempore Linum thebanum lugubres versus cecinisse. Pli. ubi de inventoribus scribit: ponit est alios: qui cythare inventionem amphioni: alios qui Orpheo: alios vero qui Lino tribuant.

Virgil, *Vergilius cum commentariis quinque, videlicet Servii, Landini, Ant. Mancinelli, Donati, Domitii* (Venice: s.n., 1501), fols. 14v–15r

Orpheus Theologus was an ancient theologian, as indeed is adjudged from the content of his hymns. The inceptor of theology was Hermes Trismegistrus; Orpheus, in truth, was a follower of Hermes. The rites of Orpheus were imitated by Aglaophemus. Those of Aglaophemus by Pythagoras. Philolaus heard them from Pythagoras, and Plato heard them from Philolaus. But I return to the Orphaea. Indeed, the mysteries were taken from the Egyptians and transferred to the Greeks, by whom they were called Orphic. And trusting to the obscurity of antiquity, all that was carried from Egyptian Thebes concerning the Theban Bacchus, whence Cadmus, as a friend of Bacchus, transferred it to Boeotian Thebes. Orpheus' poetry possessed such power, that the uncivilized, or foolish and stupid people were brought to an acceptable cult. It is said that he could subdue tigers and lions, and move trees. Therefore, as we have said, his hymns restore the profound doctrine of the ancient theology, and are remarkable for their wonderful sweetness and gravity. It is said that he was one of the Argonauts, and that he averted the terrible storm that befell them by means of his rites. They say that Mount Citheron in Boeotia took its name from his cithara, because he would often play in the rites there. Pliny [*Naturalis historia* 7.56] writes that Orpheus showed how auguries, which previously were taken from birds, could also be taken from other animals. It is true that in Thrace he had instituted that in the rites of Bacchus men should abstain from women. Some consider that, this law being made in contempt of them, their host attacked the man, who feared nothing, and tore him apart. Most, however, on the authority of Diogenes Laertius [*Vitae Philosophorum* Prologue.5–6], affirm that he perished by a lightning strike; indeed, there is a carved epigram in Dium in Macedonia, which is as follows: "Θρήϊκα χρυσολύρην τῆδ' Ὀρφέα Μοῦσαι ἔθαψαν,/ ὃν κτάνεν ὑψιμέδων Ζεὺς ψολόεντι βέλει," which is in Latin: "Here the Muses have placed their poet, golden-lyred Orpheus./ Struck by lightning from high-ruling Zeus." The Theban Linus was the poet of Apollo according to them who from 'poet' extrapolate 'son'. But Diogenes [*Vitae Philosophorum* Prologue.4] relates that he was born of Mercury and the nymph Urania, and that he perished when he was pierced by an arrow from Apollo, and moreover that he wrote of the creation of the world and the courses of the sun and moon and the origins of animals and fruits. Herein at the beginning of the poem he said everything was simultaneous, which Anaxagoras followed [when he said that] all things are born together. Plutarch in his book *On Music* [3], having said that Amphion was the first to learn the art of singing to the cithara from Jove, adds at the same time that Linus the Theban sang mournful verses. Pliny [*Naturalis historia* 7.56], where he writes of the inventors of things, mentions that some attribute the invention of the cithara to Amphion, some to Orpheus, and others to Linus.

Excerpt 3.5: Apollonius of Tyana discusses music with Canius the piper in Rhodes

Degebat tum temporis Rhodi canius tibicen: omnium, ut ferebatur aetatis suae tibicinum prestantissimus. Hunc ad se vocatum Apollonius interrogavit: quid nam arte sua tibicen efficeret: Ille vero quicquid voluerit auditor respondit: At inquit Apollonius auditorum plures ditari quam tibiarum cantus audire malunt: potes ne igitur divites illos efficere. Minime inquit ille: Quam vero id vellem inquit Apollonius: quid autem formosos ne reddere potes adolescentes: quid te audiunt: id enim maxime affectant adolescentes: Nec id quidem possum inquit ille: quamvis iocunditatis plurimum afferam: Quid est igitur inquit Apollonius: quidem auditorem velle putas? Quid aliud inquit canius: quam ut moerentibus, moerorem adimam. Laetantem vero se ipso reddam hilariorem: Amantem quoque callidiorem: Religiosum vero divino numine correptum: et ad laudandos deos paratiorem efficiam. An igitur praeterea cani efficit haec tibia: qui ex auro, aurichalcove, aut cervorum: aut asinorum cruribus compacta sit: an aliud quiddam est: quid hoc potestas efficere: aliud perfecto est inquit Apolloni: Musica namque: et modulationes: et armoniarum commixtio, earumdemque permutatio diversis moribus accommodata auditores movet: et eorum animos varie deducens tales reddit: quales tibicen esse eos voluit. Intelligo inquit Apollonius: quid ars tua possit efficere: eius enim diversitas: et in omnes modos conversio auditores varie affectos reddit: Mihi autem, praeter illa: quae abs te commemorata sunt videtur tibicen aliis quibusdam indigere: Haec autem sunt ipsius flatus: eiusque spiritus bonitas: commoditas oris: et manuum dexteritas quaedam: habet autem spiritus bonitatem, si lenis sit: ac politus: nec emissus in faucibus obstrepat: id enim indigeat inconcinam efficit vocem: Oris autem commoditatem, dico si possint labia tibiarum linguam tibicen. bene complecti neve incensa ardentique facie cantet: Manuum vero dexteritas permulti (ut arbitror) exstimanda est: ut neque manuum iuncturae infractae sint: neve digiti tardius vocis numeros insequantur: velociter enim modulari et ex alio in alium modum transire eorum esse maxime puto quam manuum dexteritate valeant: quod si haec omnia prestare potes o cani audacter tibicinariam exerce: tecumque euterpe semper erit

Philostratus of Athens, *De vita Apollonii Tyanei scriptor luculentus a Philippo Beroaldo castigatus* (Bologna: Benedetto Faelli, 1501), fol. 49r–v (*Vita Apollonii* 5.21)

There was living at that time in Rhodes Canius the piper, considered the best among all the pipers of his age. Apollonius called him to himself and asked: "What is accomplished by your art of piping?" "In truth, that which the auditor wishes," he replied. "But," said Apollonius, "many in your audience would rather become rich than listen to a piper play; surely, therefore, what you accomplish is to make them rich?" "Not at all," said he, "as much as I would like to do this." Apollonius said, "Then surely you will make the youths in your audience beautiful, for youths greatly desire this?" "No, indeed, I am not able," said he, "although I can give much pleasure." "What is it, then," said Apollonius, "that you think your audience wants?" "What else," said Canius, "than that I will save the mournful from their mourning, and moreover increase the cheerfulness of the joyful, and the ardour of lovers, and cause the religious to be more seized by divine power and better prepared to praise the gods." "This, furthermore, is achieved by the sounds of the pipe itself, whether it is made of gold or silver, or the shin of a deer or an ass? Or is it something else that has the power to accomplish this?" said Apollonius. "Indeed it is music, and modulations, and the mingling of harmonies, and their alteration, according to the requirements of different styles, that moves the audience, and, leading their souls in various ways, the piper brings them to the state that they wish for." "I understand," said Apollonius, "what your art can accomplish; by means of its diversity and the changes of mode, the listeners are given over to different moods. But, besides those things that you have mentioned, it seems to me that the piper also requires some others. And these are his blowing, and his good breath, and fitness of mouth, and a certain dexterity of the hands; and moreover the breath is good if it is smooth and well-controlled, and not noisy when sent forth from the throat, for this makes the sound inharmonious. And the mouth is fit, I say, if the lips and tongue can address the pipe well, and he does not play with a ruddy and burning face; and the dexterity of the hands is (in my view) greatly to be esteemed, requiring that the joint before the hand [i.e., the wrist] not be weak, nor the fingers slow in following the metered notes; indeed, I consider that dexterity of the hands is most particularly worthy in the ability to modulate swiftly and to pass from one mode to another. If you can demonstrate all of these, O Canius, pipe with confidence, for Euterpe will always be with you."

Excerpt 3.6: Landino translates Pliny discussing materials for pipes

Di quivi erono glinstrumenti acanti chiusi equali non sono da tacere pel resto del miracolo de la cura laquale era tale che pare da dovere perdonare a chi vole piu tosto sonare con instrumento dargento. Solevonsi taglare in tempo conveniente circa allarcturo stella insino alleta dantigene sonatore di zufoli: perche usavano ancora la musicha simplice. Et cosi preparate dopo alchuni anni cominciavano aessere utili. Ma et anchora alhora si domavano con molta exercitatione: et essi zufoli si facevano canori: perche le lingue si comprimevono se medesime: ilche era piu utile aquegli chostumi de Theatri: Ma poi che ne venne la varieta et ecanti lascivi cominciorono ataglare innanzi al solstitio. Et el terzo anno erono buone. Perche erono piu aperte lunghielle loro a reflectere ecanti. lequali sono cosi hogi. Ma alhora era una opinione che fossino congrue ciaschuna de la sua canna. El buccivo lo proximano a la radice era conveniente al sinistro. zufolo et el proximano a la vecta aldextro zufolo. Et e maravigla quanto erono piu stimate que le che el fiume Cephyso havessi bagnato

> Pliny the Elder, *Libro de l'historia naturale* (Venice: per Albertino da Lessona, 1501), fol. 115r (*Naturalis historia* 16.60)

From these [aforementioned reeds] were made the instruments for private performance, of which I will not pass over in silence the miracle of the care of them, which was such that it seems that one must pardon those who wish sooner to play with instruments of silver. They had to be cut at the appropriate time around the time of the star Arcturus, up to the time of Antigenes the player of pipes, because they were still using simple music. And thus prepared, after several years they began to be useful. But even then they were controlled with much practice, and these pipes made themselves good singers, because the tongues compressed themselves, which was more useful to the customs of the theatres. But after that came more variety and lascivious songs, and they began to be cut before the solstice. And in the third year they were good. Because they were more open at the tip [i.e., mouthpiece] to undulate the songs. As they are today. But at the time there was an opinion that each should be made consistent with its reed [i.e., both reed and pipe from the same reed]. And the trumpet nearest to the root was appropriate for the left pipe, and that nearest the top for the right pipe. And it is marvellous how esteemed were those that the river Cephisus had bathed.

Bibliographies

1. 1501 Books

We include only titles that are mentioned or discussed in the first volume of our study.

Albertus Magnus. *De secretis mulierum cum commento*. Venice: per Giovanni Luigi Varisio, 1501. 1.3

Albubather et al. *Albubather. Et Centiloquium divi Hermetis*. Venice: per Giovanni Battista Sessa, 1501. 0.3, 1.4

Alexander of Villedieu. *Doctrinale cum comento*. Venice: per Lazzaro Soardi, 1501. 1.1

——. *Doctrinale cum commento*. Venice: per Pietro Quarengi, 1501. 1.1

Allegri, Francesco degli. *Tratato di astrologia: prima di uno iudicio vero approbato: elqual dura in perpetuo dele calamita: abondantie: carestie. Item trata de li di infelici li quali sono pericolosi da far tutte le cose*. Venice: per Bernardino Vitali, 1501. 1.4

Almansore (Al Rhazes). *Libro tertio delo Almansore chiamato Cibaldone*. Venice: per Giovanni Battista Sessa, 1501. 1.3

Amaseo, Gregorio. *Gregorii Amasei Utinensis Oratoris Facuntissimi Oratio de laudibus studiorum humanitatis ac eloquentiae*. Venice: per Bernardino Benalio, 1501. 3.2

Andrelini, Publio Fausto. *Amorum libri quattuor*. Venice: per Bernardino Vitali, 1501. 2.intro, 2.1, 2.2, 2.4

Antiphonarium Romanum. [Venice: Johannes Emericus] per Lucantonio Giunta, [c.1501–02]. 0.1

Apuleius. *Commentarii a Philippo Beroaldo conditi in Asinum aureum Lucii Apuleii*. Venice: per Simone Bevilacqua, 1501. 0.3, 3.3

Aristotle. [*Opera*]. Venice: per Giovanni & Gregorio De Gregori impensa Paganino Paganini, 1501. 3.1

Aristotle et al. *Aristotelis philosophorum maximi secretum secretorum ad Alexandrum. De regum regimine: De sanitatis conservatione: De physionomia. [...] Alexandri aphrodisei Clarissimi peripatetici. de intellectu. Averrois magni commentatoris de anime beatitudine. Alexandri Achillini bononiensis de Universalibus. Alexandri macedonis in septentrione monarche de mirabilibus Indiae Ad Aristotelem.* Bologna: impensis Benefetto Faelli, 1501. 1.2

Aristotle et al. *Problemata Alexandri Aphrodisei. Georgio Valla interprete. Problemata Aristotelis. Theodorus Gaza e Graeco transtulit. Problemata Plutarchi per Ioannem Petrum Lucensem in Latinum conversa.* Venice: per Albertino da Lessona, 1501. 3.1

Aristotle et al. *Problemata Aristotelis cum duplici translatione antiqua & nova Theodori Gaze: cum expositione Petri Aponi. Tabula secundum Petrum de Tussignano Problemata Alexandri Aphrodisei. Problemata Plutarchi.* Venice: per Boneto Locatello haer. Ottaviano Scoto, 1501. 0.3, 1.3, 3.1

Bartolo da Sassoferrato. *Consilia questiones & tractatus cum additionibus novis.* Venice: per Giovanni & Gregorio De Gregori, 1501. 3.5

Bassino, Giovanni Antonio. *Modo e ordine securo da preservarse e curarse dal pestifero morbo.* Pavia: s.n., 1501. 1.3

Boattieri, Pietro, and Rolandino de Passaggeri. *Commentaria seu expositio in summa notarie Rolandini.* Milan: per Giovanni Angelo Scinzenzeler ad impensas Giovanni da Legnano, 1501. 3.5

Boiardo, Matteo Maria. *Sonetti e Canzone del Poeta Clarissimo Matheo Maria Boiardo Conte di Scandiano.* Venice: per Giovanni Battista Sessa, 1501. 2.2, 2.3, 2.4

Bonaventura da Brescia. *Regula musice plane venerabilis fratris Bonaventurae de Brixia Ordinis minorum.* Milan: per Leonhard Pachel ad impensas Giovanni da Legnano, 1501. 0.1, 1.1

Bonvesin de la Riva. *Vita scolastica.* Venice: per Giovanni Battista Sessa, 1501. 1.intro, 1.2

Borghi, Pietro. *Libro de abacho.* Venice: Giacomo Penzio per Giovanni Battista Sessa, 1501. 1.1

Bornato, Bernardino. *Opusculum de laudibus matrimonii Et de immortalitate animae.* Brescia: per Bernardino Misinta, 1501. 3.2

Bourdon, François de. *Oratio pro capessenda expeditione contra infideles habita in conspectu domini Alexandri divina providentia pape VI. Ex parte d. Petri Daubusson cardi sancti Adriani magni magistri Rhodi per fratrem Francisci de Bourdon decretorum doctorem ipsius reverendissimi domini cappellanum.* Rome: s.n., 1501. 3.2

Brandolini, Raffaello. *Parentalis oratio de obitu Dominici Ruvere Sancti Clementis presbyteri cardinalis Romae in templo Sanctae Mariae de populo ad patres e populum habita MDI.* Rome: Euchario Silber, 1501. 3.2

Burley, Walter. *In Physicam Aristotelis expositio et questiones / Super octo libros phisicorum*. Venice: per Simone Lovere iussu Andrea Torresano, 1501. 3.1

Caiado, Henrique. *Aeglogae et sylvae et epigrammata Hermici*. Bologna: Benedetto Faelli, 1501. 2.intro, 2.2, 2.4

Cantalicio, Giovanni Battista. *Canones brevissimi grammatices & metricas pro rudibus pueris*. Rome: s.n., 1501. 1.1

Canti B. numero cinquanta. Venice: Ottaviano Petrucci, 1501. 0.1

Cicero. *Commentarii Philippicarum cum annotationibus Philippi Beroaldi*. Bologna: Benedetto Faelli, 1501. 3.2

———. *Tullius De oratore cum commento et alia opera*. Venice: per Albertino da Lessona, 1501. 3.2

Ciolek, Erazm. *Ad Alexandrum sextum pontificem maximum in prestita obedientia Romae habita oratio*. Rome: Johann Besicken, 1501. 3.2

Claudian. *Commentarius primus in Raptum Proserpinae Cl. Claudiani*. Milan: in aedibus Lucio Cotta dexteritate Guillame Le Signerre, 1501. 2.1, 3.3

Commenduno, Leonardo. *Oratio d. Leonardi Comenduni Bergomatis ac militis Bergomatium legati congratulatoria ad serenissimum Venetorum principem dominum d. Leonardum Lauretanum*. Venice: per Bernardino Vitali, 1501. 3.2

Concoregio, Giovanni de. *Practica nova medicine Ioannis de Concoregio Mediolanensis. Lucidarium & flos florum medicinae nuncupata. Summula de curis febrium secundum hodiernum modum & usum compilata*. Venice: [Simone Bevilacqua], 1501. 0.3, 1.3

Dati, Agostino. *Elegantiolae faeliciter incipiunt*. Venice: per Cristoforo Pensi, 1501. 1.1

Digestum novum de Tortis. Venice: per Battista Torti, 1501. 3.5

Digestum vetus de Tortis. Venice: per Battista Torti, 1501. 3.5

Donati, Girolamo. *Ad Caesarem pro re christiana*. Venice: per Bernardino Vitali, 1501. 3.2

———. *Ad Christianiss. Ac invictiss. Gallorum Regem Oratio*. Venice: Aldo Manuzio, 1501. 3.2

———. *La oration del magnifico & clarissimo misier Hieronymo Donado orator veneto, facta al sacra maiesta de re Maximiliano*. Venice: per Bernardino Vitali, 1501. 3.2

Donatus, Aelius, et al. *Donatus Melior. Catonis Carmen de moribus. De Arte Libellus*. Milan: [Giovanni da Legnano] per Leonhard Pachel, 1501. 1.intro, 1.2

Dubravius, Roderich. *De componendis epistolis*. Venice: Pietro Quarengi, after 24 May 1501. 1.1

Duns Scotus, John. *Commentaria doctoris subtilis Ioannis Scoti in XII libros Metaphysice Aristotelis emendata & quottationibus concordantiis atque annotationibus decorata per fratrem Mauricium Hibernicum.* Venice: cura ac studio Boneto Locatello mandato & expensis haer. Ottaviano Scoto, 1501. 3.1

Durand, Guillaume. *Speculum judiciale.* Venice: Baptista de Tortis, [1501]. 3.5

Equicola, Mario. *De mulieribus ad d. Margaritam Cantelmam.* Mantua: s.n, 1501. 1.3

Ferrari, Giovanni Matteo, et al. *Tabula consiliorum d. Ioannis Mathei Gradi Mediolanensis, secundum ordinem ac viam d. Auicene ordinata, et Papie anno MCCCCCI impressa. Additis etiam De regimine sanitatis Rabi Moysi ad sultanum, necnon doctissimi Rainaldi ex Villa Nova ad Aragonum regem inclitum.* Pavia: per Giovanni Andrea Bosco impensis Bernardino Scoto, 1501. 1.3

Ficino, Marsilio. *De triplici vita libri tres.* Bologna: Benedetto Faelli, 1501. 1.intro, 1.3, 1.4

Fieschi, Stefano. *De componendis epistolis.* Venice: per Cristoforo Pensi, 1501. 1.1

Galen et al. *Commentum in veterem librorum Techni Galeni translationem. Expositio Ja. Forliviensis in nouam librorum Techni Galeni translationem. Quaestiones Ja. Forlivensis super tribus Techni Galeni libris.* Pavia: impensis ac iussu Luigi Castello, Baldassarre Gabiano & Bartolomeo Trotti: arte et industria Michele & Bernardino Garaldi, 1501. 1.3

Gareth, Benedetto. *Opera nova del Chariteo.* Venice: per Giorgio Rusconi, [1501–09]. 2.intro, 2.1, 2.2, 2.3, 2.4

———. *Opere di Chariteo stampate novamente.* [Venice]: per Manfredo Bonelli, [1501–09]. 2.intro

Gaurico, Luca. *Ex regno Neapolitano Prognosticon anni 1502.* Venice: per Bernardino Vitali, 1501 [= January 1502]. 1.4

Giles of Rome. *Questiones methaphisicales clarissimi doctoris Egidii Romani Ordinis sancti Augustini.* Venice: per Simone da Lovere mandato Andrea Torresano, 1501. 3.1

Grapaldi, Francesco Maria. *De partibus aedium libellus cum additamentis emendatissimus.* Parma: Angelo Ugoleto, 1501. 1.intro, 1.2, 3.4

Harmonice musices odhecaton. [Venice: Ottaviano Petrucci, 1501]. 0.1

Horace. *Horatius.* Venice: Aldo Manuzio, 1501. 2.3, 3.4

Jean de Jandun. *Questiones Ioannis de Ianduno de physico auditu nouiter emendate.* Venice: Boneto Locatello mandato & expensis haer. Ottaviano Scoto, 1501. 3.1

———. *Questiones Ioannis Iandoni de anima.* Venice: per Boneto Locatello impendio haer. Ottaviano Scoto, 1501. 3.1

——. *Questiones Ioannis Iandoni de celo & mundo*. Venice: Boneto Locatello mandato & expensis haer. Ottaviano Scoto, 1501. 3.1

Johannes de Sacrobosco. *Algorismus domini Ioannis de Sacro Busco noviter impressus*. Venice: per Bernardino Vitali, 1501. 1.1

Juvenal. *Argumenta Satyrarum Iuvenalis per Antonium Mancinellum. Cum quattuor commentariis*. Venice: per Giovanni Tacuino, 1501. 0.3, 3.3

——. *Argumenta satyrarum Iuvenalis per Antonium Mancinellum. Cum quattuor commentariis Sebastianus Ducius recensuit*. Milan: per Giovanni Angelo Scinzenzeler sub impensis Giovanni da Legnano, 1501. 0.3, 3.3

——. *Commentarii Ioannis Britannici in Iuuenalem, cum gratia a ducali dominio Venetiarum nequis alius eos intra decennium imprimat*. Brescia: ab Angelo & Giacomo Britannico, 1501. 0.3, 3.3

Juvenal and Persius. *Iuvenalis. Persius*. Venice: Aldo Manuzio, 1501. 1.3

Lamento di Roma fato novamente. [Milan: Alessandro Minuziano, 1501]. 2.intro

Le Battaglie date in Faienza dal duca Valentino. [Rome: Eucario Silber, 1501–09]. 2.intro

Livy. *Titi Livii Decadis*. Venice: per Giorgio Rusconi, 1501. 1.4, 3.4

Macrobius. *De Somno Scipionis: nec non de Saturnalibus libri: summa diligentia suo nitori restituti sunt: in quo plusquam ter mille errores corriguntur: Graecumque quod in olim impressis deerat fere omnibus locis reponitur. Macrobius lectoribus. Qui mutilus dudum & crebris erroribus auctus. Macrobius nulli pene legendus eram Taberii ac Pyladae cura magnoque labore. Nunc iterum mihimet redditus ecce legor*. Brescia: per Angelo Britannico, 1501. 1.3

Manuzio, Aldo. *Rudimenta grammatices Latinae linguae. De literis Graecis & diphthongis, & quemadmodum ad nos veniant. Abbreviationes, quibus frequenter Graeci utuntur. Oratio dominica, & duplex salutatio ad Virginem gloriosiss. Symbolum Apostolorum. Divi Ioannis Evangelistae evangelium. Aurea carmina Pythagorae. Phocylidis poema ad bene, beateque vivendum. Omnia haec cum interpretatione latina. Introductio per brevis ad Hebraicam linguam*. Venice: Aldo Manuzio, 1501. 1.1, 1.2

Martial. *Martialis*. Venice: in aedibus Aldo Manuzio, 1501. 3.4

Mazzolini, Silvestro. *Opere vulgare*. Bologna: per Benedetto Faielli, 1501. 0.3

——. *Incominza la vita de la seraphica e ferventissima amatrice de Iesu Cristo Salvatore Sancta Maria Magdalena: ricolta cum molte nove hystorie per il reverendo padre e maestro ne la sacra theologia frate Silvestro da Prierio de l'ordine de frati predicatori*. Bologna: per Caligola Bazalieri, 1501. 0.3

——. *Summario per confessarsi brevissimo e doctrinale*. Bologna: Giovanni Antonio Benedetti, 1501. 0.3

Mirabilia Romae. Rome: per Johann Besicken, 1501. 0.3

Missale Romanum. Venice: sumptibus & iussu Nikolaus von Frankfurt arte itemque & industria Peter Liechtenstein & Johann Hertzog Hamann, 1501. 0.1

Missale Romanum. Venice: Antonius de Zanchis, 1501. 0.1

Missale romanum noviter impressum. Venice: per Lucantonio Giunta, 1501. 0.1

Missale secundum morem Romane Curie. Venice: iussu & impensis Antonio Zanchi, 1501. 0.1

Ovid. *Epistolae Heroides Ouidii cum commentariis Antonii Volsci et Ubertini Clerici Crescentinatis*. Venice: per Giovanni Luigi Varisio, 1501. 3.3

——. *Ovidio Metamorphoseos vulgare*. Venice: per Cristoforo Pensi ad instantia de Lucantonio Giunta, 1501. 2.2, 2.4

Pasqualigo, Pietro. *Ad Hemanuelem Lusitaniae regem oratio*. Venice: per Bernardino Vitali, 1501. 3.2

Perotti, Niccolò. *Cornucopie nuper emendatum a domino Benedicto Brugnolo: ac mirifice concinnatum cum tabula prioribus aliis copiosiori: utiliori: faciliorique*. Venice: per Giovanni Tacuino, 1501. 1.1, 3.3, 3.4

——. *Rudimenta grammatices*. Turin: per Francesco Silva, 1501. 1.1

Persius. *Aulus Flaccus Persius cum glosis Scipionis Ferrarii Georgii filii de Monte Ferrato artium et medicine doctoris*. Venice: Giacomo Penzio, after 1501. 3.3

Petrarca, Francesco. *Le cose vulgari di messer Francesco Petrarcha*. Venice: Aldo Manuzio, 1501. 2.1, 2.2, 2.3, 2.4

Philostratus of Athens. *De vita Apollonii Tyanei scriptor luculentus a Philippo Beroaldo castigatus*. Bologna: Benedetto Faelli, 1501. 3.4

Pico della Mirandola, Gianfrancesco. *Liber de imaginatione*. Venice: Aldo Manuzio, 1501. 3.1

Pio, Giovanni Battista. *Praelectio in Titum Lucretium & Suetonium Tranquillum*. Bologna: s.n., 1501. 3.2, 3.4

Platina, Bartolomeo. *Platina de honesta voluptate et valitudine vulgare*. Venice: Giorgio Rusconi, 1501. 1.3

Pliny the Elder. *Libro de l'historia naturale*. Venice: per Albertino da Lessona, 1501. 1.3, 3.3, 3.4

Pliny the Younger. *Quae in isto continentur opusculo. C. Plinii iunioris epistolae per Philippum beroaldum emendatae: et unus est adiunctus liber: qui in aliis super impressis minime continebatur. Etiam eiusdem auctoris panegaerycus in laudem Trayani imperatoris: et de iuris illustribus libellus*. Venice: per Albertino da Lessona, 1501. 3.3

Pomponius Mela. *De situ orbis Hermolai Barbari fideliter emendatus*. Venice: Giovanni Battista Sessa, 1501. 3.4

Pontano, Giovanni. *Opera. De fortitudine: libri duo. De principe: liber unus. Dialogus qui Charon inscribitur. Dialogus qui Antonius inscribitur. De liberalitate: liber unus. De benificentia: liber unus. De magnificentia: liber unus. De splendore: liber unus. De coviventia: liber unus. De obedientia: libri quinque.* Venice: per Bernardino Viani, 1501. 0.3, 1.2

Porcia, Girolamo. *In Turcos Porcia declamatio.* Rome: Johann Besicken, 1501. 3.2

Questa e la discordia de tutti quanti li fati che sono stati in Italia e simel di quelli signori che sono distruti. [Venice: Manfredo Bonelli, 1501]. 2.intro

Questa sie la venuta del imperatore. [Venice]: s.n., [1501]. 2.intro

Questo sie uno libro utilissimo a chi se dilecta de intendere todescho dechiarando in lingua latina solennissimo vocabulista utilissimo. Milan: per Alessandro Pellizzoni, 1501. 1.1

Sallust. *Hoc in volumine haec continentur. Pomponii epistola ad Augustinum Maphaeum. C. Crispi Salustii bellum catilinarium cum commento Laurentii Vallae. Portii Latronis declamatio contra L. Catilinam. C. Crispi Salustii bellum iugurtinum cum commentariis preclarissimi fratris Ioannis chrysostomi Soldi brixiani. C. Crispi Salustii variae orationes ex libris eius dem historiarum exceptae. C. Crispi Salustii vita. Romae per Pomponium emendata: Mediolanique per Alexandrum Minutianum diligentissime revisa.* Milan: Alessandro Minuziano, 1501. 3.2

Sasso, Panfilo. *Opera del praeclarissimo poeta miser Pamphilo Sasso modenese. Sonetti. CCCCVII. Capituli XXXVIII. Egloge V.* Venice: Bernardino Viani, 1501. 2.intro, 2.1, 2.2, 2.3, 2.4

——. *Strambotti del clarissimo professore dele bone arte miser Sasso Modoneso.* Rome: per Johannem Besicken & Martinum de Amsterdam, 1501. 2.intro, 2.1, 2.2, 2.3, 2.4

Serafini, Domenico. *Compendium Sinonymorum.* Milan: [Giovanni da Legnano] per Leonhard Pachel, 1501. 1.1

Serafino Aquilano. *Soneti del Seraphin.* Brescia: per Bernardino Misinta, [1501]. 2.intro, 2.1, 2.3, 2.4

Sorci, Giacomo de', and anon. *La historia e la guerra del populo genovese e gentilhomini e del re di Franza. E una barzelletta dela discordia de Italia.* Naples: s.n., [1501]. 2.intro

Staccoli, Agostino. *Sonecti et canzone de miser Agostino da Urbino.* [Rome: Johann Besicken & Martin van Amsterdam, 1501]. 2.intro

Statuta magnifice communitatis regii. Reggio Emilia: Vincenzo Bertocchi impressit, 1501. 3.5

Storia overo cronica come il signor Ludovicho que duca de Milano si parti di Millano e ando in terra todesca e como torno con exercito el paese che conquistò e como al fine e stato preso. Bologna: [Giustiniano da Rubiera, c.1501]. 2.intro

Sulpizio, Giovanni. *Regulae Sulpitij*. [Venice: s.n., 1501–09]. 1.1, 3.4

Tartagni, Alessandro. *Alexander de imola super secunda veteris cum apostilis noviter editis*. Venice: per Battista Torti, 1501. 3.5

Tebaldeo, Antonio. *Soneti, capituli et egloghe*. Milan: per Giovanni Angelo Scinzenzeler, 1501. 2.intro, 2.1, 2.2, 2.3, 2.4

Terence. *Terentius cum tribus commentis. Videlicet Donati Guidonis [et] Calphurnii*. Milan: per Giovanni Angelo Scinzenzeler [et] Giovanni da Legnano, 1501. 3.3

Thomas Aquinas. *Divi Thome aquinatis in librum de anima Aristotelis expositio. Magistri Dominici de Flandria ordinis predicatorum in eundem librum acutissime questiones et annotationes*. Venice: per Pietro Quarengi, 1501. 3.1

Tiberti, Dario. *Epithome Plutarchi*. Ferrara: Lorenzo Rossi, 1501. 3.4

Tortelli, Giovanni. *Orthographia. Ioannis Tortelii Lima quaedam per Georgium Vallam tractatum de orthographia*. Venice: per Bartolomeo Zani, 1501. 1.1, 3.3, 3.4

Uberti, Fazio degli. *Opera di Faccio Degliuberti Fiorentino Chiamato Ditta Mundi. Vuolgare*. Venice: Lucantonio Giunta per Cristoforo Pensi, 1501. 2.1

Valerius Flaccus. *Argonautica diligenter accurateque emendata & suo nitori reddita in hoc volumine continentur*. Venice: per Cristoforo Pensi, 1501. 2.1, 3.4

Valla, Giorgio. *De expetendis et fugiendis rebus opus*. Venice: in aedibus Aldo Manuzio impensa ac studio Giampietro Valla, 1501. 0.4, 3.3

Virgil. *Vergilius cum commentariis quinque, videlicet Servii, Landini, Ant. Mancinelli, Donati, Domitii*. Venice: s.n., 1501. 2.1, 3.3

——. *Vergilius*. Venice: ex aedibus Aldo Manuzio, 1501. 3.4

Vita di sancti padri vulgariter historiada. Venice: per Otino Luna, 1501. 0.3

Xenophon. *Opera*. Milan: Alessandro Minuziano, c.1501–02. 3.4

2. Other Primary Sources

Albertus Magnus (Pseudo). *Woman's Secrets: A Translation of Pseudo-Albertus Magnus' De Secretis Mulierum with Commentaries*. Translated by Helen Rodnite Lemay. New York: State University of New York Press, 1992.

Albumasar. *Flores astrologie*. Venice: Giovanni Battista Sessa, c.1500–06.

Apuleius. *Metamorphoses (The Golden Ass), Volume I: Books 1–6*. Edited and translated by J. Arthur Hanson. Loeb Classical Library 44. Cambridge, MA: Harvard University Press, 1996. https://doi.org/10.4159/dlcl.apuleius-metamorphoses.1996

Aristotle. *The Complete Works of Aristotle: The Revised Oxford Translation*. Edited by Jonathan Barnes. 2 vols. Princeton: Princeton University Press, 1984. https://doi.org/10.1515/9781400835843 https://doi.org/10.1515/9781400835850

Augustus Moravus. *Iudicium Anno Domini 1494*. Padua: s.n., 1494.

Barber, Richard, trans. *Bestiary*. Woodbridge: Boydell & Brewer, 1992.

Beroaldo, Filippo. *Annotationes Centum*. Edited by Lucia A. Ciapponi. Binghampton, NY: Centre for Medieval and Early Renaissance Studies, 1995.

Boiardo, Matteo Maria. *Amorum Libri: The Lyric Poems of Matteo Maria Boiardo*. Edited by Andrea di Tommaso. Binghampton: Medieval & Renaissance Texts and Studies, 1993.

Brandolini, Raffaele. *On Music and Poetry*. Translated by Ann E. Moyer and Marc Laureys. Tempe, AZ: Arizona Centre for Medieval and Renaissance Studies, 2001.

Burzio, Nicolò. *Musices opusculum*. Bologna: Ugo Rugerius per Benedictus Hectoris, 1487.

—. *Musices opusculum*. Translated by Clement A. Miller. Neuhausen-Stuttgart: Hänssler-Verlag, 1983.

Castiglione, Baldassare. *Il Libro del Cortegiano*. Edited by Giulio Preti. Turin: Einaudi, 1965.

Cicero. *On the Orator: Book 3. On Fate. Stoic Paradoxes. Divisions of Oratory*. Translated by H. Rackham. Loeb Classical Library 349. Cambridge, MA: Harvard University Press, 1942. https://doi.org/10.4159/DLCL.marcus_tullius_cicero-de_oratore.1942

—. *On the Ideal Orator*. Translated by James M. May and Jakob Wisse. Oxford: Oxford University Press, 2001. https://doi.org/10.1093/actrade/9780195091984.book.1

Collettanee grece, latine, e vulgari per diversi auctori moderni, nella morte de l'ardente Seraphino Aquilano per Gioanne Philoteo Achillino bolognese in uno corpo ridutte. E alla diva Helisabetta Feltria da Gonzaga duchessa di Urbino dicate. Bologna: Caligola Bazalieri, 1504.

Columella. *On Agriculture, Vol. 2: Books 5–9*. Edited and translated by E. S. Forster and Edward H. Heffner. Loeb Classical Library 407. Cambridge, MA: Harvard University Press, 1954. https://doi.org/10.4159/DLCL.columella-agriculture.1941

Costa, Stefano. *Tractatus de Ludo*. Pavia: Franciscus de Sancto Petro, 1478.

Decor Puellarum. [Venice]: Nicolaus Jensen, [1471].

Dio Chrysostom. *Dion de Regno*. Bologna: Franciscus de Benedictis, 1493.

Engel, Johann. *Astrolabium planum in tabulis ascendens*. Venice: per Lucantonio Giunta, 1502.

Fedele, Cassandra. *Clarissimae Feminae Cassandrae Fidelis venetae Epistolae et orationes*. Edited by Jacopo Filippo Tomasini. Padua: Franciscus Bolzetta, 1636.

———. *Letters and Orations*. Edited and translated by Diana Robin. Chicago, IL: University of Chicago Press, 2000. https://doi.org/10.7208/chicago/9780226239330.001.0001

Ficino, Marsilio. *Consiglio contro la pestilenza*. Florence: Jacobum de Ripolis, 1481.

———. *Three Books on Life: A Critical Edition and Translation with Introduction and Notes*. Edited and translated by Carol V. Kaske and John R. Clark. Tempe, AZ: Medieval & Renaissance Texts and Studies, 1998.

Fiore di virtù. Florence: [Bartolommeo di Libri], 1489.

Froctola dilectevole da mandar via lotoi et la malinconia. [Florence]: Zanobi, n.d.

Gafori, Franchino. *Practica musicae*. Milan: Guillaume le Signerre, 1496.

Galen. *On the Constitution of the Art of Medicine. The Art of Medicine. A Method of Medicine to Glaucon*. Edited and translated by Ian Johnston. Loeb Classical Library 523. Cambridge, MA: Harvard University Press, 2016. https://doi.org/10.4159/DLCL.galen-constitution_art_medicine.2016

Gareth, Benedetto. *Le Rime di Benedetto Gareth, detto il Chariteo*. Edited by Erasmo Percopo. 2 vols. Naples: [Tipografia dell'Accademia delle scienze], 1892.

Horace. *Satires. Epistles. The Art of Poetry*. Translated by H. Rushton Fairclough. Loeb Classical Library 194. Cambridge, MA: Harvard University Press, 1926. https://doi.org/10.4159/DLCL.horace-satires.1926

———. *Odes and Epodes*. Edited and translated by Niall Rudd. Loeb Classical Library 33. Cambridge, MA: Harvard University Press, 2004. https://doi.org/10.4159/DLCL.horace-odes.2004

Isidore of Seville. *Etymologiae*. Venice: Petrus Löslein, 1483.

———. *The Etymologies of Isidore of Seville*. Edited and translated by Stephen A. Barney, W. J. Lewis, J. A. Beach, and Oliver Berghof. Cambridge, UK: Cambridge University Press, 2006. https://doi.org/10.1017/cbo9780511482113

Juvenal and Persius. *Juvenal and Persius*. Edited and translated by Susanna Morton Braund. Loeb Classical Library 91. Cambridge, MA: Harvard University Press, 2004. https://doi.org/10.4159/DLCL.juvenal-satires.2004

Kallendorf, Craig W., ed. and trans. *Humanist Educational Treatises*. The I Tatti Renaissance Library 5. Cambridge, MA: Harvard University Press, 2002.

Le malitie dei vilani con alquanti stramotti alla Bergamascha. S.l.: s.n, n.d.

Livy. *History of Rome, Volume I: Books 1–2*. Translated by B. O. Foster. Loeb Classical Library 114. Cambridge, MA: Harvard University Press, 1919. https://doi.org/10.4159/DLCL.livy-history_rome_1.1919

———. *History of Rome, Volume II: Books 3–4*. Translated by B. O. Foster. Loeb Classical Library 133. Cambridge, MA: Harvard University Press, 1922. https://doi.org/10.4159/DLCL.livy-history_rome_3.1922

———. *History of Rome, Volume III: Books 5–7*. Translated by B. O. Foster. Loeb Classical Library 172. Cambridge, MA: Harvard University Press, 1924. https://doi.org/10.4159/DLCL.livy-history_rome_5.1924

———. *History of Rome, Volume IV: Books 8–10*. Translated by B. O. Foster. Loeb Classical Library 191. Cambridge, MA: Harvard University Press, 1926. https://doi.org/10.4159/DLCL.livy-history_rome_8.1926

———. *History of Rome, Volume XI: Books 38–40*. Edited and translated by J. C. Yardley. Loeb Classical Library 313. Cambridge, MA: Harvard University Press, 2018. https://doi.org/10.4159/DLCL.livy-history_rome_38.2018

Lucretius. *On the Nature of Things*. Translated by W. H. D. Rouse, revised by Martin F. Smith. Loeb Classical Library 181. Cambridge, MA: Harvard University Press, 1924. https://doi.org/10.4159/DLCL.lucretius-de_rerum_natura.1924

Martial. *Epigrams, Vol. 2: Books 6–10*. Edited and translated by D. R. Shackleton Bailey. Loeb Classical Library 95. Cambridge, MA: Harvard University Press, 1993. https://doi.org/10.4159/DLCL.martial-epigrams.1993

———. *Epigrams, Vol. 3: Books 11–14*. Edited and translated by D. R. Shackleton Bailey. Loeb Classical Library 480. Cambridge, MA: Harvard University Press, 1993. https://doi.org/10.4159/DLCL.martial-epigrams.1993

———. *Martial's Epigrams: Book Two*. Edited and translated by Craig A. Williams. Oxford: Oxford University Press, 2003. https://doi.org/10.1093/actrade/9780195155310.book.1

Musica Plutarchi a Charolo Valgulio Brixiano Versa in latinum, published together with his *Prooemium in Musicam Plutarchi*. Brescia: Angelo Britannico, 1507.

Ovid. *Heroides. Amores*. Translated by Grant Showerman, revised by G. P. Goold. Loeb Classical Library 41. Cambridge, MA: Harvard University Press, 1914. https://doi.org/10.4159/DLCL.ovid-heroides.1914

Petrarca, Francesco. *Petrarcha con doi commenti sopra li sonetti & canzone. El primo del ingeniosissimo misser Francesco Philelpho. Laltro del sapientissimo misser Antonio da Tempo, novamente addito. Ac etiam con lo commento del eximio misser Nicolo Peranzone, overo Riccio marchesiano sopra li Triumphi, con infinite nove acute et excellente expositione.* Venice: per Albertino da Lessona, 1503.

———. *Il Petrarcha colla spositione di Misser Giovanni Andrea Gesualdo*. Venice: per Giovanni Antonio Nicolini da Sabbio & fratres, 1533.

———. *Petrarch: The Canzoniere, or Rerum Vulgarium Fragmenta*. Translated by Mark Musa. Bloomington: Indiana University Press, 1999.

———. *Canzoniere*. Translated by J. G. Nichols. Manchester: Carcanet Press, 2002.

Pico della Mirandola, Gianfrancesco. *On the Imagination*. Translated by Harry Caplan. New Haven, CT: Yale University Press, 1930.

———. *L'immaginazione*. Edited and translated by Francesco Molinarolo. Pisa: Edizioni della Normale, 2022.

Pietro d'Abano. *Expositio Problematum (XIX)*. Edited by Christian Meyer. Leuven: Leuven University Press, 2022. https://doi.org/10.2307/j.ctv1ccbg33

Plato. [*Opera*]. Edited and translated by Marsilio Ficino. Florence: Lorenzo d'Alopa, [1484–85].

Plutarch. *Lives, Vol. 7*. Translated by Bernadotte Perrin. Loeb Classical Library 99. Cambridge, MA: Harvard University Press, 1919. https://doi.org/10.4159/DLCL.plutarch-lives_demosthenes.1919

Poliziano, Angelo. *Rime*. Edited by Daniela Delcorno Branca. Florence: Accademia della Crusca, 1986.

Pontano, Giovanni. *I libri delle virtù sociali*. Edited by Francesco Tateo. Rome: Bulzone Editore, 1999.

———. *Dialogues, vol. 1: Charon and Antonius*. Edited and translated by Julia Haig Gaisser. Cambridge, MA: Harvard University Press, 2012.

Ptolemy. *Tetrabiblos*. Translated by F. E. Robbins. Loeb Classical Library 435. Cambridge, MA: Harvard University Press, 1940. https://doi.org/10.4159/DLCL.ptolemy-tetrabiblos.1940

Questo sie uno libreto utilissimo a chi non sapesse littere de imparare presto elqual se chiama Babuino. Venice: Giovanni Battista Sessa, 1505.

Quintilian. *The Orator's Education, Volume I: Books 1–2*. Edited and translated by Donald A. Russell. Loeb Classical Library 124. Cambridge, MA: Harvard University Press, 2002. https://doi.org/10.4159/DLCL.quintilian-orators_education.2002

Ramos de Pareja, Bartolomé. *Musica Practica*. Bologna: [Balthasar de Ruberia and Henricus de Colonia], 1482.

Sasso, Panfilo. *Strambotti*. Edited by Folke Gernert. Trier: Romanica Treverensis, 2017.

Serafino Aquilano. *Opere del facundissimo Seraphino Aquilano collette per Francescio Flavio. Sonetti LXXXIX. Egloghe III. Epistole VI. Capitoli IX Strammotti CCVI Barzellette X*. Venice: Manfredo Bonelli, 1502.

—. *Opere del facundissimo Serafino Aquilano collette per Francesco Flauio Sonetti lxxxix Egloghe. iii Epistole yi Capitoli ix. Strasmmoti ccyi barzelette. X*. Bologna: Girolamo Ruggeri, 1503.

Statius. *Silvae*. Edited and translated by D. R. Shackleton Bailey, revised by Christopher A. Parrott. Loeb Classical Library 206. Cambridge, MA: Harvard University Press, 2015. https://doi.org/10.4159/DLCL.statius-silvae.2015

Strabo. *Geographia, libri XVI*. [Venice]: Johannes Rubeus, 1495.

Suetonius. *Lives of the Caesars, vol. 2*. Edited and translated by J. C. Rolfe. Loeb Classical Library 38. Cambridge, MA: Harvard University Press, 1914. https://doi.org/10.4159/DLCL.suetonius-lives_caesars_book_v_claudius.1914

The Digest of Justinian. Volume 4. Translated by Alan Watson. Philadelphia: University of Pennsylvania Press, 1985.

Thomas Aquinas. *A Commentary on Aristotle's* De anima. Translated by Robert Pasnau. New Haven, CT: Yale University Press, 1999.

Valerius Flaccus. *Argonautica*. Translated by J. H. Mozley. Loeb Classical Library 286. Cambridge, MA: Harvard University Press, 1934. https://doi.org/10.4159/DLCL.valerius_flaccus-argonautica.1934

Vitalis, Ludovico. *Prognosticon in annum Domini 1506*. Bologna: s.n., 1505/6.

Vitruvius. *De architectura*. [Rome: Eucharius Silber, 1486].

Zerbi, Gabriele. *Gerontocomia*. Rome: Eucharius Silber, 1489.

—. *Gerontocomia*. Edited and translated by L. R. Lind. Philadelphia, PN: American Philosophical Society, 1988.

3. Modern Literature

Abramov-Van Rijk, Elena. *Singing Dante: The Literary Origins of Cinquecento Monody*. Farnham: Ashgate, 2014. https://doi.org/10.4324/9781315609157

Ajmar-Wollheim, Marta, and Flora Dennis, ed. *At Home in Renaissance Italy*. London: V&A, 2006.

Allen, Don Cameron. *The Star-Crossed Renaissance: The Quarrel about Astrology and its Influence in England*. London: Frank Cass, 1966.

Alpers, Paul. *What is Pastoral?* Chicago, IL: The University of Chicago Press, 1996.

Arcangeli, Alessandro. "Dance and Health: The Renaissance Physicians' View." *Journal of the Society for Dance Research* 18.1 (2000): 3–30. https://doi.org/10.3366/1291009

———. *Recreation in the Renaissance: Attitudes towards Leisure and Pastimes in European Culture, c. 1425–1675*. New York: Palgrave Macmillan, 2003.

Askari, Nasrin. *The Medieval Reception of the Shāhnāma as a Mirror for Princes*. Leiden: Brill, 2016. https://doi.org/10.1163/9789004307919

Atkinson, Niall. *The Noisy Renaissance: Sound, Architecture, and Florentine Urban Life*. University Park, PA: Penn State University Press, 2016. https://doi.org/10.5325/j.ctv14gp0cj

Austin, J. L. *How to Do Things with Words*. Oxford: Oxford University Press, 1962. https://doi.org/10.1093/acprof:oso/9780198245537.001.0001

Avelar de Carvalho, Helena. *An Astrologer at Work in Late Medieval France: The Notebooks of S. Belle*. Leiden: Brill, 2021. https://doi.org/10.1163/9789004463387

Azzolini, Monica. *The Duke and the Stars: Astrology and Politics in Renaissance Milan*. Cambridge, MA: Harvard University Press, 2013. https://doi.org/10.4159/harvard.9780674067912

Bayer, Andrea, ed. *Art and Love in Renaissance Italy*. New York: Metropolitan Museum of Art, 2008.

Bejczy, István Pieter, and Cary J. Nederman, ed. *Princely Virtues in the Middle Ages, 1200–1500*. Turnhout: Brepols, 2007. https://doi.org/10.1484/m.disput-eb.6.09070802050003050106090607

Bell, Rudolph M. *How To Do It: Guides to Good Living for Renaissance Italians*. Chicago, IL: University of Chicago Press, 1999. https://doi.org/10.7208/chicago/9780226041834.001.0001

Bellomo, Manilo. *The Common Legal Past of Europe, 1000–1800*. Translated by Lydia Cochrane. Washington, DC: The Catholic University of America Press, 1995. https://doi.org/10.2307/j.ctt4cg8mj

Benavent, Julia, Maria Josep Bertomeu, and Alessio Bonafe. "Le battaglie date a Faienza dal duca Valentino." *Revista Borja* 1 (2007): 63–102.

Bent, Margaret. "Sense and Rhetoric in Late Medieval Polyphony." In *Music in the Mirror: Reflections on the History of Music Theory and Literature for the 21st Century*, edited by Andreas Giger and Thomas J. Mathiesen, 45–59. Lincoln: University of Nebraska Press, 2002.

———. "Grammar and Rhetoric in Late Medieval Polyphony: Modern Metaphor or Old Simile?" In *Rhetoric Beyond Words: Delight and Persuasion in the Arts of the Middle Ages*, edited by Mary Carruthers, 52–71. Cambridge, UK: Cambridge University Press, 2010.

———. "Performative Rhetoric and Rhetoric as Validation." In *Inventing a Path: Studies in Medieval Rhetoric in Honour of Mary Carruthers*, edited by Laura Iseppi De Filippis, 43–62. *Nottingham Medieval Studies* 56 (2012). https://doi.org/10.1484/j.nms.1.102751

Bistagne, Florence. "Pontano, Castiglione, Guazzo: facétie et normes de comportement dans la trattatistica de la Renaissance." *Cahiers d'études italiennes* 6 (2007): 183–192. https://doi.org/10.4000/cei.860

Black, Robert. *Humanism and Education in Medieval and Renaissance Italy*. Cambridge, UK: Cambridge University Press, 2001. https://doi.org/10.1017/cbo9780511496684

Blackburn, Bonnie J. "Music Theory and Musical Thinking after 1450." In *Music as Concept and Practice in the Late Middle Ages*, edited by Reinhard Strohm and Bonnie J. Blackburn, 301–45. Oxford: Oxford University Press, 2001. https://doi.org/10.1093/oso/9780198162056.003.0007

———. "The Fifteenth-Century Afterlives of the *Speculum musicae* by Jacobus of Liege." *Journal of the Alamire Foundation* 16.2 (2024): 244–78. https://doi.org/10.1484/j.jaf.5.142077

Blackburn, Bonnie J., Edward Lowinsky, and Clement A. Miller, ed. *A Correspondence of Renaissance Musicians*. Oxford: Clarendon, 1990.

Blair, Ann. "Reading Strategies for Coping with Information Overload ca.1550–1700." *Journal of the History of Ideas* 64.1 (2003): 11–28. https://doi.org/10.1353/jhi.2003.0014

Blume, Dieter. "Children of the Planets: The Popularisation of Astrology in the 15th Century." *Micrologus* 12 (2004): 549–63.

Boorman, Stanley. *Ottaviano Petrucci: A catalogue raisonné*. New York: Oxford University Press, 2006.

Borghetti, Vincenzo, and Tim Shephard. "Politics: Staging Power." In *A Cultural History of Music in the Renaissance*, edited by Jeanice Brooks and Richard Freedman, 91–120. London: Bloomsbury, 2023. https://doi.org/10.5040/9781350075566.ch-3

Bortoletti, Francesca. "Serafino Aquilano and the Mask of *Poeta*: A Denunciation in the Eclogue of *Tyrinto e Menandro* (1490)." In *Voices and Texts in Early Modern Italian Society*, edited by Stefano Dall'Aglio, Brian Richardson, and Massimo Rospocher, 139–52. New York: Routledge, 2017. https://doi.org/10.4324/9781315547893

Bowd, Stephen D. *Venice's Most Loyal City: Civic Identity in Renaissance Brescia*. Cambridge, MA: Harvard University Press, 2010. https://doi.org/10.4159/9780674060562

Brand, Benjamin. "A Medieval Scholasticus and Renaissance Choirmaster: A Portrait of John Hothby at Lucca." *Renaissance Quarterly* 63.3 (2010): 754–806. https://doi.org/10.1086/656928

Brown, Howard M., and Rebecca Stewart. "Workshop IV. Voice Types in Josquin's Music." In *Proceedings of the Josquin Symposium. Cologne, 11–15 July 1984*, published as *Tijdschrift van de Vereniging voor Nederlandse Muziekgeschiedenis* 35.1–2 (1985): 97–193.

Brown, Patricia Fortini. *Private Lives in Renaissance Venice*. New Haven, CT: Yale University Press, 2004.

Brundin, Abigail, Deborah Howard, and Mary Laven. *The Sacred Home in Renaissance Italy*. Oxford: Oxford University Press, 2018. https://doi.org/10.1093/oso/9780198816553.001.0001

Bullard, Melissa Meriem. "The Inward Zodiac: A Development in Ficino's Thought on Astrology." *Renaissance Quarterly* 43.4 (1990): 687–708. https://doi.org/10.2307/2862785

Burke, Jill. *The Italian Renaissance Nude*. New Haven, CT: Yale University Press, 2018. https://doi.org/10.37862/aaeportal.00310

Burke, Peter. *The Fortunes of the Courtier: The European Reception of Castiglione's Cortegiano*. University Park, PA: Penn State University Press, 1995.

Burnett, Charles. "Sound and Its Perception in the Middle Ages." In *The Second Sense: Studies in Hearing and Musical Judgement from Antiquity to the Seventeenth Century*, edited by Charles Burnett, Michael Fend, and Penelope M. Gouk, 43–69. London: Warburg Institute, 1991.

———. "Hearing and Music in Book XI of Pietro d'Abano's Expositio Problematum Aristotelis." In *Tradition and Ecstasy: The Agony of the Fourteenth Century*, edited by Nancy van Deusen, 153–90. Ottawa: Institute of Medieval Music, 1997.

Busse Berger, Anna Maria. *Medieval Music and the Art of Memory*. Berkeley, CA: University of California Press, 2005. https://doi.org/10.1525/california/9780520240285.001.0001

Caldwell, Mary Channon. "Singing Cato: Grammar and Moral Citation in Medieval Latin Song." *Music and Letters* 102.2 (2021): 191–233. https://doi.org/10.1093/ml/gcaa090

Calogero, Elena Laura. "'Sweet alluring harmony': Heavenly and Earthly Sirens in Sixteenth- and Seventeenth-Century Literary and Visual Culture." In *Music of the Sirens*, edited by Linda Phyllis Austern and Inna Naroditskaya, 140–75. Bloomington, IN: Indiana University Press, 2006.

Campbell, Stephen. *The Cabinet of Eros: Renaissance Mythological Painting and the Studiolo of Isabella d'Este*. New Haven, CT: Yale University Press, 2006.

Canguilhem, Philippe. "Singing Horace in Sixteenth-Century France: A Reappraisal of the Sources and Their Interpretation." In *Horace across the Media: Textual, Visual and Musical Receptions of Horace from the 15th to the 18th Century*, edited by K. A. E. Enkel and Marc Laureys, 422–41. Leiden: Brill, 2022. https://doi.org/10.1163/9789004373730_009

Carpenter, Nan Cooke. *Music in the Medieval and Renaissance Universities*. Norman, OK: University of Oklahoma Press, 1958.

Casanova-Robin, Hélène. "La rhétorique de la légitimité: Droits et devoirs du prince dans le de Principe de Pontano." *Rhetorica: A Journal of the History of Rhetoric* 32.4 (2014): 348–61. https://doi.org/10.1353/rht.2014.0001

Cattin, Giulio. "Nomi di rimatori per la polifonia profana Italiana del secondo quattrocento." *Rivista Italiana di Musicologia* 25.2 (1990): 209–311.

Cattin, Giulio, and Patrizia Dalla Vecchia, ed. *Venezia 1501: Petrucci e la stampa musicale*. Venice: Fondazione Levi, 2005.

Cavallo, Sandra, and Tessa Storey. *Healthy Living in Late Renaissance Italy*. New York: Oxford University Press, 2013. https://doi.org/10.1093/acprof:oso/9780199678136.001.0001

Cavicchi, Camilla. "The cantastorie and His Music in 15th- and 16th-Century Italy." *Troja—Jahrbuch für Renaissancemusik* 13 (2017): 105–33. https://doi.org/10.25371/troja.v20142585

Cazelles, Brigitte. *Soundscape in Early French Literature*. Tempe, AZ: Arizona Center for Medieval and Renaissance Studies, 2005.

Chiu, Remi. *Plague and Music in the Renaissance*. Cambridge, UK: Cambridge University Press, 2017. https://doi.org/10.1017/9781316271476

Cinelli, Luciano. "Domenico di Fiandra: La carriera di un frate predicatore del quattrocento fra Bologna e Firenze." In *Università, teologia e studium domenicano dal 1360 alla fine del medioevo*, edited by Roberto Lambertini, 147–69. Florence: Nerbini, 2014.

Clarke, Eric, Nicola Dibben, and Stephanie Pitts. *Music and Mind in Everyday Life*. Oxford: Oxford University Press, 2010. https://doi.org/10.1093/acprof:oso/9780198525578.001.0001

Coelho, Victor, and Keith Polk. *Instrumentalists and Renaissance Culture, 1420–1600*. Cambridge, UK: Cambridge University Press, 2016. https://doi.org/10.1017/cbo9781316536186

Coleman, James K. *A Sudden Frenzy: Improvisation, Orality, and Power in Renaissance Italy*. Toronto: University of Toronto Press, 2022. https://doi.org/10.3138/9781487563455

Comboni, Andrea, and Tiziano Zanato, ed. *Atlante dei canzonieri del Quattrocento*. Florence: Edizioni del Galluzzo, 2017.

Comiati, Giacomo. "Horace in the Italian Renaissance." PhD dissertation, University of Warwick, 2015.

Conti, Alessandro D. "Giles of Rome's Questions on the Metaphysics." In *A Companion to the Latin Medieval Commentaries on Aristotle's Metaphysics*, edited by Gabriele Galluzzo and Fabrizio Amerini, 255–76. Leiden: Brill, 2013. https://doi.org/10.1163/9789004261297_008

Copenhaver, Brian P., and C. Schmitt. *Renaissance Philosophy*. Oxford: Oxford University Press, 1992.

Corn, Alan M. "'Thus Nature Ordains': Juvenal's Fourteenth Satire." *Illinois Classical Studies* 17.2 (1992): 309–22.

Cosgrove, Charles H. *Music at Social Meals in Greek and Roman Antiquity: From the Archaic Period to the Age of Augustine*. Cambridge, UK: Cambridge University Press, 2022. https://doi.org/10.1017/9781009161060

Cummings, Anthony M. "Music and Feasts in the Fifteenth Century." In *The Cambridge History of Fifteenth-Century Music*, edited by Anna Maria Busse Berger and Jesse Rodin, 361–73. Cambridge, UK: Cambridge University Press, 2015. https://doi.org/10.1017/cho9781139057813.027

Da Col, Paolo. "Silent Voices: Professional Singers in Venice." In *A Companion to Music in Sixteenth-Century Venice*, edited by Katelijne Schiltz, 231–71. Leiden: Brill, 2018. https://doi.org/10.1163/9789004358300_010

Degl'Innocenti, Luca, and Massimo Rospocher. "Street Singers: An Interdisciplinary Perspective." *Italian Studies* 71.2 (2016): 149–53. https://doi.org/10.1080/00751634.2016.1175713

———. "Urban Voices: The Hybrid Figure of the Street Singer in Renaissance Italy." *Renaissance Studies* 33.1 (2019): 17–41. https://doi.org/10.1111/rest.12529

Deitch, Judith. "The Girl He Left Behind: Ovidian imitatio and the Body of Echo in Spenser's 'Epithalamion'." In *Ovid and the Renaissance Body*, edited by Goran V. Stanivukovic, 224–38. Toronto: University of Toronto Press, 2001. https://doi.org/10.3138/9781442678194-014

Delcorno, Carlo. "Medieval Preaching in Italy." In *The Sermon*, edited by Beverly Mayne Kienzle and René Noël, 449–560. Turnhout: Brepols, 2000.

Delcorno, Pietro. *In the Mirror of the Prodigal Son: The Pastoral Uses of a Biblical Narrative (c. 1200–1550)*. Leiden: Brill, 2018. https://doi.org/10.1163/9789004349582

Dennis, Flora. "Sound and Domestic Space in Fifteenth- and Sixteenth-Century Italy." *Studies in the Decorative Arts* 16.1 (2008–9): 7–19. https://doi.org/10.1086/652811

———. "Resurrecting Forgotten Sound: Fans and Handbells in Early Modern Italy." In *Everyday Objects: Medieval and Early Modern Material Culture and Its Meanings*, edited by Tara Hamling and Catherine Richardson, 191–210. New York: Routledge, 2010. https://doi.org/10.4324/9781315255798-28

———. "Scattered Knives and Dismembered Song: Cutlery, Music and the Rituals of Dining." *Renaissance Studies* 24.1 (2010): 156–84. https://doi.org/10.1111/j.1477-4658.2009.00634.x

———. "Unlocking the Gates of Chastity: Music and the Erotic in the Domestic Sphere in Fifteenth- and Sixteenth-Century Italy." In *Erotic Cultures of Renaissance Italy*, edited by Sara F. Matthews-Grieco, 223–45. Ashgate: Aldershot, 2010. https://doi.org/10.4324/9781315094380-8

———. "Cooking Pots, Tableware, and the Changing Sounds of Sociability in Italy." *Sound Studies* 6.2 (2020): 174–95. https://doi.org/10.1080/20551940.2020.1794650

DeNora, Tia. *Music in Everyday Life*. Cambridge, UK: Cambridge University Press, 2000. https://doi.org/10.1017/cbo9780511489433

Dillon, Emma. *The Sense of Sound: Musical Meaning in France 1260–1330*. Oxford: Oxford University Press, 2012. https://doi.org/10.1093/acprof:oso/9780199732951.001.0001

Di Tommaso, Andrea. "Introduction." In *Boiardo, Amorum Libri: The Lyric Poems of Matteo Maria Boiardo*, edited by di Tommaso, 1–26. Binghampton: Medieval & Renaissance Texts and Studies, 1993.

Dondi, Cristina. "From the Corpus Iuris to 'psalterioli da puti' on Parchment, Bound, Gilt… The Price of Any Book Sold in Venice 1484–1488." *Studi di storia* 13 (2020): 577–99. https://doi.org/10.30687/978-88-6969-332-8/020

Dooley, Brendan. "Introduction." In *A Companion to Astrology in the Renaissance*, edited by Dooley, 1-16. Leiden: Brill, 2014. https://doi.org/10.1163/9789004262300_002

Doyle, Oliver. "Beyond the Courtier: Music and Lifestyle Literature in Italy 1480–1530." PhD dissertation, University of Sheffield, 2024.

———. "Musicianship and the Masteries of the Stars: Music and Musicians in the Liber Nativitatum." *Renaissance Studies* 38.4 (2024): 494–518. https://doi.org/10.1111/rest.12912

Dronzek, Anna. "Gendered Theories of Education in Fifteenth Century Conduct Books." In *Medieval Conduct*, edited by Kathleen Ashley and Robert L. A. Clark, 135–59. Minnesota, MN: University of Minnesota Press, 2001.

Duggan, Mary Kay. *Italian Music Incunabula: Printers and Type*. Berkeley, CA: University of California Press, 1992.

Eamon, William. "Astrology and Society." In *A Companion to Astrology in the Renaissance*, edited by Brendan Dooley, 141–92. Leiden: Brill, 2014. https://doi.org/10.1163/9789004262300_007

Enekel, Karl A. E. "The Neo-Latin Epigram: Humanist Self-Definition in a Learned and Witty Discourse." In *The Neo-Latin Epigram: A Learned and Witty Genre*, edited by Susanna De Beer, Karl A.E. Enenkel, and David Rijsser, 1–24. Leuven: Leuven University Press, 2009.

Fanti, Claudia. "L'elegia properziana nella lirica amorosa del Cariteo." *Italianistica* 14 (1985): 23–44.

Feng, Aileen Astorga. *Writing Beloveds: Humanist Petrarchism and the Politics of Gender*. Toronto: University of Toronto Press, 2017. https://doi.org/10.3138/9781487511791

Fenlon, Iain, and Richard Wistreich, ed. *The Cambridge History of Sixteenth Century Music*. Cambridge, UK: Cambridge University Press, 2019. https://doi.org/10.1017/9780511675874

Fenzi, Enrico. "Benet Garret, detto Cariteo." In *Atlante dei canzonieri del Quattrocento*, edited by Andrea Comboni and Tiziano Zanato, 348–57. Florence: Edizioni del Galluzzo, 2017.

Frick, Carole Collier. *Dressing Renaissance Florence: Families, Fortunes and Fine Clothing*. Baltimore, MD: Johns Hopkins University Press, 2002. https://doi.org/10.56021/9780801869396

Friedman, John Block. *Orpheus in the Middle Ages*. Cambridge, MA: Harvard University Press, 1970.

Gambassi, Osvaldo. *"Pueri cantores" nelle cattedrali d'Italia tra Medioevo ed età moderna*. Florence: Olschki, 1997.

Gandolfi, Giangiacomo. "Two Illustrated Horoscopes of the Italian Renaissance." *Paragone: Past and Present* 4 (2023): 45–69. https://doi.org/10.1163/24761168-00401002

Gansten, Martin. "Samarasiṃha and the Early Transmission of Tājika Astrology." *Journal of South Asian Intellectual History* 1 (2018): 79–132. https://doi.org/10.1163/25425552-12340005

Gerbino, Giuseppe. *Music and the Myth of Arcadia in Renaissance Italy*. Cambridge, UK: Cambridge University Press, 2009.

Gomez-Aranda, Mariano. "The Contribution of the Jews of Spain to the Transmission of Science in the Middle Ages." *European Review* 16.2 (2008): 169–81. https://doi.org/10.1017/s1062798708000161

Gouk, Penelope. "Raising Spirits and Restoring Souls: Early Modern Medical Explanations for Music's Effects." In *Hearing Cultures: Essays on Sound, Listening and Modernity*, edited by Veit Erlmann, 87–105. New York: Routledge, 2004. https://doi.org/10.5040/9781474214865.ch-005

——. "Harmony, Health and Healing: Music's Role in Early Modern Paracelsian Thought." In *The Practice of Reform in Health, Medicine, and Science, 1500–2000*, edited by Margaret Pelling and Scott Mandelbrote, 23–42. New York: Routledge, 2005. https://doi.org/10.4324/9781315237626-2

Grafton, Anthony. *Cardano's Cosmos: The Worlds and Works of a Renaissance Astrologer*. Cambridge, MA: Harvard University Press, 1999.

Green, Jonathan, Frank McIntyre, and Paul Needham. "The Shape of Incunable Survival and Statistical Estimation of Lost Editions." *The Papers of the Bibliographical Society of America* 105.2 (2011): 141–75.

Greenfield, Concetta Carestia. *Humanist and Scholastic Poetics, 1250–1500*. London: Associated University Presses, 1981.

Grendler, Paul F. *Schooling in Renaissance Italy: Literacy and Learning, 1300–1600*. Baltimore, MD: John Hopkins University Press, 1989.

———. *The Universities of the Italian Renaissance*. Baltimore, MD: John Hopkins University Press, 2002. https://doi.org/10.56021/9780801866319

Grieco, Allen J. *Food, Social Politics and the Order of Nature in Renaissance Italy*. Florence: I Tatti—The Harvard Centre for Italian Renaissance Studies, 2019.

Haar, James. "The Frontispiece of Gafori's *Practica Musicae* (1496)." *Renaissance Quarterly* 27.1 (1974): 7–22.

———. "The Courtier as Musician: Castiglione's View of the Science and Art of Music." In *Castiglione: The Ideal and the Real in Renaissance Culture*, edited by Robert Hanning and David Rosand, 165–90. New Haven, CT: Yale University Press, 1983.

Hankins, James, ed. *Renaissance Civic Humanism: Reappraisals and Reflections*. Cambridge, UK: Cambridge University Press, 2000. https://doi.org/10.1017/cbo9780511558474

———. "Humanism and Music in Italy." In *The Cambridge History of Fifteenth-Century Music*, edited by Anna Maria Busse Berger and Jesse Rodin, 231–62. Cambridge, UK: Cambridge University Press, 2015. https://doi.org/10.1017/cho9781139057813.020

———. *Virtue Politics: Soulcraft and Statecraft in Renaissance Italy*. Cambridge, MA: Harvard University Press, 2019. https://doi.org/10.4159/9780674242517

Havelock, Eric A. *The Muse Learns to Write: Reflections on Orality and Literacy from Antiquity to the Present*. London: Yale University Press, 1986.

Henry, Chriscinda. "Alter Orpheus: Masks of Virtuosity in Renaissance Portraits of Musical Improvisers." *Italian Studies* 71.2 (2016): 238–58. https://doi.org/10.1080/00751634.2016.1175721

Holford-Strevens, Leofranc. "Sirens in Antiquity and the Middle Ages." In *Music of the Sirens*, edited by Linda Phyllis Austern and Inna Naroditskaya, 16–51. Bloomington, IN: Indiana University Press, 2006.

Holmes, Olivia. *Assembling the Lyric Self: Authorship from Troubadour Song to Italian Poetry Book*. Minneapolis, MN: University of Minnesota Press, 2000.

Horden, Peregrine, ed. *Music as Medicine: The History of Music Therapy since Antiquity*. New York: Routledge, 2016. https://doi.org/10.4324/9781315090894

Howard, Peter. "A Landscape of Preaching: Bartolomeo Lapacci Rimbertini OP." In *Mendicant Cultures in the Medieval and Early Modern World: Word, Deed, and Image*, edited by Sally Cornelison, Nirit Ben Debby, and Peter Howard, 45–64. Turnout: Brepols, 2016. https://doi.org/10.1484/m.es-eb.5.108256

Huot, Sylvia. *From Song to Book: The Poetics of Writing in Old French Lyric and Lyrical Narrative Poetry*. Ithaca, NY: Cornell University Press, 1987.

Hyde, Thomas. *The Poetic Theology of Love: Cupid in Renaissance Literature*. Newark, DE: University of Delaware Press, 1986.

Ignesti, Alessandra. "Music Teaching in Montagnana: Organization, Methods, and Repertories." In *Music in Schools from the Middle Ages to the Modern Age*, edited by Paola Dessì, 171–94. Turnhout: Brepols, 2021.

Ilic, Ljubica. "In Pursuit of Echo: Sound, Space and the History of Self." In *Music, Myth and Story in Medieval and Early Modern Culture*, edited by Katherine Butler and Samantha Bassler, 156–68. Woodbridge: Boydell, 2019. https://doi.org/10.1017/9781787444409.010

Jarcho, Saul. "Galen's Six Non-Naturals: A Bibliographic Note and Translation." *Bulletin of the History of Medicine* 44.4 (1970): 372–77.

Jones, Ann Rosalind. "New Song for the Swallow: Ovid's Philomena in Tullia d'Aragona and Gaspara Stampa." In *Refiguring Woman: Perspectives on Gender and the Italian Renaissance*, edited by Marilyn Migiel and Juliana Schesari, 263–78. New York: Cornell University Press, 1991.

Kaborycha, Lisa. *A Corresponding Renaissance: Letters Written by Italian Women, 1375–1650*. New York: Oxford University Press, 2016.

Kallendorf, Craig W. "Cristoforo Landino's Aeneid and the Humanist Critical Tradition." *Renaissance Quarterly* 36.4 (1983): 519–46. https://doi.org/10.2307/2860732

——. *Printing Virgil: The Transformation of the Classics in the Renaissance*. Leiden: Brill, 2020. https://doi.org/10.1163/9789004421356

Kennedy, William J. *Jacopo Sannazaro and the Uses of Pastoral*. London: University Press of New England, 1983.

——. *Authorizing Petrarch*. New York: Cornell University Press, 1994.

——. "Citing Petrarch in Naples: The Politics of Commentary in Cariteo's Endimione." *Renaissance Quarterly* 55.4 (2002): 1196–221. https://doi.org/10.2307/1262101

——. *The Site of Petrarchism: Early Modern National Sentiment in Italy, France, and England*. Baltimore, MD: Johns Hopkins University Press, 2003.

Kent, Dale. *Cosimo de' Medici and the Florentine Renaissance: The Patron's Oeuvre*. New Haven, CT: Yale University Press, 2000.

Kirk, W. H. "The Syntax of the Gerund and the Gerundive, II." *Transactions and Proceedings of the American Philological Association* 76 (1945): 166–76.

Klapisch-Zuber, Christiane. *Women, Family and Ritual in Renaissance Italy*. Chicago, IL: University of Chicago Press, 1985.

Knecht, Ross. "'Invaded by the World': Passion, Passivity, and the Object of Desire in Petrarch's Rime sparse." *Comparative Literature* 63.3 (2011): 235–52. https://doi.org/10.1215/00104124-1335727

Kraye, Jill. "The Printing History of Aristotle in the Fifteenth Century: A Bibliographical Approach to Renaissance Philosophy." *Renaissance Studies* 9.2 (1995): 189–211. https://doi.org/10.1111/j.1477-4658.1995.tb00309.x

Kristeller, Paul Oskar. "Thomism and the Italian Thought of the Renaissance." In *Kristeller, Medieval Aspects of Renaissance Learning: Three Essays by Paul Oskar Kristeller*, edited and translated by Edward P. Mahoney, revised edition, 29–94. New York: Columbia University Press, 1992.

Krueger, Roberta L. "Introduction. Teach Your Children Well: Medieval Conduct Guides for Youths." In *Medieval Conduct Literature: An Anthology of Vernacular Guides to Behaviour for Youths with English Translations*, edited by Mark D. Johnston, ix–xxxiii. Toronto: University of Toronto Press, 2009. https://doi.org/10.3138/9781442697614-002

Kunkel, Wolfgang. *An Introduction to Roman Legal and Constitutional History*. Translated by J. M. Kelly. Oxford: Clarendon Press, 1966.

La Face Bianconi, Giuseppina, and Antonio Rossi. *Le Rime di Serafino Aquilano in Musica*. Florence: Olschki, 1999.

Leach, Elizabeth Eva. *Sung Birds: Music, Nature, and Poetry in the Later Middle Ages*. Ithaca, NY: Cornell University Press, 2007. https://doi.org/10.7591/9781501727573

Lemay, Richard. *Abu Ma'shar and Latin Aristotelianism in the Twelfth Century: The Recovery of Aristotle's Natural Philosophy through Arabic Astrology*. Beirut: American University of Beirut, 1962.

Lev, Efraim, and Zohar Amar. *Practical Materia Medica of the Medieval Eastern Mediterranean According to the Cairo Genizah*. Leiden: Brill, 2008. https://doi.org/10.1163/ej.9789004161207.i-621

LeVen, Pauline A. *Music and Metamorphosis in Graeco-Roman Thought*. Cambridge, UK: Cambridge University Press, 2020. https://doi.org/10.1017/9781316563069

Lines, David A. *The Dynamics of Learning in Early Modern Italy: Arts and Medicine at the University of Bologna*. Cambridge, MA: Harvard University Press, 2023. https://doi.org/10.2307/j.ctv32nxzh8

Lucentini, Paolo, and Vittoria Perrone Compagni. *I testi e i codici di Ermete nel Medioevo*. Florence: Edizioni Polistampa, 2001.

Luisi, Francesco. *La musica vocale nel Rinascimento: Del cantar a libro… o sulla viola: studi sulla musica vocale profana in Italia nei secoli XV e XVI*. Turin: ERI, 1977.

——, ed. *Laudario Giustinianeo. Vol. 1*. Venice: Edizioni Fondazione Levi, 1983.

MacCarthy, Evan. "'This is another and greater subject': Leonardo Bruni on Music." In *Renaissance Then and Now: Danza, musica e teatra per un nuovo Rinascimento*, edited by Stefano U. Baldassari, 101–09. Pisa: Edizioni ETS, 2014.

———. "The English Voyage of Pietrobono Burzelli." *Journal of Musicology* 35.4 (2018): 431–59. https://doi.org/10.1525/jm.2018.35.4.431

Mack, Peter. *A History of Renaissance Rhetoric*. Oxford: Oxford University Press, 2011. https://doi.org/10.1093/acprof:osobl/9780199597284.001.0001

MacNeil, Anne. "'A Voice Crying in the Wilderness': Issues of Authorship, Performance, and Transcription in the Italian Frottola." *The Italianist* 40.3 (2020): 463–76. https://doi.org/10.1080/02614340.2020.1901458

Malinverni, Massimo. "Un caso di incrocia fra tradizione autorizzata e letteratura populare: I 'sonetti e capitula' di Panfilo Sasso e un opuscolo sulle guerre di fine '400'." *Diacritica* 5.6 (2019): 45–53.

Mann, Nicholas. "From Laurel to Fig: Petrarch and the Structures of the Self." *Proceedings of the British Academy* 105 (2000): 17–42.

Marsh, David. "Cicero in the Renaissance." In *The Cambridge Companion to Cicero*, edited by Catherine Steel, 306–17. Cambridge, UK: Cambridge University Press, 2013. https://doi.org/10.1017/cco9781139048750.020

Martinez, Ronald L. "Mourning Laura in the Canzoniere: Lessons from Lamentations." *MLN* 118.1 (2003): 1–45. https://doi.org/10.1353/mln.2003.0025

Matthews-Grieco, Sara F., ed. *Erotic Cultures of Renaissance Italy*. Aldershot: Ashgate, 2010. https://doi.org/10.4324/9781315094380

McGee, Timothy J. "Cantare all'improvviso: Improvising to Poetry in Late Medieval Italy." In *Improvisation in the Arts of the Middle Ages and Renaissance*, edited by McGee, 31–70. Kalamazoo, MI: Medieval Institute Publications, Western Michigan University, 2003.

McLaughlin, Martin. "Biography and Autobiography in the Italian Renaissance." In *Mapping Lives: The Uses of Biography*, edited by Peter France and William St. Clair, 37–65. Oxford: Oxford University Press, 2002. https://doi.org/10.5871/bacad/9780197263181.003.0004

Meriani, Angelo. "Notes on the Prooemium in Musicam Plutarchi ad Titum Pyrrhynum by Carlo Valgulio (Brescia 1507)." *Greek and Roman Musical Studies* 3 (2015): 116–36. https://doi.org/10.1163/22129758-12341031

Moyer, Ann E. *Musica Scientia: Musical Scholarship in the Italian Renaissance*. Ithaca, NY: Cornell University Press, 1992. https://doi.org/10.7591/9781501737275

Musacchio, Jacqueline Marie. *Art, Marriage and Family in the Florentine Renaissance Palace*. New Haven, CT: Yale University Press, 2008.

Nazarian, Cynthia N. *Love's Wounds: Violence and the Politics of Poetry in Early Modern Europe*. New York: Cornell University Press, 2017. https://doi.org/10.7591/9781501708268

Nuovo, Angela. "Private Libraries in Sixteenth Century Italy." In *Early Printed Books as Material Objects*, edited by Bettina Wagner and Marcia Reed, 229–40. Berlin: De Gruyter Saur, 2010. https://doi.org/10.1515/9783110255300.229

———. *The Book Trade in the Italian Renaissance*. Translated by Lydia G. Cochrane. Leiden: Brill, 2013. https://doi.org/10.1163/9789004208490

O'Flaherty, Ciara. "Performative Constructions of Authorship in Italian Vernacular Verse 1470–1550." PhD dissertation, University of Sheffield, 2025.

O'Flaherty, Ciara, and Tim Shephard. "Commenting on Music in Juvenal's Sixth Satire." *Renaissance Studies* 38.4 (2024): 541–62. https://doi.org/10.1111/rest.12914

Palisca, Claude V. *Humanism in Italian Renaissance Musical Thought*. New Haven, CT: Yale University Press, 1985.

———. "Mode Ethos in the Renaissance." In *Essays in Musicology: A Tribute to Alvin Johnson*, edited by Lewis Lockwood and Edward Roesner, 126–39. Philadelphia: American Musicological Society, 1990.

Pantani, Italo. "Agostino Staccoli." In *Atlante dei canzonieri del Quattrocento*, edited by Andrea Comboni and Tiziano Zanato, 565–74. Florence: Edizioni del Galluzzo, 2017.

Parker, Holt N. "Renaissance Latin Elegy." In *A Companion to Roman Love Elegy*, edited by Barbara K. Gold, 476–90. Newark, DE: Wiley, 2012. https://doi.org/10.1002/9781118241165.ch29

Percival, W. Keith. "Grammar, Humanism and Renaissance Italy." *Mediterranean Studies* 16 (2007): 94–119. https://doi.org/10.2307/41167006

———. *Studies in Renaissance Grammar*. Abingdon: Routledge, 2016.

Pettegree, Andrew. *The Book in the Renaissance*. New Haven, CT: Yale University Press, 2010. https://doi.org/10.12987/9780300168358

Piperno, Franco. "Suoni della sovranità: Le cappelle musicali fra storiografia generale e storia della musica." In *Cappelle musicali fra corte, stato e chiesa nell'Italia del Rinascimento*, edited by Piperno, Gabriella Biagi Ravenni, and Andrea Chegai, 11–36. Florence: Olschki, 2007.

Pirrotta, Nino. "Music and Cultural Tendencies in 15th-Century Italy." *Journal of the American Musicological Society* 19 (1966): 127–61. https://doi.org/10.2307/830579

Pirrotta, Nino, and Elena Povoledo. *Music and Theatre from Poliziano to Monteverdi*. Translated by Karen Eales. Cambridge, UK: Cambridge University Press, 1982.

Plebani, Tiziana. *Alle donne che niente sanno: Mestieri femminili, alfabetizzazione e stampa nella Venezia del Rinascimento*. Venice: Marsilio, 2022.

Prins, Jacomien. *Echoes of an Invisible World: Marsilio Ficino and Francesco Patrizi on Cosmic Order and Music Theory*. Boston: Brill, 2015. https://doi.org/10.1163/9789004281769

Prizer, William F. "Una 'Virtù Molto Conveniente a Madonne': Isabella d'Este as a Musician." *Journal of Musicology* 17 (1999): 10–49. https://doi.org/10.2307/764010

———. "Cardinals and Courtesans: Secular Music in Rome, 1500–1520." In *Italy and the European Powers: The Impact of War, 1500–1530*, edited by Christine Shaw, 253–78. Boston: Brill, 2006. https://doi.org/10.1163/9789047409748_017

Puig, Josep. "The Transmission and Reception of Arabic Philosophy in Christian Spain (Until 1200)." In *The Introduction of Arabic Philosophy into Europe*, edited by Charles E. Butterworth and Blake Andrée Kessel, 7–20. New York: Brill, 1994. https://doi.org/10.1163/9789004451926_004

Raninen, Sanna. "No Country for Old Men? Aging and Men's Musicianship in Italian Renaissance Art." In *Music and Visual Culture in Renaissance Italy*, edited by Chriscinda Henry and Tim Shephard, 268–80. New York: Routledge, 2023. https://doi.org/10.4324/9781003029380-16

Rebecchini, Guido. "The Book Collection and Other Possessions of Baldassare Castiglione." *Journal of the Warburg and Courtauld Institutes* 61 (1998): 17–52. https://doi.org/10.2307/751243

Reynolds, Susan. "Medieval Law." In *The Medieval World*, edited by Peter Linehan and Janet L. Nelson, 485–502. New York: Routledge, 2001. https://doi.org/10.4324/9781315102511-34

Richardson, Brian. *Printing, Writers and Readers in Renaissance Italy*. Cambridge, UK: Cambridge University Press, 1999.

———. "*Recitato e Cantato*: The Oral Diffusion of Lyric Poetry in Sixteenth-Century Italy." In *Theatre, Opera, and Performance in Italy from the Fifteenth Century to the Present: Essays in Honour of Richard Andrews*, edited by Brian Richardson, Simon Gilson, and Catherine Keen (Leeds: Society for Italian Studies, 2004), 67–82.

———. "Isabella d'Este and the Social Uses of Books." *La Bibliofilía* 114.3 (2012): 293–326.

Reidemeister, Peter, ed. *Ottaviano Petrucci 1501–2001*, published as *Basler Jahrbuch für historische Musikpraxis* 25 (2001).

Rizzi, Andrea. "Editing and Translating Pliny in Renaissance Italy: Agency, Collaboration and Visibility." In *Issues in Translation Then and Now: Renaissance Theories and Translation Studies Today*, edited by Annet den Haan, Brenda Hosington, Marianne Pade, and Anne Wegener. *Renaessanceforum* 14 (2018): 117–38.

Robbins, Jillian Curry. "The Art of History: Livy's Ab Urbe Condita and the Visual Arts of the Early Italian Renaissance." PhD dissertation, Florida State University, 2004.

Roick, Matthias. *Pontano's Virtues: Aristotelian Moral and Political Thought in the Renaissance*. London: Bloomsbury, 2017. https://doi.org/10.5040/9781474281881

Rospocher, Massimo. "Songs of War: Historical and Literary Narratives of the 'Horrendous Italian Wars' (1494–1559)." In *Narrating War: Early Modern and Contemporary Perspectives*, edited by Marco Mondini and Massimo Rospocher, 79–98. Bologna: Mulino, 2013.

Rospocher, Massimo, and Rosa Salzberg. "An Evanescent Public Sphere: Voices, Spaces, and Publics in Venice during the Italian Wars." In *Beyond the Public Sphere: Opinions, Publics, Spaces in Modern Europe*, edited by Massimo Rospocher, 93–114. Bologna: Mulino, 2012.

Ross, Sarah Gwyneth. *Everyday Renaissances: The Quest for Cultural Legitimacy in Venice*. Cambridge, MA: Harvard University Press, 2016. https://doi.org/10.4159/9780674969957

Rossi, Antonio. *Serafino Aquilano e la poesia cortigiana*. Brescia: Morcelliana, 1980.

Rosso, Paolo. "La politica culturale dei Paleologi fra Quattro e Cinquecento e i suoi riflessi nell'editoria del marchesato." In *Trino e l'arte tipografica nel XVI secolo*, edited by Magda Balboni, 71–90. Novara: Interlinea, 2014.

Rubsamen, Walter H. *Literary Sources of Secular Music in Italy (ca.1500)*. New York: Da Capo Press, 1972.

Russo, Attilio. "Costantino Lascaris tra fama e oblio nel Cinquecento messinese." *Archivio Storico Messinese* 84–85 (2003–04): 5–87.

Saggio, Francesco. "Improvvisazione e scrittura nel tardo-quattrocento cortese: Lo strambotto al tempo di Leonardo Giustinian e Serafino Aquilano." In *Cantar ottave: Per una storia culturale dell'intonazione cantata in ottava rima*, edited by Maurizio Agamennone, 25–46. Lucca: LIM, 2017.

Salzberg, Rosa. "In the Mouths of Charlatans: Street Performers and the Dissemination of Pamphlets in Renaissance Italy." *Renaissance Studies* 24.5 (2010): 638–53. https://doi.org/10.1111/j.1477-4658.2010.00670.x

———. *Ephemeral City: Cheap Print and Urban Culture in Renaissance Venice*. Manchester: Manchester University Press, 2014. https://doi.org/10.7228/manchester/9780719087035.001.0001

Sansom, Helena. "Introduction. Women and Conduct in the Italian Tradition, 1470–1900: An Overview." In *Conduct Literature for and about Women in Italy 1470–1900: Prescribing and Describing Life*, edited by Helena Sanson and Francesco Lucioli, 9–38. Paris: Classiques Garnier, 2016.

Schmitt, Charles B. *Aristotle and the Renaissance*. Cambridge, MA: Harvard University Press, 1983.

Shailor, Barbara A. *The Medieval Book*. Toronto: University of Toronto Press, 1991.

Shapiro, Marianne. *From the Critic's Workbench: Essays in Literature and Semiotics*. Edited by Michael Shapiro. New York: Peter Lang, 2005.

Shephard, Tim. *Echoing Helicon: Music, Art and Identity in the Este Studioli*. Oxford: Oxford University Press, 2014. https://doi.org/10.1093/acprof:oso/9780199936137.001.0001

———. "Musical Classicisms in Italy Before the Madrigal." *Music and Letters* 101.4 (2020): 690–712. https://doi.org/10.1093/ml/gcaa047

———. "24. Venus." In *The Museum of Renaissance Music*, edited by Vincenzo Borghetti and Tim Shephard, 119–24. Turnhout: Brepols, 2023. https://doi.org/10.1484/m.em-eb.5.119587

———. "The Domestic Life of the Syrinx." In *The Media of Secular Music in the Medieval and Early Modern Period*, edited by Vincenzo Borghetti and Alexandros Maria Hatzikiriakos, 217–38. New York: Routledge, 2024. https://doi.org/10.4324/9781003194637-14

Shephard, Tim, and Patrick McMahon. "Foolish Midas: Representing Musical Judgement and Moral Judgement in Italy c.1520." In *Music, Myth and Story in Medieval and Early Modern Culture*, edited by Katherine Butler and Samantha Bassler, 87–104. Woodbridge: Boydell, 2019. https://doi.org/10.1017/9781787444409.006

Shephard, Tim, and Charlotte Hancock. "Looking Up Music in Two 'Encyclopedias' Printed in 1501." *Renaissance Studies* 38.4 (2024): 564–95. https://doi.org/10.1111/rest.12915

Shephard, Tim, and Melany Rice. "Giovanni Pontano Hears the Street Soundscape of Naples." *Renaissance Studies* 38.4 (2024): 519–41. https://doi.org/10.1111/rest.12913

Shephard, Tim, Sanna Raninen, Serenella Sessini, and Laura Ștefănescu, *Music in the Art of Renaissance Italy 1420–1540*. London: Harvey Miller, 2020.

Shumaker, Wayne. *The Occult Sciences in the Renaissance: A Study in Intellectual Patterns*. Berkeley, CA: University of California Press, 1979.

Siraisi, Nancy G. "The Music of Pulse in the Writings of Italian Academic Physicians (Fourteenth and Fifteenth Centuries)." *Speculum* 50.4 (1975): 689–710. https://doi.org/10.2307/2855474

———. *Medieval and Early Renaissance Medicine: An Introduction to Knowledge and Practice*. Chicago, IL: University of Chicago Press, 1990. https://doi.org/10.7208/chicago/9780226761312.001.0001

Skafte Jensen, Minna. "Performance." In *A Companion to Ancient Epic*, edited by John Miles Foley, 45–54. Oxford: Blackwell, 2005. https://doi.org/10.1002/9780470996614.ch5

Stevens, Kevin M. "Books Fit for a Portuguese Queen: The Lost Library of Catherine of Austria and the Milan Connection (1540)." In *Documenting the Early Modern Book World: Inventories and Catalogues in Manuscript and Print*, ed. Malcolm Walsby and Natasha Constantinidou, 86–116. Leiden: Brill, 2013. https://doi.org/10.1163/9789004258907_005

Sturm-Maddox, Sara. *Petrarch's Laurels*. Philadelphia, PN: University of Pennsylvania Press, 1992.

Strunk, Oliver, and Leo Treitler, ed. *Source Readings in Music History*. Revised edition. New York: Norton, 1998.

Sullivan, J. P. *Martial: The Unexpected Classic*. Cambridge, UK: Cambridge University Press, 1991. https://doi.org/10.1017/cbo9780511582639

Sulprizio, Chiara. *Gender and Sexuality in Juvenal's Rome: Satire 2 and Satire 6*. Norman, OK: University of Oklahoma Press, 2020.

Syson, Luke, and Dora Thornton. *Objects of Virtue: Art in Renaissance Italy*. London: British Museum, 2001.

Thorndike, Lynn. "A Roman Astrologer as a Historical Source: Julius Firmicus Maternus." *Classical Philology* 8.4 (1913): 415–35.

———. *A History of Magic and Experimental Science*. Vol. 1. New York: Columbia University Press, 1923.

Thornton, Dora. *The Scholar in his Study: Ownership and Experience in Renaissance Italy*. New Haven, CT: Yale University Press, 1997.

Tomlinson, Gary. *Music in Renaissance Magic: Towards a Historiography of Others*. Chicago, IL: The University of Chicago Press, 1993.

Ventura, Iolanda. "Translating, Commenting, Retranslating: Some Considerations on the Latin Translations of the Pseudo-Aristotelian *Problemata* and Their Readers." In *Science Translated: Latin and Vernacular Translations of Scientific Treatises in Medieval Europe*, edited by Michèle Goyens, Pieter de Leemans, and An Smets, 123–54. Leuven: Leuven University Press, 2008. https://doi.org/10.2307/j.ctt9qf0d5.12

Versnel, H. S. "The Festival for Bona Dea and the Thesmophoria." *Greece and Rome* 39.1 (1992): 31–55. https://doi.org/10.1017/s0017383500023974

Vickers, Nancy J. "Diana Described: Scattered Woman and Scattered Rhymes." *Critical Inquiry* 8.2 (1981): 265–79. https://doi.org/10.1086/448154

Voss, Angela. "The Music of the Spheres: Marsilio Ficino and Renaissance Harmonia." *Culture and Cosmos* 2.2 (1998): 16–38.

———. "Diligentia et divina sorte: Oracular Intelligence in Marsilio Ficino's Astral Magic." In *Innovation in Esotericism from the Renaissance to the Present*, edited by Georgiana D. Hedesan and Tim Rudbøg, 33–62. London: Macmillan, 2021. https://doi.org/10.1007/978-3-030-67906-4_2

Walker, D. P. "Orpheus the Theologian and Renaissance Platonists." *Journal of the Warburg and Courtauld Institutes* 16.1–2 (1953): 100–20. https://doi.org/10.2307/750229

———. *Spiritual and Demonic Magic: From Ficino to Campanella*. London: Warburg Institute, 1958.

Walsby, Malcolm. "Booklists and their meaning." In *Documenting the Early Modern Book World: Inventories and Catalogues in Manuscript and Print*, ed. Malcolm Walsby and Natasha Constantinidou, 1–24. Leiden: Brill, 2013. https://doi.org/10.1163/9789004258907_002

Ward, John O. "Renaissance Commentators on Ciceronian Rhetoric." In *Renaissance Eloquence: Studies in the Theory and Practice of Renaissance Rhetoric*, edited by James J. Murphy, 126–73. Berkeley, CA: University of California Press, 1983.

Warden, John. "Orpheus and Ficino." in *Orpheus: The Metamorphoses of a Myth*, edited by John Warden, 85–110. Toronto: University of Toronto Press, 1982.

Warner, Christopher J. "Quick Eloquence in the Late Renaissance: Agostino Dati's 'Elegantiolae'." *Humanistica Lovaniensia* 61 (2012): 65–240.

Webb, Jennifer D. "All Is Not Fun and Games: Conversation, Play, and Surveillance at the Montefeltro Court in Urbino." *Renaissance studies* 26.3 (2012): 417–40. https://doi.org/10.1111/j.1477-4658.2011.00745.x

Weber, Henri. "Deux théoriciens de la facétie: Pontano et Castiglione." *Réforme, Humanisme, Renaissance* 7 (1978): 74–78. https://doi.org/10.3406/rhren.1977.1062

Welch, Evelyn. *Shopping in the Renaissance: Consumer Cultures in Italy 1400–1600*. New Haven, CT: Yale University Press, 2005.

Westman, Robert S. *The Copernican Question: Prognostication, Skepticism and Celestial Order*. Berkeley, CA: University of California Press, 2011. https://doi.org/10.1525/9780520948167

Willan, Anne, and Mark Cherniavsky. *The Cookbook Library: Four Centuries of the Cooks, Writers, and Recipes That Made the Modern Cookbook*. Berkeley, CA: University of California Press, 2012. https://doi.org/10.1525/9780520352612

Williams, Steven J. *The Secret of Secrets: The Scholarly Career of a Pseudo-Aristotelian Text in the Latin Middle Ages*. Ann Arbor: University of Michigan Press, 2003. https://doi.org/10.3998/mpub.17841

Wilson, Blake. "The Cantastorie/Canterino/Cantimbanco as Musician." *Italian Studies* 71 (2016): 154–70. https://doi.org/10.1080/00751634.2016.1175714

———. *Singing to the Lyre in Renaissance Italy*. Cambridge, UK: Cambridge University Press, 2020. https://doi.org/10.1017/9781108768887

———. *Apollo Volgare: Serafino Aquilano and the Performance of Vernacular Poetry in Renaissance Italy*. Lucca: Libreria musicale italiana, 2024.

Wood, Rega. "Walter Burley's *Physics* Commentaries." *Franciscan Studies* 44 (1984): 275–327. https://doi.org/10.1353/frc.1984.0002

Yinger, Melissa A. "Echo-Critical Poetic Narcissisms: Being Transformed in Petrarch, Ronsard, and Shakespeare." PhD dissertation, University of California Santa Cruz, 2016.

Young, Abigail Anne. "Plays and Players: The Latin Terms for Performance." *Records of Early English Drama* 9.2 (1984): 56–72.

Zanovello, Giovanni. "'In the Church and in the Chapel': Music and Devotional Spaces in the Florentine Church of Santissima Annunziata." *Journal of the American Musicological Society* 67.2 (2014): 379–428. https://doi.org/10.1525/jams.2014.67.2.379

———. "'You will take this sacred book': The Musical Strambotto as a Learned Gift." *Journal of the Royal Musicological Association* 141.1 (2016): 1–26. https://doi.org/10.1080/02690403.2016.1151230

———. "The Frottola in the Veneto." In *A Companion to Music in Sixteenth-Century Venice*, edited by Katelijne Schiltz, 395–414. Leiden: Brill, 2018. https://doi.org/10.1163/9789004358300_016

Zolli, Daniel M., and Christopher Brown. "Bell on Trial: The Struggle for Sound after Savonarola." *Renaissance Quarterly* 72.1 (2019): 54–96. https://doi.org/10.1017/rqx.2018.6

Zorzi, Andrea. "Justice." In *The Italian Renaissance State*, edited by Andrea Gamberini and Isabella Lazzarini, 490–514. Cambridge, UK: Cambridge University Press, 2012. https://doi.org/10.1017/cbo9780511845697.028

Index

academies 128, 212–213, 259
Accursius (Accorso da Bagnolo) 296–298
Achilles 67, 259–260, 288
acoustics 123, 141, 144–147, 161, 196–197, 199–200, 205, 295, 297
actor. *See* player (theatrical)
Aeetes 290
Aeschines 210–211
Aglaophemus 265, 328
Albertino da Lessona 78, 81, 187, 197, 207, 228, 268
Albertus Magnus 77, 80, 189
Albubather (Abu Bakr al-Hassan ibn al-Khasib) 8–9, 99, 103, 105
Albucasis (Abu al-Qasim Khalaf ibn al-Abbas al-Zahrawi) 78
Albumasar (Abu Maʿshar al-Balkhi) 105, 111
Alcibiades 58
Alexander of Aphrodisias 9, 233
Alexander of Villedieu 32, 35–36, 39
Alexander the Great 54, 67, 250–251
Alexander VI, Pope 208
Alfonso II, King of Naples 53–55, 72
Alfonso X, King of Castile 103
Alighieri, Dante 45, 134–135, 258
Ali ibn Ridwan 79
Amaryllis 61–62
Amaseo, Gregorio 207, 209
Amphion 43, 241, 256, 261–264, 275–276, 327–329
Anagnostes 61
Andrelini, Publio Fausto 121–122, 128, 131–132, 136, 140–141, 144–145, 167
Antiope 263
Antonio di Guido 44–45
Antonius Andreas 190

Apollo 49, 64, 113, 150, 174, 176, 242, 255–256, 262, 266, 287, 306, 328
Apollonius of Tyana 274, 277, 284, 292, 329
Apuleius 8, 17, 228, 247–248, 254–256
 Asinus aureus 8, 247, 249–250, 253–254
 Florida 254, 256
Arcadia 61, 260
architecture 16, 23
Argives 263
Argonautica Orphica 265–266
Argonauts 265, 276, 328
Arion 43, 174, 251, 262, 264
Aristophanes 17
Aristotle 8–9, 17, 43, 51–52, 59–60, 68, 77–78, 88, 183, 186–194, 196–197, 200–202, 205–206, 212, 255, 267, 276, 306, 310–311, 324
 De anima 184, 189–190, 192–194, 197–200, 202, 205, 306, 311, 324
 De caelo et mundo 190, 192, 205, 307
 De generatione et corruptione 190
 Metaphysics 190, 192, 200, 205
 Physics 190–192, 205
 Politics 59, 255
 Posterior Analytics 192
 Problemata (pseudo-Aristotle) 8–9, 17, 77, 88, 187, 197–198, 233, 276
 Regum regimine (pseudo-Aristotle) 54, 67, 69, 117
Aristoxenus 213
Arnaldus de Villa Nova 17, 80
Aron, Pietro 19
astrology 7, 10, 31, 99–104, 109, 111–114, 119, 185, 216–217, 270, 303–304, 309, 326
 birth chart 102
 horoscope 13, 105, 303–304

prognostication 13, 18
stars, the 6, 32, 82, 99–101, 103, 115, 166, 177
zodiac 104–105
Athena 58
Athens 285
Augustine, Saint 39, 52
Aulus Gellius 54, 61, 117, 251
Averroes (Ibn Rushd) 78, 190
Avicenna (Ibn Sina) 17, 78–79, 98, 198

Bacchanalia 239–240
Bacchus 240, 265, 308, 328. *See also* Dionysus
banquet. *See* feast
Barbaro, Ermolao 75, 271
Bartholomew of Messina 198
Bartolo da Sassoferrato 295–296
Bassino, Giovanni Antonio 12, 77, 80, 97
Beccadelli, Antonio (Il Panormita) 55
Bembo, Pietro 2, 56, 122, 125, 310
  Gli Asolani 2, 56
  Le cose vulgari di messer Francesco Petrarcha 122, 133, 140, 156, 167
Benedetti, Vincenzo 36
Bentivoglio family
  Bentivoglio, Anton 275
  Bentivoglio, Giovanni 100
Bergamo 19
Beroaldo, Filippo 209, 229, 247–256, 258, 268, 274
Besicken, Johann 11, 121, 126, 133, 140, 156, 168, 207
birds 147–149, 151–156, 176, 178, 328
  nightingale 151–154, 180
  swallow 151
  swan 150
  turtledove 150–151
Boethius 116, 195, 206, 267, 320
Boiardo, Matteo Maria 121–122, 127, 140, 142–143, 146, 148–149, 151, 153–154, 156–157, 159–160, 163, 167, 169–173, 175–176, 179, 247

Bologna 128, 183–184, 186, 192, 209, 229, 272, 274, 285, 288, 296
Bona Dea 237–240
Bonaventura da Brescia 5, 32, 35
Bonisoli, Ognibene 211, 213–217, 219–220, 222–226, 324
Bonvesin de la Riva 29, 31, 51, 53, 73
Borghi, Pietro 32
Borgia, Cesare 57
Bracciolini, Poggio 39, 57
Brandolini, Raffaele 47, 60–61, 206–207, 209, 305
Brennus 290
Brescia 35, 57, 124, 126–127, 209, 230, 271–272
Briseis 259
Britannico family
  Britannico, Angelo 35, 78, 228
  Britannico, Giacomo 228
  Britannico, Giovanni 230, 233, 236, 238, 240, 242–246, 254, 260
Bruni, Leonardo 16, 29, 211, 226
Burley, Walter 187, 189–191
Burzelli, Pietrobono 44
Burzio, Nicolò 19, 90
Bussi, Giovanni Andrea 247, 271

Caiado, Henrique 121–122, 128, 131, 140–142, 146, 167, 173–174
Caius Gracchus 225
Calderini, Domizio 229–230, 234, 241–242, 244, 259, 261–262, 275
Calfurnio, Giovanni 229
Calvo, Andrea 16
Cambyses 289
Campano, Giovanni Antonio 272
Canius 279, 329–330
Canossa, Ludovico 57, 69, 117
Cantalicio, Giovanni Battista 32, 49
cantare. See singing
canto. See song
Cara, Marchetto 34, 126, 305
Castiglione, Baldassare 2, 16–18, 53, 56–58, 60–61, 63–64, 66–69, 117–118, 206, 270, 288, 305

Catherine, Queen of Portugal 15–17
Cato 16, 53, 209
Celsus 232–233
Cesena 127, 272
Chigi, Agostino 102
chironomy 101
Cicero 16–17, 38–40, 47, 52, 107, 183, 202, 207, 209–227, 267, 307, 324
  De claris oratoribus (aka *Brutus*) 210
  De optimo genere oratorum (pseudo-Cicero) 210
  De oratore 38, 183, 210–214, 216–227, 307–308, 324
  De partitione oratio 210
  De petitione consulatus (pseudo-Cicero) 210
  Epistulae ad familiares 16
  Orator 17, 210
  Philippics 209
  Rhetorica ad Herennium (aka *Rhetorica nova*) 45, 210, 227
  Rhetorica vetus 210
  Topica 210
Ciolek, Erazm 207–208
clapping 69, 109, 234
Claudius Claudianus 132, 134, 228, 256, 262
Clement V, Pope 80
Cleopatra 292
Clerico, Ubertino 229, 259–260
cognition 90, 188, 202–204, 206, 307
Colli, Vincenzo (Il Calmeta) 2
Colocci, Angelo 176
Columella 232–233
Commenduno, Leonardo 207–208
commonplace book 45–47, 80, 242, 269
complexion 21, 82–85, 87, 92, 94–96, 99, 308–309
Concoreggio, Giovanni de 79, 83, 96–98, 118
conduct literature 6–7, 29–30, 52, 54, 73, 75, 113, 116–118
confession 6
contracts 34, 44, 297

Corpus Juris Civilis 184–185, 295
Cortenese, Jacopo 129
Cortesi, Paolo 2, 206, 270
Corybantes 256, 283, 294
Costa, Stefano 60
counterpoint. *See* polyphony
Ctesiphus 210
Cupid 64
Curialti, Pietro 198
Cybele 240, 283, 308
Cyrus, King of Persia 274, 281, 289

Damon 213
Damophyle 209, 280
dance 33, 36, 49, 66, 75–77, 98–99, 108–109, 112, 115, 117, 145, 204, 236, 248, 252, 275, 283, 285, 287, 291–292, 304–305
Da Tempo, Antonio 151
Dati, Agostino 32, 36, 42, 46
deafness 195, 201, 297
Degli Allegri, Francesco 99, 101
Della Barba, Zanobi 45
Della Fonte, Bartolomeo 229
Della Rovere, Domenico, Cardinal 209
Demetrius 280
Demosthenes 211
Des Prez, Josquin 12
devotion 6–7, 13, 18, 22, 24, 36
Diana 280
dictionary 43, 54, 243, 252–254
Dio Chrysostom 250
Diodorus Siculus 256, 265
Diogenes Laertius 266, 327–328
Dionysiodorus 234–235, 277
Dionysus 265, 285. *See also* Bacchus
Dioscorides 75
disability 38, 297. *See also* deafness
Dominicans 10, 189
Dominic of Flanders 189–190, 192, 311
Domitian 244
Donati, Girolamo 207–208

Donatus, Aelius 29, 35–37, 40, 42, 51, 53, 275, 305
   Ars maior (pseudo-Donatus) 37
   De partibus orationis ars minor 37
   Ianua 37, 53, 305
Dubravius, Roderich 32, 46–47

ear 80, 84, 130, 164–166, 193–196, 198, 204, 206, 218–221, 226, 233, 257, 307, 319
Echo 144–147, 151, 156, 161, 178–180, 306
Egypt 265, 328
eloquence 37, 40, 42, 44, 45, 58, 63, 106, 107, 108, 109, 110, 112, 117, 188, 210, 219, 265, 269, 270, 276.
   See also oratory; *See also* rhetoric
Emanuel I, King of Portugal 128
emotions 21, 47, 75, 95, 99, 136, 141, 143, 148–149, 166, 168–171, 182, 197, 203–204, 206, 223–224, 305
Engel, Johannes 102, 112
Epicles 280
Equicola, Mario 77, 92
Eratosthenes 242, 260
Este family
   Este, Ercole I d' 127, 298
   Este, Ippolito d' 108
   Este, Isabella d' 15, 17–18, 92, 108, 126
Eugenius IV, Pope 34

Faelli, Benedetto 29, 77, 99, 121, 140, 167, 207, 209, 275, 278, 329
Faienza 121, 129
farming 74, 101
feast 47–48, 55, 57, 61, 70–72, 88, 118–119, 235, 255, 282
Fedele, Cassandra 127
Ferdinand I, King of Naples 271
Ferrara 33, 46, 127, 184, 296
Ferrari, Giovanni Matteo 77, 79, 91
Ferrari, Scipione 229
festival 70, 284–285, 287, 293–294
Festus 224, 253–254
fever 96–97

fibula (buckle) 231–233, 245
Ficino, Marsilio 29, 31, 61, 77, 82, 90–91, 93–94, 97–99, 101, 113–116, 119, 257, 263–265
   Argonautica Orphica, translation of 265
   Consiglio contro la pestilenza 97
   Corpus Hermeticum, translation of 265–266
   De vita libri tres 31, 82, 90, 93, 99
   De amore 61
Fieschi, Stefano 32, 46
Filelfo, Francesco 151, 272, 274
Fiore di virtù 30, 55, 76–77
Flavio, Francesco 124–125
Florentius de Faxolis 270
foodstuffs 22, 81, 83, 89–90, 92, 96, 118
   alliums 87–88
      chive 87–88
      garlic 87–89
      leek 87–88, 94, 309
      onion 88–89
   almond 89
   borage 89, 94
   eggs 89
   honey 89
   nuts 89, 309
   pomegranate 89
   rosemary 89, 309
   thyme 89
Forman, Simon 101
Fortune 159–160, 169
France 48, 80, 185
François de Bourdon 207–208
Fregoso, Federico 57, 61, 64

Gafori, Franchino 2, 18–19, 34, 51, 116, 270
   Fioretti di musica 18
   Practica musicae 2, 50
Gaius Duilius 71
Gaius (Roman jurist) 295
Galatea 60–62
Galen 24, 78–79, 82–86, 310

Gareth, Benedetto (Il Cariteo) 121–122, 133, 140, 156, 167
gaudium (joy) 21, 83, 96–97, 99, 112, 116, 118, 148, 153, 159, 169, 171, 204–205, 221, 248–249, 255, 308
Gauls 290–291
Gaurico, Luca 99–100, 112
Gaza, Teodoro 197
Genoa 130
Gerard of Cremona 80
Gesualdo, Giovanni Andrea 151
Giles of Rome 12, 187, 189–190, 200
Giolito, Gabriele 30
Giustiniani, Leonardo 272
Gomez, Gonzalo 15
Gonzaga family 70, 80
grammar 10, 15–16, 18, 31, 34–40, 42–49, 51, 53, 72, 119, 183, 185, 211–212, 215–217, 228, 230, 304–305, 326
Grapaldi, Francesco Maria 29, 31, 52, 54, 61, 71, 118, 268, 280
Guarini, Battista 46
Guarino da Verona 17, 33, 36, 40, 238, 261, 272
  Erotemata 17
  Grammaticales regulae 36
Gupalatino, Niccolò 198

Haly Abbas (Ali ibn-'al-Abbas al-Majusi) 78
Hannibal 74, 289
harmony 21, 32, 39, 92–94, 114, 130, 149, 196–197, 200, 205, 212, 214, 243, 248, 252, 254, 257–258, 283, 303, 307
health 6, 18, 22, 31, 53, 77, 81–84, 87, 91, 93, 95, 98–99, 114, 116, 119, 195, 232, 303, 308
  catarrh 84–85, 89, 91
  coryza 84–86
  diet 6, 81–82, 86–87, 90, 92–93, 102, 303, 309
  digestion 81, 98, 308
  humours 21, 32, 74, 82–83, 89, 94, 118–119, 203

medicine 13, 16, 21, 79–82, 92, 96, 100, 159, 183–186, 188
  non-naturals 83
  qualities 32, 83–86, 88–89, 97, 104
  regimen 6, 29, 31, 53, 79, 81–83, 86, 90–92, 98–99, 103, 303
  surgery 79, 185
hearing 1, 3, 5, 7, 44–45, 72, 74, 76, 84, 86, 105, 116, 138, 159, 162, 188–189, 192–198, 200–202, 204, 206, 221, 289, 300, 308, 317–321
Helenius Acron 252, 274
Heraclides Ponticus 263
Hermes Trismegistus 265, 328
Herodotus 251, 264
Hippias 211
Hippocrates 78
history 6, 24, 128–129, 188, 266, 268–270, 276, 283–284, 288
Holy Roman Empire 208
Homer 163–164, 180–181, 255
  Iliad 255
  Odyssey 164
Horace 63, 156, 158, 229, 252, 254, 262, 265, 268, 274, 276, 279, 281, 283–284
  Ars poetica 229, 252, 265
  Odes 158, 262
hornbook 15, 34
Hothby, John 38
humanism 16, 20, 40, 47, 50, 55, 58, 60–61, 79, 117, 130–131, 134, 185–186, 188–190, 192, 202, 223, 227, 236, 246–247, 256, 267, 269, 305, 310
Hyagnis 254
Hyginus 242–243, 261
Hypnerotomachia Poliphili 2

imagination 195, 197, 203, 205–206, 321
improvisation 32, 45, 47, 60, 128–129, 131–132, 139, 284, 304
inventories 14–18, 41, 56, 118
Isidore of Seville 39, 64, 267
Ismenias 234–235, 242, 277–278, 280

Jean de Jandun 187–190, 192
Jensen, Nicolaus 41, 55
Jerome, Saint 52, 272
Johannes de Sacrobosco 17, 32, 34
   Algorismus 34
   De sphaera mundi 17
John Duns Scotus 187, 189–190
Jove 263, 328
Juba II, King of Mauritania 75
Julius Caesar 209
Julius Firmicus Maternus 100
   Mathesis 100
Julius II, Pope 100
Juno 283
Jupiter 104, 106, 107, 108, 110, 111, 112, 113, 114, 116, 119, 258, 282, 304. *See also* Zeus
Justinian, Roman Emperor 295
Juvenal 10, 12, 14, 16–17, 25–26, 78, 90, 183, 228–231, 234–237, 243–247, 259, 283, 294, 307

Laberius 68
Lactantius 265
Lamia 280–281
Landino, Cristoforo 81, 229, 242, 256–258, 263–266, 271, 275, 327, 330
   commentary on Dante's *Commedia* 258
   commentary on Virgil's *Aeneid* 256, 258, 264
   commentary on Virgil's *Eclogues* 263
   translation of Pliny's *Naturalis historia* 78, 81, 87, 90, 92, 228, 242, 268, 275, 277, 279, 288, 330–331
landscape 123, 129, 140–149, 153, 156, 161, 165–167, 174–179, 182, 306
Lascaris, Constantine 17, 53
laughter 69, 98, 158, 161–163
Lauro, Antonio 9, 103
law 6, 24–25, 128, 183–188, 218, 251–252, 293, 295–300, 306, 309, 328
Leoniceno, Niccolò 79

Leo X, pope 126
Leto, Pomponio 128, 259
Linus 241, 264, 266, 275, 327–329
Lithuania 209
Livy 71, 74, 99, 109, 239–240, 246, 268, 270–272, 281–284, 288–291
logic 24, 185–186, 208, 216–217, 303
Loredan, Leonardo 208
Lucian 55
Lucretius 243, 246, 272
luxuria (lust) 36, 48, 61–62, 74, 76, 89, 116–118, 203–204, 206, 236–239, 294, 300
Lycurgus 248–249, 285, 287

Macrobius 17, 78, 93, 237–238, 246–249
   Saturnalia 237–238, 247
   Somnium Scipionis 17
Madiis, Francesco de 30, 36
maenads 237, 239–240, 266, 276
magic 43
Maimonides (Rabi Moysi) 79, 95, 97
Mancinelli, Antonio 53, 229–230, 275
Manfred, King of Sicily 9, 104
Mantua 33, 35, 211
Manuel I, King of Portugal 208
Manuzio, Aldo 17, 33, 40–41, 48, 52–53, 56, 78–79, 133, 140, 156, 167, 188, 207, 228, 268, 274
Mark Antony 209, 291
marriage 38, 157, 210, 297. *See also* wedding
Mars 104–105, 107–110, 113–114, 283
Marsyas 254, 256, 275
Martial 17, 60, 62, 229, 232–234, 246, 254, 268, 274–275, 281, 283, 292, 294, 307
Martinus de Amsterdam 54
Massaria, Domenico 198
mathematics 100, 185, 212, 215–217, 326
Mathias Moravus 11, 54
mattinata 66, 299
Maturanzio, Francesco 209

Maximilian I, Holy Roman Emperor 202, 208
Mazzolini, Silvestro 10, 13
medicine. *See* health: medicine
melancholy 83, 91, 96, 115
memento mori 54, 62
memory 39, 45–47, 51, 81, 85–86, 93, 119, 160, 163, 182, 201, 203, 206, 213, 304
Mercury 55, 93, 104–114, 116, 119, 242, 260, 262, 266, 275–276, 304, 328
Merula, Giorgio 230, 232, 241, 259, 275
metaphysics 185–186
metrics 37, 39, 49, 51, 226, 304
Milan 19, 29, 126, 209, 230, 270, 274
Minuziano, Alessandro 121, 208–209
Misinta, Bernardino 121, 124, 126, 132, 156, 167, 207
modes 84, 116, 263, 280
Mona Dianora 33
Moreto, Antonio 40
Moro, Domenico 95
Muscovy 209
Muses 243, 255, 257–258, 260, 328
  Urania 104, 266, 327–328
musical instruments 43–44, 67, 76, 96, 111, 195–196, 238, 240–244, 246, 256, 307, 322
  aera 283
  aulos 232, 234–236, 253
  cithara 40–41, 44, 64, 94, 108, 127, 224, 232, 241–244, 255–256, 260–266, 275–276, 292–294, 328–329
  cornu 42, 117, 231, 237, 283, 288–290
  cymbala 283
  fistula 44, 117, 225
  harp 241
  lira da braccio 60, 131, 273
  litus 231
  lute 94, 131, 205
  lyre 44, 47, 50, 60–61, 68, 93–94, 122, 127, 130–131, 134, 174, 223–224, 227, 240–241, 243–244, 256, 258, 260–262, 264, 276, 281, 292, 294, 307, 322–323
  organa 241, 243
  psaltria 281
  rotta 108
  sambuca 44
  simphonia 44
  tibia 44, 71, 235–238, 242, 248, 252–254, 285, 322–323, 329
  trombone 57
  trumpet 43–44, 58–59, 67, 72, 118, 130, 288–289, 300, 331
  tuba 58, 71, 118, 288
  tympana 283
  viella 131
  viola 57–58, 60, 65

Naples 11, 19, 53–54, 72, 75, 125, 132, 184, 208, 259, 271
Narcissus 144–145, 147
Negri, Francesco 49
Nereus 247
Nero 87–88, 235, 292–294
Nicholas of Lyra 54
Nicomachus 235, 242, 277, 325–326
non-verbal 297
notary 18, 44
Numa, King of Rome 281
nuns 299–300

Obrecht, Jacob 12
Odysseus 75, 164
oratory 39, 208–213, 215, 218–219, 221, 223, 225–227, 301, 307, 309, 325–326. *See also* eloquence; *See also* rhetoric
Order of St John of Jerusalem 208
Orpheus 43, 173–174, 176–178, 238, 242, 255–256, 260–262, 264–266, 275–276, 306, 309, 327–329
Ottoman Empire 208
Ovid 6, 16–17, 52, 127, 140, 144–145, 167, 210, 228–229, 234, 246, 259–260, 267, 276
  Ars amatoria 127

Heroides 16, 259, 262
Metamorphoses 16–17, 144, 234
Pachel, Leonardo 126
Pallas 251, 285
Pallavicino, Gaspar 68
Pan 144, 249–250, 275
Paris 128, 188, 202
Pasqualigo, Pietro 207–208
passions 83, 84, 99, 305. *See also* emotions
Paul II, Pope 271
Peleus 64
perception 7, 84–85, 202, 204
Periander 264
Perotti, Niccolò 17–18, 33, 35–36, 40, 43, 45, 48, 228–229, 254, 268, 281
  Cornucopiae 17–18, 254, 281
  Rudimenta grammatices 17, 33, 35, 40, 45
Perses 290
Persius 78, 228–230, 238, 246, 294
Pesenti, Michele 34, 50
Petrarca, Francesco 122, 133, 140, 151–152, 156, 167
Petrucci, Ottaviano 5, 50
Philolaus 265, 293, 327–328
Philomena 151–156, 178–180
philosophy 6, 20, 24, 30, 80, 94, 101, 158, 183, 185–188, 190, 192, 205, 214–216, 226, 269, 300, 306, 326
  moral philosophy 185–186, 214, 226, 269
  natural philosophy 6, 20, 24, 183, 185–188, 190, 192, 205, 300, 306
Philostratus of Athens 17, 268, 273–274, 277–280, 284, 292, 329
Phocylides 53, 72
physiology 188
Piccolomini, Enea Silvio 29
Pico della Mirandola family
  Pico della Mirandola, Gianfrancesco 188, 202
  Pico della Mirandola, Giovanni Pico 202

Pietro d'Abano 189, 197–198, 205, 275
Pio, Giovanni Battista 207, 209, 268, 272, 285
pitch 87, 195, 197, 205–206, 213, 223, 225, 227, 307, 323
plainchant 1, 5
planets/spheres 92, 102–113, 116, 119, 205, 257–258, 303, 307
  harmony of the spheres 205, 257–258, 303, 307
  Jupiter 104, 106–108, 110–114, 116, 119, 258, 282, 304
  Mars 104–105, 107–110, 113–114, 283
  Mercury 55, 93, 104–114, 116, 119, 242, 260, 262, 266, 275–276, 304, 328
  Moon 104, 108–110
  Saturn 104–105, 107, 113–115
  Sun 104, 113, 116
  Venus 36, 104–106, 108–114, 116, 119, 150, 153, 233, 252, 260, 292, 304
Platina, Bartolomeo 78, 81, 87, 118
Plato 9, 43, 61, 92, 104, 107, 205, 213, 215, 247–249, 255, 257–258, 265, 267, 293, 327–328
  Laws 61, 247–248
  Republic 61
  Timaeus 92
Plato Tiburtinus 9, 104
player (of musical instruments) 43, 47, 57–60, 71–72, 94, 98, 108, 110, 117–118, 234–235, 240, 242, 253–254, 277, 279, 281, 283, 289, 292, 294, 331
  choraules 231–232, 234–236, 242, 267
  citharoedus 174, 232
  herald 72, 118, 130, 292–293
  lyre-player 44, 59–60, 62–64, 66, 72, 117, 281, 292, 294
  piper 43, 71, 118, 225, 235–236, 242, 250, 252–253, 275, 277–279, 281–284, 287–289, 292, 294, 308, 329–330

trumpeter 43–44, 58–59, 63, 67, 70, 72, 118, 130, 288, 300
player (theatrical) 68, 98, 108–110, 112, 148, 151, 155, 157, 165–166, 173, 221, 223, 231–232, 245, 283–284, 292–293
Pliny the Elder 78, 81, 87, 90, 228, 241–242, 246, 250, 253–254, 256, 261, 263–264, 266, 268, 270–272, 275–277, 279–280, 284, 288, 328, 330–331
Pliny the Younger 16, 228, 249
Plotinus 101
Plutarch 9, 58, 234–235, 237–238, 246, 248, 263, 266, 272–274, 278, 280, 287, 291, 328
  De musica 263, 266
  Problemata 77, 187
poetics 21, 39, 124, 220, 226, 229, 256, 304. *See also* metrics
poetry
  canzoni 125, 128
  capitoli 125–126
  carmen 40, 43, 49, 54, 65, 74, 251, 298–299
  chivalric epic 127, 131
  classical epic 136
  classical Latin 6, 50
  didactic 53
  eclogue 61–62, 108, 126, 128, 140–141, 263
  elegy 128
  epigram 17, 128
  frottole 125
  lyric 20, 47, 50–51, 60–61, 122–123, 126–127, 129, 136–137, 142, 144, 146–147, 151, 154, 156–158, 160, 162–163, 166, 173–175, 178, 181–182, 303, 305–306, 308
  madrigal 148
  neo-Latin 44, 122, 128–129, 131, 136, 140–141, 144, 146–147, 156, 173, 178, 181
  recitation 32, 50, 58, 131–132, 182, 222–223, 233, 305

  sestine 125, 128
  sonnet 45, 125–126, 128, 138, 153–154, 157
  strambotti 124–126, 131, 139, 177
  sung performance 182
  terza rima 135
  vernacular 122, 125–126, 137, 140, 142, 156, 181
politics 208
Poliziano, Angelo 128, 145
Polyphemus 60, 62
polyphony 1, 23, 32, 41, 50, 114, 151
Pomponius Mela 268, 271–272, 276
Pomponius Porphyrio 275
Pontano, Giovanni 10, 16–17, 52–64, 66–69, 71–72, 74–75, 117–119
  Antonius 54–55, 59–60, 62, 65–67, 72, 74, 117–118
  Charon 52, 54–55
  De aspiratione 54, 56
  De beneficentia 54
  De conviventia 54
  De fortitudine 52, 54–55
  De liberalitate 52, 54, 63, 72
  De magnificentia 52, 54
  De oboedientia 54
  De principe 52–55, 68–69
  De splendore 52, 54
  Opera 10, 16, 55, 117–118
Porcia, Girolamo 207–208
Portugal 15, 128, 185, 208
prayer 12, 40–41, 172, 304
primer 34–35, 41
Procne 151, 154–155, 178–180
prognostication 79, 101–102
pronuntiatio 48, 226
psalterium 34–35, 44
Psyche 64
Ptolemy I Soter 280
Ptolemy of Alexandria 104–105, 109, 267, 326
Pucci, Antonio 45
Pythagoras 53, 76, 92, 265, 285, 327–328

Quintilian 20, 38–39, 107, 210, 231, 267

Ramos de Pareja, Bartolomé 19, 114, 186
Ratdolt, Erhard 34, 102
Regazola, Thomas 54
Rhazes (Abu Bakr al-Razi) 78, 80
rhetoric 6, 8, 16, 21, 24, 37, 38, 49, 51, 107, 117, 128, 133, 182–183, 185, 187, 208–212, 216–217, 226–230, 259, 269, 271–272, 288, 301, 306, 326. *See also* eloquence; *See also* oratory
rhythm 39, 50, 131, 206, 212–213, 218–220, 226–227, 304, 307
Rinuccini, Alamanno 274
Rome 12, 126, 128, 136, 184, 200, 229–231, 239, 247, 259, 281–282, 286, 289–290, 293
Ruffo, Vincenzo 34

Sabellico, Marco Antonio 271
Sabino 230, 235
Saladin 79
Salii 283
Salllust
  Bellum Catilinae 209
Sallust 207, 209
  Histories 209
Sannazaro, Jacopo 2
Sappho 241, 259, 261, 280
Sasso, Panfilo 121–122, 124, 126–127, 130, 133, 139–140, 147, 149–151, 154–159, 161, 163, 165, 168, 173, 178–181, 306
Savonarola, Girolamo 20
Scaliger, Julius Caesar 61
Scandiano 127
scholasticism 40
school 13, 31, 33–34, 47, 51, 53, 55, 66, 73, 117, 229
Scuola di San Marco, Venice 209
Seneca 247–249
Serafini, Domenico 33, 44

Serafino Aquilano 2, 37, 45, 121–126, 128, 130, 132, 137, 147, 156, 165, 167, 171–172, 176–178, 306
sermon 6, 13–14, 110
Servius 42, 50, 252–253, 264, 275
Sessa, Giovanni Battista 29, 32, 34, 41, 51, 54, 73, 78, 99, 121, 140, 156, 167, 268
sexual intercourse 22, 36, 82–83, 90–92, 114, 118, 232–233, 236, 239–240, 244–245, 307
Sforza family 80
  Sforza, Galeazzo Maria 119
  Sforza, Ludovico Maria 100
Sidonius 249
silence 59, 69, 71, 74, 151, 285–286, 331
Simonides 261, 275
singer 2, 34, 44, 82, 84, 86–87, 89–92, 105, 110, 112, 127, 132, 139, 231–232, 234, 236, 241–242, 244–245, 277, 279, 283–284, 292–294, 305–309, 331
  canterino 131
  cantimbanco 131
  cantimpanco 44–45, 47
  cantor ad lyram 44, 47, 50, 60
  cantor letus 105, 108, 112
  chorus 87, 148, 232, 234–236, 247–249, 252, 287
  singing voice 38, 81, 88, 156, 167, 305–306
singing 5, 8, 38, 42–43, 45, 48, 50–51, 57, 62–65, 76, 81–82, 86–90, 96, 117, 119, 122–123, 130–131, 134–139, 148, 150, 152–156, 161, 166–172, 176, 180–182, 217, 222, 227, 231, 233, 236, 238, 241, 244–245, 248–249, 251, 256, 258, 261–262, 264, 275, 279–280, 283, 287, 290, 293, 298, 300, 305–306, 328
Sirens 62, 163–167, 178, 180–181, 258, 306
sleep 74, 76, 83, 96–97, 288–289
Socrates 67
Soldi, Giangrisostomo 209

song 8, 32, 43, 47, 50, 53, 57–58, 60–65, 68, 72–73, 82, 86–88, 94–96, 98–99, 110, 112–117, 123, 130–132, 135, 138, 145, 149–150, 152–154, 158–159, 161, 163–164, 166, 169–171, 174, 177–178, 182, 197, 204, 206, 218–219, 222, 227, 238, 241, 245, 247, 250–252, 255–256, 258, 260–262, 276, 284–285, 287, 290, 292, 299–301, 304–306, 309, 331
soul 47, 67, 83, 93–94, 96–97, 111, 159, 172, 195, 197–198, 201–206, 258, 279, 307, 321–323, 330
soundscape 8, 23, 123, 129–130, 133, 143, 145–146, 148–151, 155, 157, 162–163, 165, 167, 170, 173, 175, 178, 181–182, 306
Sparta 248–249, 285–288, 291
Spataro, Giovanni 19
Speculum principis 52, 54
speech. *See* voice: speech
Staccoli, Agostino 121–122, 128
Statius 16–17, 128, 262
Stephen of Messina 9, 104
Strabo 261
Suetonius 87, 234–235, 244, 246, 262, 272
Sulpizio, Giovanni 33, 49–50, 117, 199, 268, 285–286
sweetness 21, 152, 154, 158–159, 164, 256, 280, 328
Sylvester, Saint 76
Syrinx (nymph) 250

Tartagni, Alessandro 295–296
Tebaldeo, Antonio 128
Telesina 60, 62
Terence 16–17, 228–229, 307
Tereus 152, 155
Terpander 256, 261, 275
Thamyras 256, 261
theatre 66, 98, 156, 200, 217, 221, 231, 235, 253, 267, 283–284, 289, 293–294, 307, 331
Thebes 234, 264, 276, 328

Themistocles 280
theology 6, 18, 24, 184–185, 190, 258, 265, 328
Theseus 273
Thetis 64
Thomas Aquinas, Saint 188, 192–193, 311, 316, 322–324
Tiburti, Dario 272, 278, 287, 291–292
Tifernate, Gregorio 250, 261
Tigellius Hermogenes 279
tightrope walker 108
Timotheus 250–251, 261, 275
Tinctoris, Johannes 2, 19
Titus Quinctius 288
Tortelli, Giovanni 17–18, 33, 43, 228, 243, 256, 260, 265, 268, 281
Trastámara family 66
Tresser, Johannes 54
Tromboncino, Bartolomeo 126
Turin 184, 259

Ubaldi, Baldo degli 296
Uberti, Fazio degli 133–135
Udine 209
Ulpian 295, 297–298
University
    of Bologna 44, 101, 183–184, 209, 272, 285, 288, 296
    of Catania 184
    of Ferrara 184, 296
    of Florence 128, 184, 192, 229, 258
    of Naples 184
    of Oxford 188
    of Padua 79, 184, 186, 229, 296
    of Paris 188
    of Pavia 79, 184, 230, 259, 296
    of Perugia 184, 209
    of Pisa 184, 192–193
    of Rome 184
    of Siena 184
    of Turin 184
Urbino 56, 128

Valagussa, Giorgio 46

Valerius Flaccus 133, 268, 275–276, 290
Valla, Giorgio 20, 209, 228–230, 232–235, 239–241, 243–244, 283
Valla, Lorenzo 17, 209
Valturio, Roberto 288
varietas. *See* variety
variety 14, 21, 30, 125, 132, 148, 175, 196, 221–223, 225, 227, 323, 331
Varisio, Giovanni Luigi 77, 228, 259
Varro, Marcus Terentius 252–254
Venice 10, 19, 34, 41, 49–50, 54–57, 66, 80–81, 102–103, 197–198, 209, 230, 259, 270–271, 274
Venus 36, 104–106, 108–114, 116, 119, 150, 153, 233, 252, 260, 292, 304
Vergerio, Pier Paolo 20, 36, 83, 259, 269, 272, 274
Verino, Michele 44–45
Verona 34, 127
Veronica, Saint 11–12
Vespasian 277, 293
Viani, Bernardino 11, 52, 54, 121, 133, 140, 157, 168
Vicenza 211
Villani, Giovanni 34
Virgil 6, 14, 17, 40, 42, 46, 48, 52, 61–62, 133–134, 141, 183, 210, 228–229, 254, 256–258, 262, 266–268, 274–276, 279, 283, 294, 307, 327–328
　Aeneid 48, 134, 183, 229, 252, 256, 258, 263–264, 283
　Eclogues 42, 61, 262–263, 276, 279
virtue 37, 52, 56, 76, 107, 111, 119, 214, 217, 287, 323
Vitali, Bernardino 32, 99, 101, 121, 132, 140, 167, 207
Vitruvius 199–200, 267
Vittorino da Feltre 33, 48, 211
voice 7–8, 38, 58, 68–69, 73, 81–82, 84–94, 98, 105, 107–108, 111, 113–114, 134–137, 141–142, 144–150, 156, 158–160, 162–164, 166–168, 170–174, 178–181, 192–193, 195–198, 205–206, 217, 219–220, 222–227, 232–233, 241, 248, 251, 255–256, 262, 266, 299, 304–309, 321–322
　differing from oratory 219
　speech 8, 14, 37, 47, 63, 69, 73–75, 106, 108, 114, 123, 131–132, 138, 147, 158–160, 162, 198, 206, 208, 218–220, 224–225, 285, 298, 323
Volsco, Antonio 229, 259–260

warfare 67, 101, 129, 204, 208, 250–251, 287, 290–291, 294, 308
wedding 59, 64, 66, 209, 256
wellbeing. *See* health
wills 44, 239, 297
women 10, 16, 18, 30, 41, 55, 60, 65, 68, 74–77, 80, 91–92, 101, 117, 157, 231, 233, 236–240, 244–246, 248, 259, 280–281, 299, 303, 328

Xenophilus of Chalcidice 279
Xenophon 268, 273–274, 280–281, 285–287, 289

Zerbi, Gabriele 81, 89–90, 102, 114
Zethus 263, 276
Zeus 266, 328. *See also* Jupiter

About the Team

Alessandra Tosi was the managing editor for this book.

Adèle Kreager proof-read this manuscript. Adèle and Hannah Shakespeare compiled the index.

Jeevanjot Kaur Nagpal designed the cover. The cover was produced in InDesign using the Fontin font.

Annie Hine typeset the book in InDesign. The main text font is Tex Gyre Pagella and the heading font is Californian FB.

Jeremy Bowman produced the PDF, paperback, and hardback editions and created the EPUB.

The conversion to the HTML edition was performed with epublius, an open-source software which is freely available on our GitHub page at https://github.com/OpenBookPublishers

Hannah Shakespeare was in charge of marketing.

This book was peer-reviewed by Prof Jason Stoessel (University of New England, Australia), and two anonymous referees. Experts in their field, these readers give their time freely to help ensure the academic rigour of our books. We are grateful for their generous and invaluable contributions.

This book need not end here...

Share

All our books — including the one you have just read — are free to access online so that students, researchers and members of the public who can't afford a printed edition will have access to the same ideas. This title will be accessed online by hundreds of readers each month across the globe: why not share the link so that someone you know is one of them?

This book and additional content is available at
https://doi.org/10.11647/OBP.0473

Donate

Open Book Publishers is an award-winning, scholar-led, not-for-profit press making knowledge freely available one book at a time. We don't charge authors to publish with us: instead, our work is supported by our library members and by donations from people who believe that research shouldn't be locked behind paywalls.

Join the effort to free knowledge by supporting us at
https://www.openbookpublishers.com/support-us

We invite you to connect with us on our socials!

BLUESKY	MASTODON	LINKEDIN
@openbookpublish.bsky.social	@OpenBookPublish@hcommons.social	open-book-publishers

Read more at the Open Book Publishers Blog
https://blogs.openbookpublishers.com

You may also be interested in:

Acoustemologies in Contact
Sounding Subjects and Modes of Listening in Early Modernity
Edited by Emily Wilbourne and Suzanne G. Cusick
https://doi.org/10.11647/OBP.0226

The Juggler of Notre Dame and the Medievalizing of Modernity
Volume 1: The Middle Ages
Jan M. Ziolkowski
https://doi.org/10.11647/OBP.0132

Denis Diderot 'Rameau's Nephew' — 'Le Neveu de Rameau'
A Multi-Media Bilingual Edition
Denis Diderot. Marian Hobson (ed.), Kate E. Tunstall (trans.), Caroline Warman (trans.), Pascal Duc (music editor)
https://doi.org/10.11647/OBP.0098

Gallucci's Commentary on Dürer's 'Four Books on Human Proportion'
Renaissance Proportion Theory
James Hutson
https://doi.org/10.11647/OBP.0198

www.ingramcontent.com/pod-product-compliance
Lightning Source LLC
Chambersburg PA
CBHW051535230426
43669CB00015B/2602